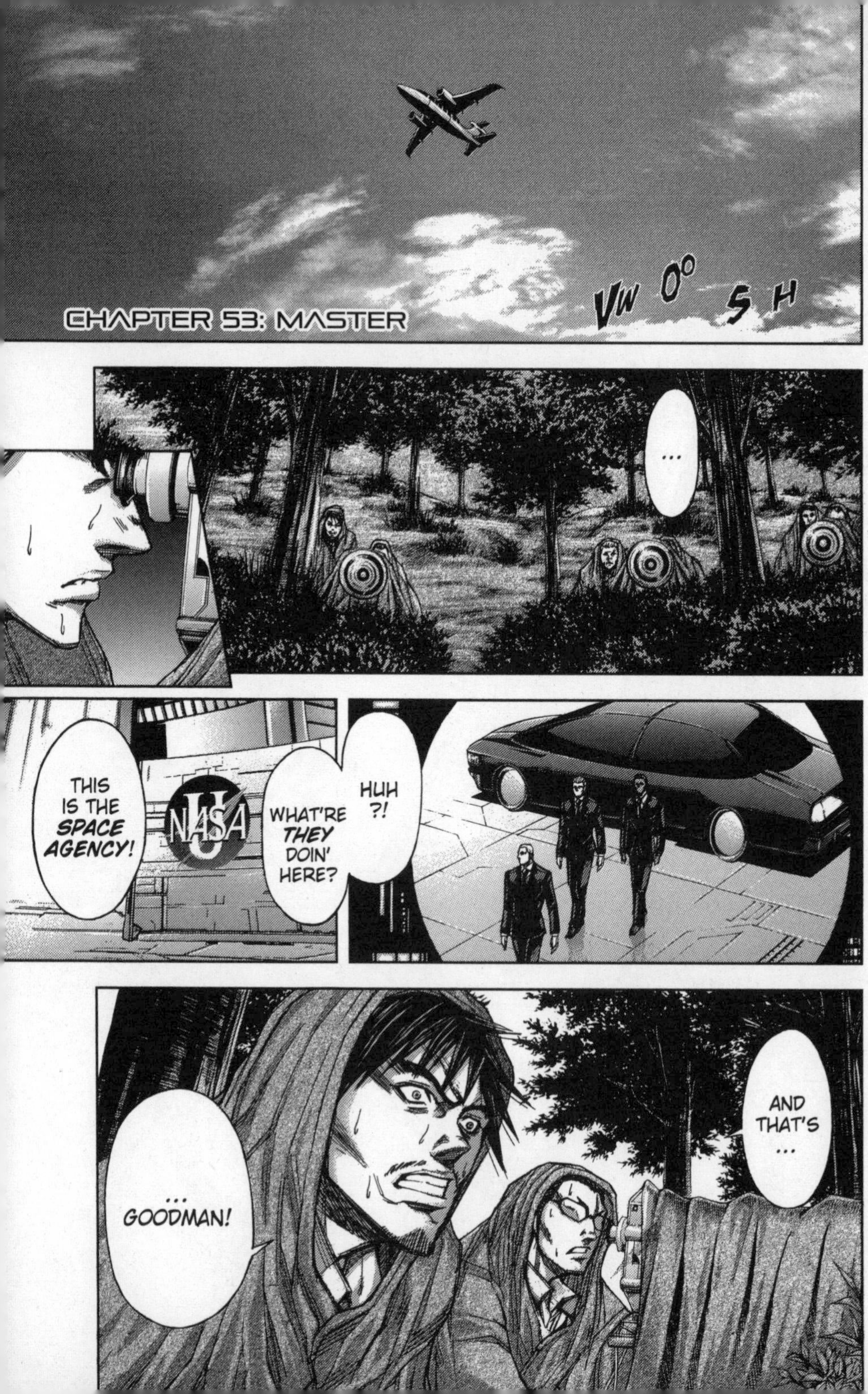
VWOOSH
CHAPTER 53: MASTER
...
HUH ?!
WHAT'RE THEY DOIN' HERE?
THIS IS THE SPACE AGENCY!
NASA
AND THAT'S ...
... GOODMAN!

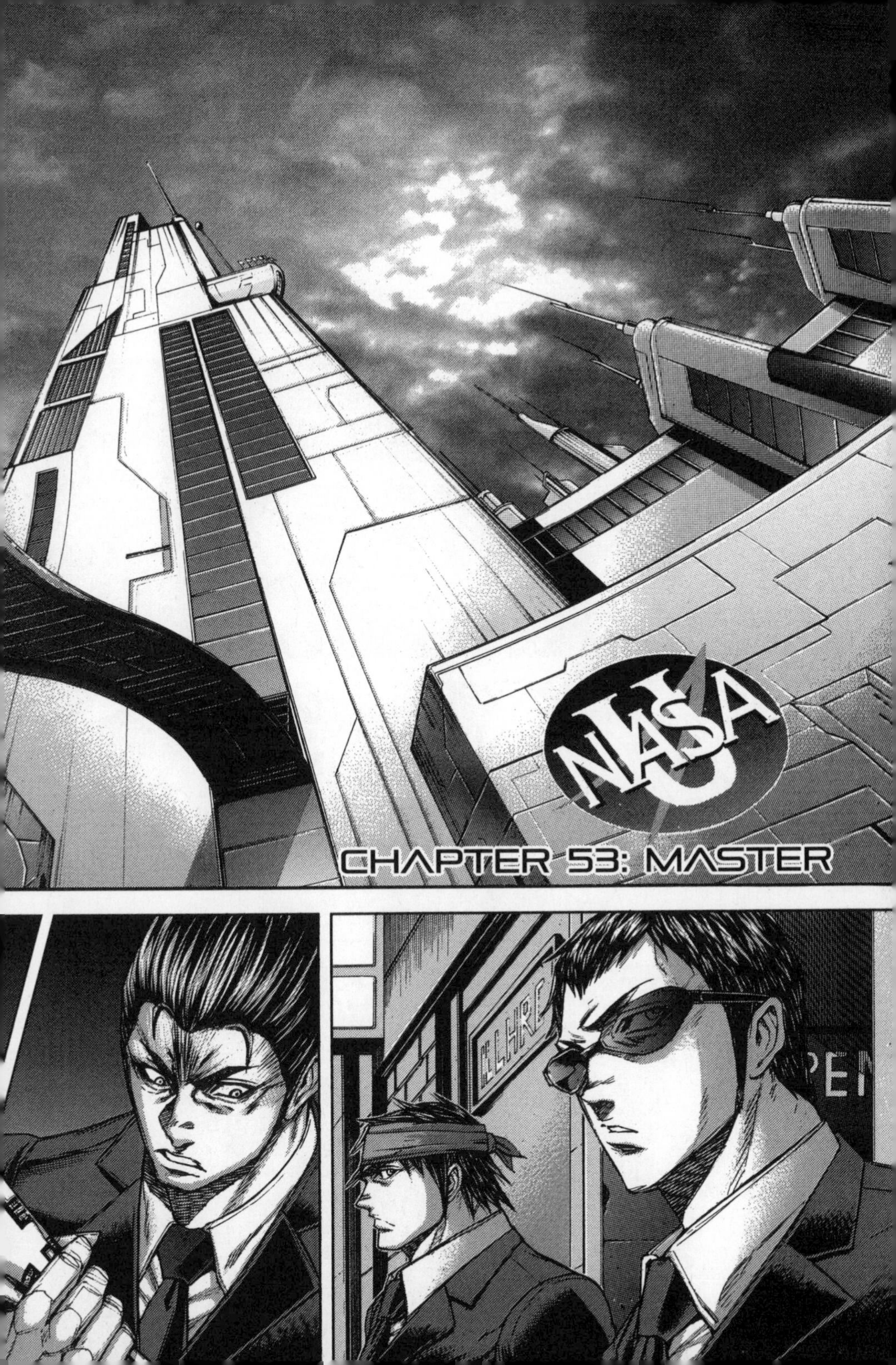
NASA
CHAPTER 53: MASTER

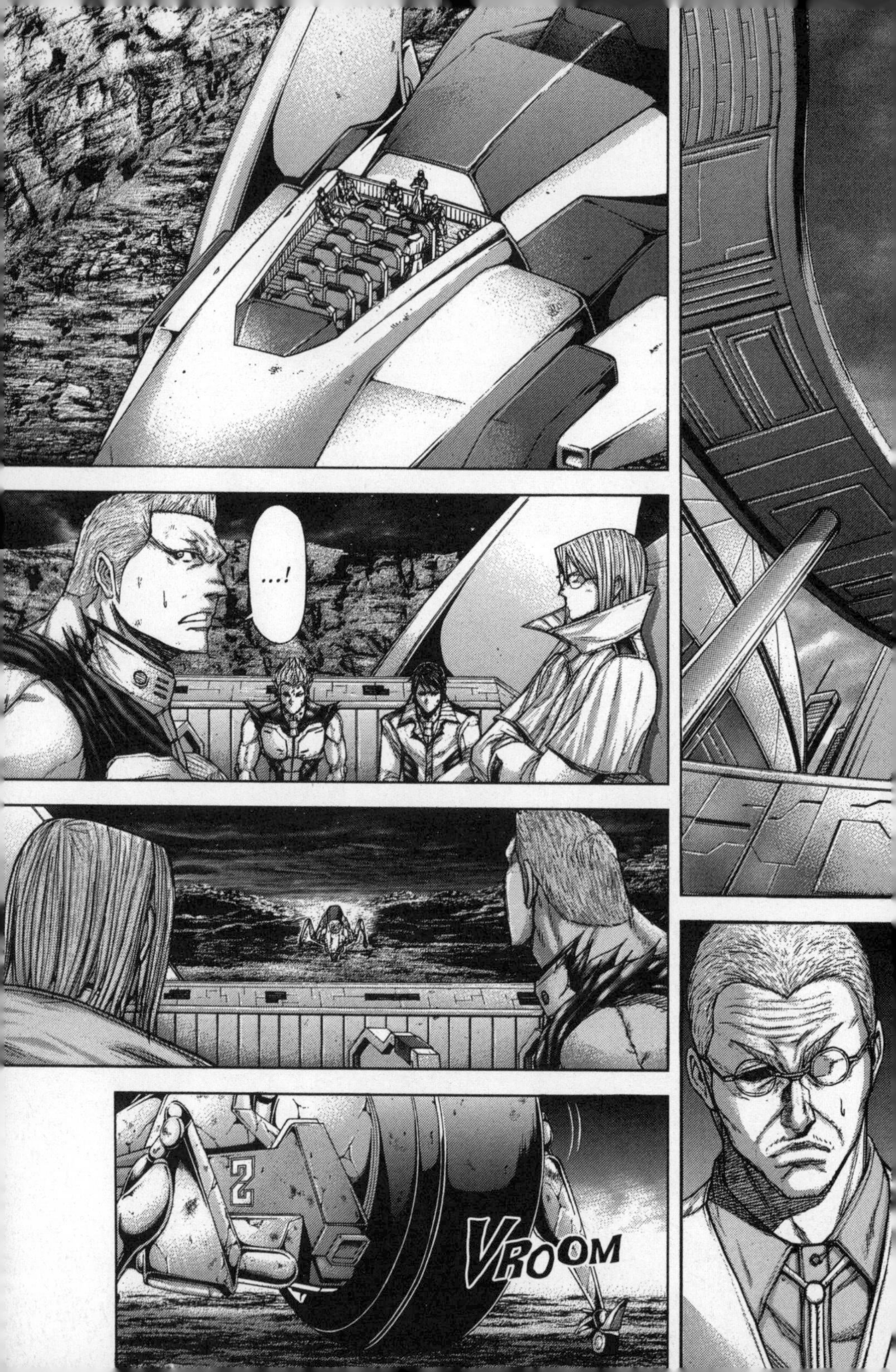
...!
VROOM

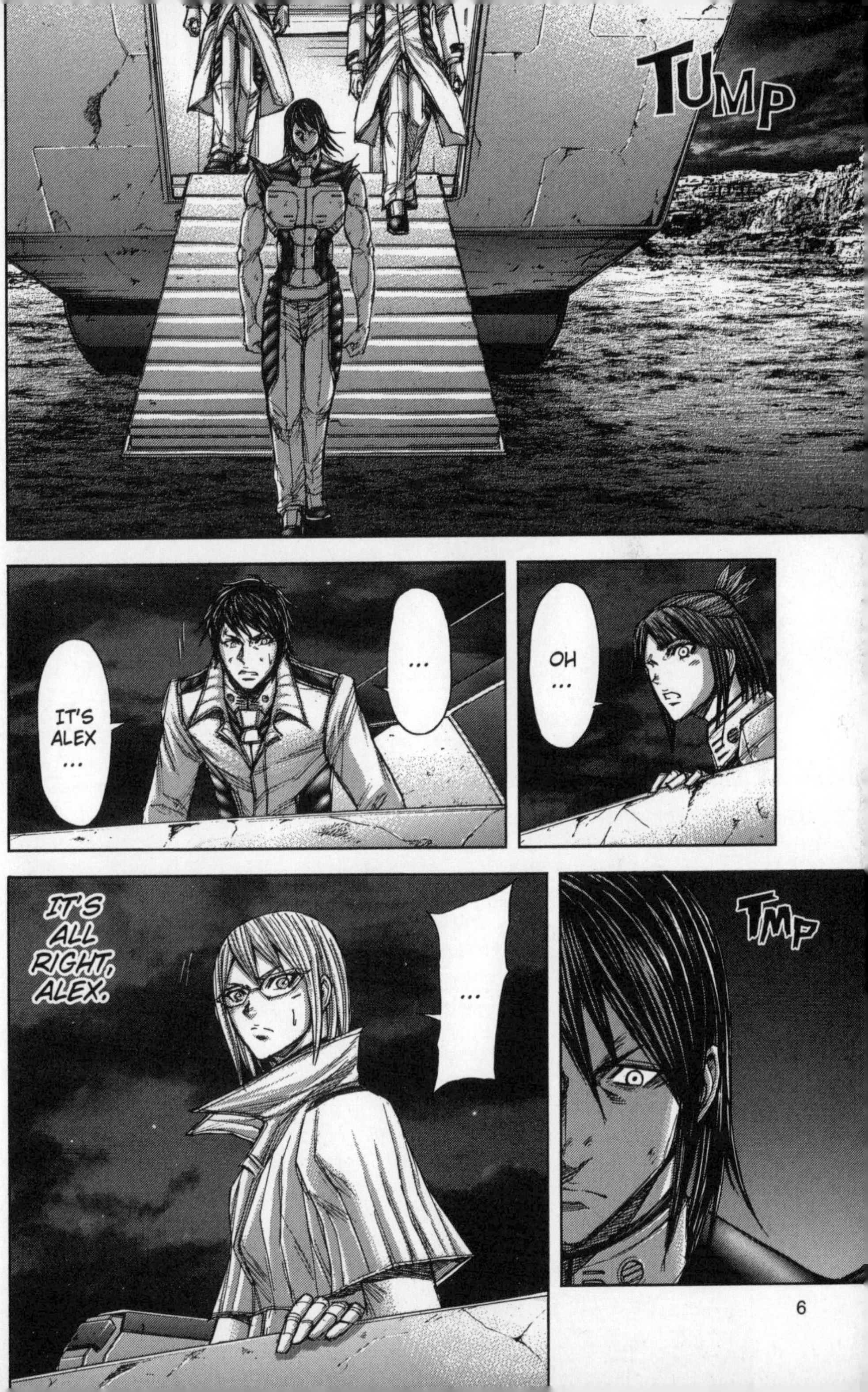
TUMP
OH ...
...
IT'S ALEX ...
TMP
...
IT'S ALL RIGHT, ALEX.

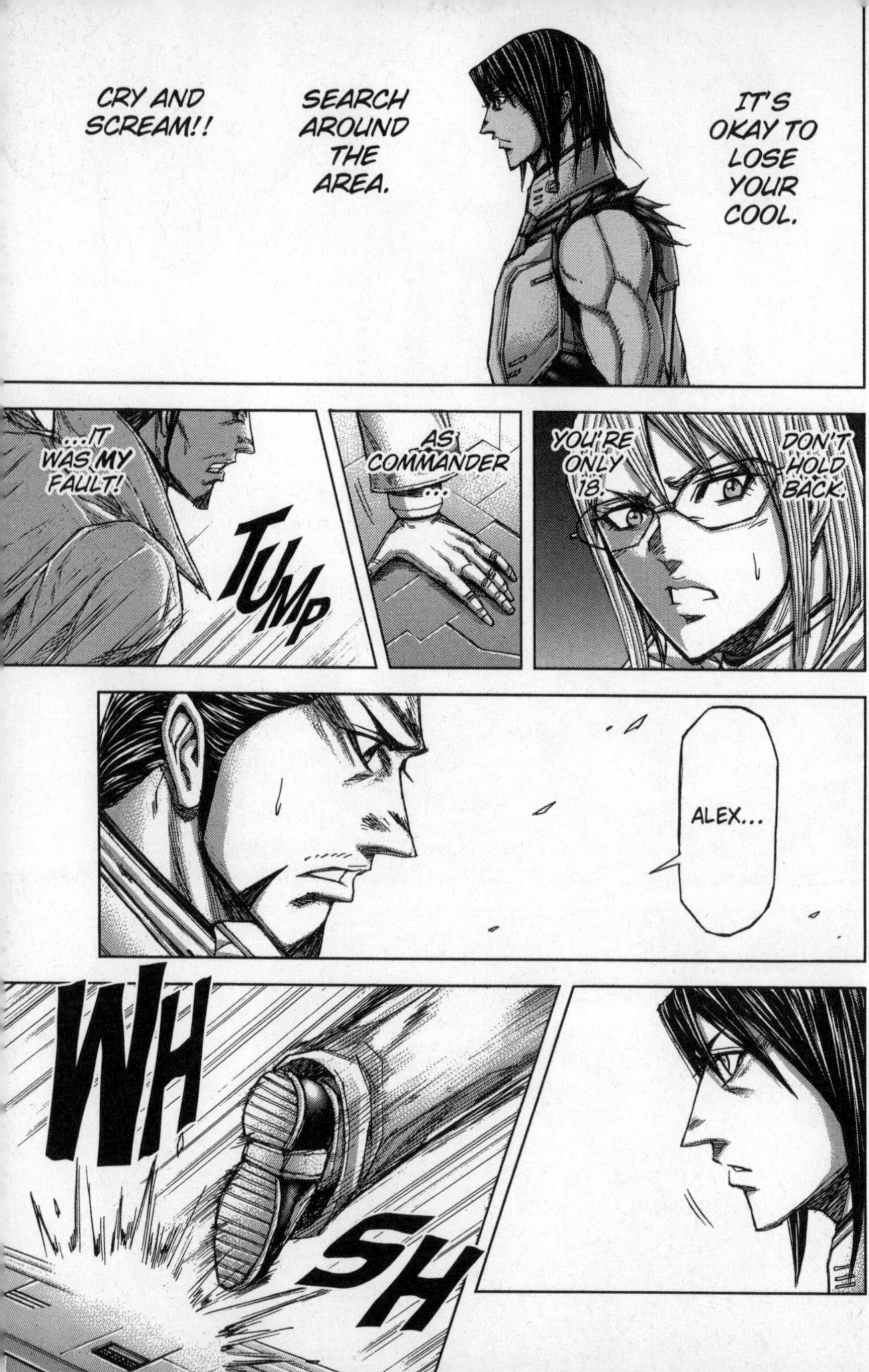
IT'S OKAY TO LOSE YOUR COOL.
SEARCH AROUND THE AREA.
CRY AND SCREAM!!
DON'T HOLD BACK.
YOU'RE ONLY 18.
AS COMMANDER...
...IT WAS MY FAULT!
TUMP
ALEX...
WHSH

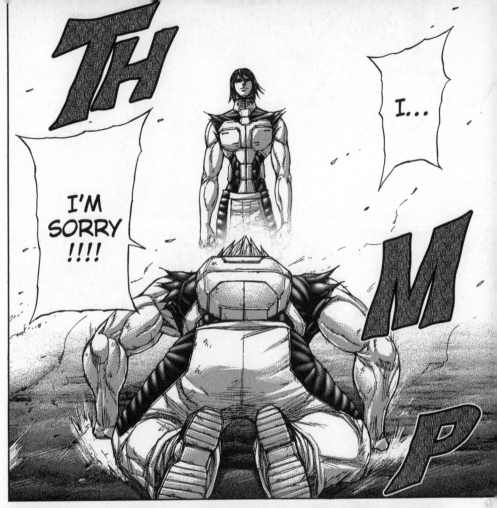

TH
UMP

I...

I'M SORRY!!!!

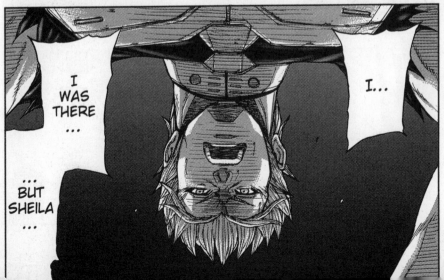

I WAS THERE...

...BUT SHEILA...

I...

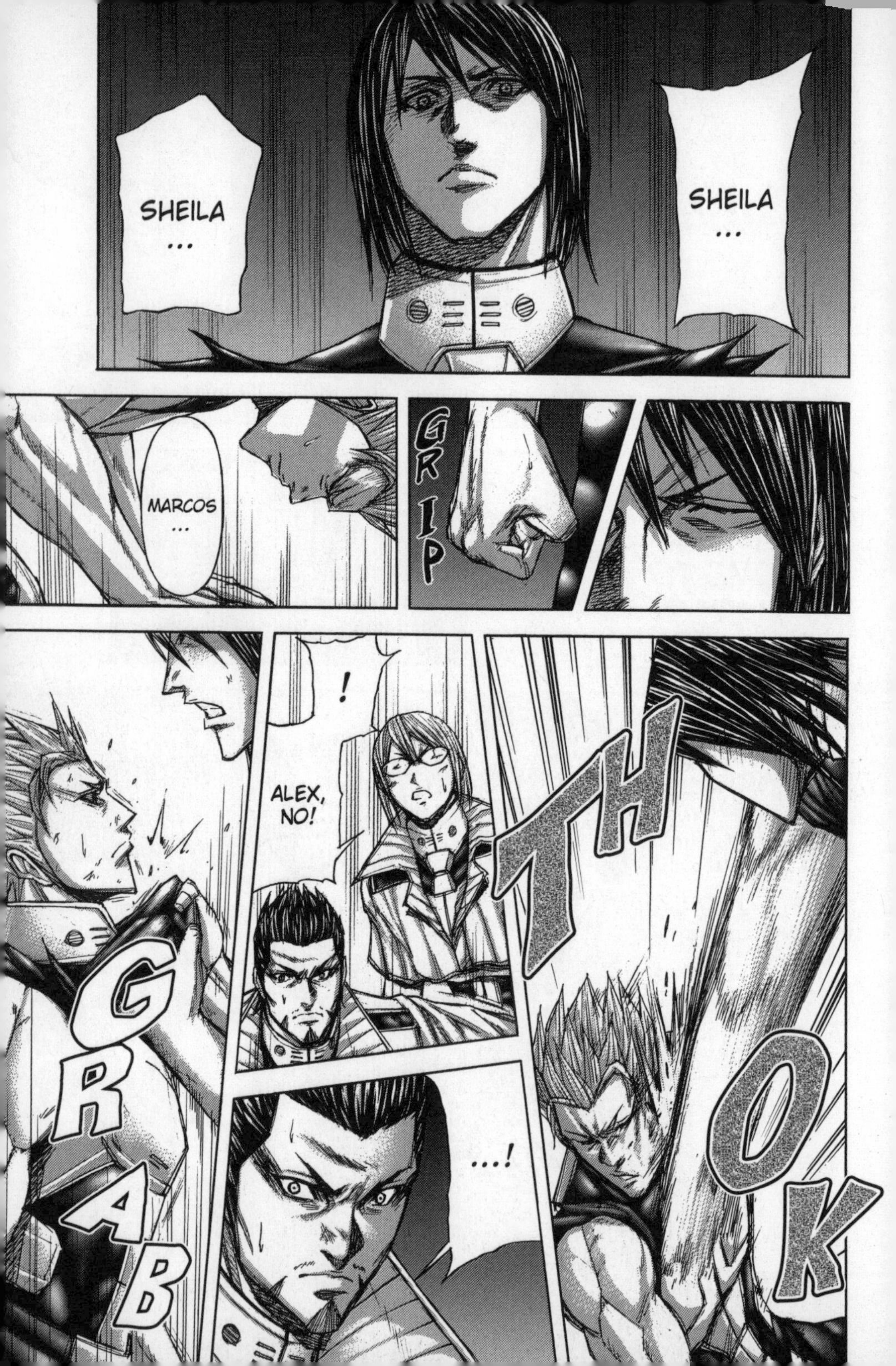

SHEILA ...
SHEILA ...
GRIP
MARCOS ...
THOOK
!
ALEX, NO!
...!
GRAB

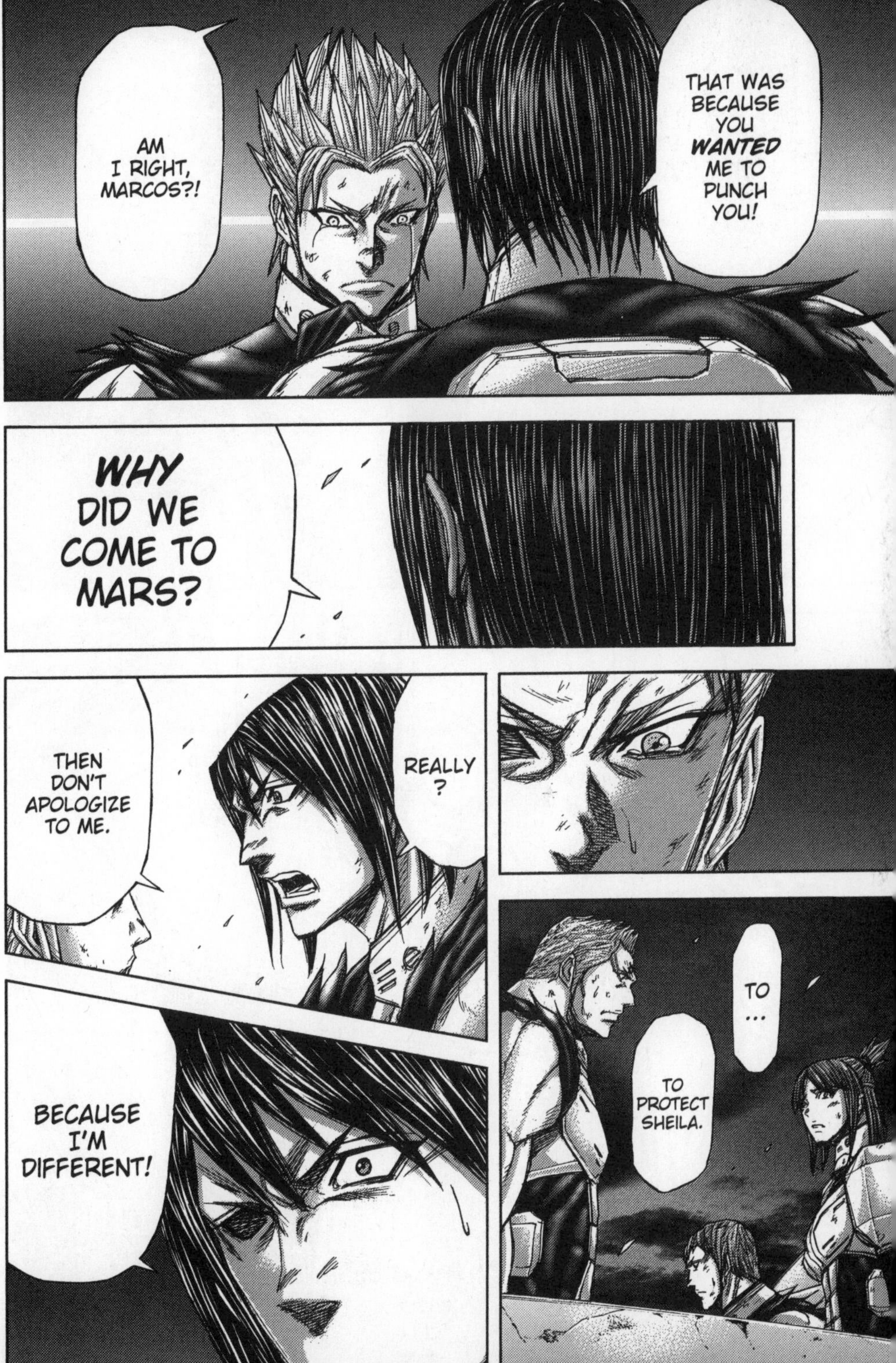

THAT WAS BECAUSE YOU ***WANTED*** ME TO PUNCH YOU!
AM I RIGHT, MARCOS?!
WHY DID WE COME TO MARS?
REALLY?
THEN DON'T APOLOGIZE TO ME.
TO...
TO PROTECT SHEILA.
BECAUSE I'M DIFFERENT!

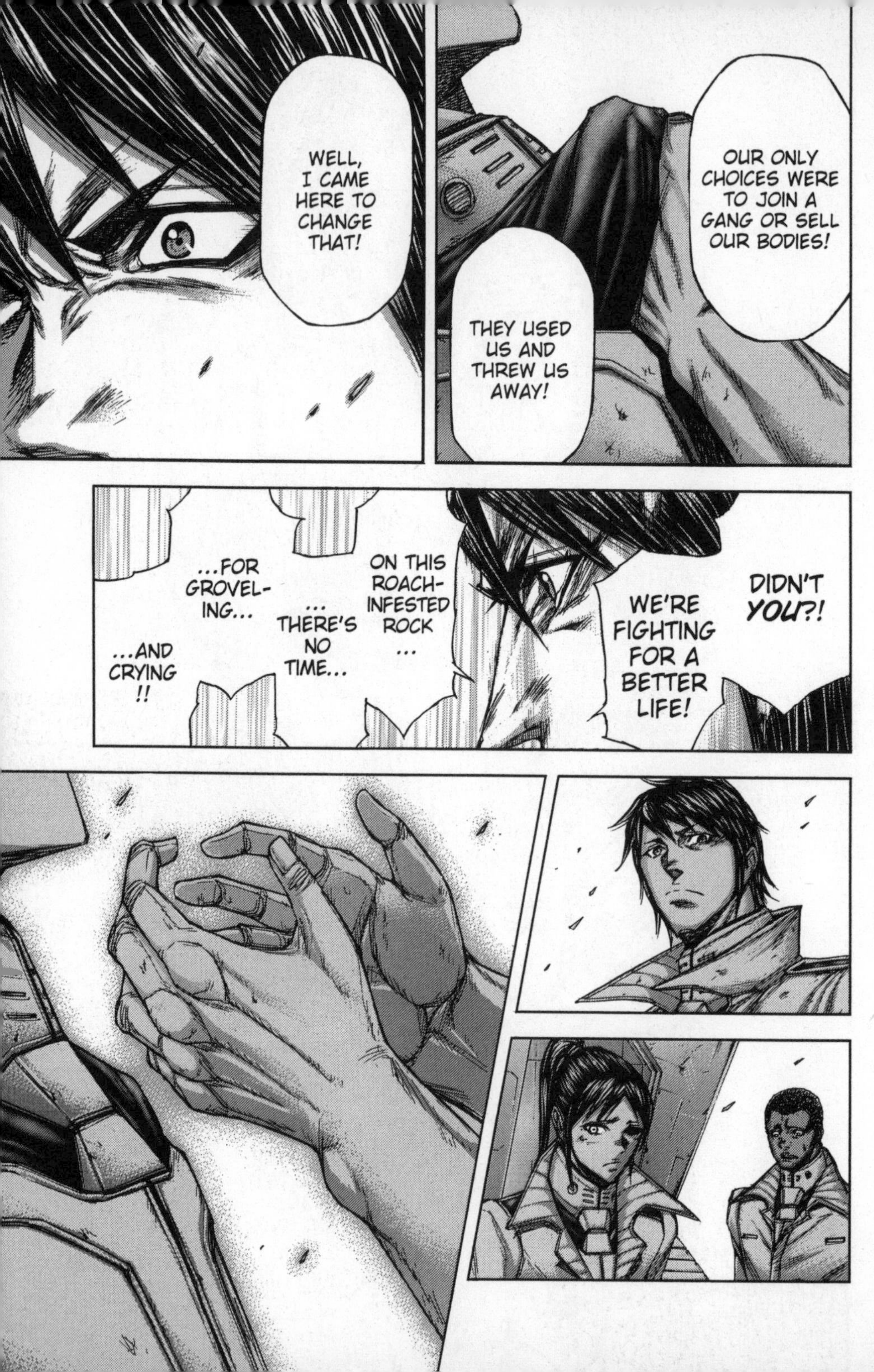
OUR ONLY CHOICES WERE TO JOIN A GANG OR SELL OUR BODIES!
THEY USED US AND THREW US AWAY!
WELL, I CAME HERE TO CHANGE THAT!
DIDN'T *YOU*?!
WE'RE FIGHTING FOR A BETTER LIFE!
ON THIS ROACH-INFESTED ROCK...
...THERE'S NO TIME...
...FOR GROVEL-ING...
...AND CRYING!!

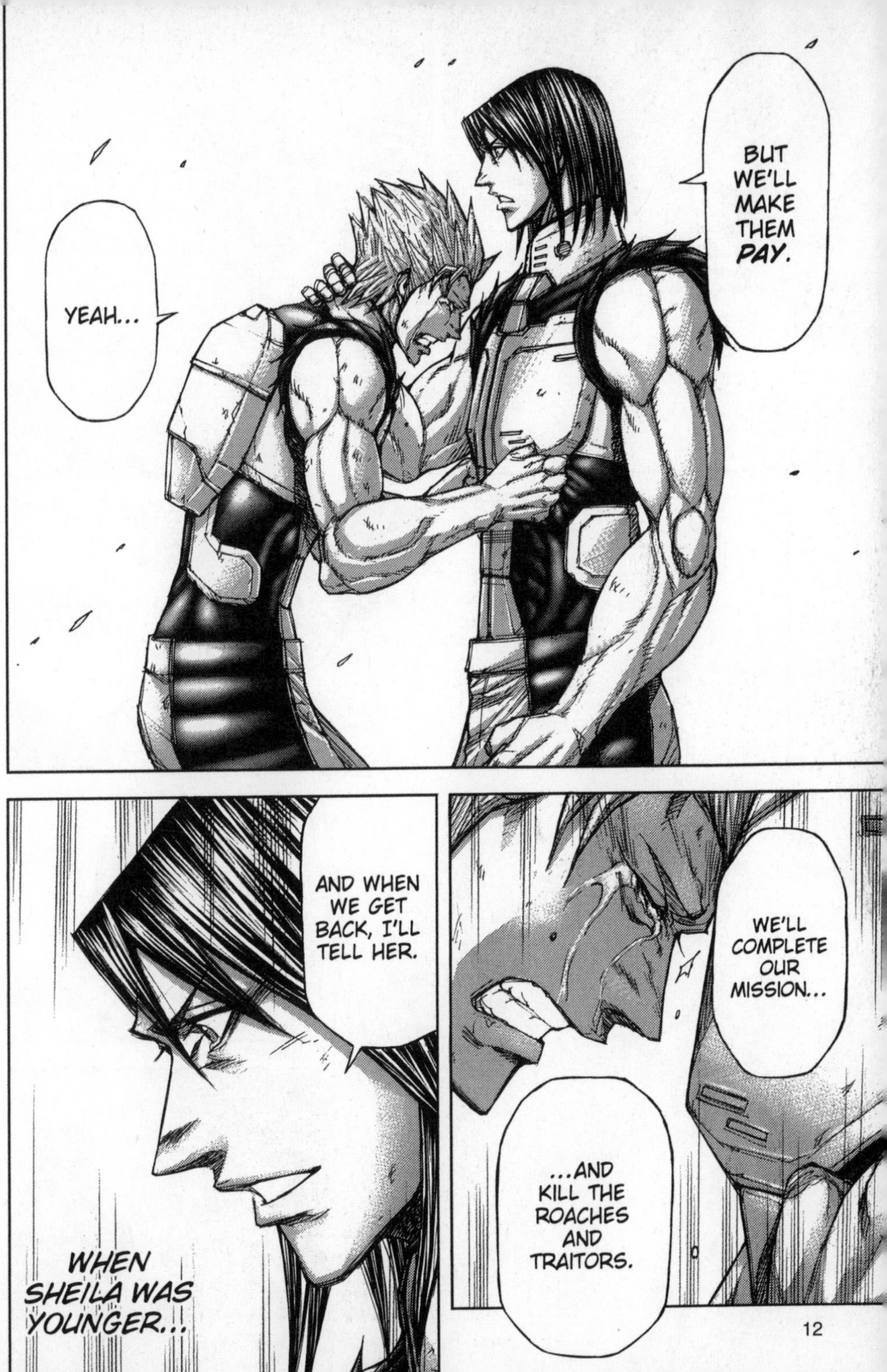
BUT WE'LL MAKE THEM PAY.
YEAH...
WE'LL COMPLETE OUR MISSION...
...AND KILL THE ROACHES AND TRAITORS.
AND WHEN WE GET BACK, I'LL TELL HER.
WHEN SHEILA WAS YOUNGER...

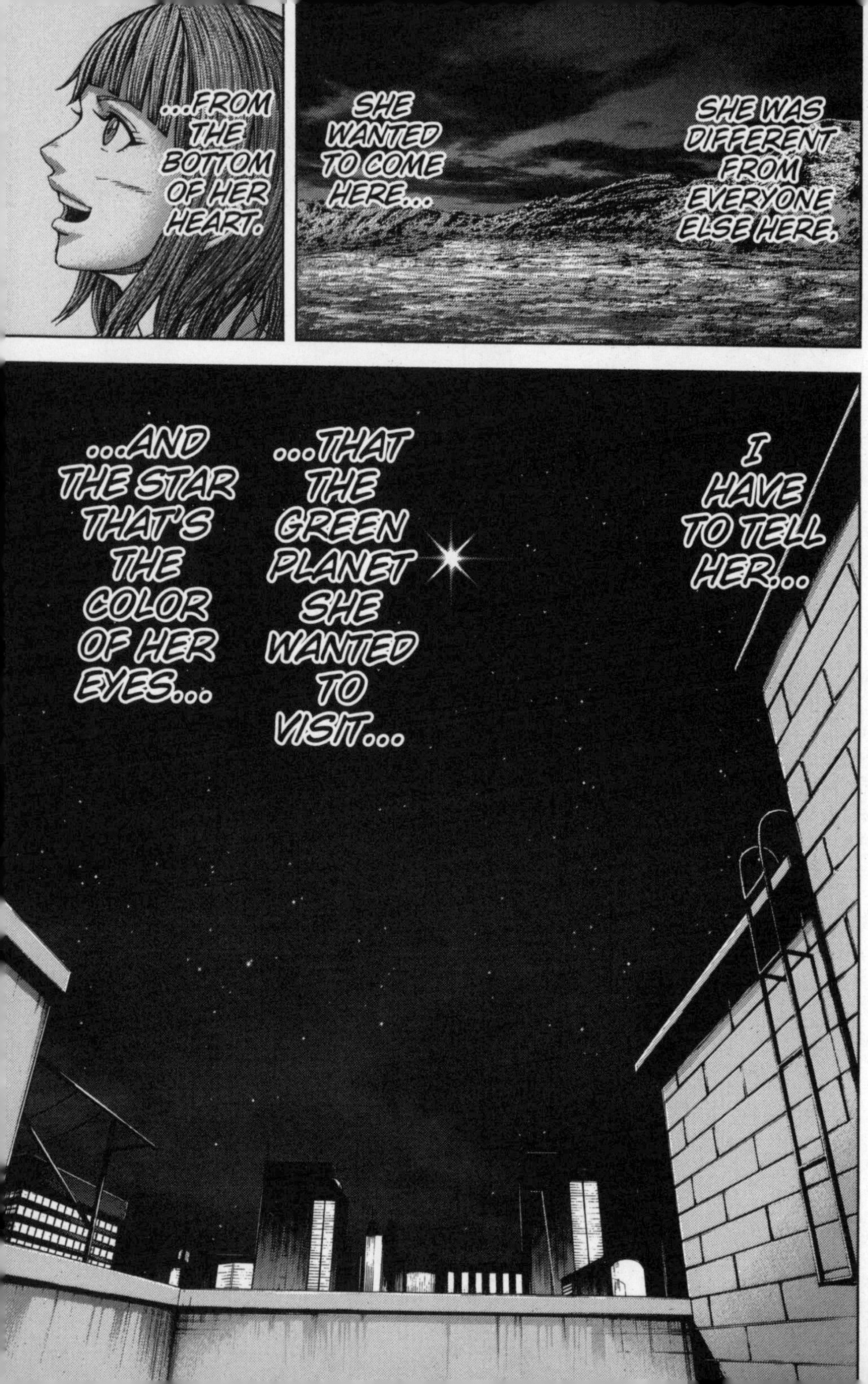
SHE WAS DIFFERENT FROM EVERYONE ELSE HERE.
SHE WANTED TO COME HERE...
...FROM THE BOTTOM OF HER HEART.
I HAVE TO TELL HER...
...THAT THE GREEN PLANET SHE WANTED TO VISIT...
...AND THE STAR THAT'S THE COLOR OF HER EYES...

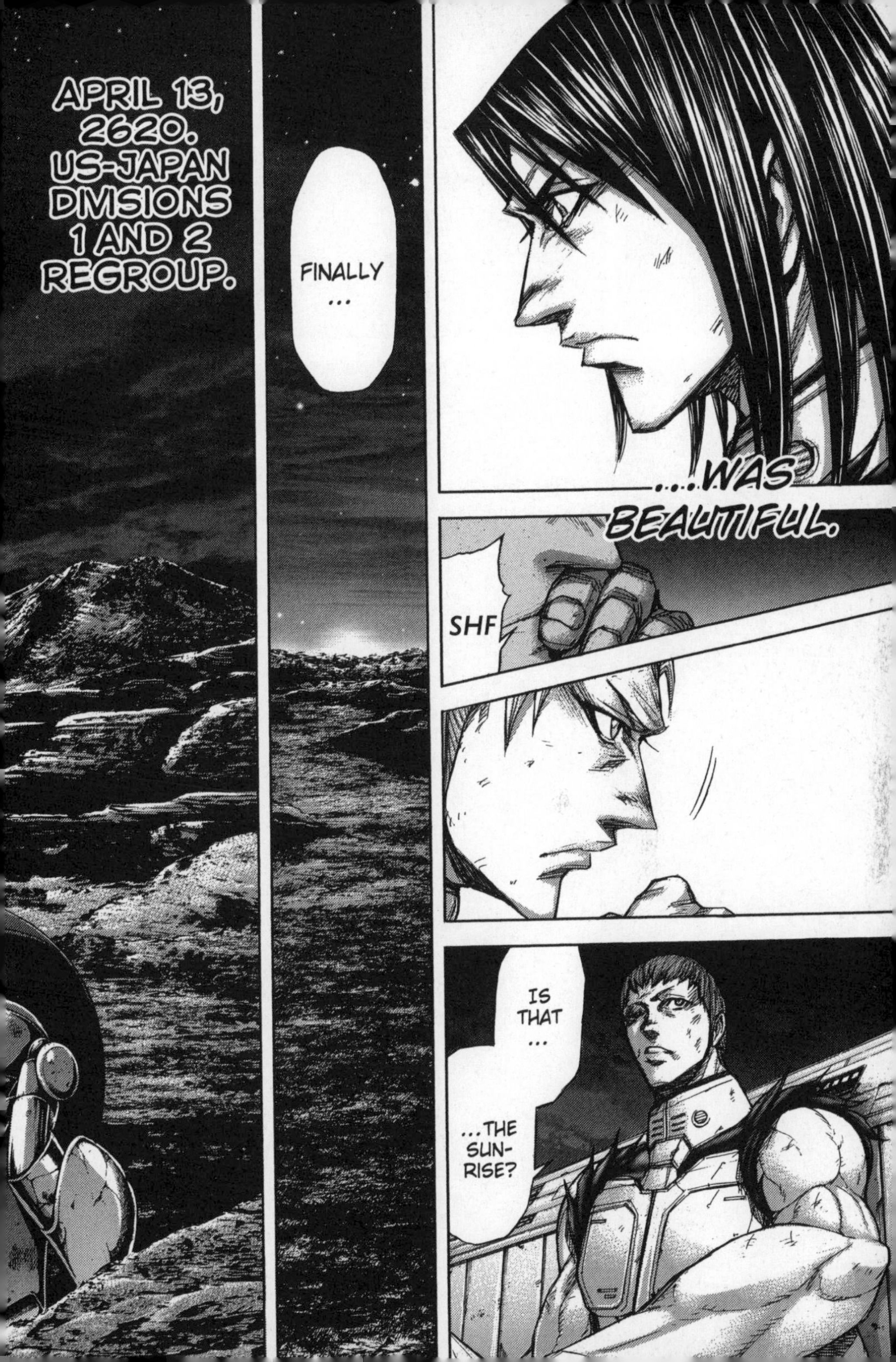
APRIL 13, 2620. US-JAPAN DIVISIONS 1 AND 2 REGROUP.
FINALLY ...
...WAS BEAUTIFUL.
SHF
IS THAT ...
...THE SUN-RISE?

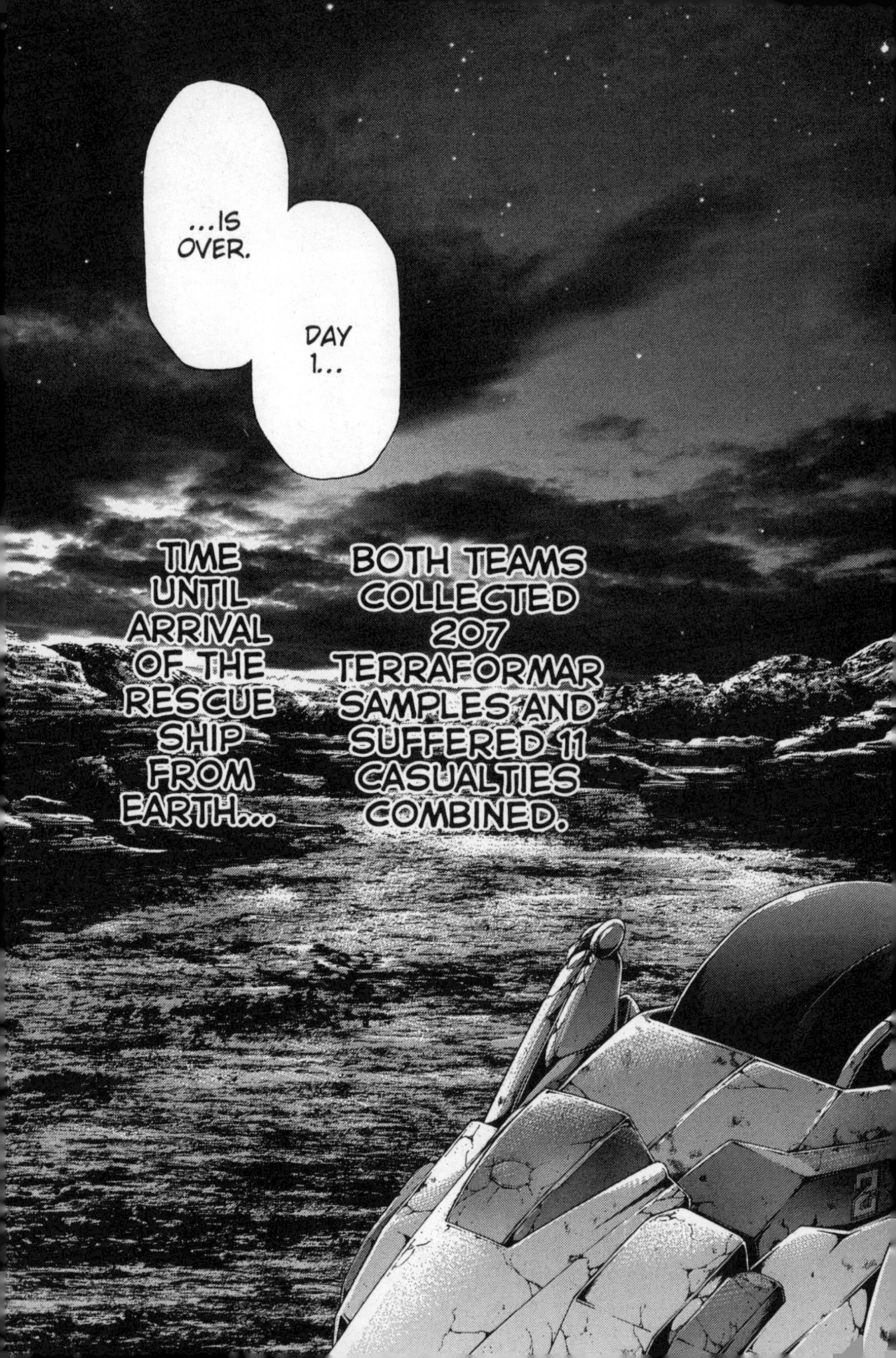
DAY 1...
...IS OVER.
BOTH TEAMS COLLECTED 207 TERRAFORMAR SAMPLES AND SUFFERED 11 CASUALTIES COMBINED.
TIME UNTIL ARRIVAL OF THE RESCUE SHIP FROM EARTH...

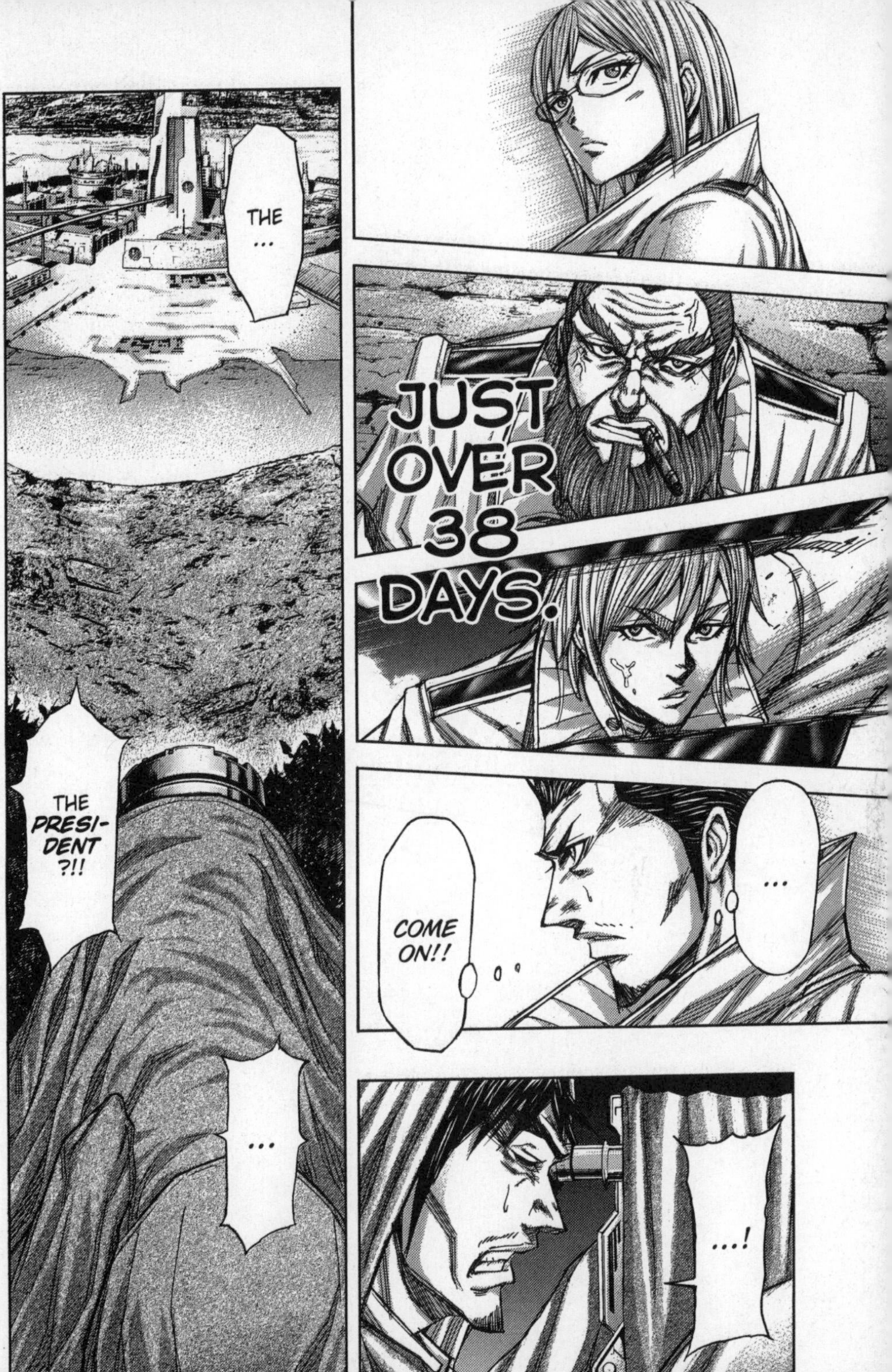
JUST OVER 38 DAYS.
...
COME ON!!
...!
THE ...
THE PRESIDENT?!!
...

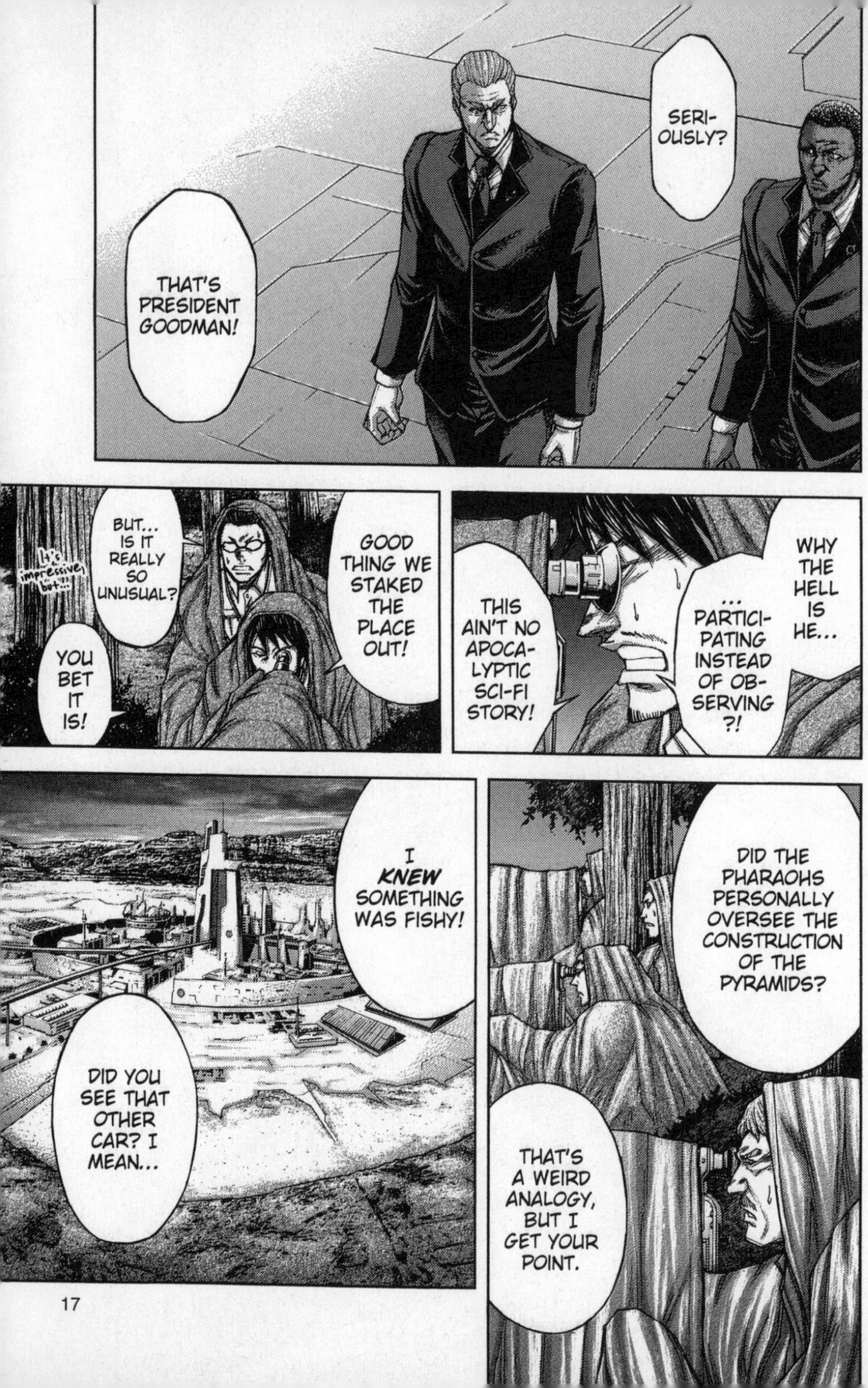
SERI-OUSLY?
THAT'S PRESIDENT GOODMAN!
WHY THE HELL IS HE...
...PARTICIPATING INSTEAD OF OB-SERVING?!
THIS AIN'T NO APOCA-LYPTIC SCI-FI STORY!
GOOD THING WE STAKED THE PLACE OUT!
BUT... IS IT REALLY SO UNUSUAL?
It's impressive, but...
YOU BET IT IS!
DID THE PHARAOHS PERSONALLY OVERSEE THE CONSTRUCTION OF THE PYRAMIDS?
THAT'S A WEIRD ANALOGY, BUT I GET YOUR POINT.
I *KNEW* SOMETHING WAS FISHY!
DID YOU SEE THAT OTHER CAR? I MEAN...

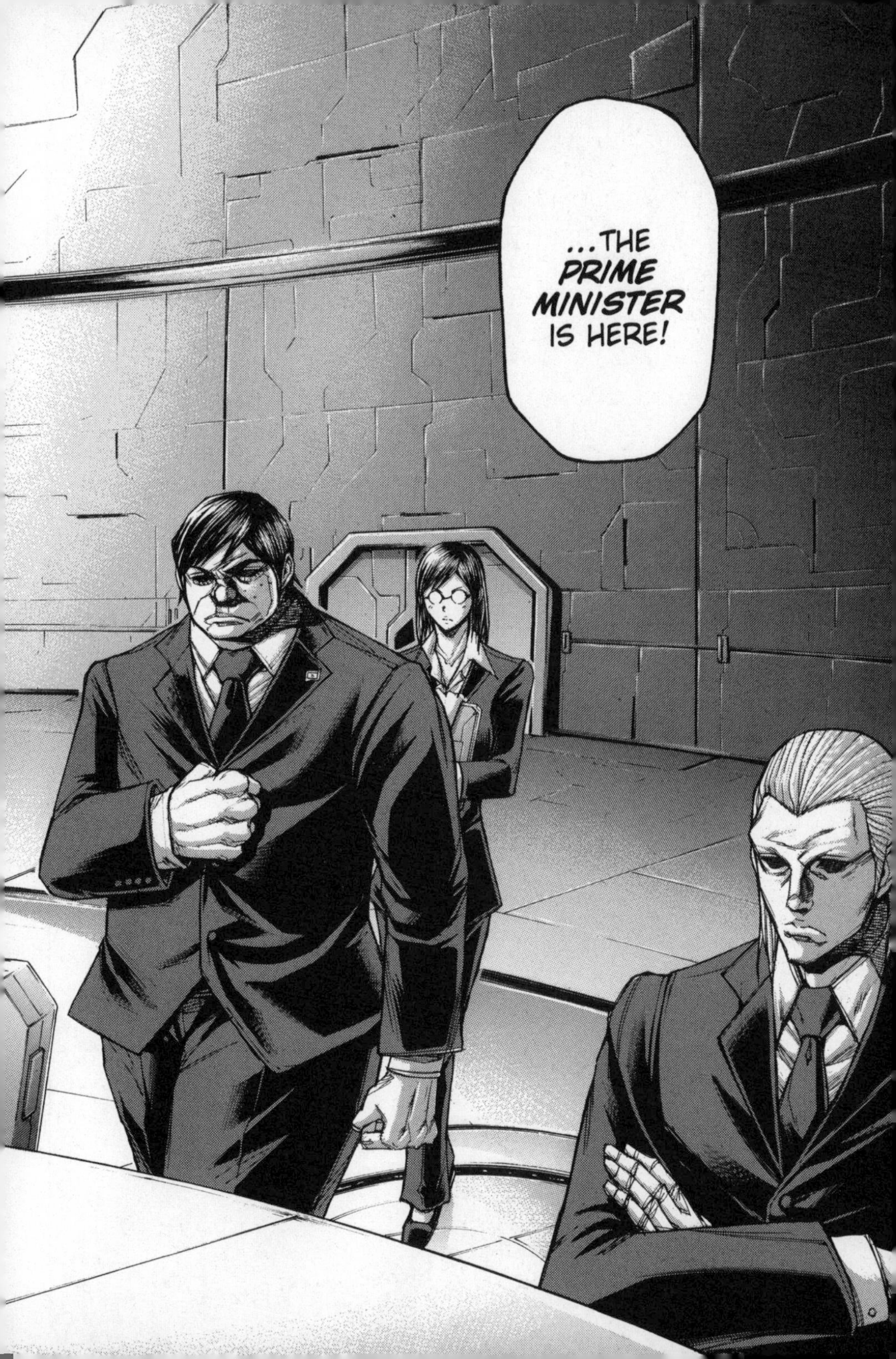
...THE *PRIME MINISTER* IS HERE!

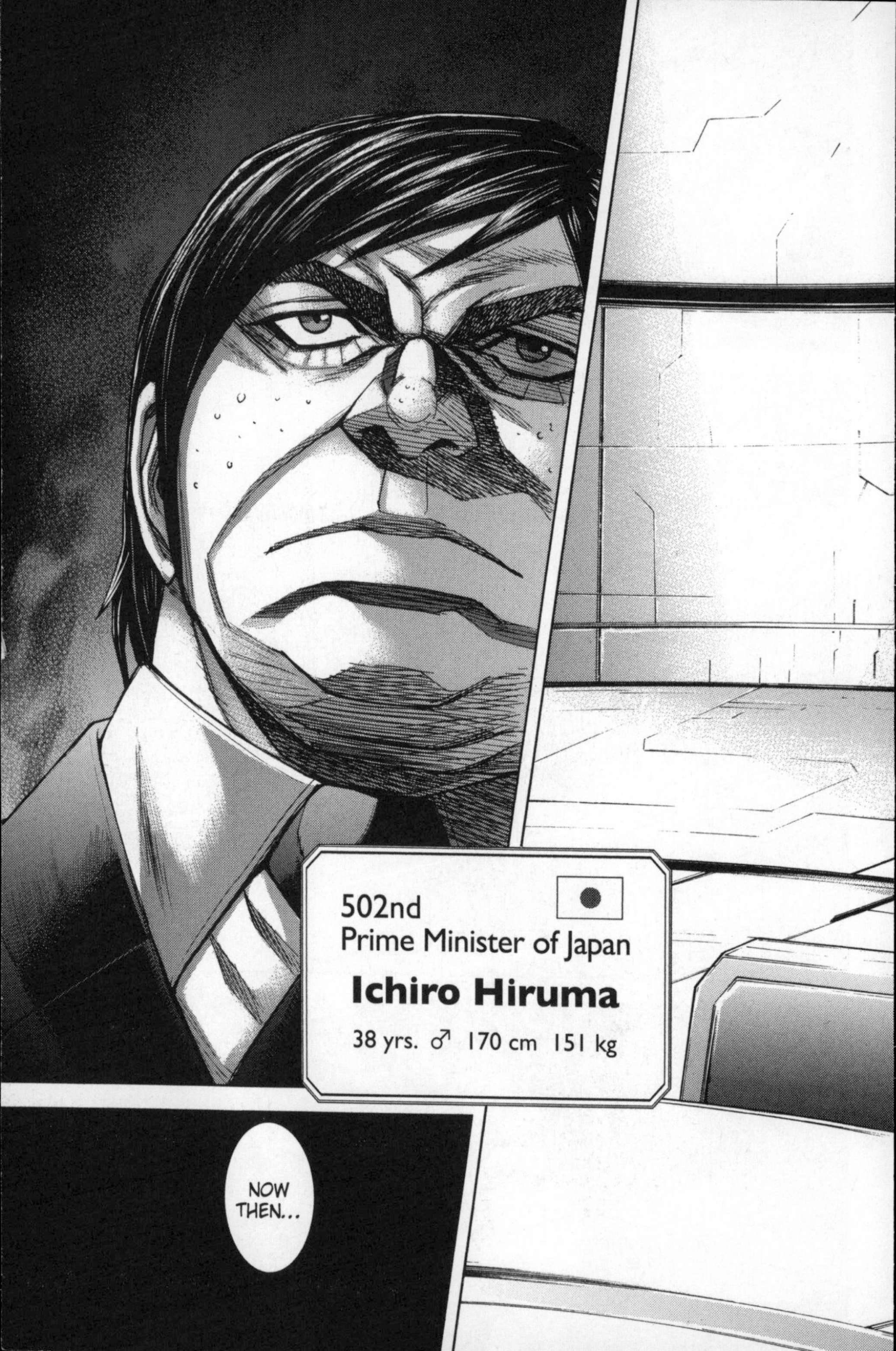
502nd
Prime Minister of Japan
Ichiro Hiruma
38 yrs. ♂ 170 cm 151 kg
NOW THEN...

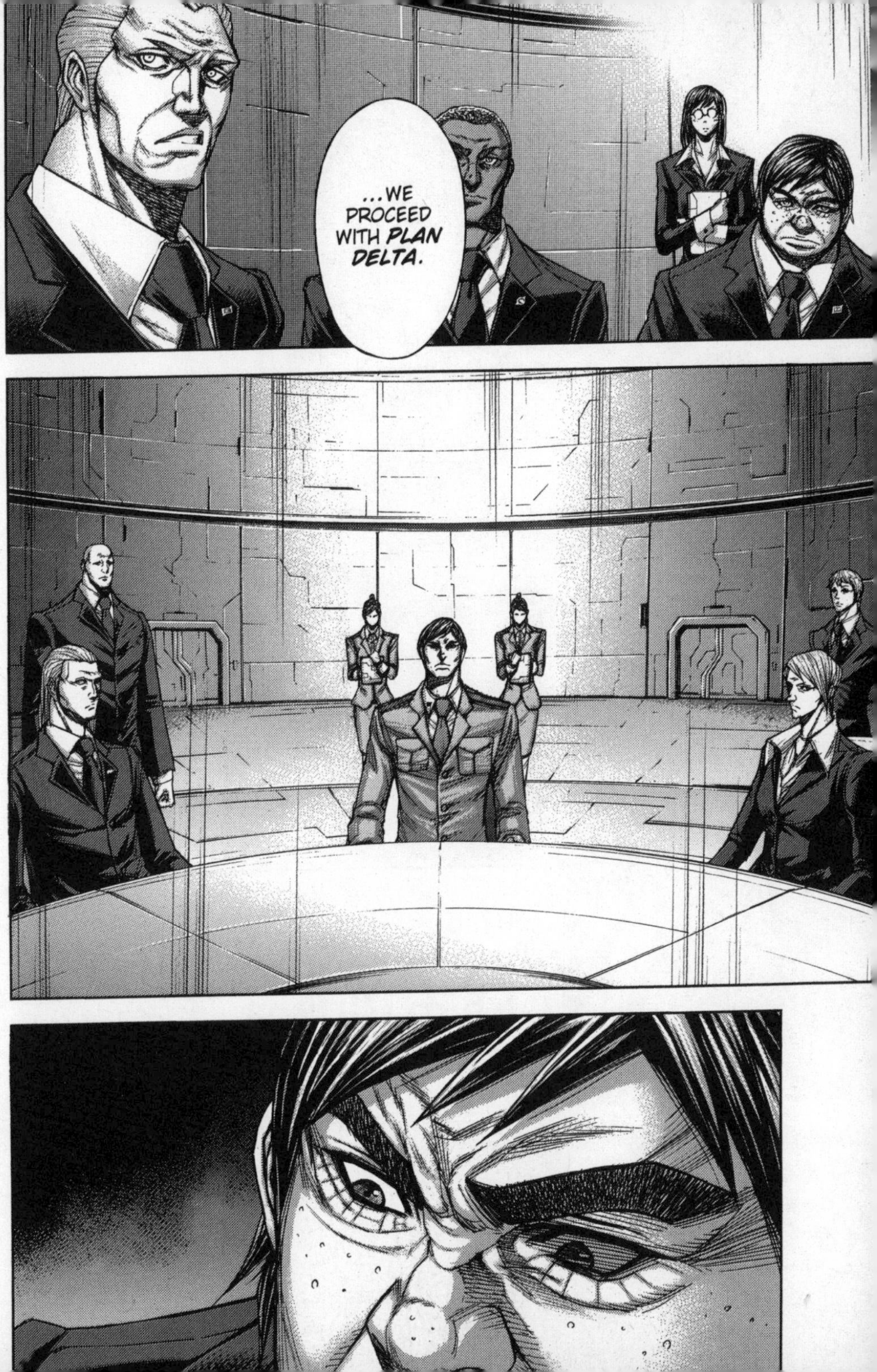
...WE PROCEED WITH PLAN DELTA.

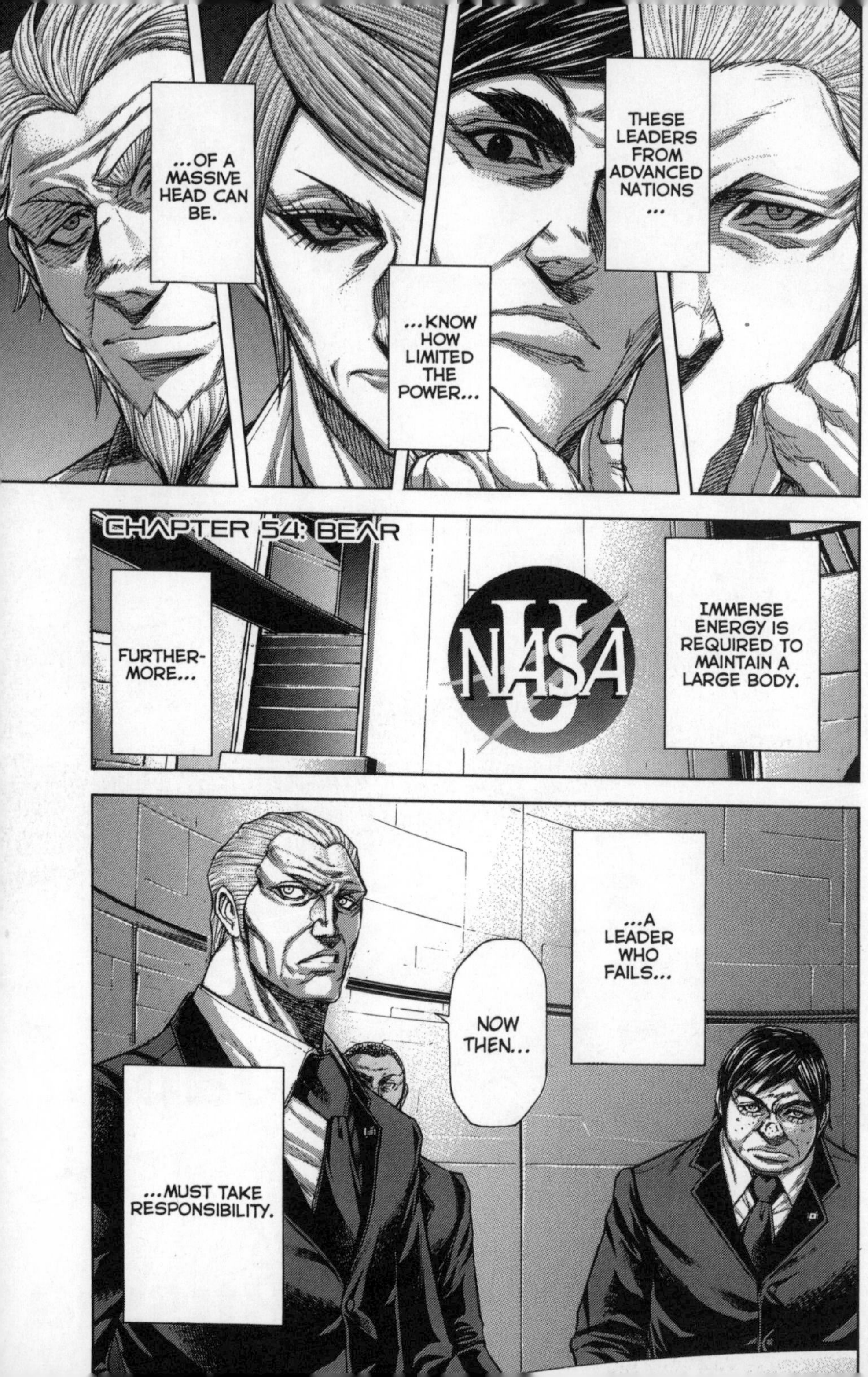
THESE LEADERS FROM ADVANCED NATIONS ...
...KNOW HOW LIMITED THE POWER...
...OF A MASSIVE HEAD CAN BE.
CHAPTER 54: BEAR
IMMENSE ENERGY IS REQUIRED TO MAINTAIN A LARGE BODY.
U NASA
FURTHER-MORE...
...A LEADER WHO FAILS...
NOW THEN...
...MUST TAKE RESPONSIBILITY.

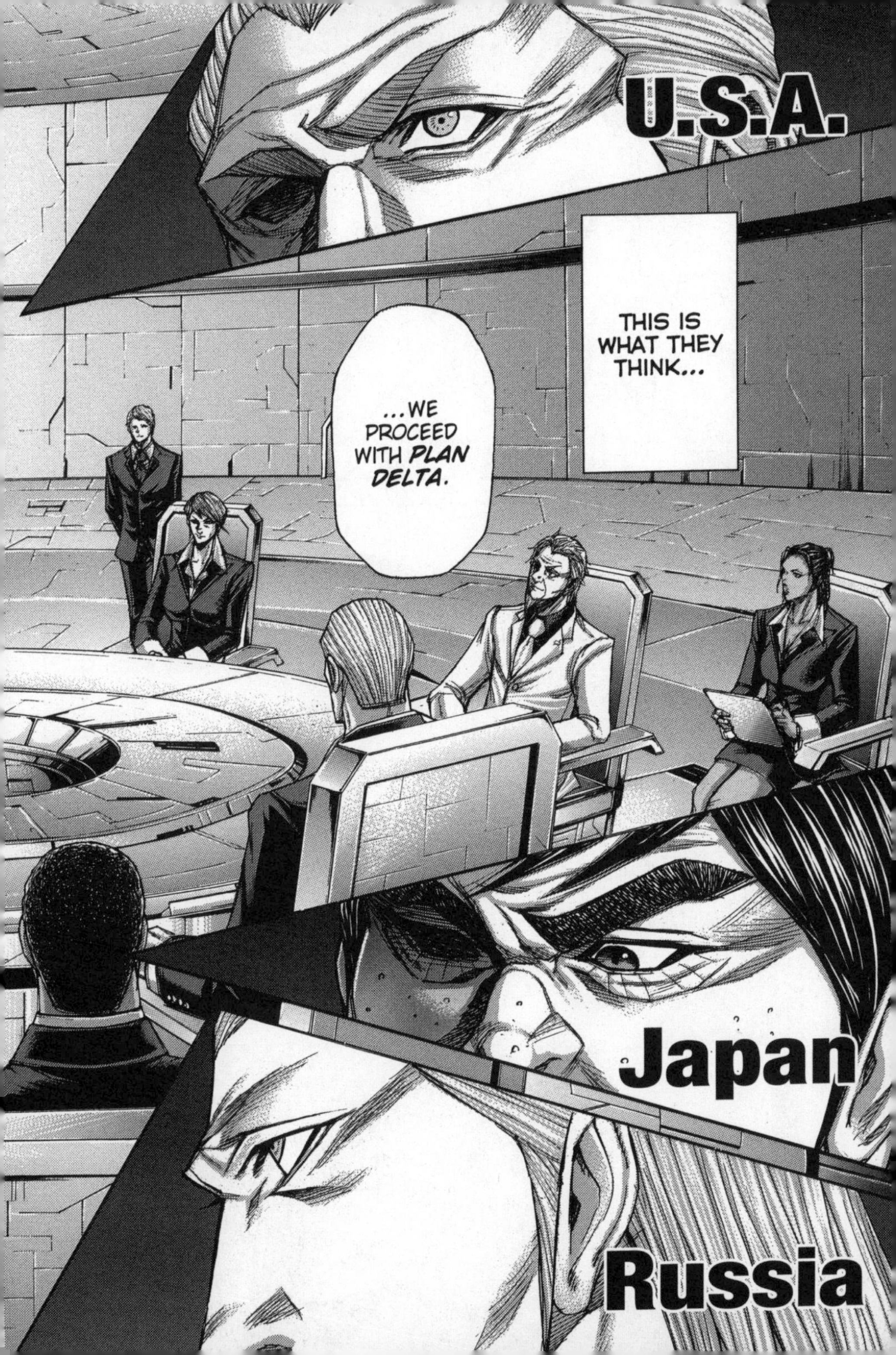
U.S.A.
THIS IS WHAT THEY THINK...
...WE PROCEED WITH *PLAN DELTA*.
Japan
Russia

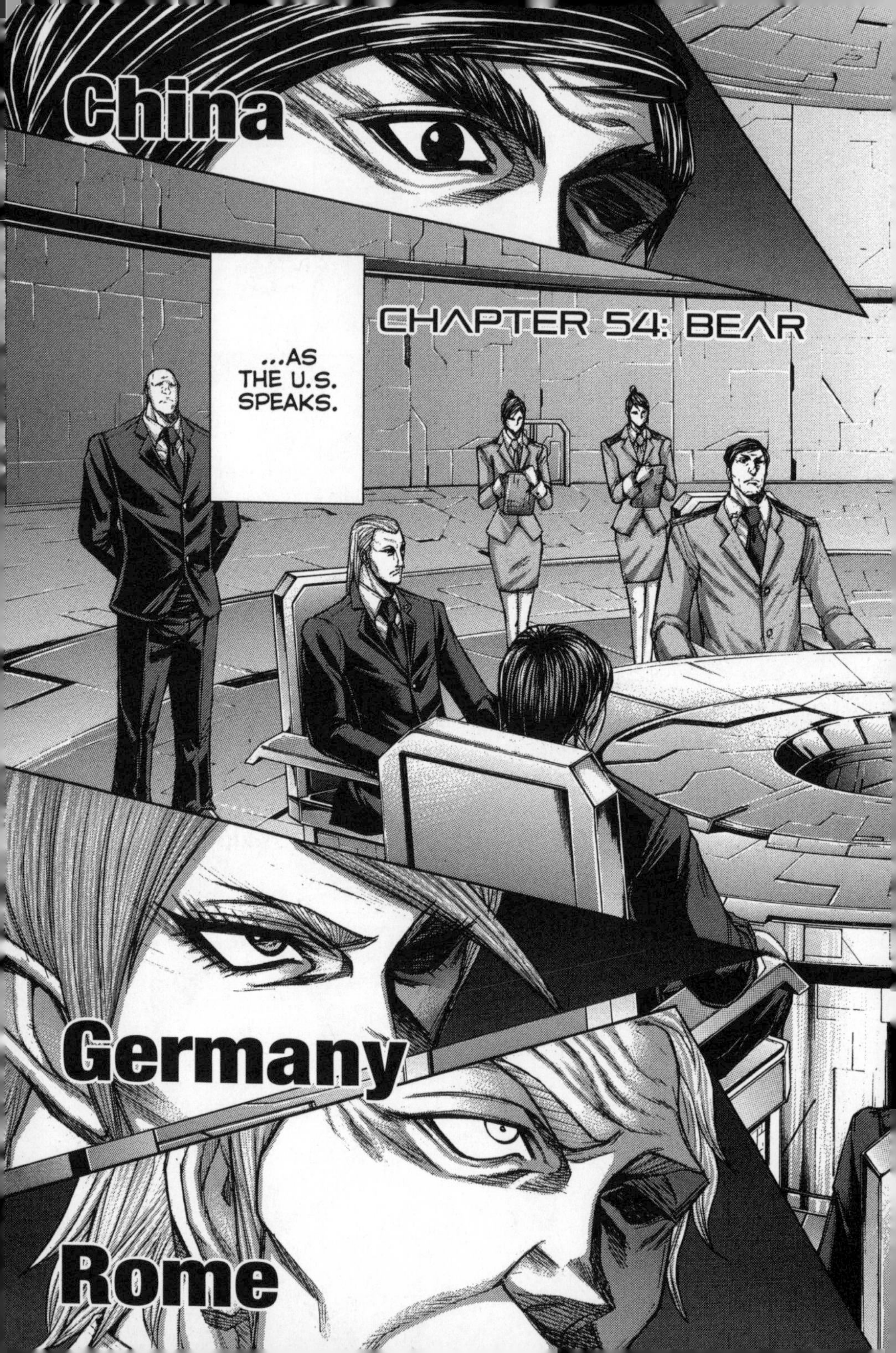
China
CHAPTER 54: BEAR
...AS THE U.S. SPEAKS.
Germany
Rome

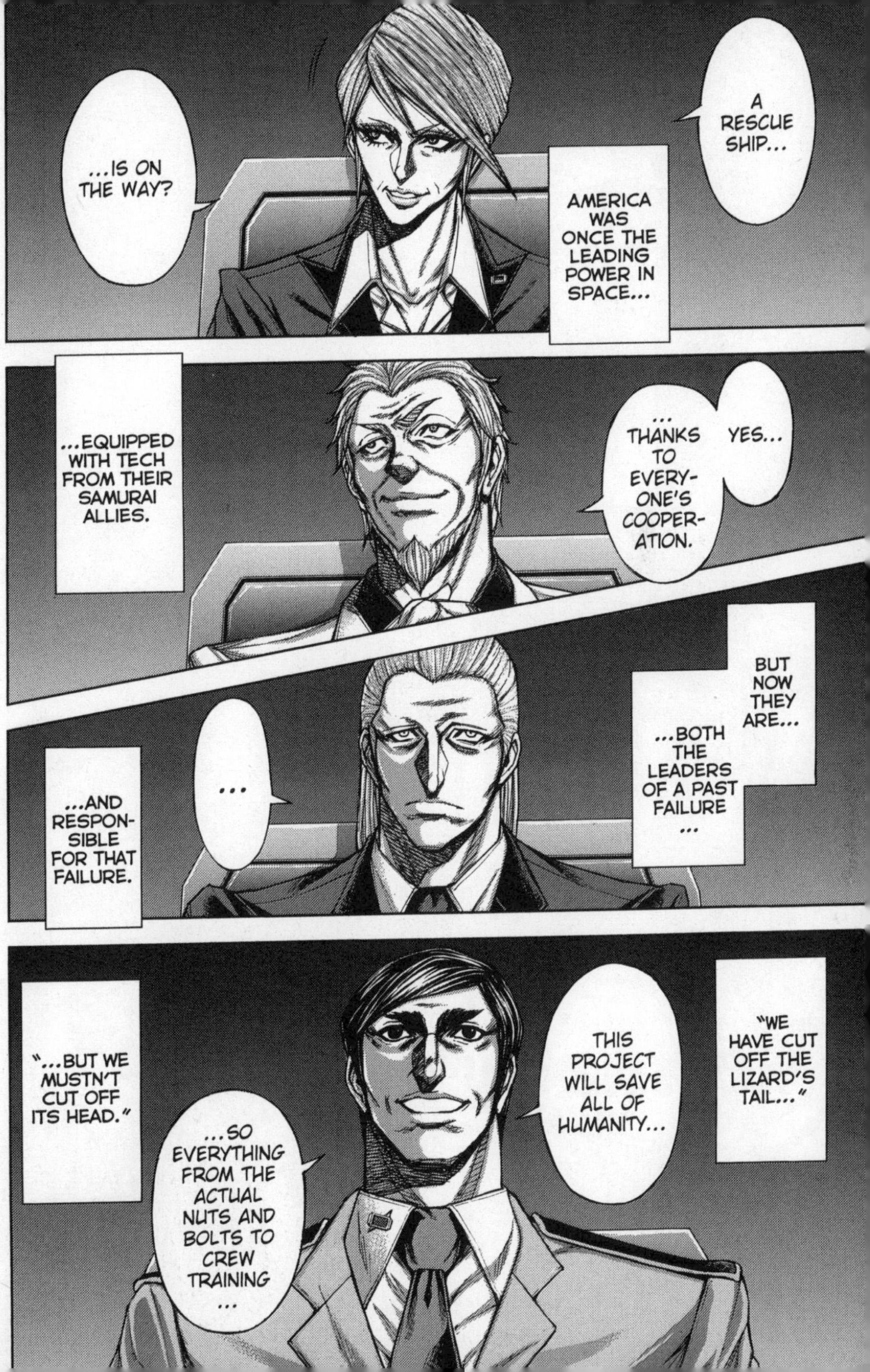
A RESCUE SHIP...
AMERICA WAS ONCE THE LEADING POWER IN SPACE...
...IS ON THE WAY?
YES...
...THANKS TO EVERY-ONE'S COOPER-ATION.
...EQUIPPED WITH TECH FROM THEIR SAMURAI ALLIES.
BUT NOW THEY ARE...
...BOTH THE LEADERS OF A PAST FAILURE...
...
...AND RESPON-SIBLE FOR THAT FAILURE.
"WE HAVE CUT OFF THE LIZARD'S TAIL..."
THIS PROJECT WILL SAVE ALL OF HUMANITY...
...SO EVERYTHING FROM THE ACTUAL NUTS AND BOLTS TO CREW TRAINING...
"...BUT WE MUSTN'T CUT OFF ITS HEAD."

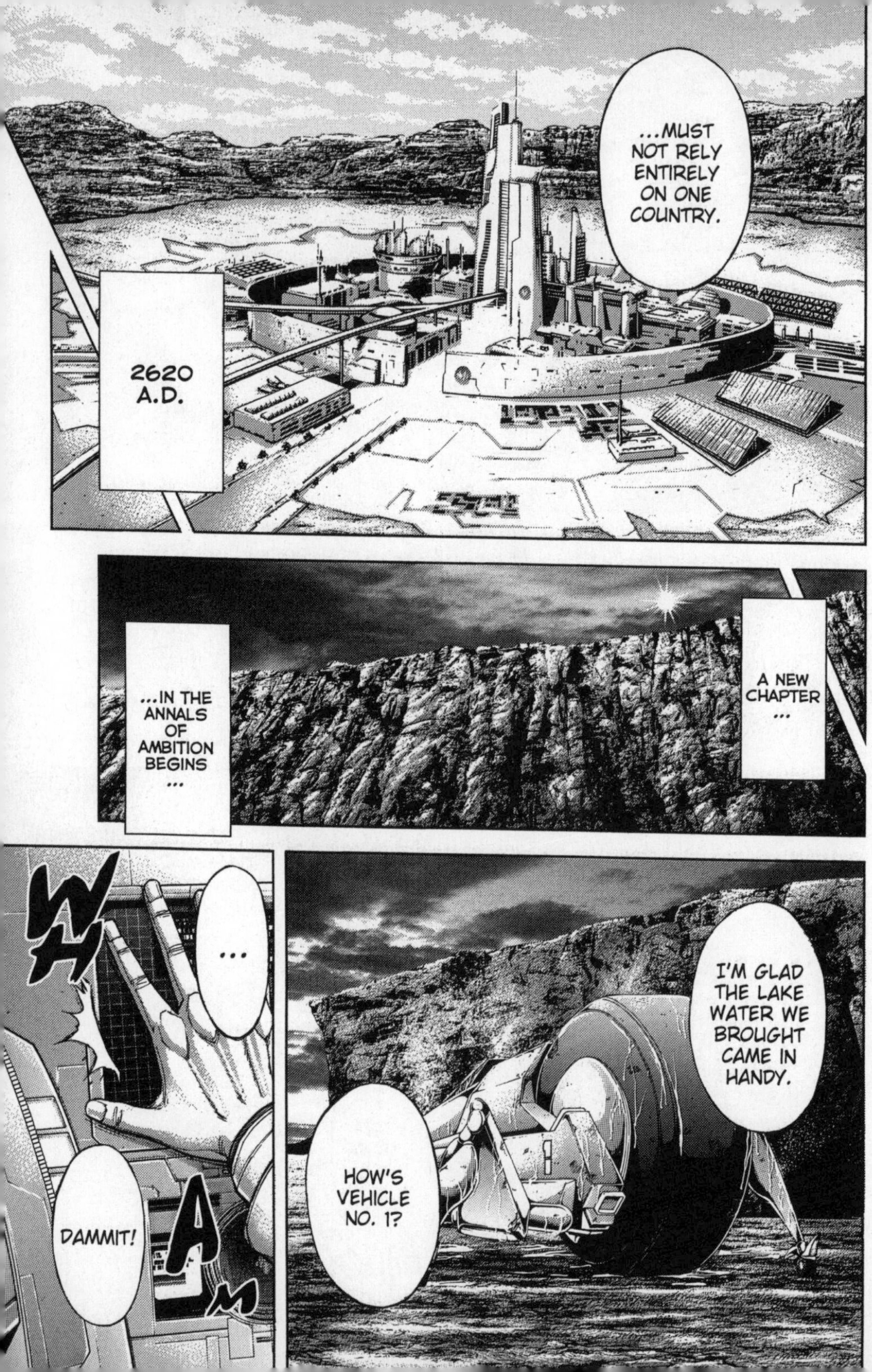
...MUST NOT RELY ENTIRELY ON ONE COUNTRY.
2620 A.D.
A NEW CHAPTER ...
...IN THE ANNALS OF AMBITION BEGINS ...
I'M GLAD THE LAKE WATER WE BROUGHT CAME IN HANDY.
HOW'S VEHICLE NO. 1?
WHAM
...
DAMMIT!

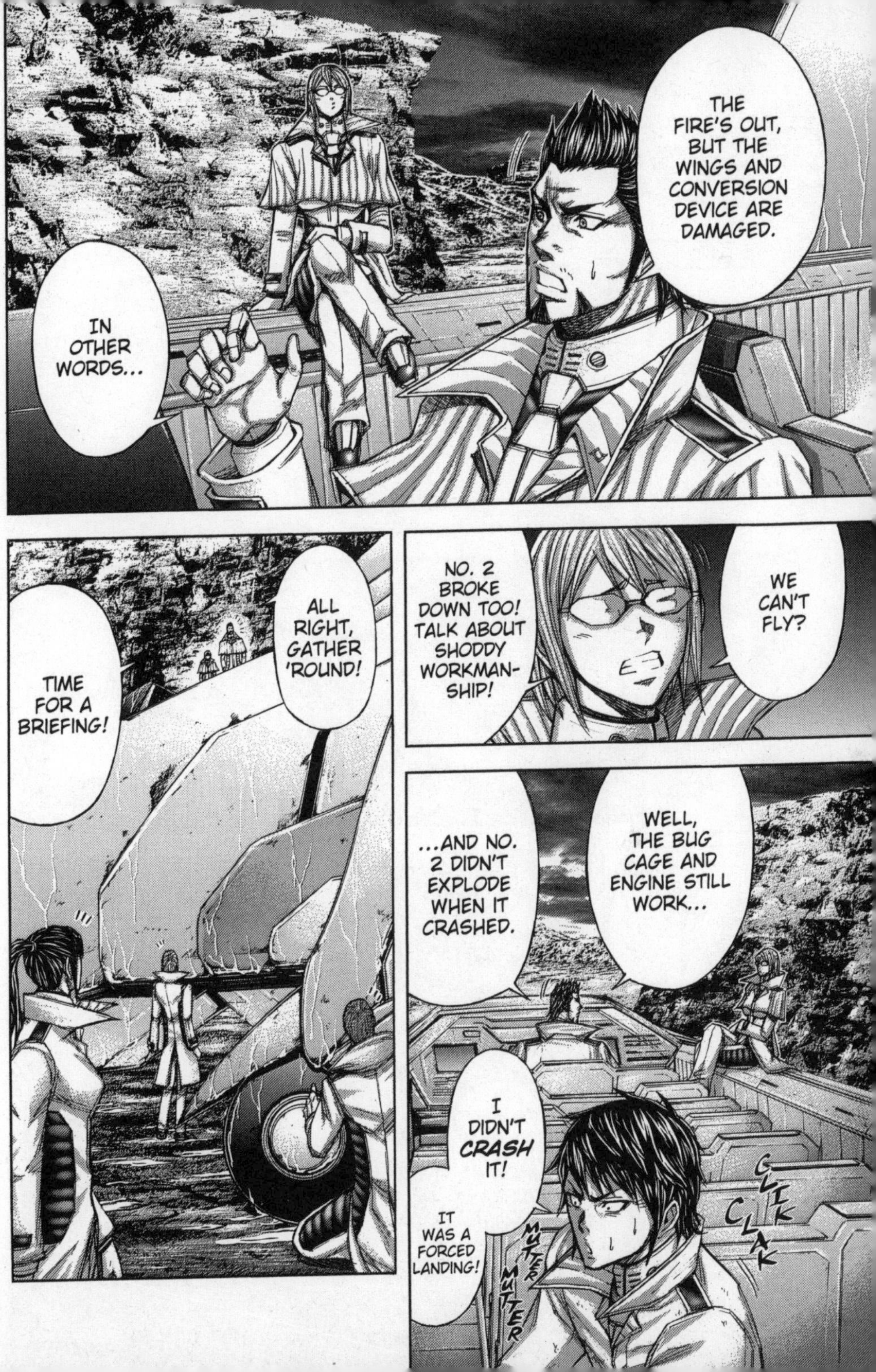
THE FIRE'S OUT, BUT THE WINGS AND CONVERSION DEVICE ARE DAMAGED.
IN OTHER WORDS...
WE CAN'T FLY?
NO. 2 BROKE DOWN TOO! TALK ABOUT SHODDY WORKMAN-SHIP!
WELL, THE BUG CAGE AND ENGINE STILL WORK...
...AND NO. 2 DIDN'T EXPLODE WHEN IT CRASHED.
I DIDN'T CRASH IT!
IT WAS A FORCED LANDING!
MUTTER MUTTER
CLIK CLAK
ALL RIGHT, GATHER 'ROUND!
TIME FOR A BRIEFING!

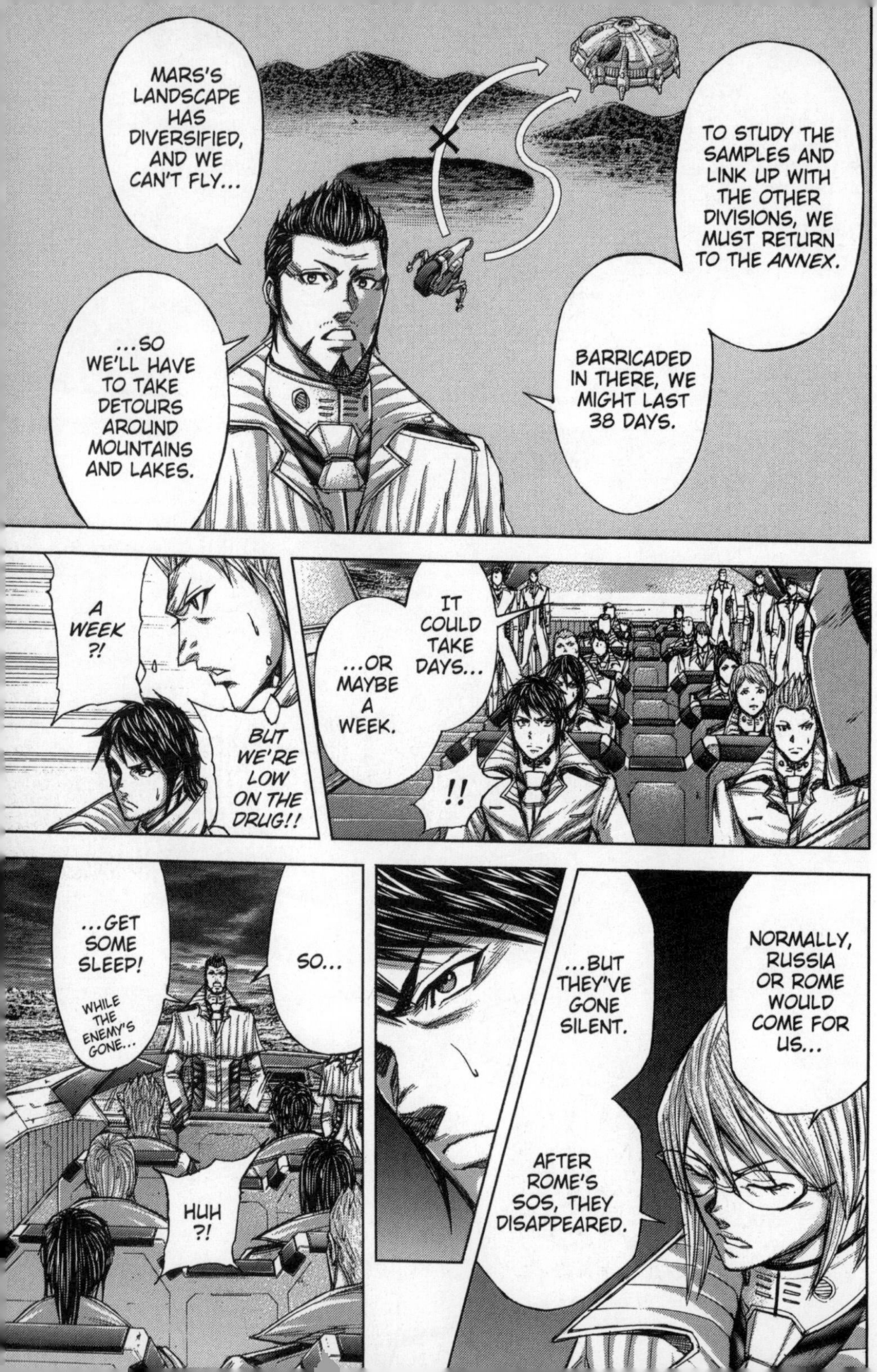
MARS'S LANDSCAPE HAS DIVERSIFIED, AND WE CAN'T FLY...
...SO WE'LL HAVE TO TAKE DETOURS AROUND MOUNTAINS AND LAKES.
TO STUDY THE SAMPLES AND LINK UP WITH THE OTHER DIVISIONS, WE MUST RETURN TO THE *ANNEX*.
BARRICADED IN THERE, WE MIGHT LAST 38 DAYS.
IT COULD TAKE DAYS...
...OR MAYBE A WEEK.
!!
A WEEK?!
BUT WE'RE LOW ON THE DRUG!!
NORMALLY, RUSSIA OR ROME WOULD COME FOR US...
...BUT THEY'VE GONE SILENT.
AFTER ROME'S SOS, THEY DISAPPEARED.
SO...
...GET SOME SLEEP!
WHILE THE ENEMY'S GONE...
HUH?!

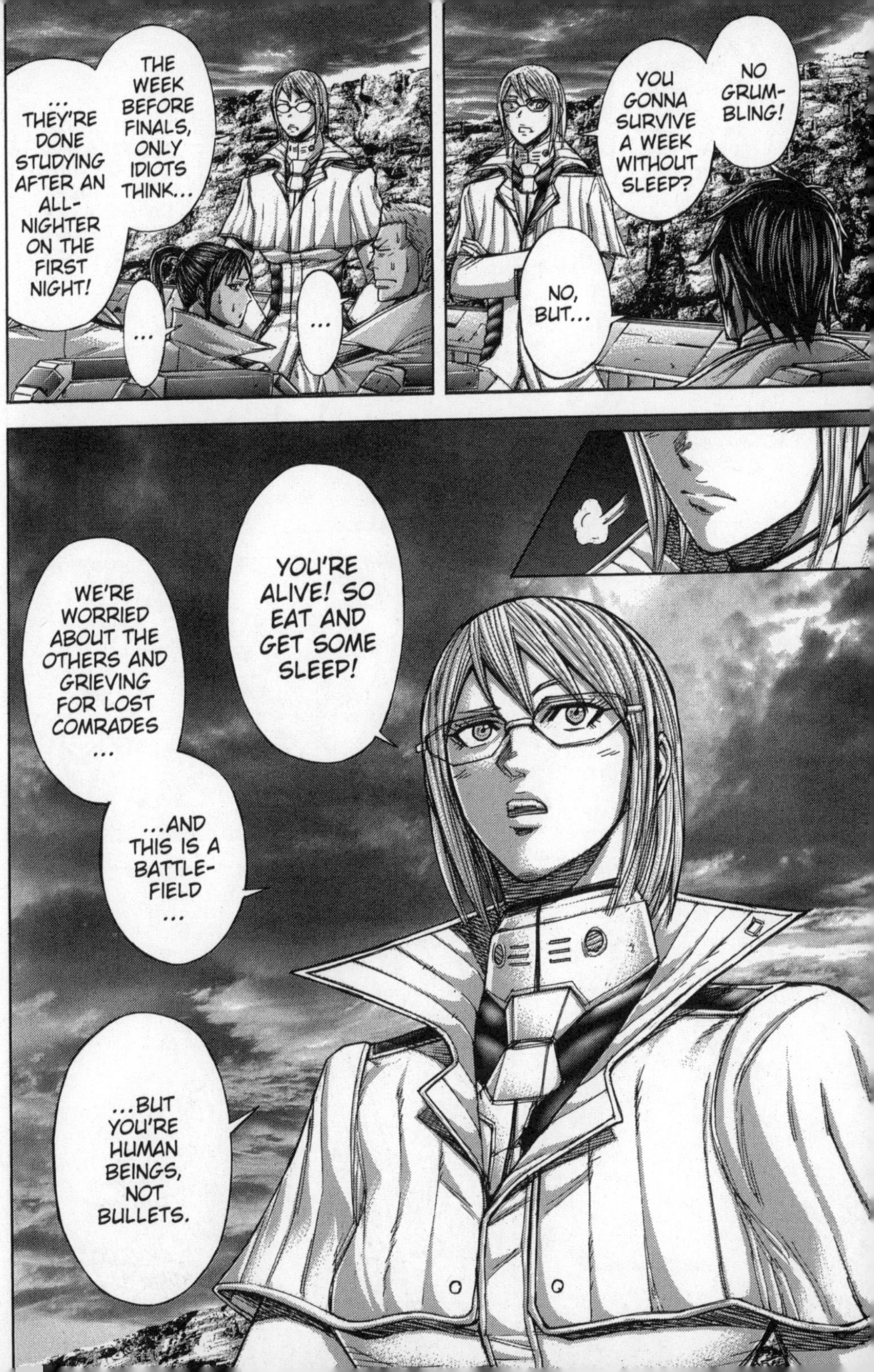
NO GRUMBLING!
YOU GONNA SURVIVE A WEEK WITHOUT SLEEP?
NO, BUT...
THE WEEK BEFORE FINALS, ONLY IDIOTS THINK...
...THEY'RE DONE STUDYING AFTER AN ALL-NIGHTER ON THE FIRST NIGHT!
...
...
YOU'RE ALIVE! SO EAT AND GET SOME SLEEP!
WE'RE WORRIED ABOUT THE OTHERS AND GRIEVING FOR LOST COMRADES...
...AND THIS IS A BATTLEFIELD...
...BUT YOU'RE HUMAN BEINGS, NOT BULLETS.

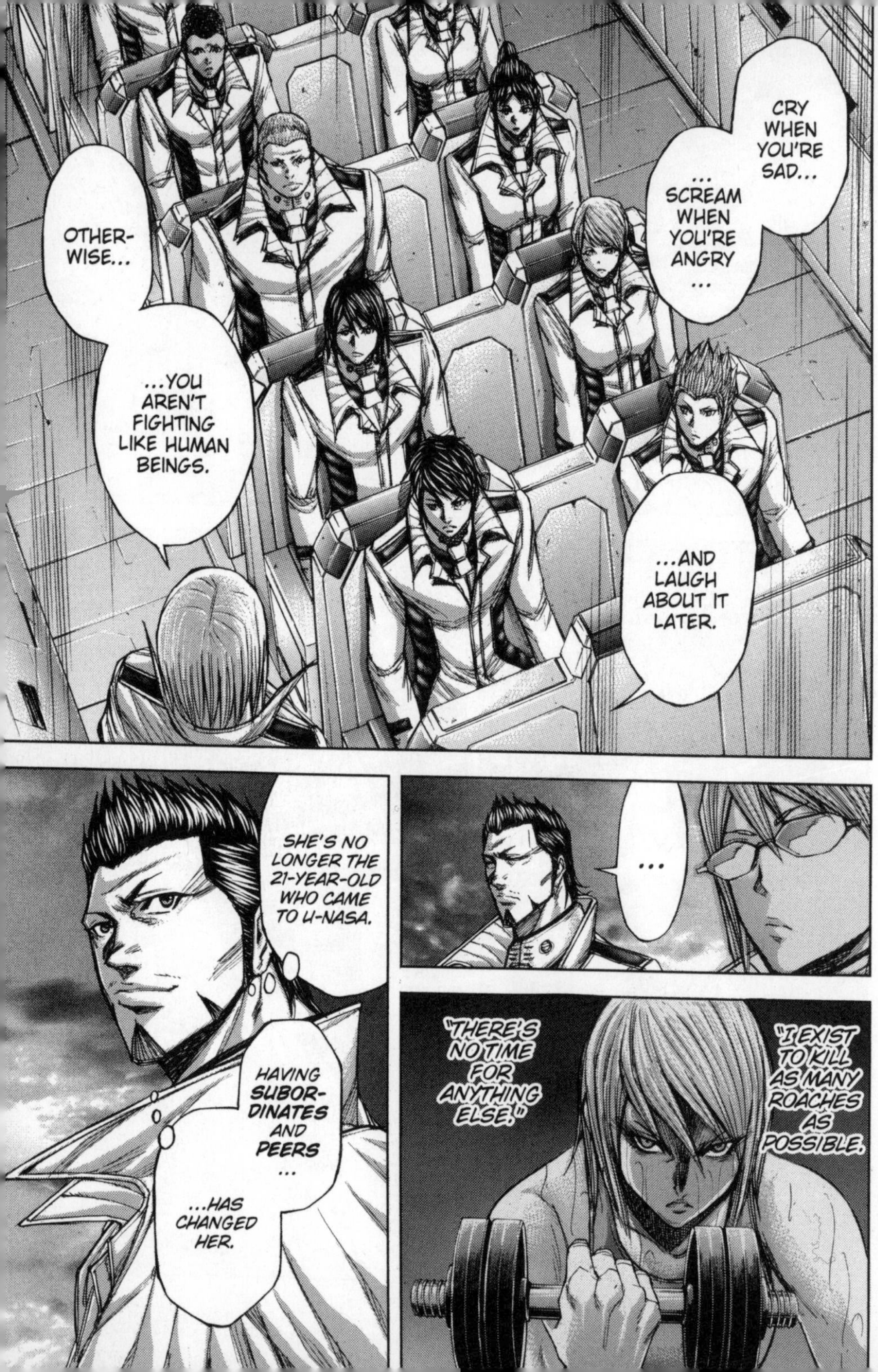
CRY WHEN YOU'RE SAD...
...SCREAM WHEN YOU'RE ANGRY...
...AND LAUGH ABOUT IT LATER.
OTHER-WISE...
...YOU AREN'T FIGHTING LIKE HUMAN BEINGS.
...
"I EXIST TO KILL AS MANY ROACHES AS POSSIBLE.
"THERE'S NO TIME FOR ANYTHING ELSE."
SHE'S NO LONGER THE 21-YEAR-OLD WHO CAME TO U-NASA.
HAVING SUBOR-DINATES AND PEERS...
...HAS CHANGED HER.

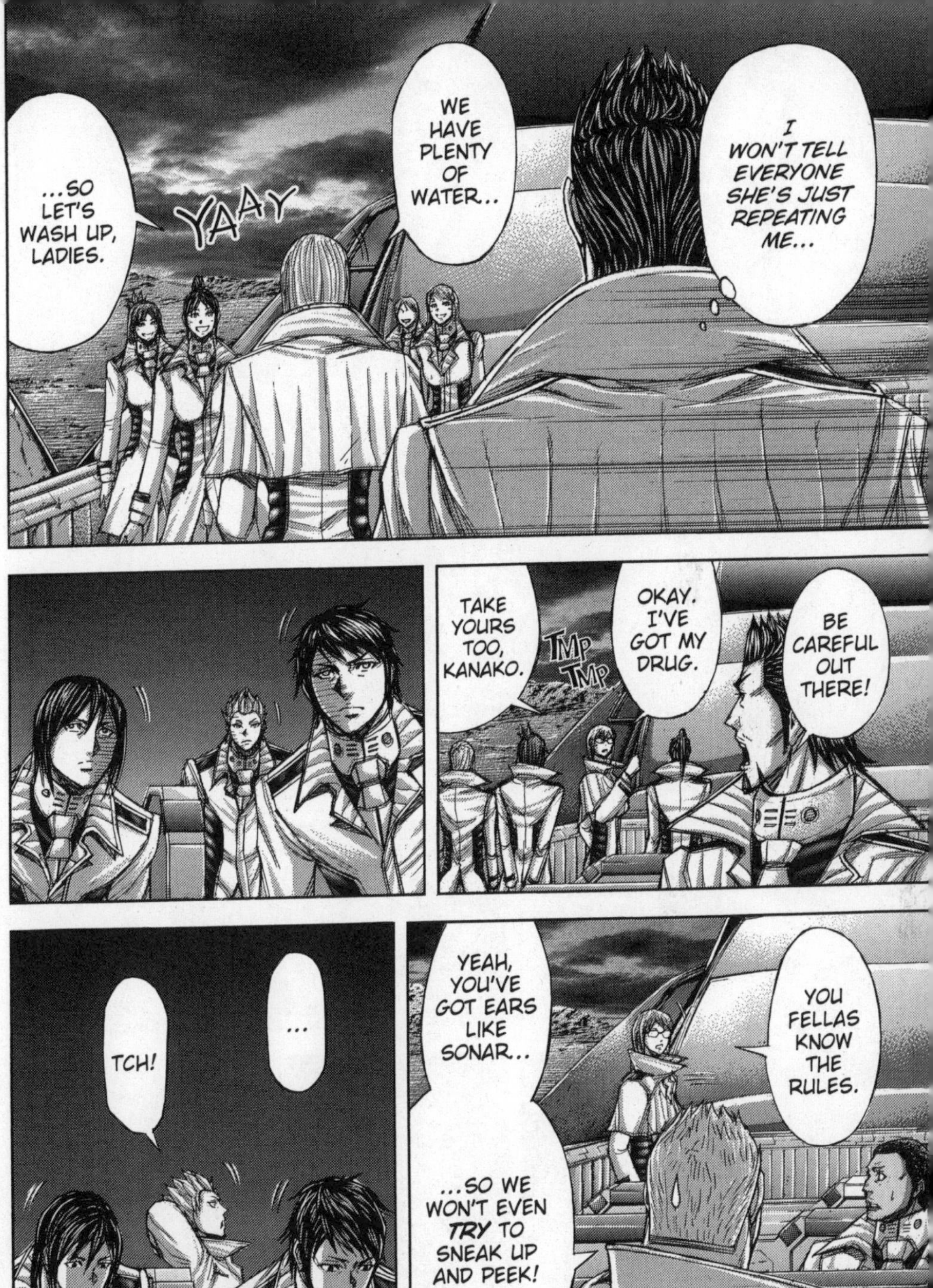
I WON'T TELL EVERYONE SHE'S JUST REPEATING ME...
WE HAVE PLENTY OF WATER...
...SO LET'S WASH UP, LADIES.
YAAY
BE CAREFUL OUT THERE!
OKAY. I'VE GOT MY DRUG.
TMP TMP
TAKE YOURS TOO, KANAKO.
YOU FELLAS KNOW THE RULES.
YEAH, YOU'VE GOT EARS LIKE SONAR...
...SO WE WON'T EVEN *TRY* TO SNEAK UP AND PEEK!
...
TCH!

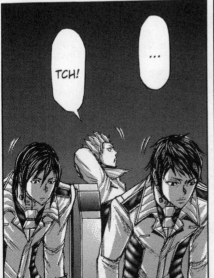

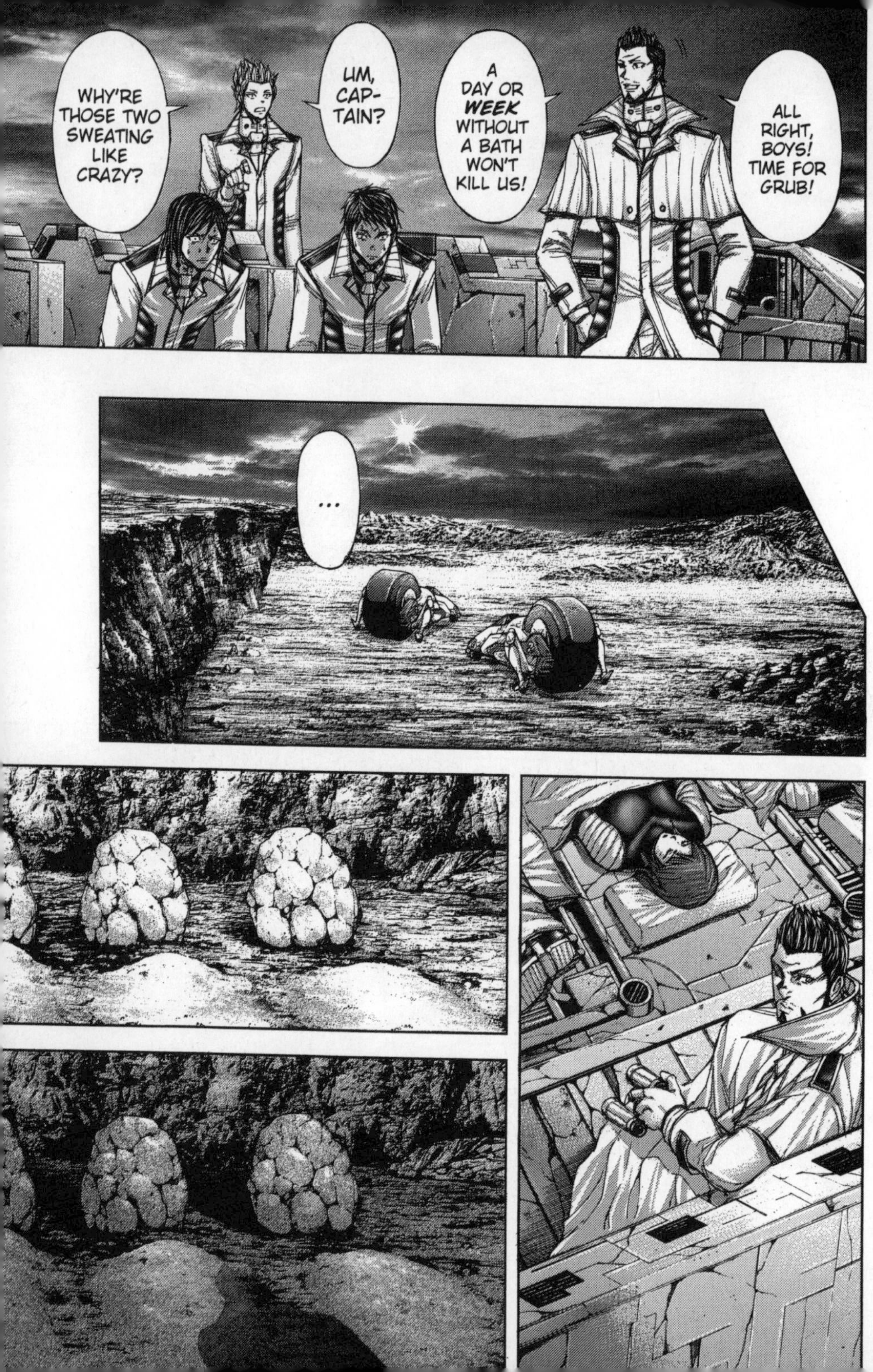
ALL RIGHT, BOYS! TIME FOR GRUB!
A DAY OR **WEEK** WITHOUT A BATH WON'T KILL US!
UM, CAP-TAIN?
WHY'RE THOSE TWO SWEATING LIKE CRAZY?
...

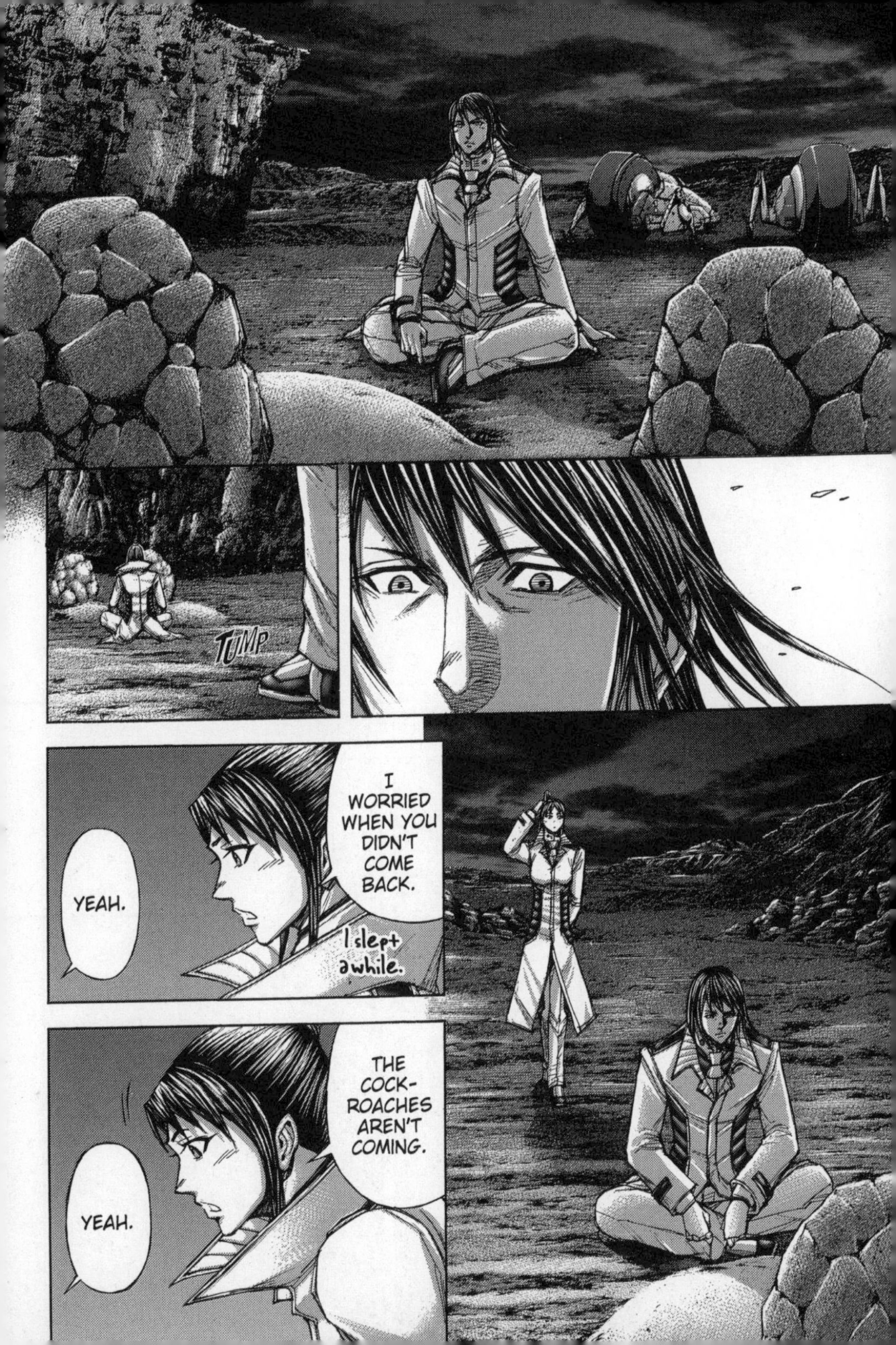
TUMP
I WORRIED WHEN YOU DIDN'T COME BACK.
I slept awhile.
YEAH.
THE COCK-ROACHES AREN'T COMING.
YEAH.

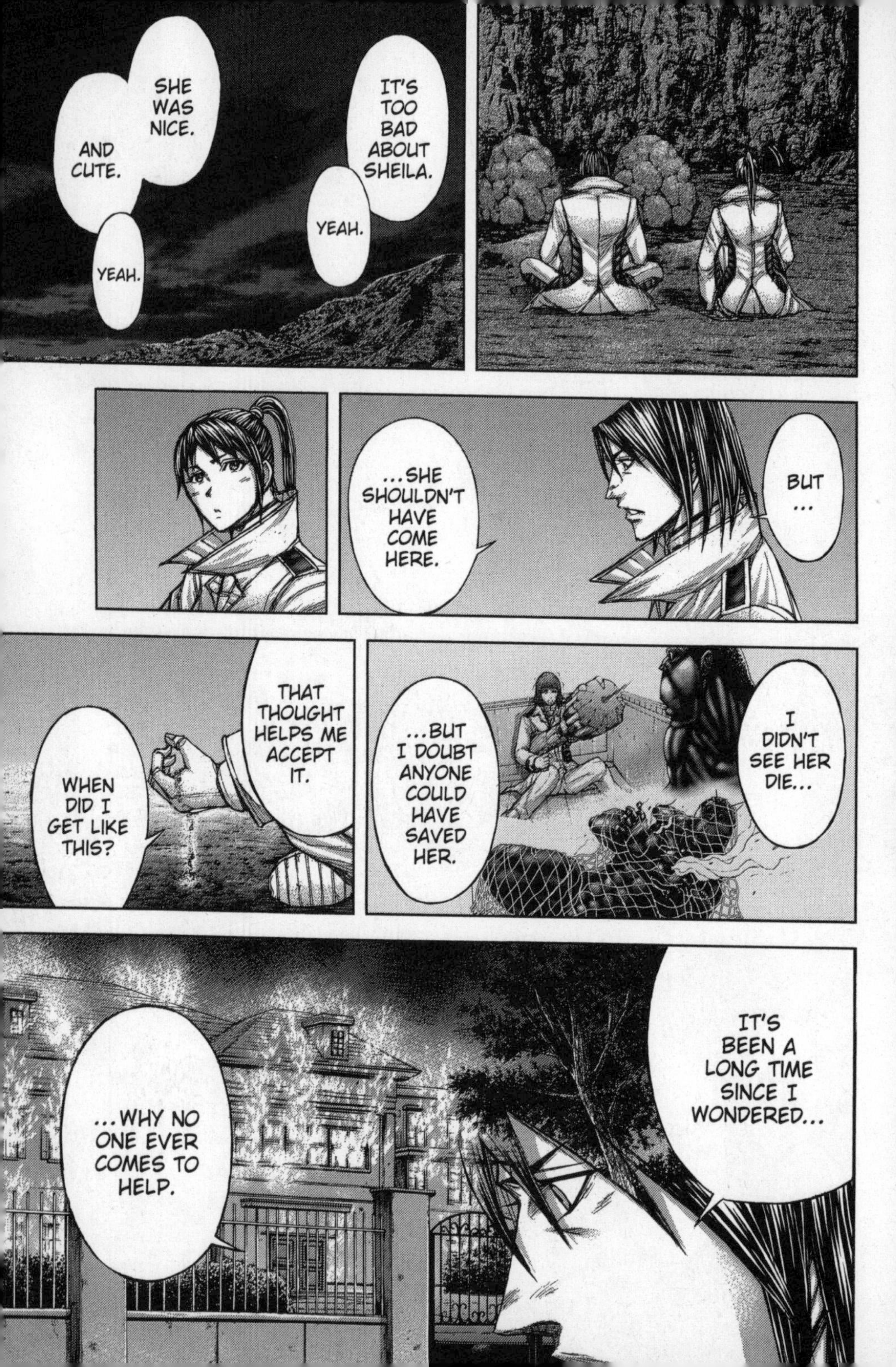
IT'S TOO BAD ABOUT SHEILA.
YEAH.
SHE WAS NICE.
AND CUTE.
YEAH.
BUT ...
...SHE SHOULDN'T HAVE COME HERE.
I DIDN'T SEE HER DIE...
...BUT I DOUBT ANYONE COULD HAVE SAVED HER.
THAT THOUGHT HELPS ME ACCEPT IT.
WHEN DID I GET LIKE THIS?
IT'S BEEN A LONG TIME SINCE I WONDERED...
...WHY NO ONE EVER COMES TO HELP.

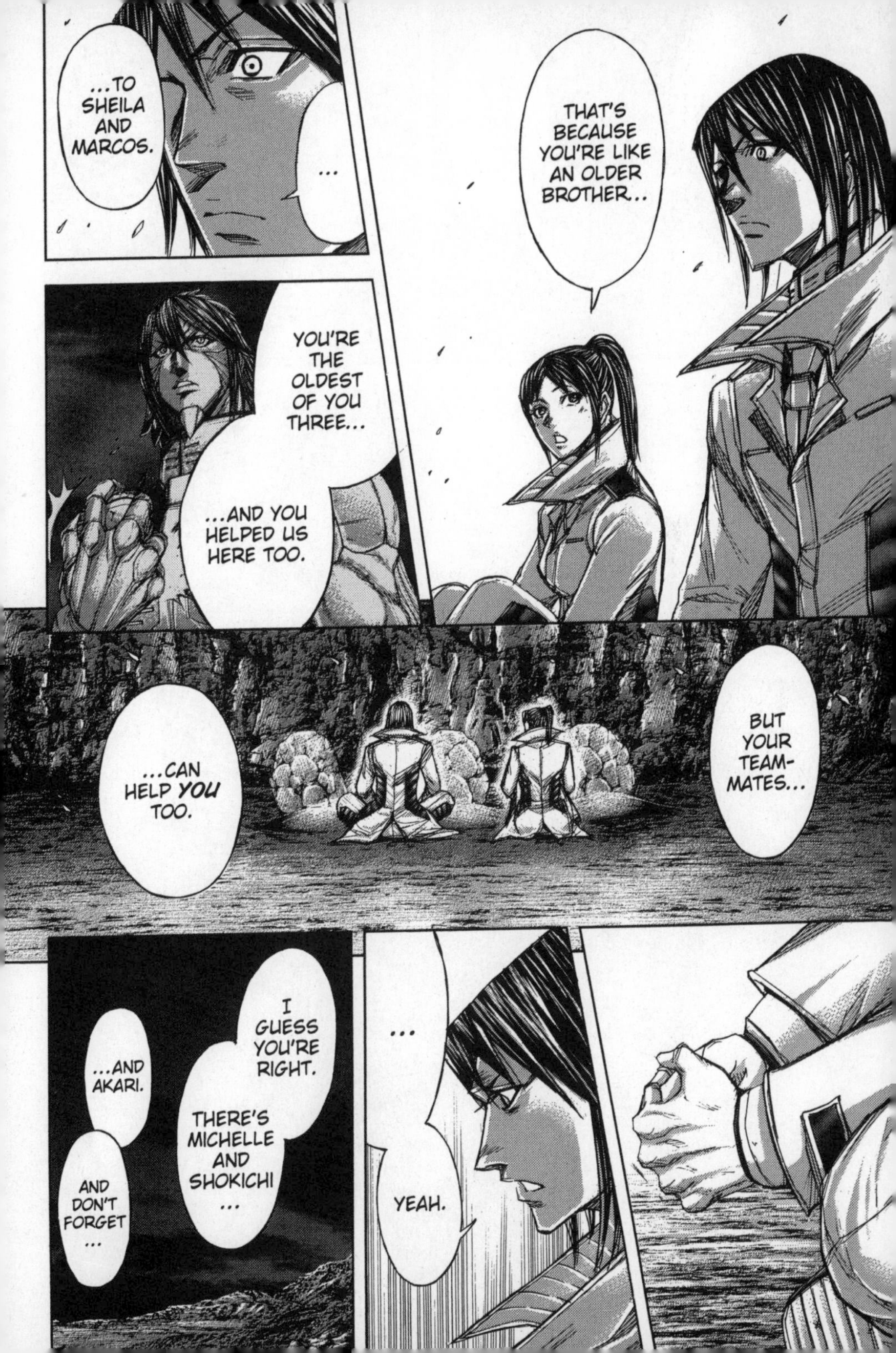
THAT'S BECAUSE YOU'RE LIKE AN OLDER BROTHER...
...TO SHEILA AND MARCOS.
...
YOU'RE THE OLDEST OF YOU THREE...
...AND YOU HELPED US HERE TOO.
BUT YOUR TEAM-MATES...
...CAN HELP *YOU* TOO.
...
YEAH.
I GUESS YOU'RE RIGHT.
THERE'S MICHELLE AND SHOKICHI...
AND DON'T FORGET...
...AND AKARI.

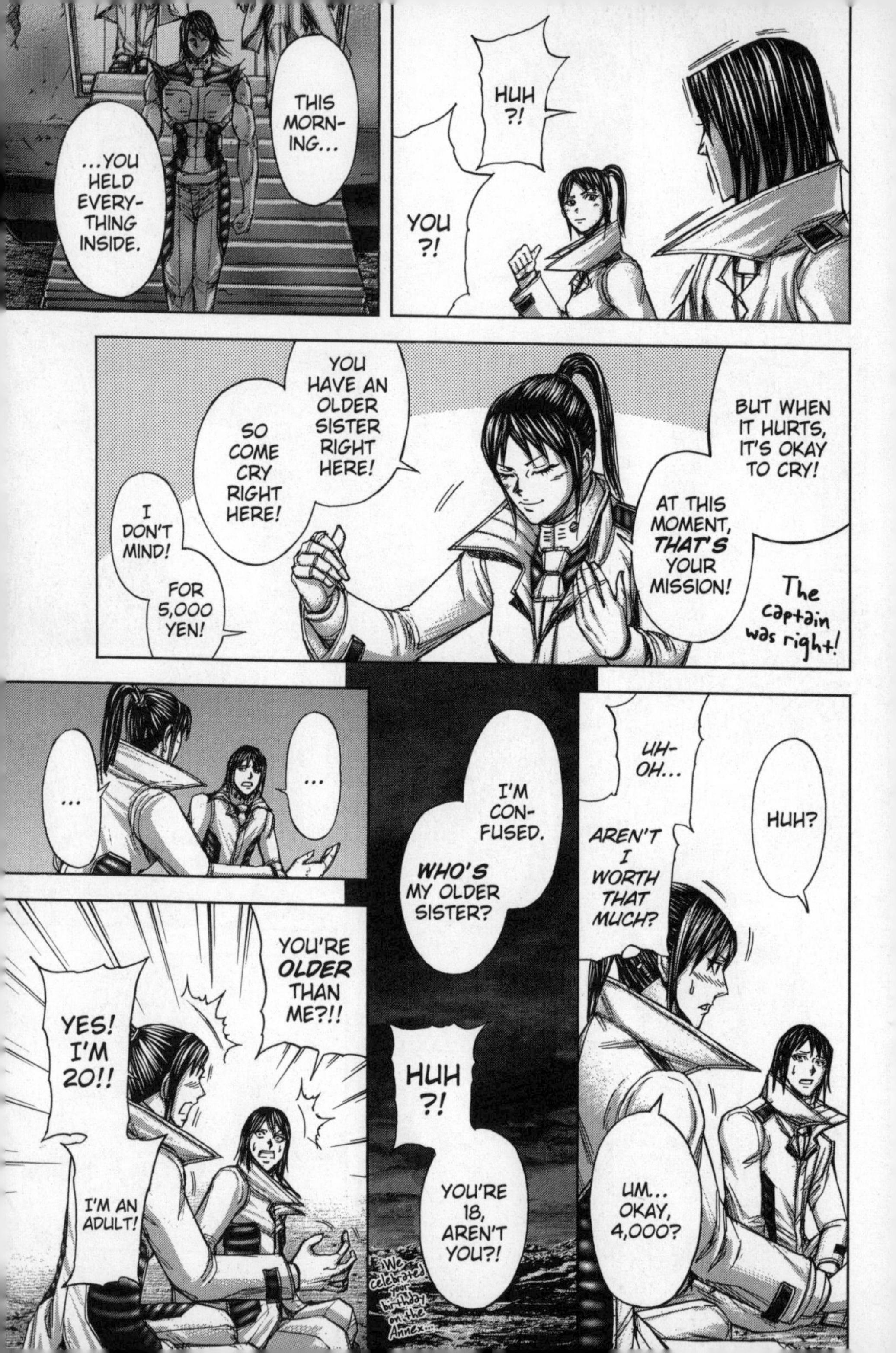
HUH ?!
YOU ?!
THIS MORNING-ING...
...YOU HELD EVERYTHING INSIDE.
BUT WHEN IT HURTS, IT'S OKAY TO CRY!
AT THIS MOMENT, *THAT'S* YOUR MISSION!
The captain was right!
YOU HAVE AN OLDER SISTER RIGHT HERE!
SO COME CRY RIGHT HERE!
I DON'T MIND!
FOR 5,000 YEN!
UH-OH...
HUH?
AREN'T I WORTH THAT MUCH?
UM... OKAY, 4,000?
I'M CON-FUSED.
WHO'S MY OLDER SISTER?
HUH ?!
YOU'RE 18, AREN'T YOU?!
We celebrated your birthday on the Annex...
...
...
YOU'RE *OLDER* THAN ME?!!
YES! I'M 20!!
I'M AN ADULT!

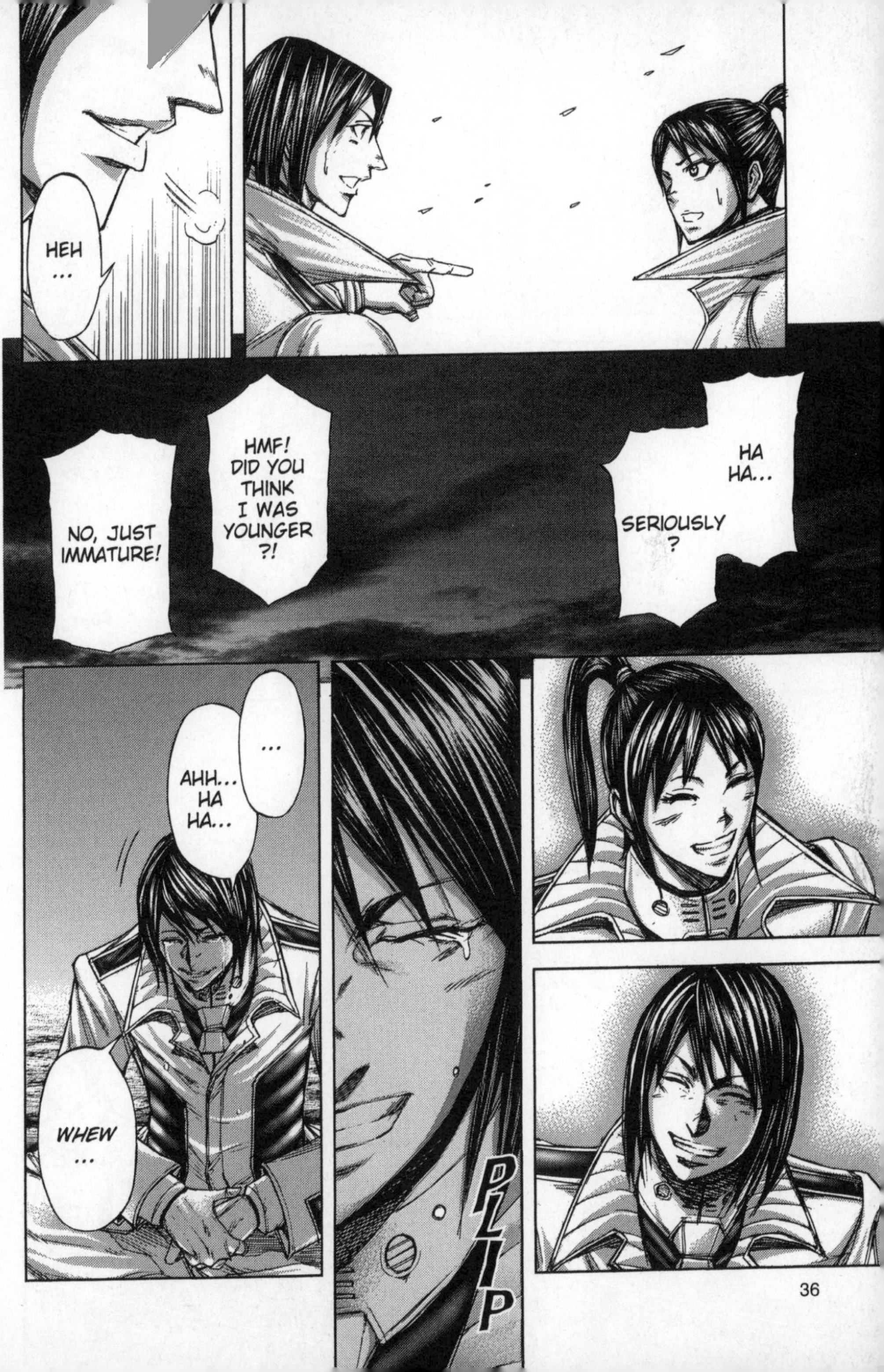
HEH ...
HA HA...
SERIOUSLY ?
HMF! DID YOU THINK I WAS YOUNGER ?!
NO, JUST IMMATURE!
PLIP
...
AHH... HA HA...
WHEW ...

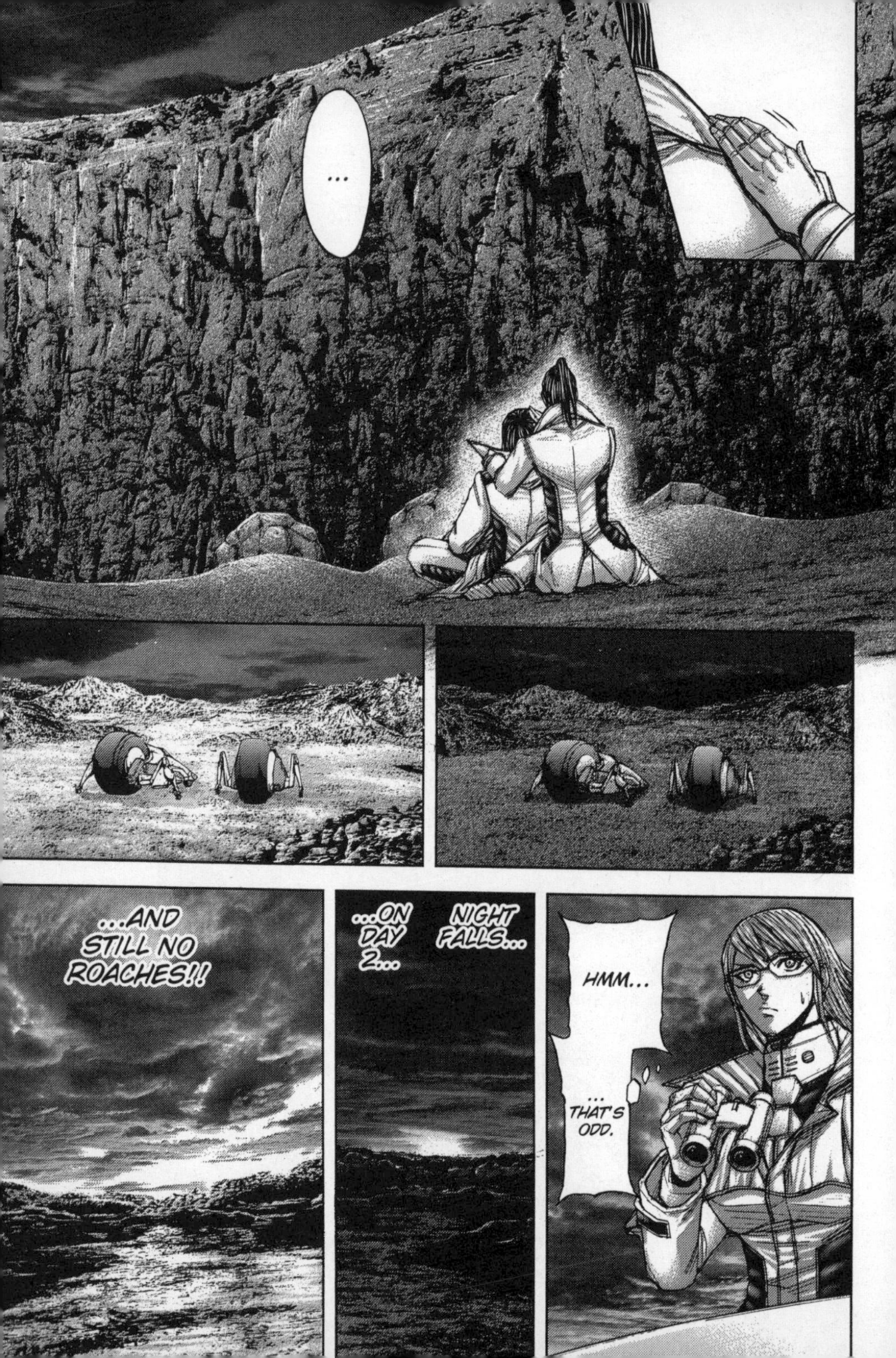
...
HMM...
... THAT'S ODD.
NIGHT FALLS...
...ON DAY 2...
...AND STILL NO ROACHES!!

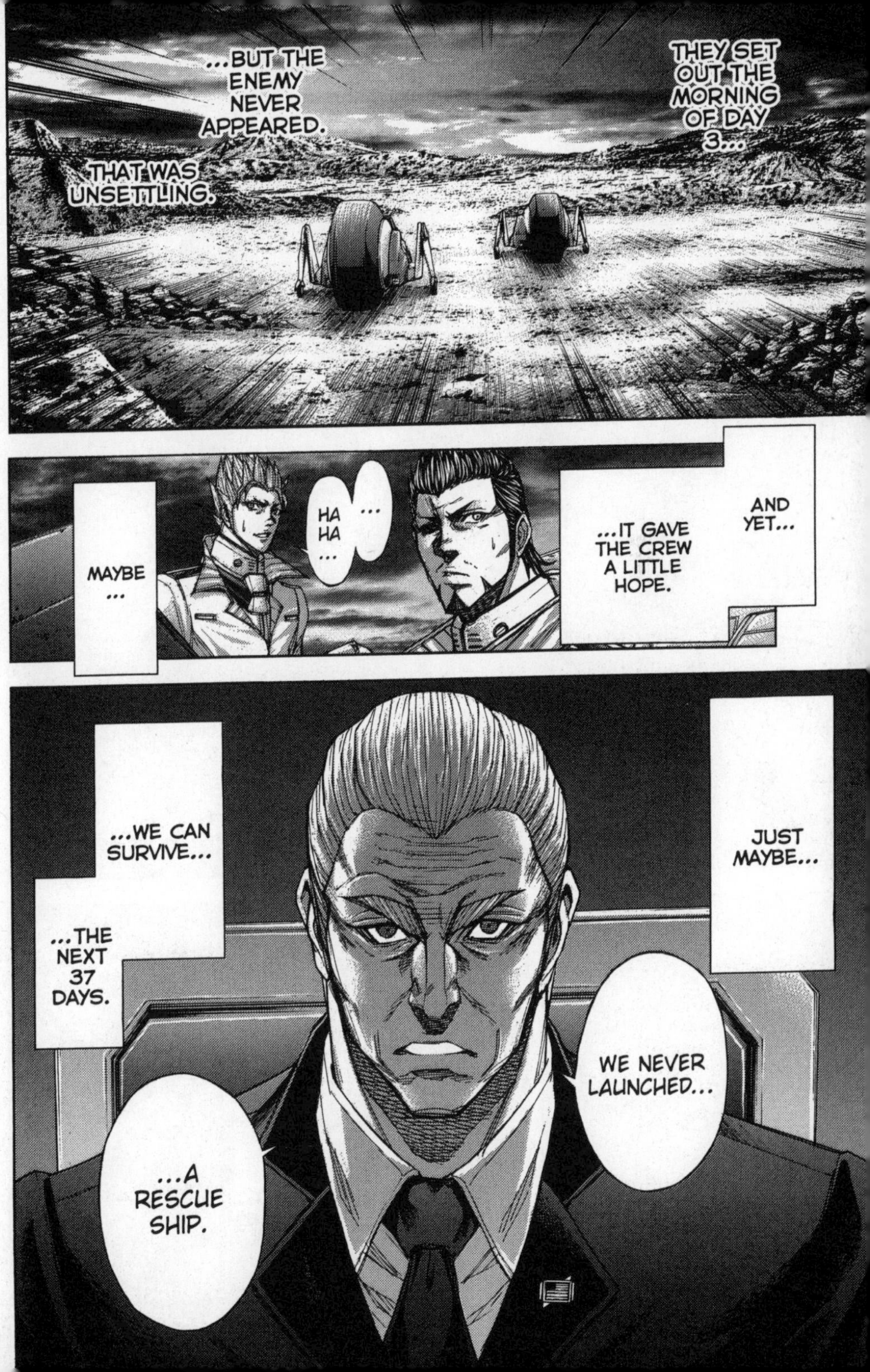
THEY SET OUT THE MORNING OF DAY 3...
...BUT THE ENEMY NEVER APPEARED.
THAT WAS UNSETTLING.
AND YET...
...IT GAVE THE CREW A LITTLE HOPE.
...
HA HA ...
MAYBE ...
JUST MAYBE...
...WE CAN SURVIVE...
...THE NEXT 37 DAYS.
WE NEVER LAUNCHED...
...A RESCUE SHIP.

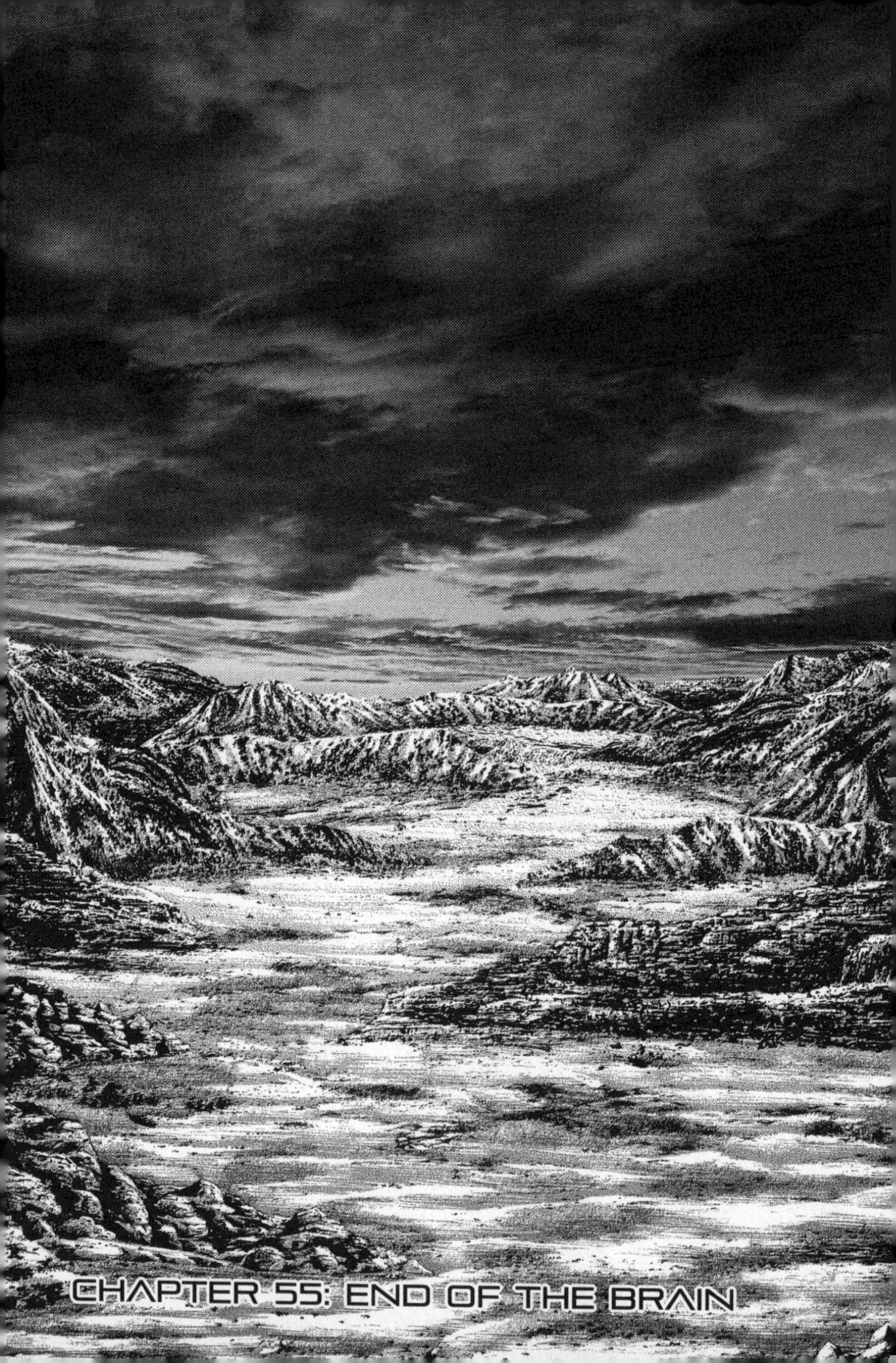

CHAPTER 55: END OF THE BRAIN

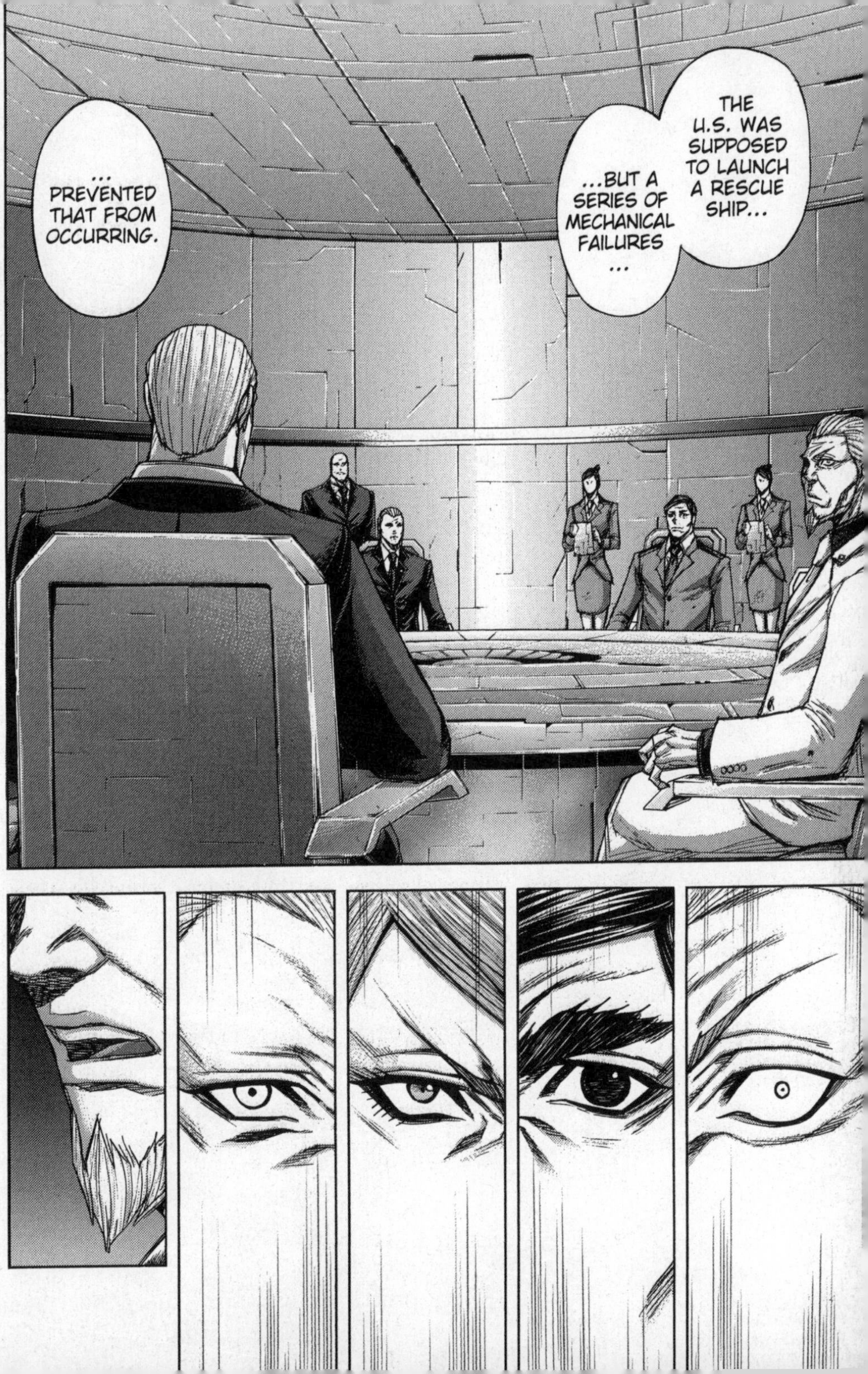
THE U.S. WAS SUPPOSED TO LAUNCH A RESCUE SHIP...
...BUT A SERIES OF MECHANICAL FAILURES ...
... PREVENTED THAT FROM OCCURRING.

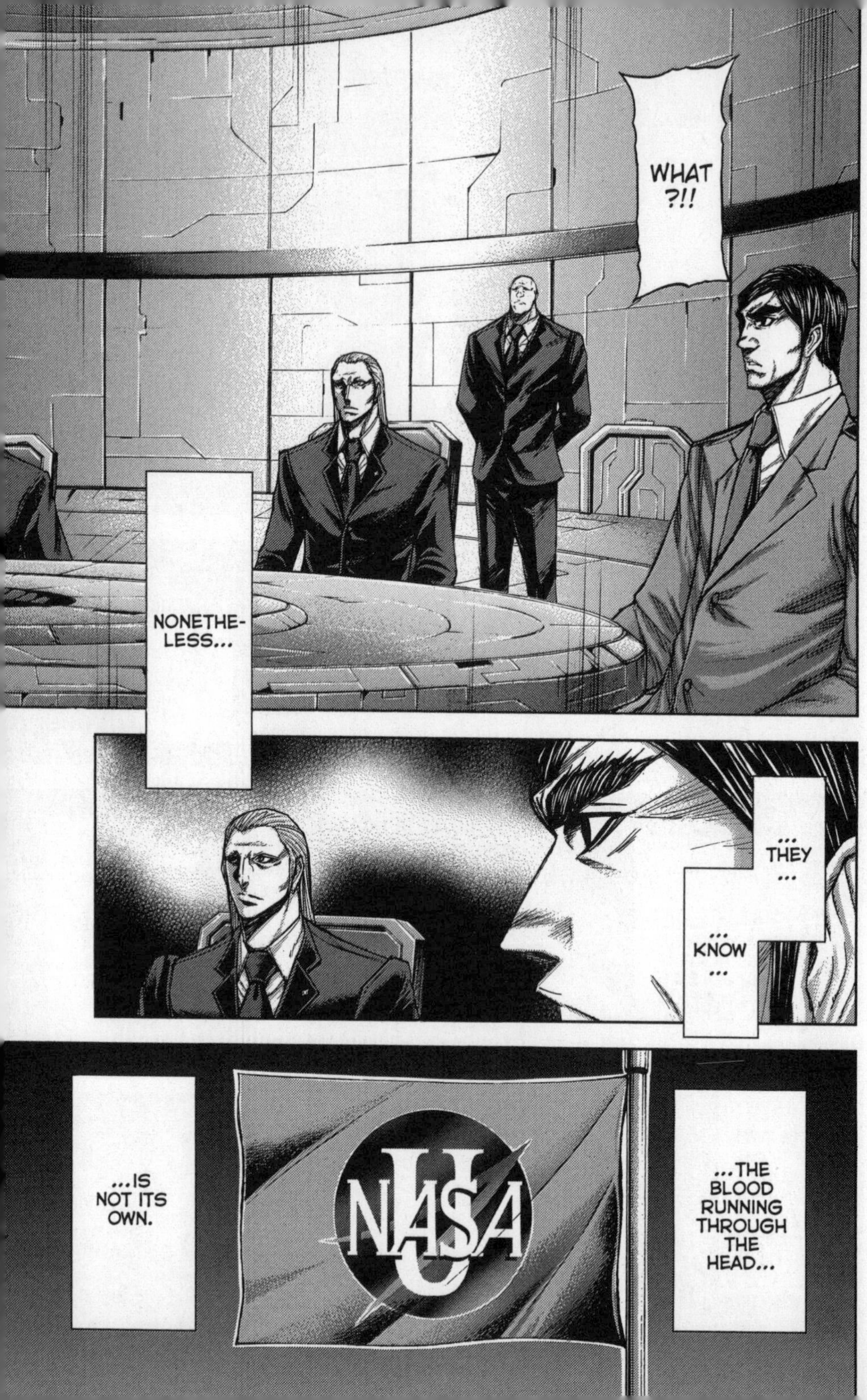
WHAT?!!
NONETHE-LESS...
...THEY...
...KNOW...
...THE BLOOD RUNNING THROUGH THE HEAD...
...IS NOT ITS OWN.

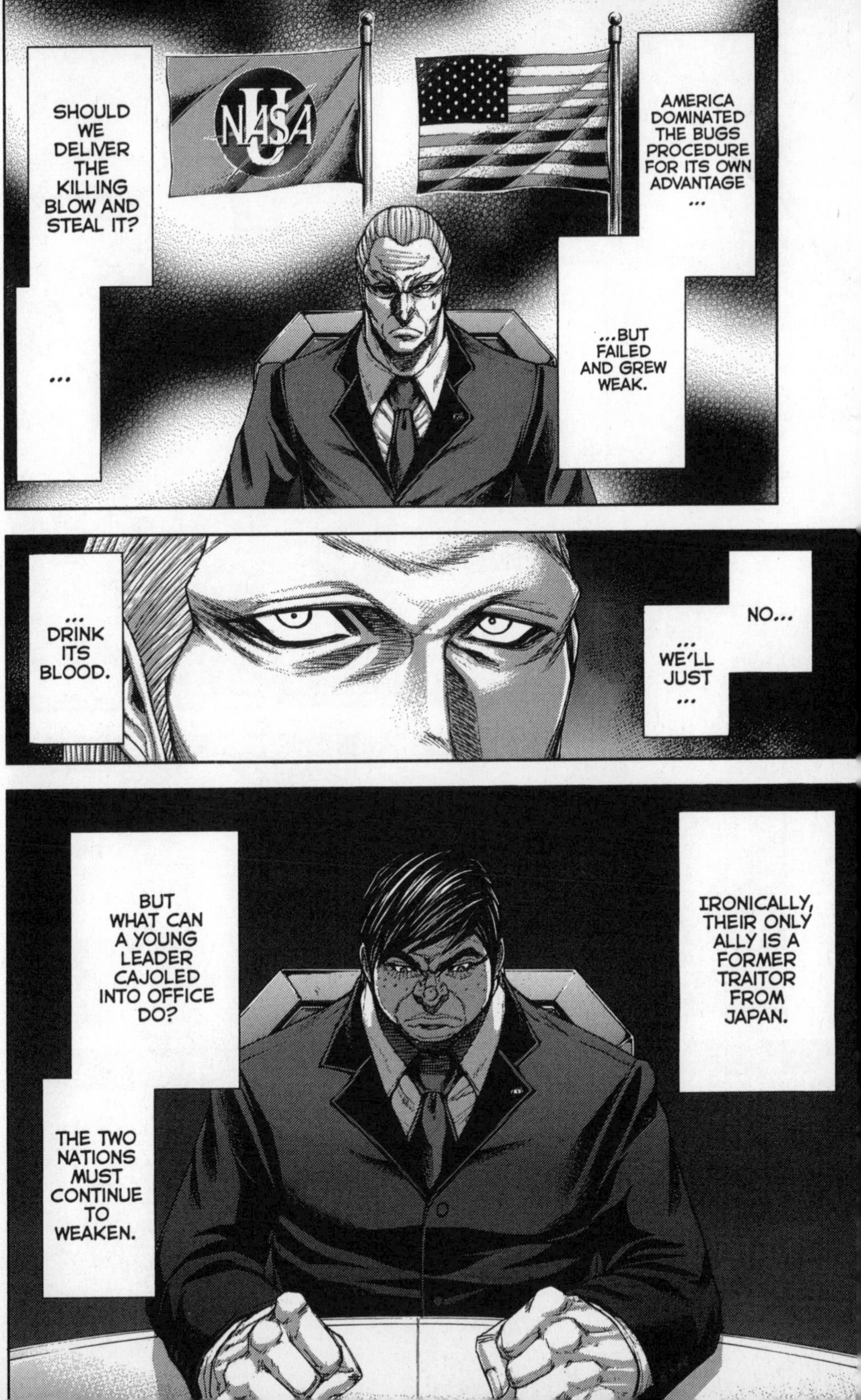
AMERICA DOMINATED THE BUGS PROCEDURE FOR ITS OWN ADVANTAGE ...
...BUT FAILED AND GREW WEAK.
SHOULD WE DELIVER THE KILLING BLOW AND STEAL IT?
...
NO...
... WE'LL JUST ...
... DRINK ITS BLOOD.
IRONICALLY, THEIR ONLY ALLY IS A FORMER TRAITOR FROM JAPAN.
BUT WHAT CAN A YOUNG LEADER CAJOLED INTO OFFICE DO?
THE TWO NATIONS MUST CONTINUE TO WEAKEN.

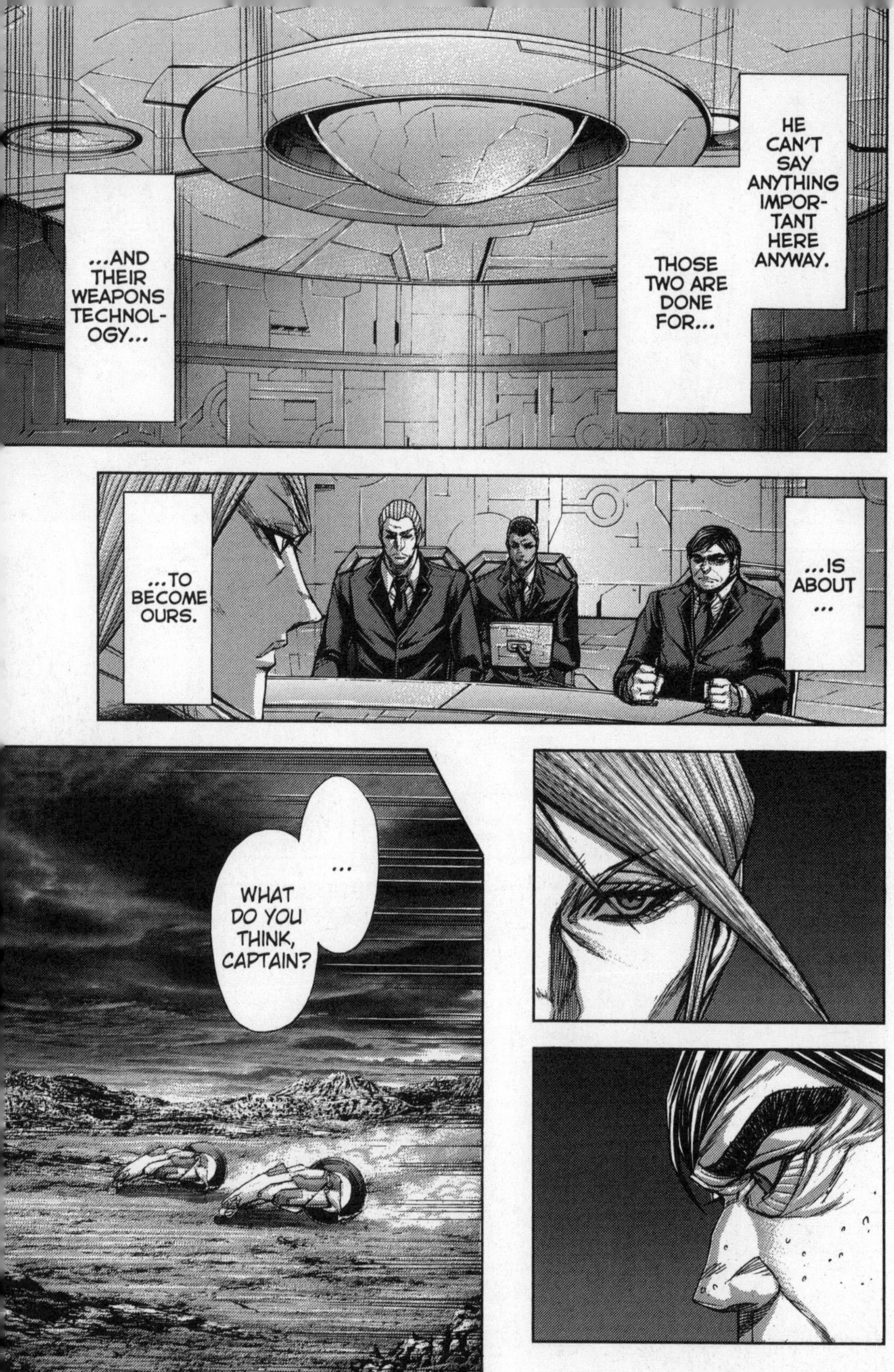
HE CAN'T SAY ANYTHING IMPOR-TANT HERE ANYWAY.
THOSE TWO ARE DONE FOR...
...AND THEIR WEAPONS TECHNOL-OGY...
...IS ABOUT ...
...TO BECOME OURS.
... WHAT DO YOU THINK, CAPTAIN?

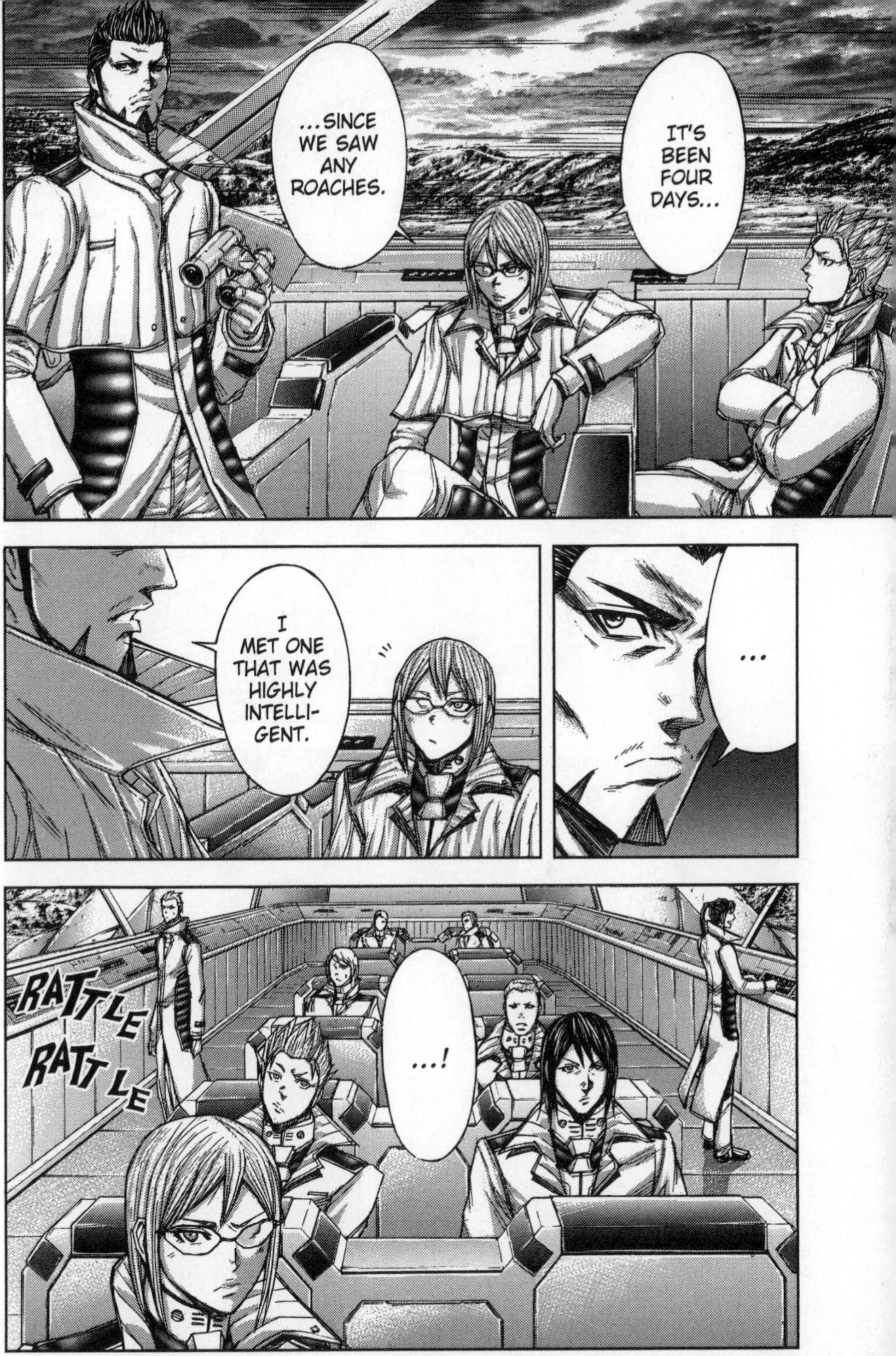
IT'S BEEN FOUR DAYS...
...SINCE WE SAW ANY ROACHES.
...
I MET ONE THAT WAS HIGHLY INTELLI-GENT.
...!
RATTLE RATTLE

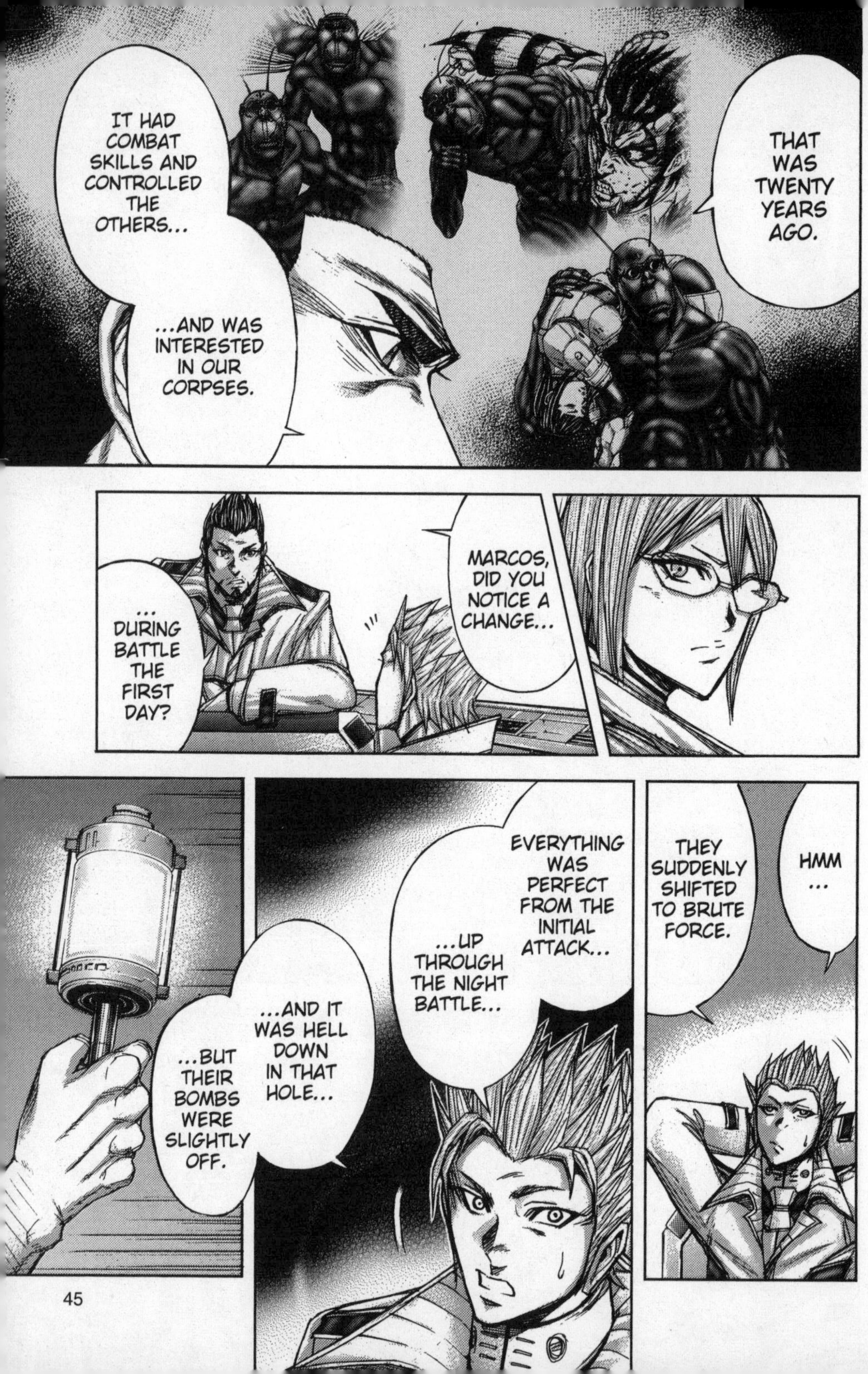
THAT WAS TWENTY YEARS AGO.
IT HAD COMBAT SKILLS AND CONTROLLED THE OTHERS...
...AND WAS INTERESTED IN OUR CORPSES.
MARCOS, DID YOU NOTICE A CHANGE...
...DURING BATTLE THE FIRST DAY?
HMM ...
THEY SUDDENLY SHIFTED TO BRUTE FORCE.
EVERYTHING WAS PERFECT FROM THE INITIAL ATTACK...
...UP THROUGH THE NIGHT BATTLE...
...AND IT WAS HELL DOWN IN THAT HOLE...
...BUT THEIR BOMBS WERE SLIGHTLY OFF.

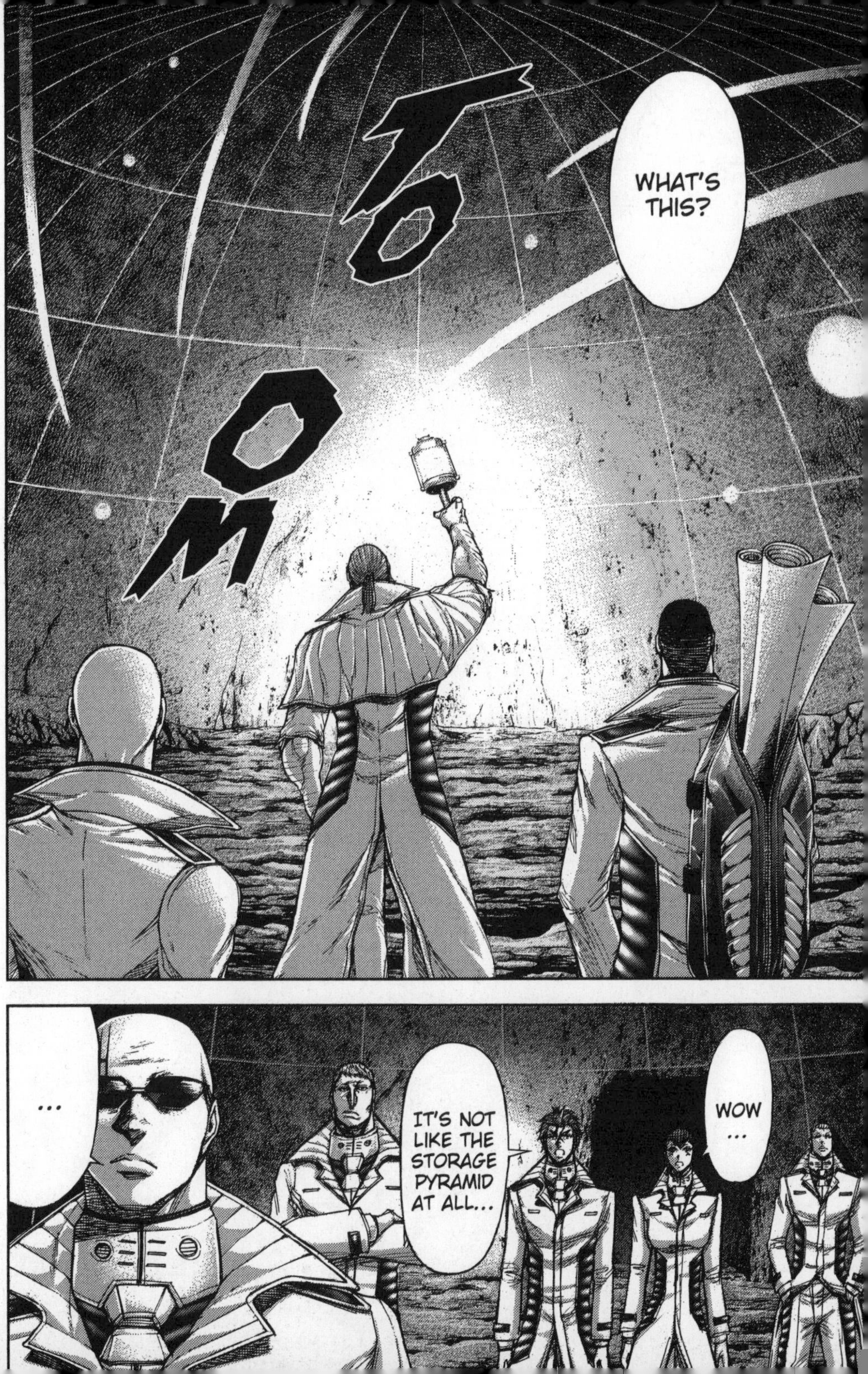
WHAT'S THIS?
TOOM
WOW ...
IT'S NOT LIKE THE STORAGE PYRAMID AT ALL...
...

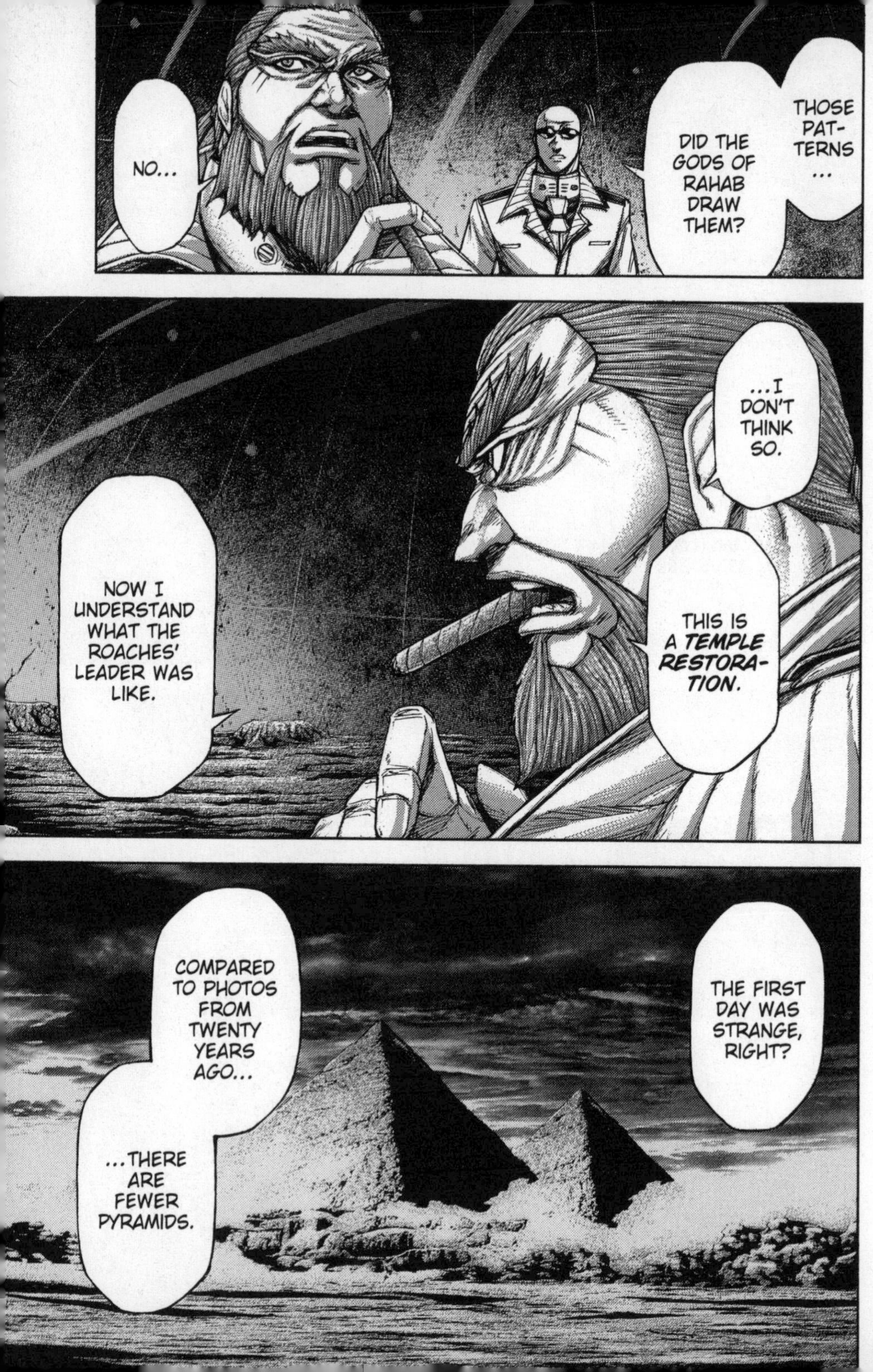
THOSE PAT-TERNS...
DID THE GODS OF RAHAB DRAW THEM?
NO...
...I DON'T THINK SO.
THIS IS A *TEMPLE RESTORATION*.
NOW I UNDERSTAND WHAT THE ROACHES' LEADER WAS LIKE.
THE FIRST DAY WAS STRANGE, RIGHT?
COMPARED TO PHOTOS FROM TWENTY YEARS AGO...
...THERE ARE FEWER PYRAMIDS.

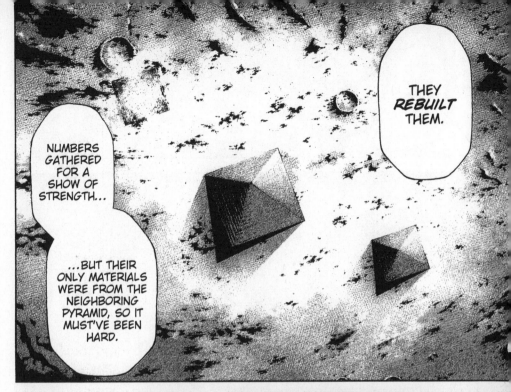

THEY *REBUILT* THEM.

NUMBERS GATHERED FOR A SHOW OF STRENGTH...

...BUT THEIR ONLY MATERIALS WERE FROM THE NEIGHBORING PYRAMID, SO IT MUST'VE BEEN HARD.

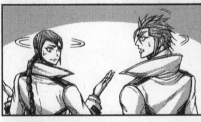

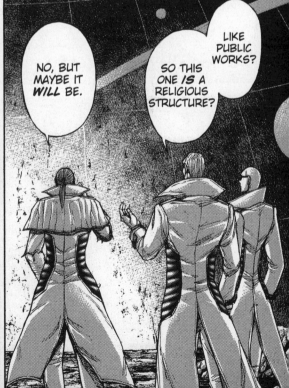

LIKE PUBLIC WORKS?

SO THIS ONE *IS* A RELIGIOUS STRUCTURE?

NO, BUT MAYBE IT *WILL* BE.

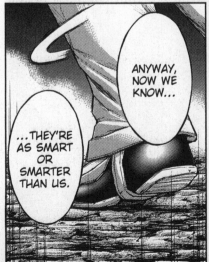

ANYWAY, NOW WE KNOW...

...THEY'RE AS SMART OR SMARTER THAN US.

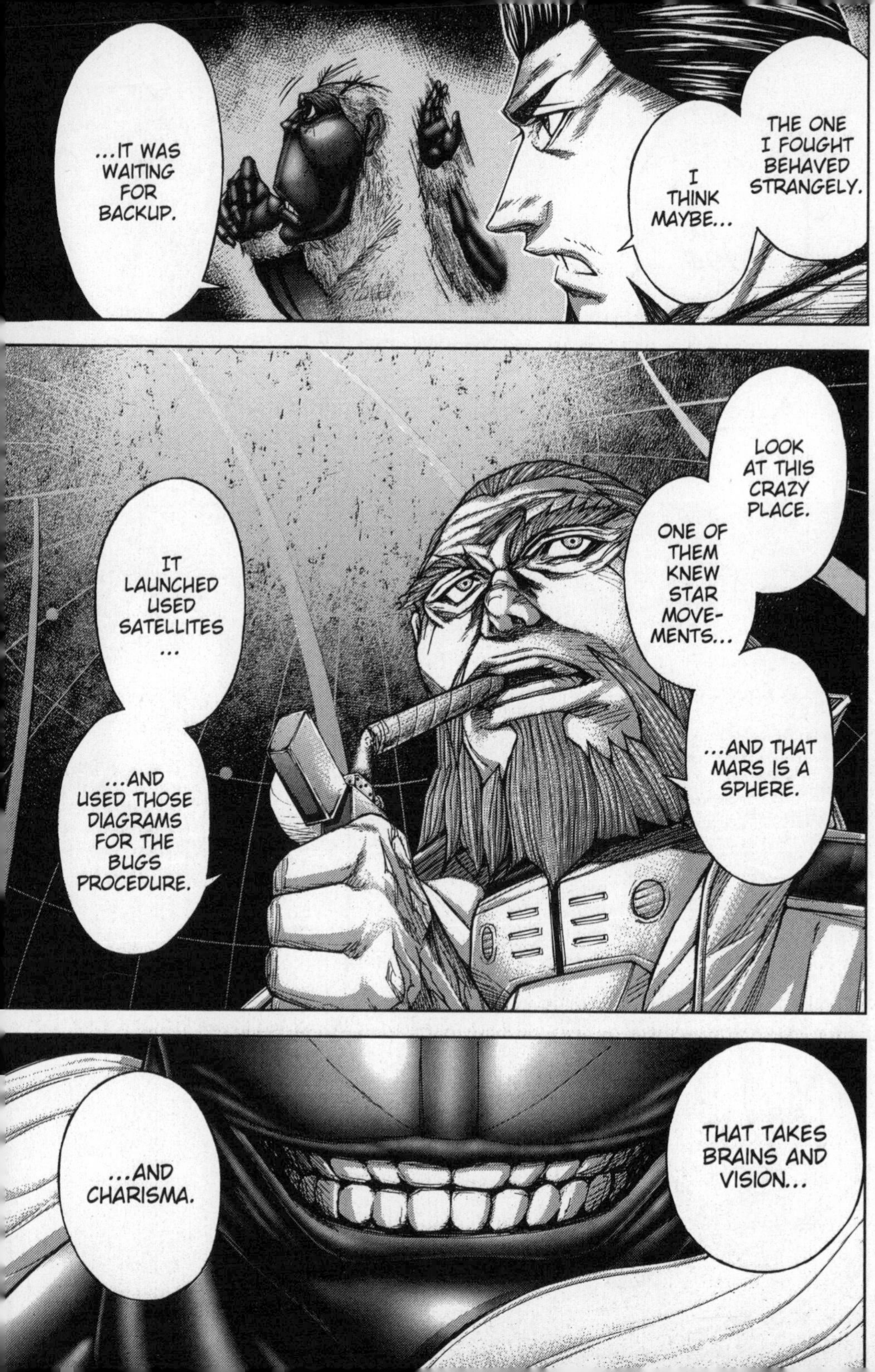
THE ONE I FOUGHT BEHAVED STRANGELY.
I THINK MAYBE...
...IT WAS WAITING FOR BACKUP.
LOOK AT THIS CRAZY PLACE.
ONE OF THEM KNEW STAR MOVEMENTS...
...AND THAT MARS IS A SPHERE.
IT LAUNCHED USED SATELLITES...
...AND USED THOSE DIAGRAMS FOR THE BUGS PROCEDURE.
THAT TAKES BRAINS AND VISION...
...AND CHARISMA.

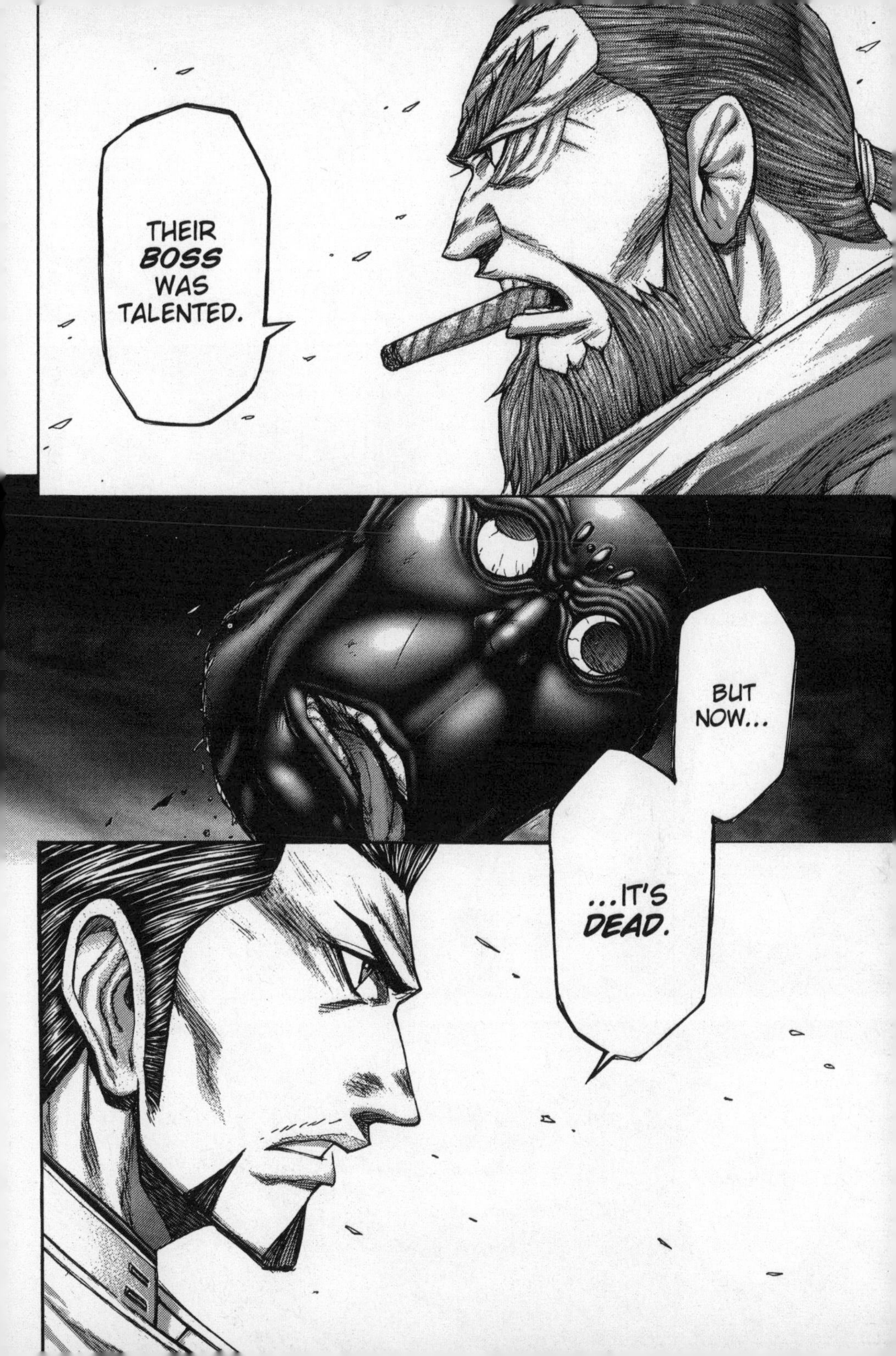
THEIR *BOSS* WAS TALENTED.
BUT NOW...
...IT'S *DEAD*.

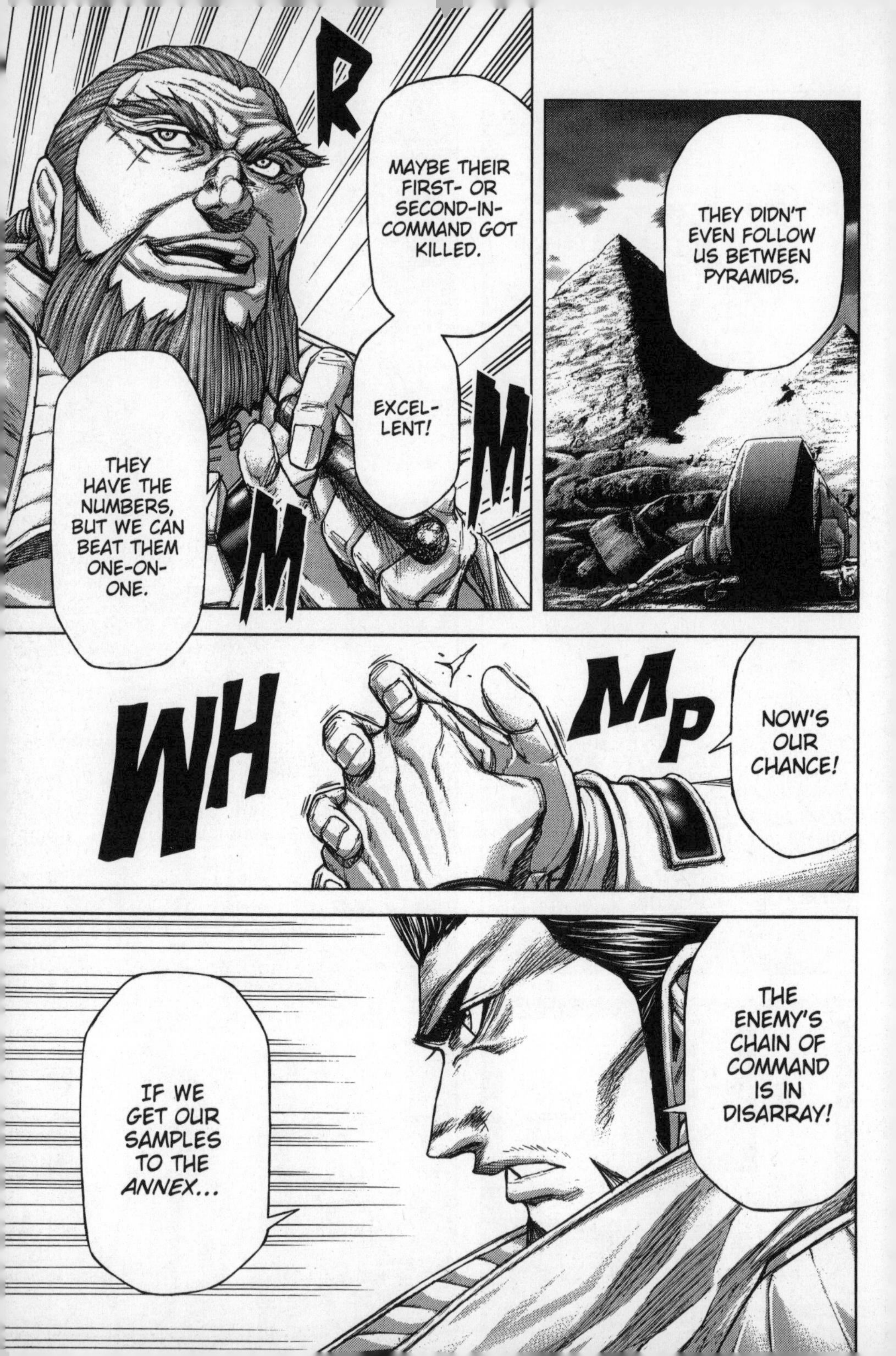
THEY DIDN'T EVEN FOLLOW US BETWEEN PYRAMIDS.
MAYBE THEIR FIRST- OR SECOND-IN-COMMAND GOT KILLED.
EXCEL-LENT!
RMM
THEY HAVE THE NUMBERS, BUT WE CAN BEAT THEM ONE-ON-ONE.
NOW'S OUR CHANCE!
WHMP
THE ENEMY'S CHAIN OF COMMAND IS IN DISARRAY!
IF WE GET OUR SAMPLES TO THE *ANNEX*...

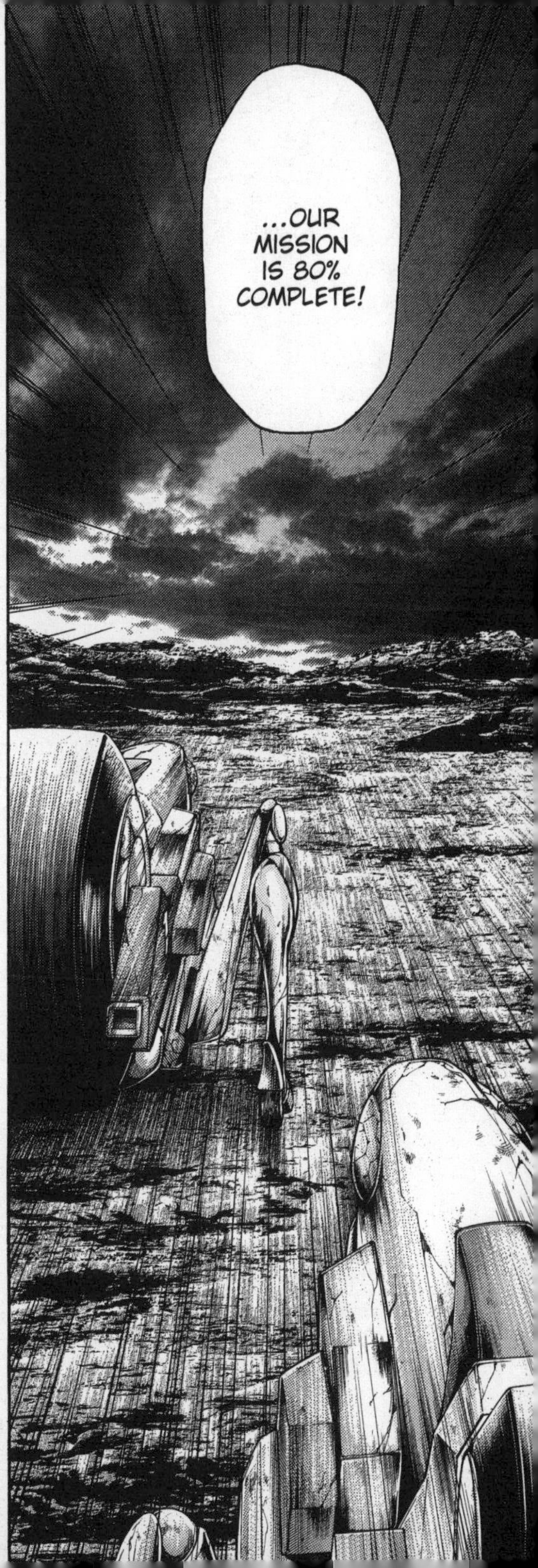
...OUR MISSION IS 80% COMPLETE!

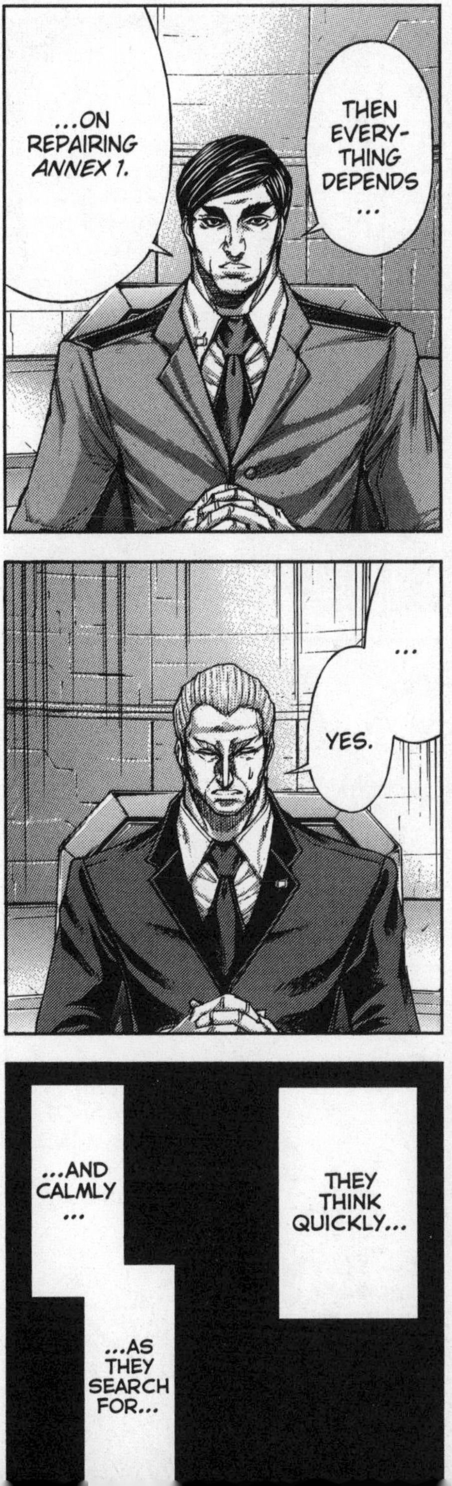
THEN EVERY-THING DEPENDS...
...ON REPAIRING ANNEX 1.
...
YES.
THEY THINK QUICKLY...
...AND CALMLY...
...AS THEY SEARCH FOR...

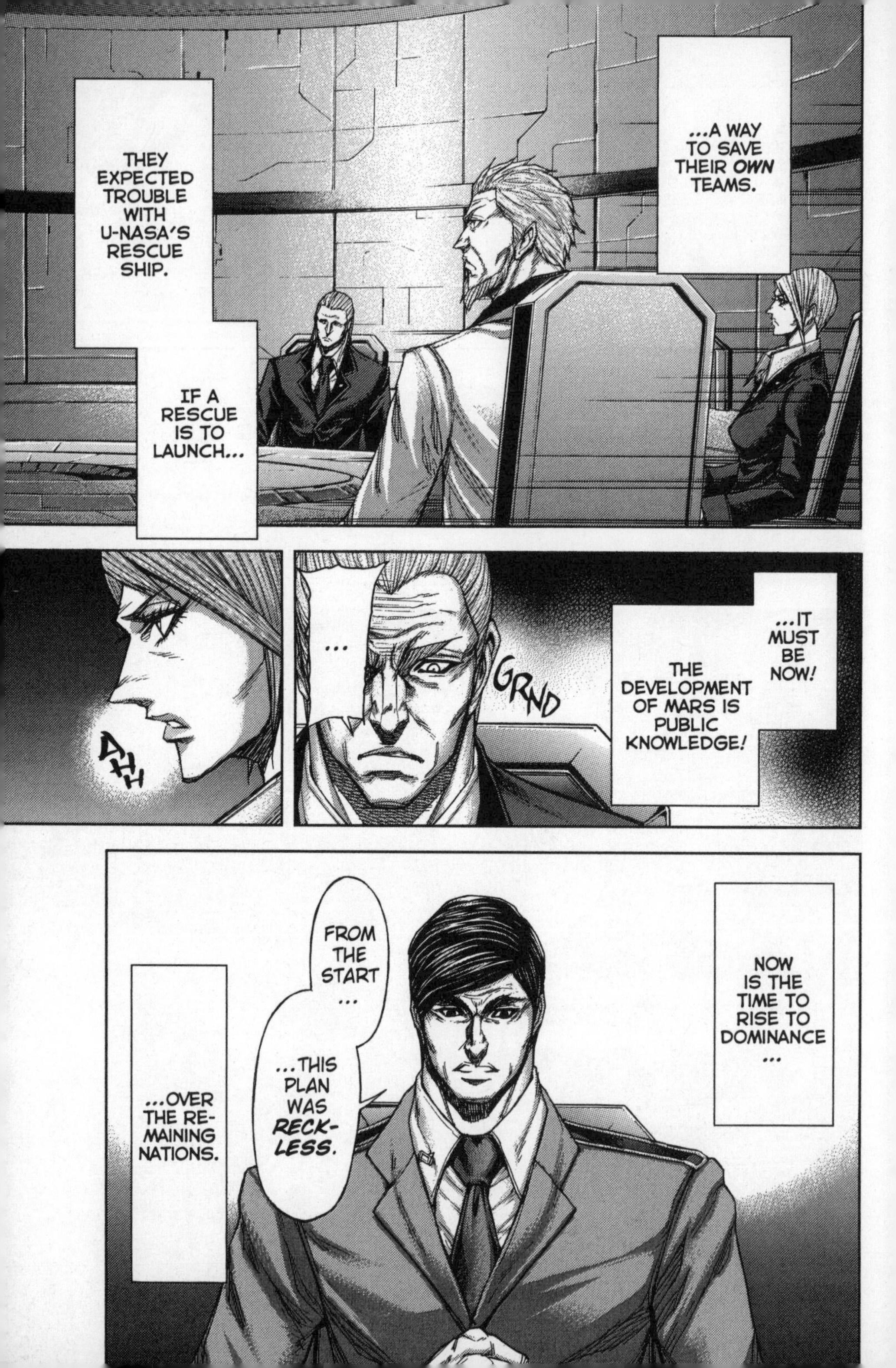
...A WAY TO SAVE THEIR *OWN* TEAMS.
THEY EXPECTED TROUBLE WITH U-NASA'S RESCUE SHIP.
IF A RESCUE IS TO LAUNCH...
...IT MUST BE NOW!
THE DEVELOPMENT OF MARS IS PUBLIC KNOWLEDGE!
GRND
...
AHH
NOW IS THE TIME TO RISE TO DOMINANCE...
FROM THE START...
...THIS PLAN WAS *RECK-LESS*.
...OVER THE RE-MAINING NATIONS.

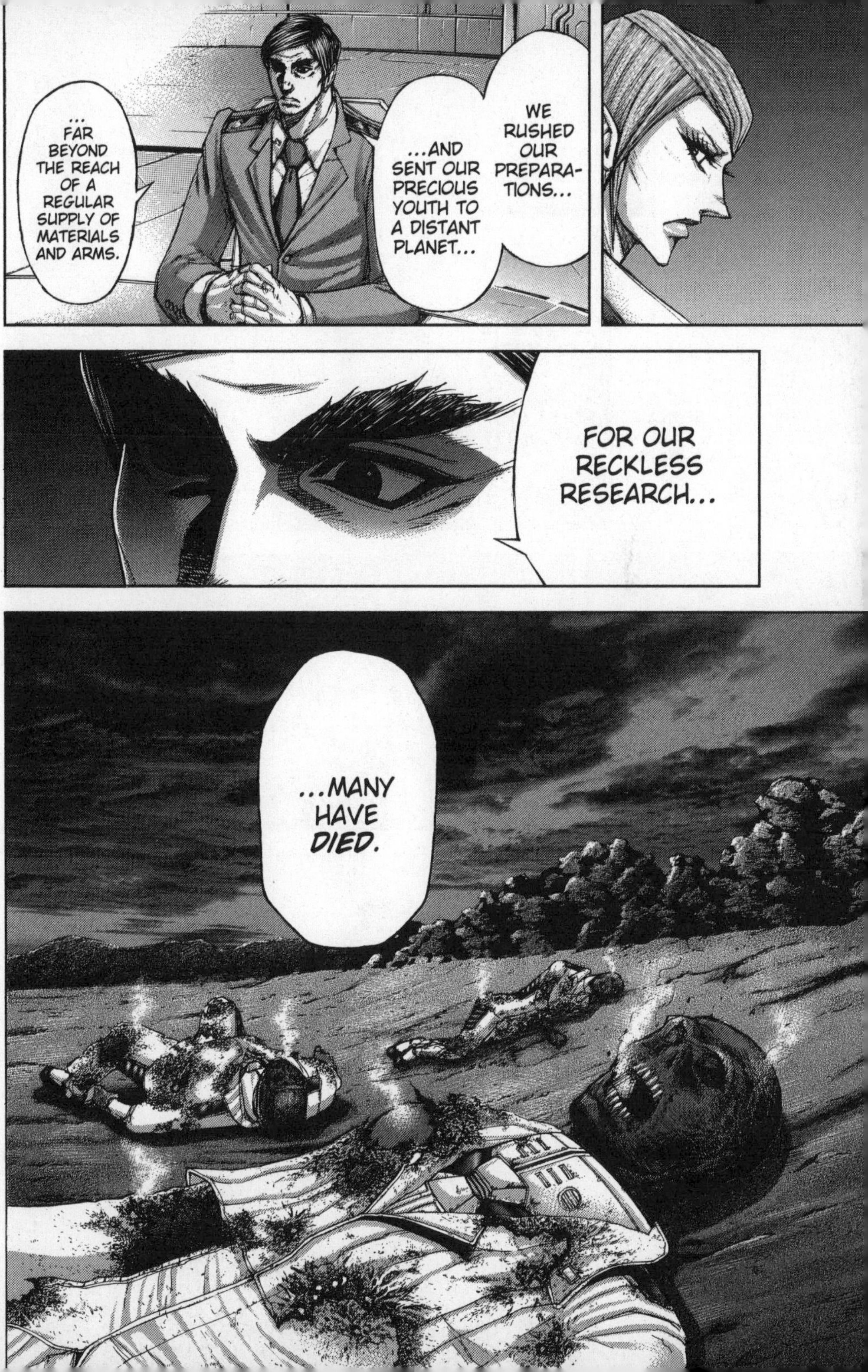
WE RUSHED OUR PREPARATIONS...
...AND SENT OUR PRECIOUS YOUTH TO A DISTANT PLANET...
...FAR BEYOND THE REACH OF A REGULAR SUPPLY OF MATERIALS AND ARMS.
FOR OUR RECKLESS RESEARCH...
...MANY HAVE *DIED*.

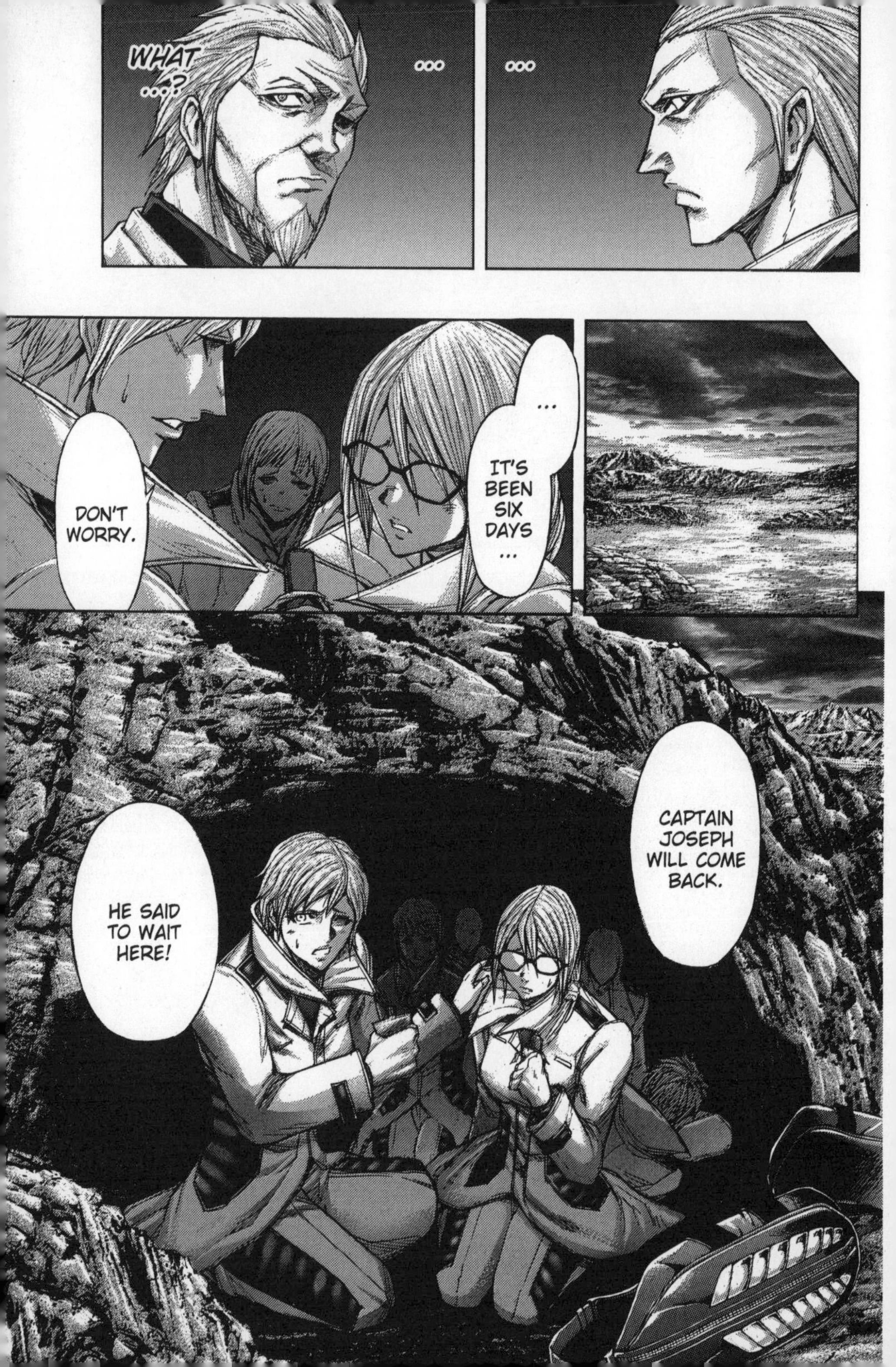
...
...
WHAT ...?
...
IT'S BEEN SIX DAYS ...
DON'T WORRY.
CAPTAIN JOSEPH WILL COME BACK.
HE SAID TO WAIT HERE!

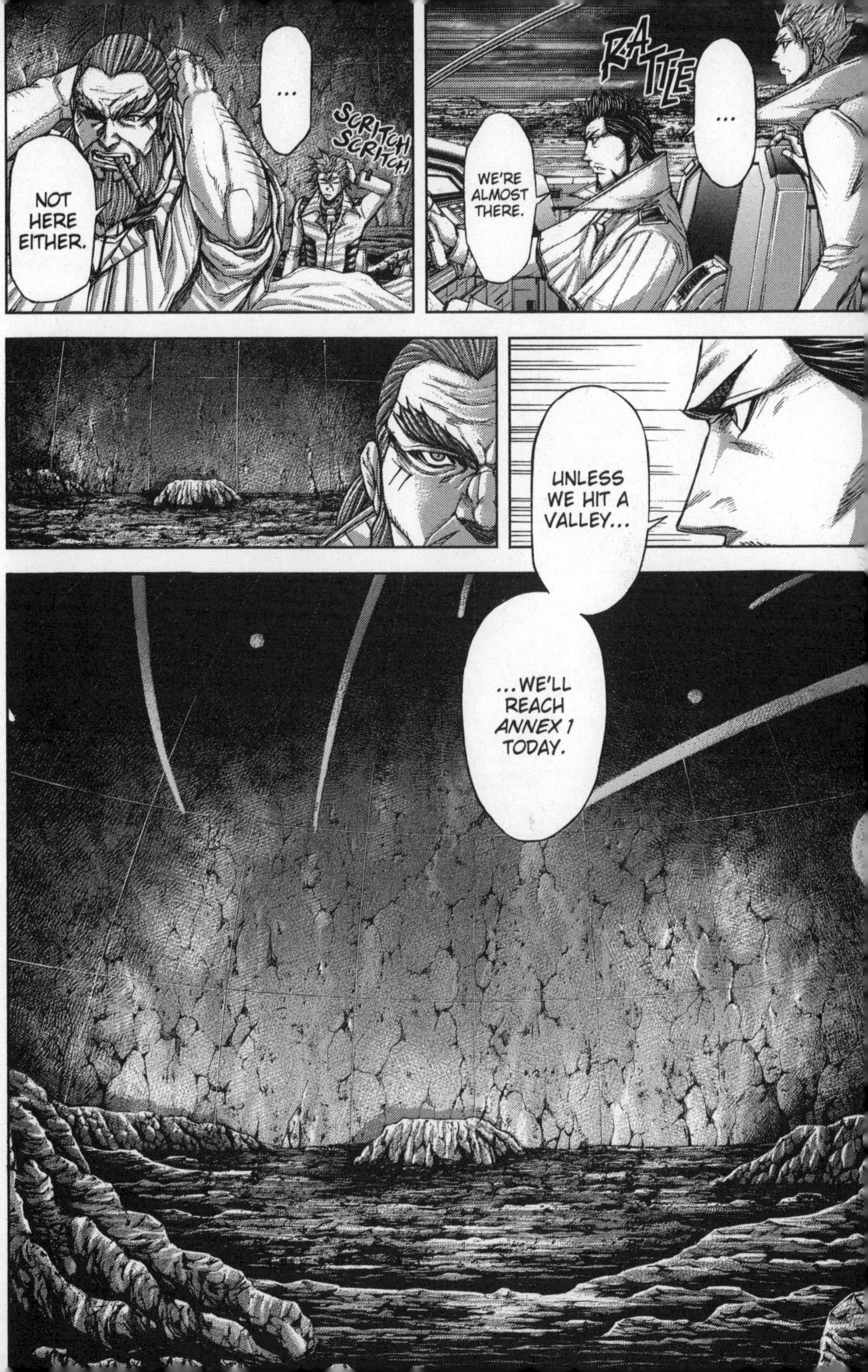
RATTLE
...
WE'RE ALMOST THERE.
...
SCRITCH SCRITCH
NOT HERE EITHER.
UNLESS WE HIT A VALLEY...
...WE'LL REACH ANNEX 1 TODAY.

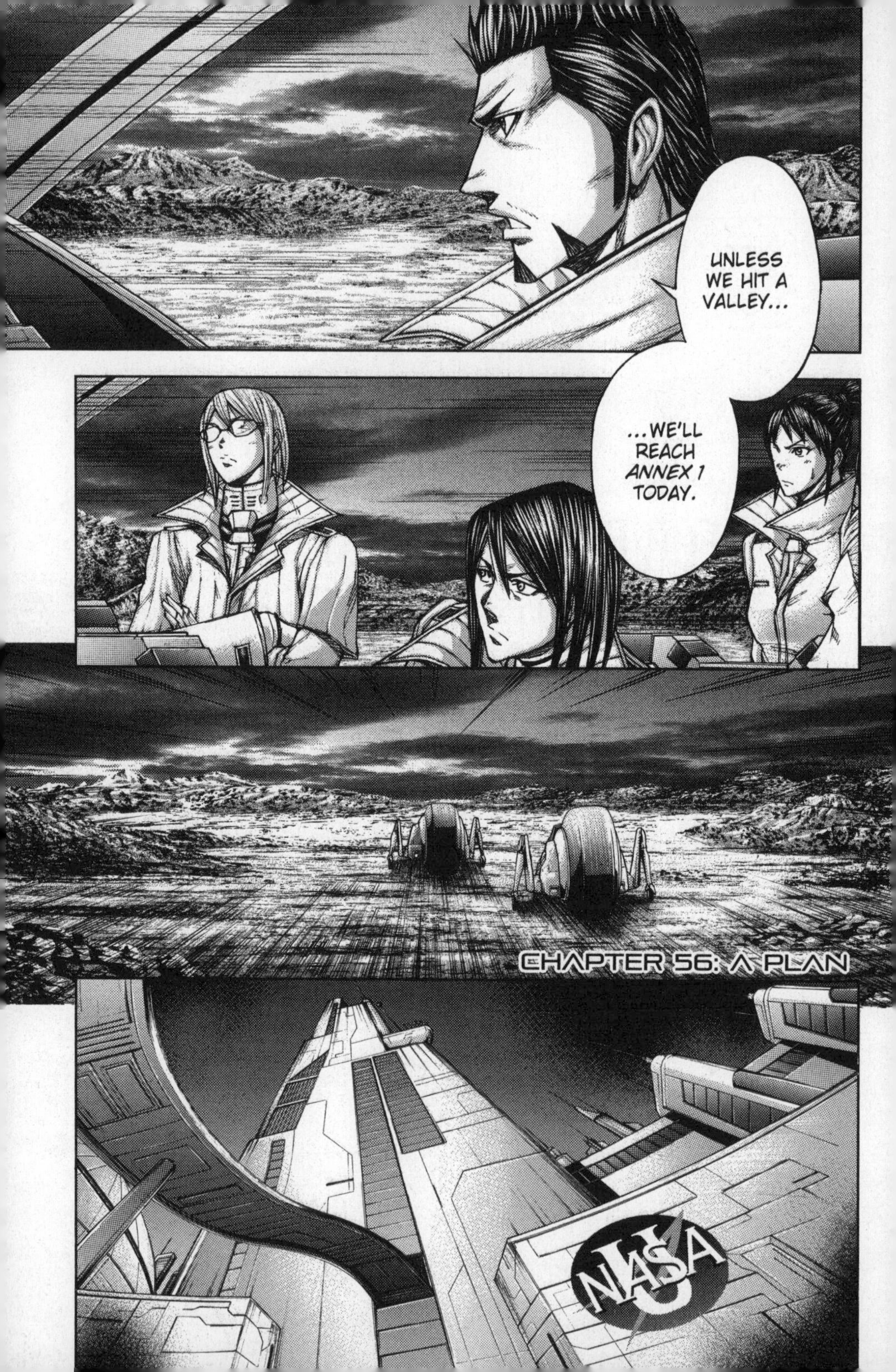
UNLESS WE HIT A VALLEY...
...WE'LL REACH ANNEX 1 TODAY.
CHAPTER 56: A PLAN
NASA

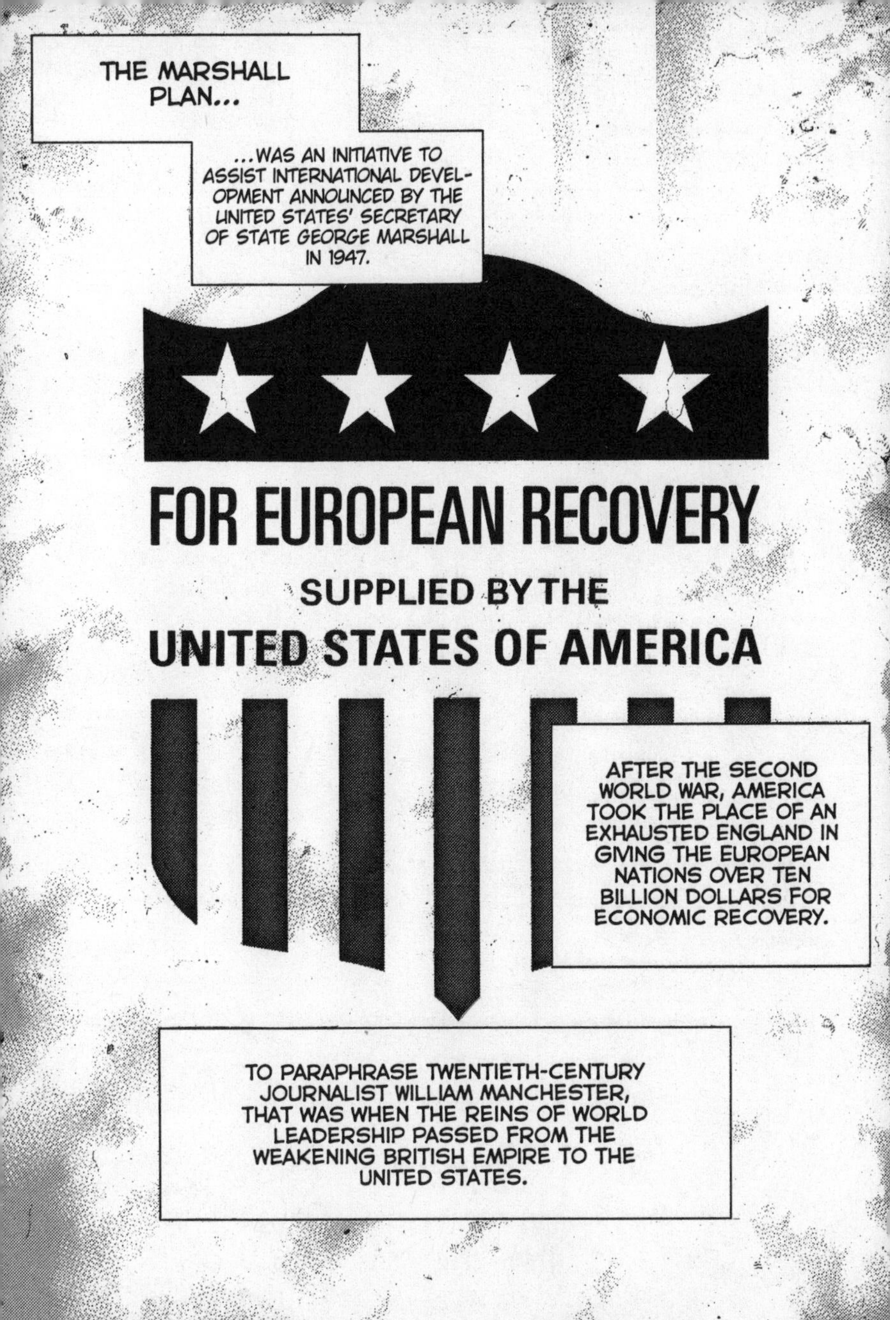
THE MARSHALL PLAN...
...WAS AN INITIATIVE TO ASSIST INTERNATIONAL DEVELOPMENT ANNOUNCED BY THE UNITED STATES' SECRETARY OF STATE GEORGE MARSHALL IN 1947.
FOR EUROPEAN RECOVERY
SUPPLIED BY THE
UNITED STATES OF AMERICA
AFTER THE SECOND WORLD WAR, AMERICA TOOK THE PLACE OF AN EXHAUSTED ENGLAND IN GIVING THE EUROPEAN NATIONS OVER TEN BILLION DOLLARS FOR ECONOMIC RECOVERY.
TO PARAPHRASE TWENTIETH-CENTURY JOURNALIST WILLIAM MANCHESTER, THAT WAS WHEN THE REINS OF WORLD LEADERSHIP PASSED FROM THE WEAKENING BRITISH EMPIRE TO THE UNITED STATES.

CHAPTER 56: A PLAN

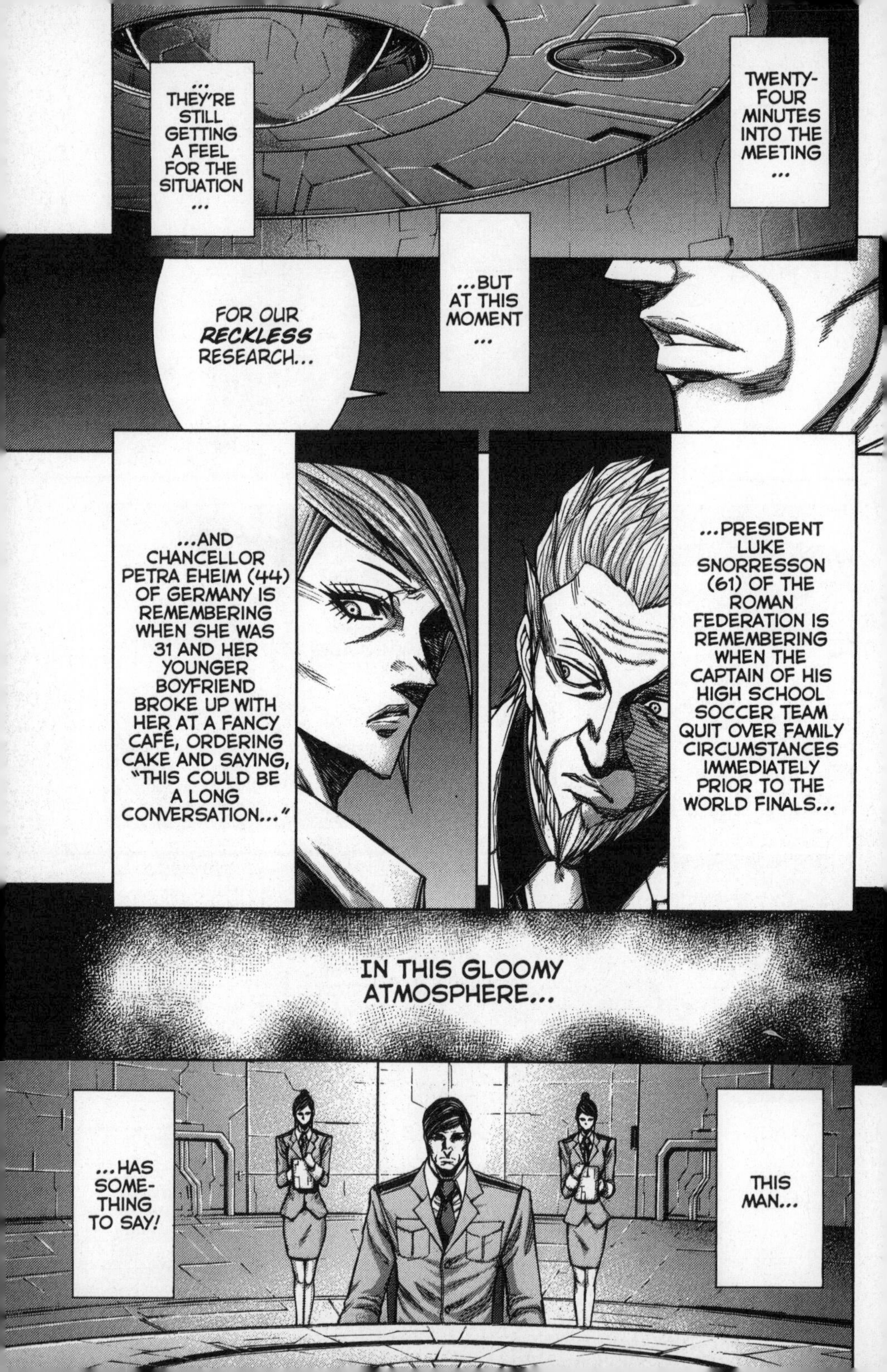
TWENTY-FOUR MINUTES INTO THE MEETING...
...THEY'RE STILL GETTING A FEEL FOR THE SITUATION...
...BUT AT THIS MOMENT...
FOR OUR *RECKLESS* RESEARCH...
...PRESIDENT LUKE SNORRESSON (61) OF THE ROMAN FEDERATION IS REMEMBERING WHEN THE CAPTAIN OF HIS HIGH SCHOOL SOCCER TEAM QUIT OVER FAMILY CIRCUMSTANCES IMMEDIATELY PRIOR TO THE WORLD FINALS...
...AND CHANCELLOR PETRA EHEIM (44) OF GERMANY IS REMEMBERING WHEN SHE WAS 31 AND HER YOUNGER BOYFRIEND BROKE UP WITH HER AT A FANCY CAFÉ, ORDERING CAKE AND SAYING, "THIS COULD BE A LONG CONVERSATION..."
IN THIS GLOOMY ATMOSPHERE...
THIS MAN...
...HAS SOME-THING TO SAY!

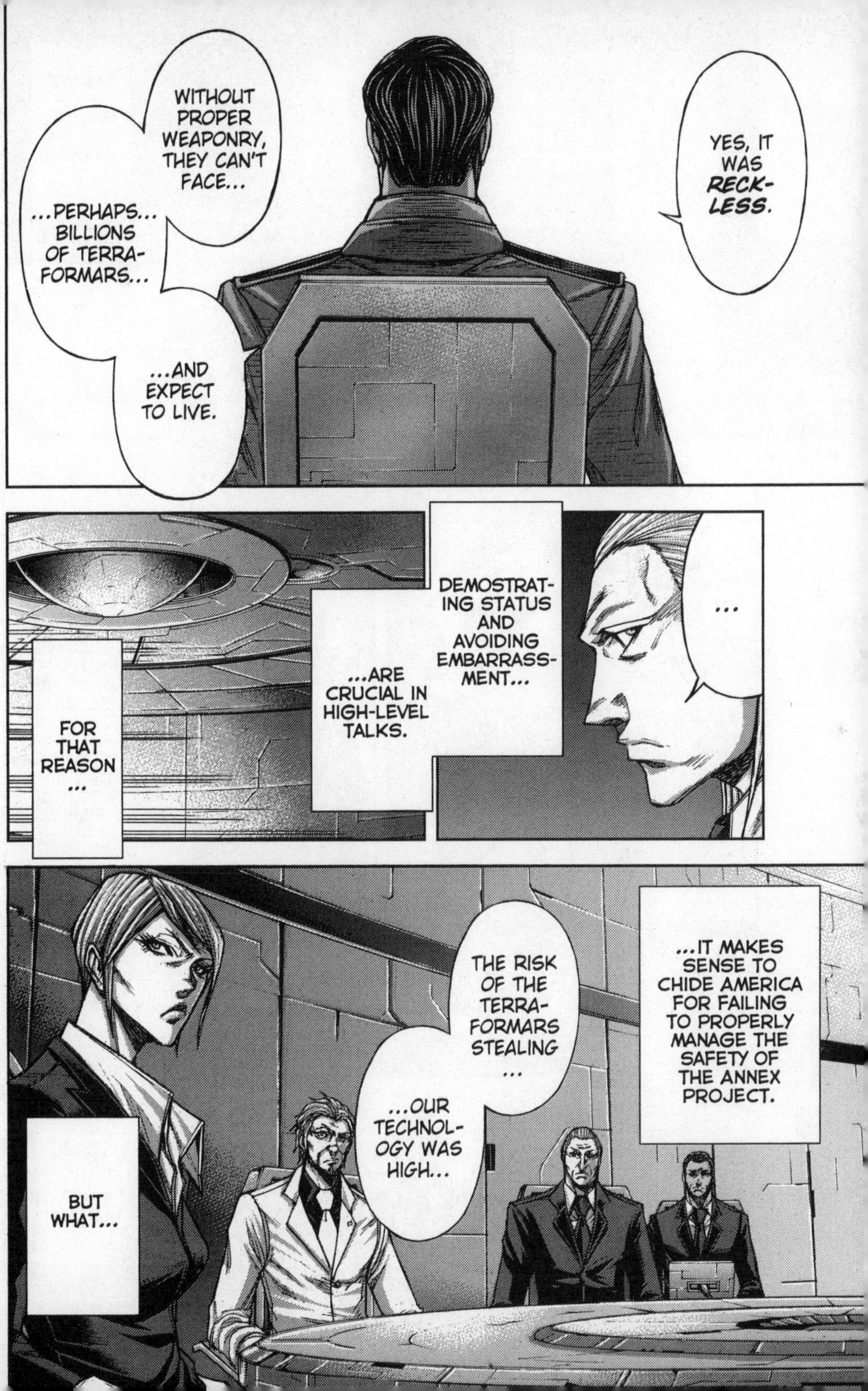
YES, IT WAS RECKLESS.
WITHOUT PROPER WEAPONRY, THEY CAN'T FACE...
...PERHAPS... BILLIONS OF TERRA-FORMARS...
...AND EXPECT TO LIVE.
...
DEMOSTRATING STATUS AND AVOIDING EMBARRASSMENT...
...ARE CRUCIAL IN HIGH-LEVEL TALKS.
FOR THAT REASON...
...IT MAKES SENSE TO CHIDE AMERICA FOR FAILING TO PROPERLY MANAGE THE SAFETY OF THE ANNEX PROJECT.
THE RISK OF THE TERRA-FORMARS STEALING...
...OUR TECHNOLOGY WAS HIGH...
BUT WHAT...

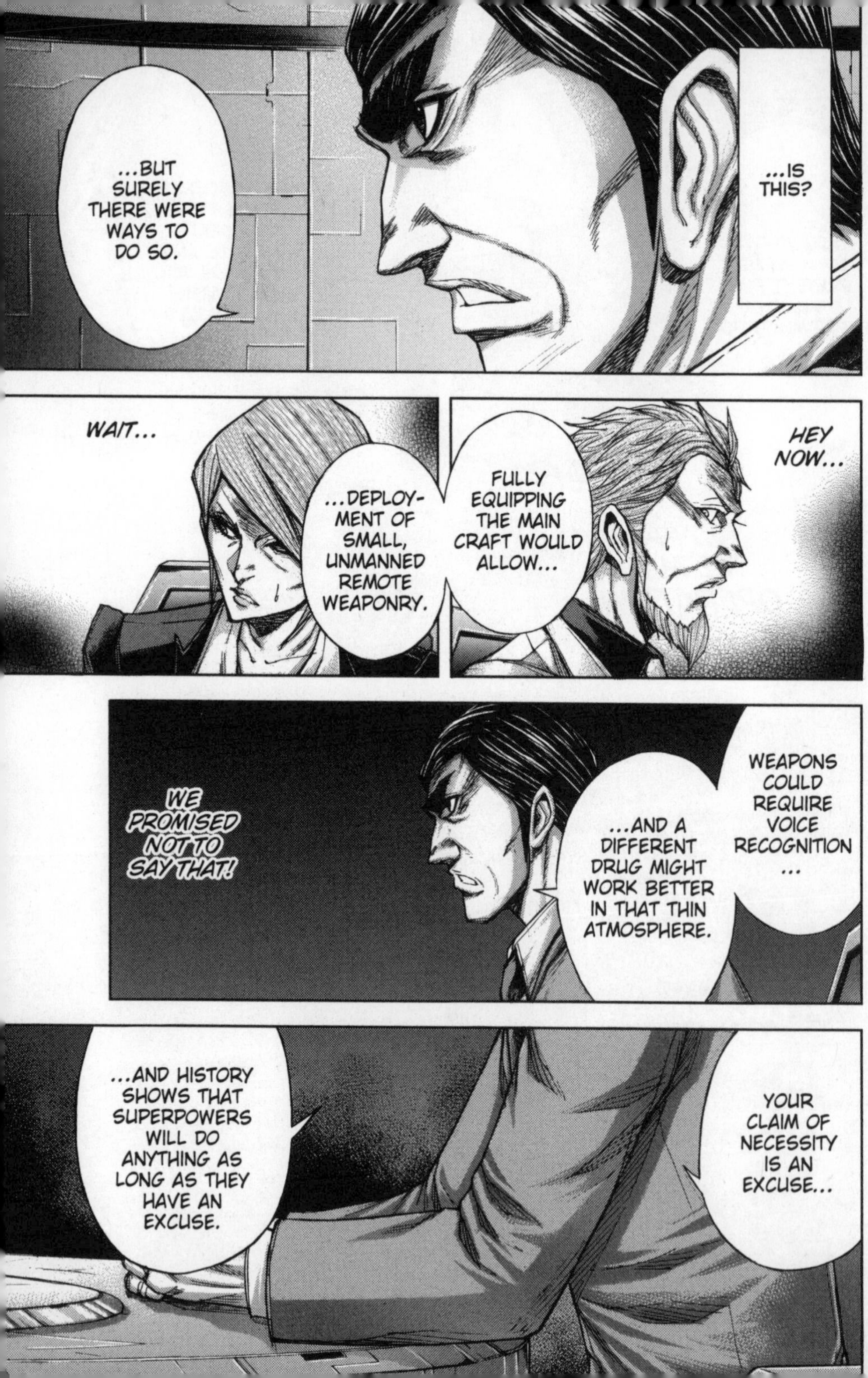
...IS THIS?
...BUT SURELY THERE WERE WAYS TO DO SO.
HEY NOW...
FULLY EQUIPPING THE MAIN CRAFT WOULD ALLOW...
...DEPLOY-MENT OF SMALL, UNMANNED REMOTE WEAPONRY.
WAIT...
WEAPONS COULD REQUIRE VOICE RECOGNITION ...
...AND A DIFFERENT DRUG MIGHT WORK BETTER IN THAT THIN ATMOSPHERE.
WE PROMISED NOT TO SAY THAT!
YOUR CLAIM OF NECESSITY IS AN EXCUSE...
...AND HISTORY SHOWS THAT SUPERPOWERS WILL DO ANYTHING AS LONG AS THEY HAVE AN EXCUSE.

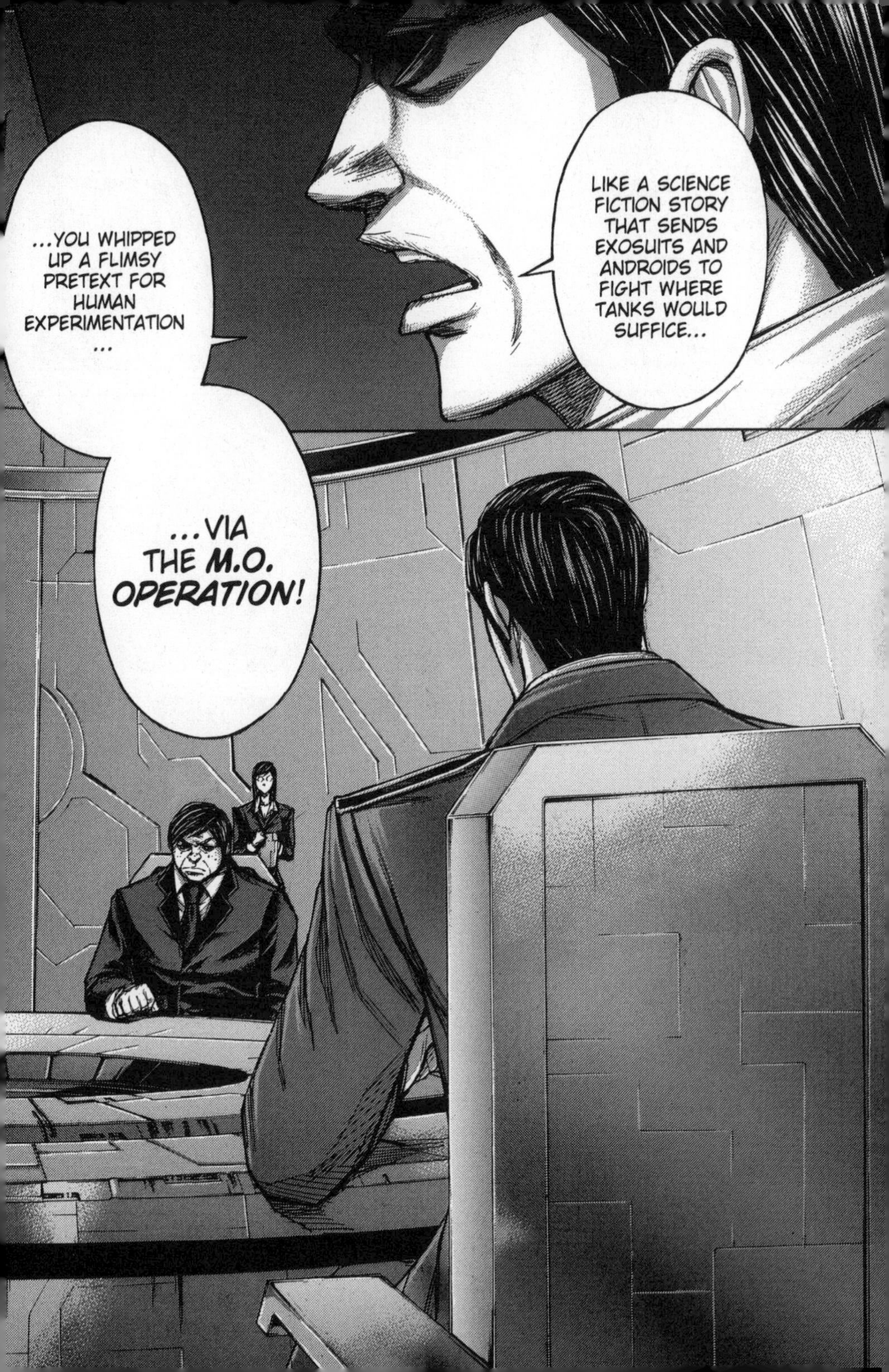
LIKE A SCIENCE FICTION STORY THAT SENDS EXOSUITS AND ANDROIDS TO FIGHT WHERE TANKS WOULD SUFFICE...
...YOU WHIPPED UP A FLIMSY PRETEXT FOR HUMAN EXPERIMENTATION ...
...VIA THE ***M.O. OPERATION***!

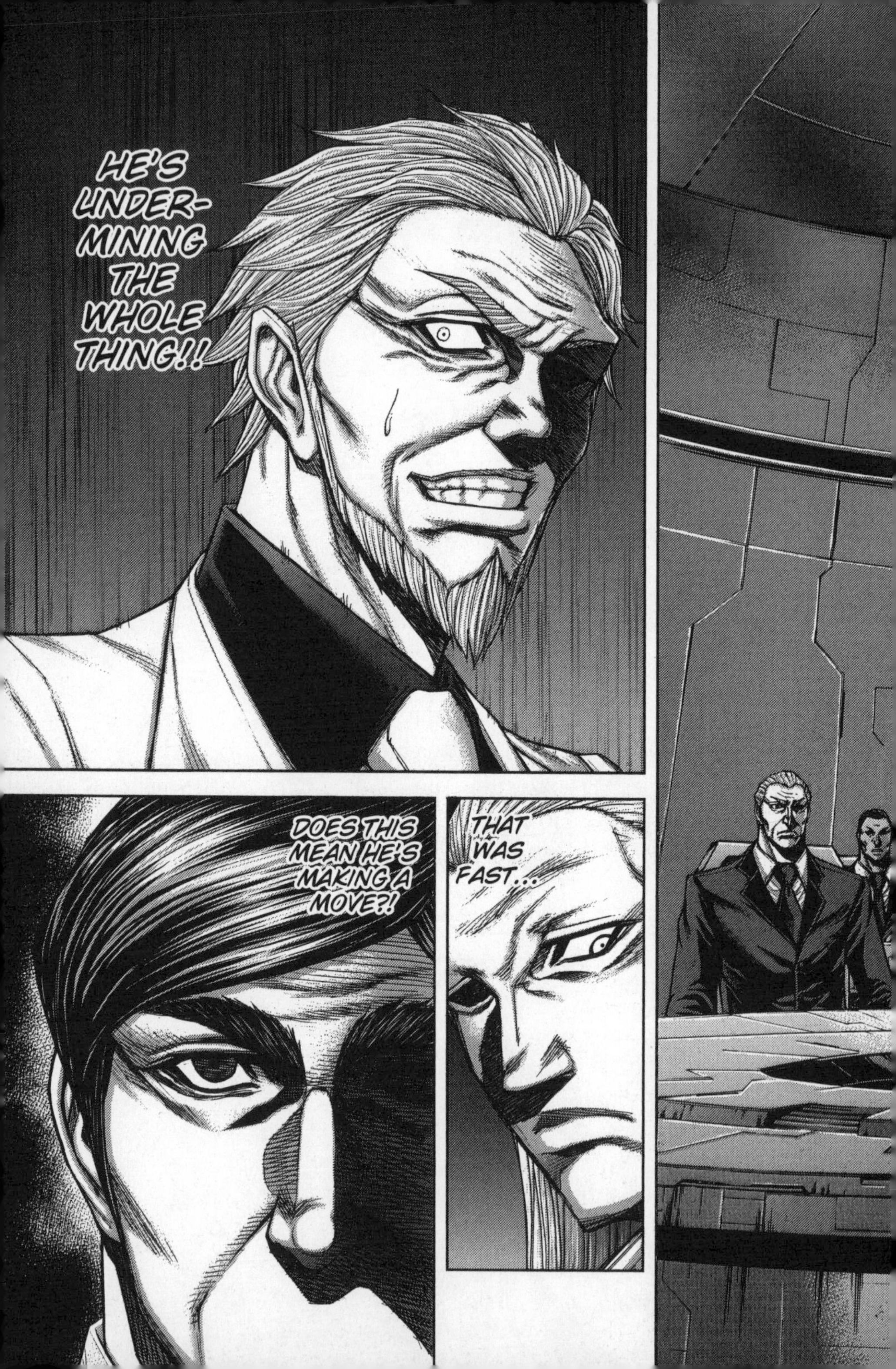
HE'S UNDER-MINING THE WHOLE THING!!
THAT WAS FAST...
DOES THIS MEAN HE'S MAKING A MOVE?!

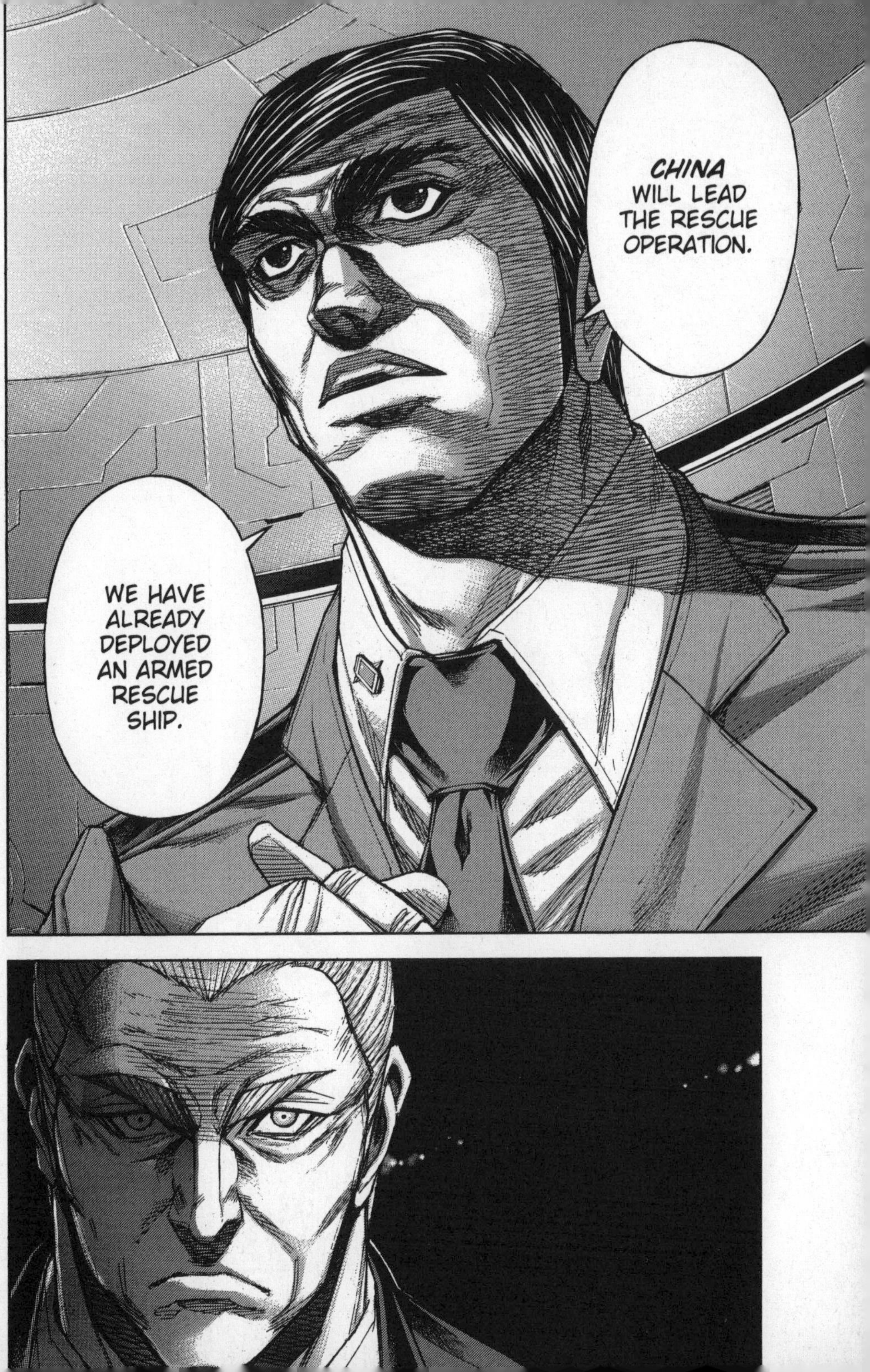
CHINA WILL LEAD THE RESCUE OPERATION.
WE HAVE ALREADY DEPLOYED AN ARMED RESCUE SHIP.

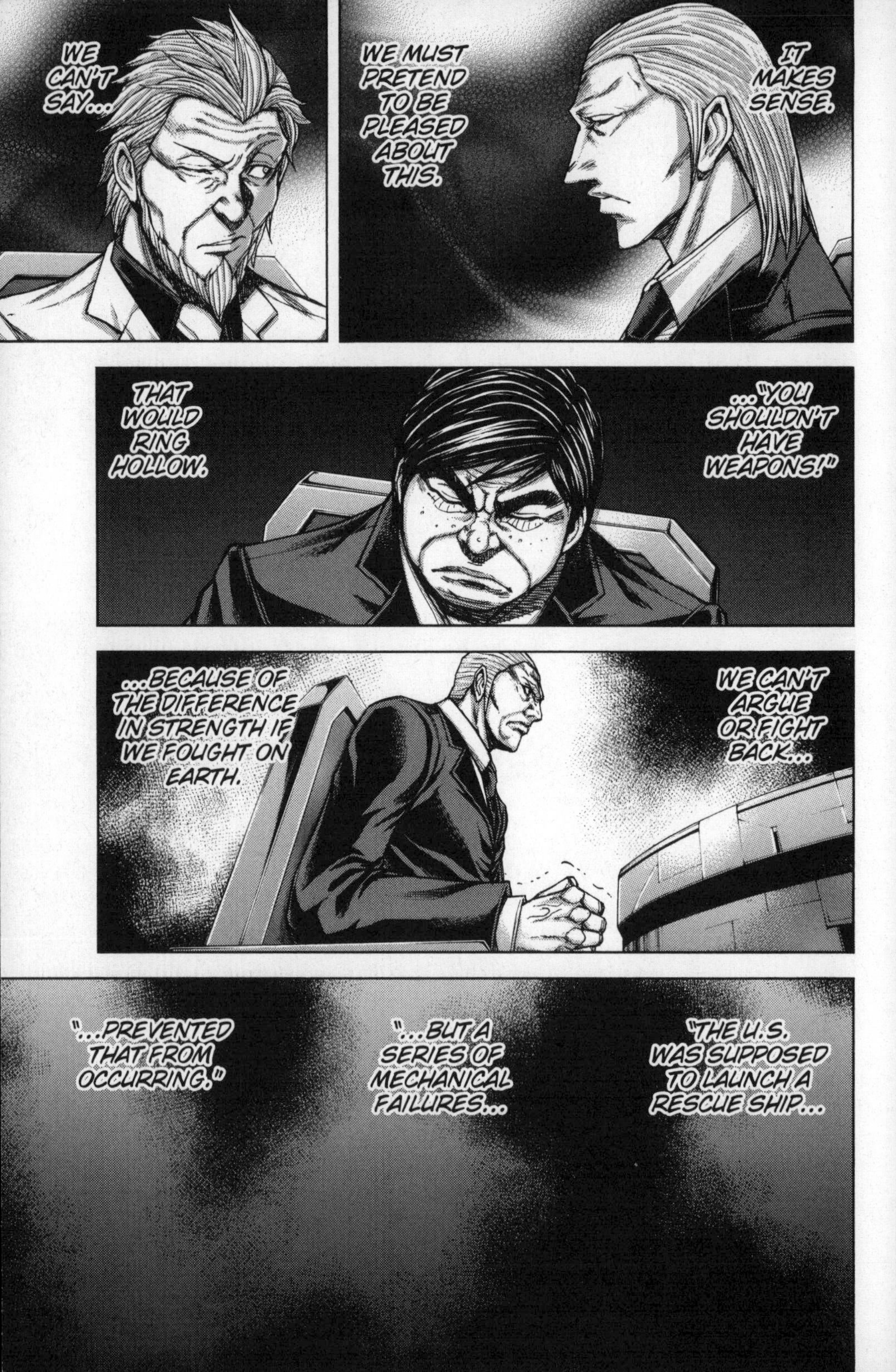
IT MAKES SENSE.
WE MUST PRETEND TO BE PLEASED ABOUT THIS.
WE CAN'T SAY...
..."YOU SHOULDN'T HAVE WEAPONS!"
THAT WOULD RING HOLLOW.
WE CAN'T ARGUE OR FIGHT BACK...
...BECAUSE OF THE DIFFERENCE IN STRENGTH IF WE FOUGHT ON EARTH.
"THE U.S. WAS SUPPOSED TO LAUNCH A RESCUE SHIP...
"...BUT A SERIES OF MECHANICAL FAILURES...
"...PREVENTED THAT FROM OCCURRING."

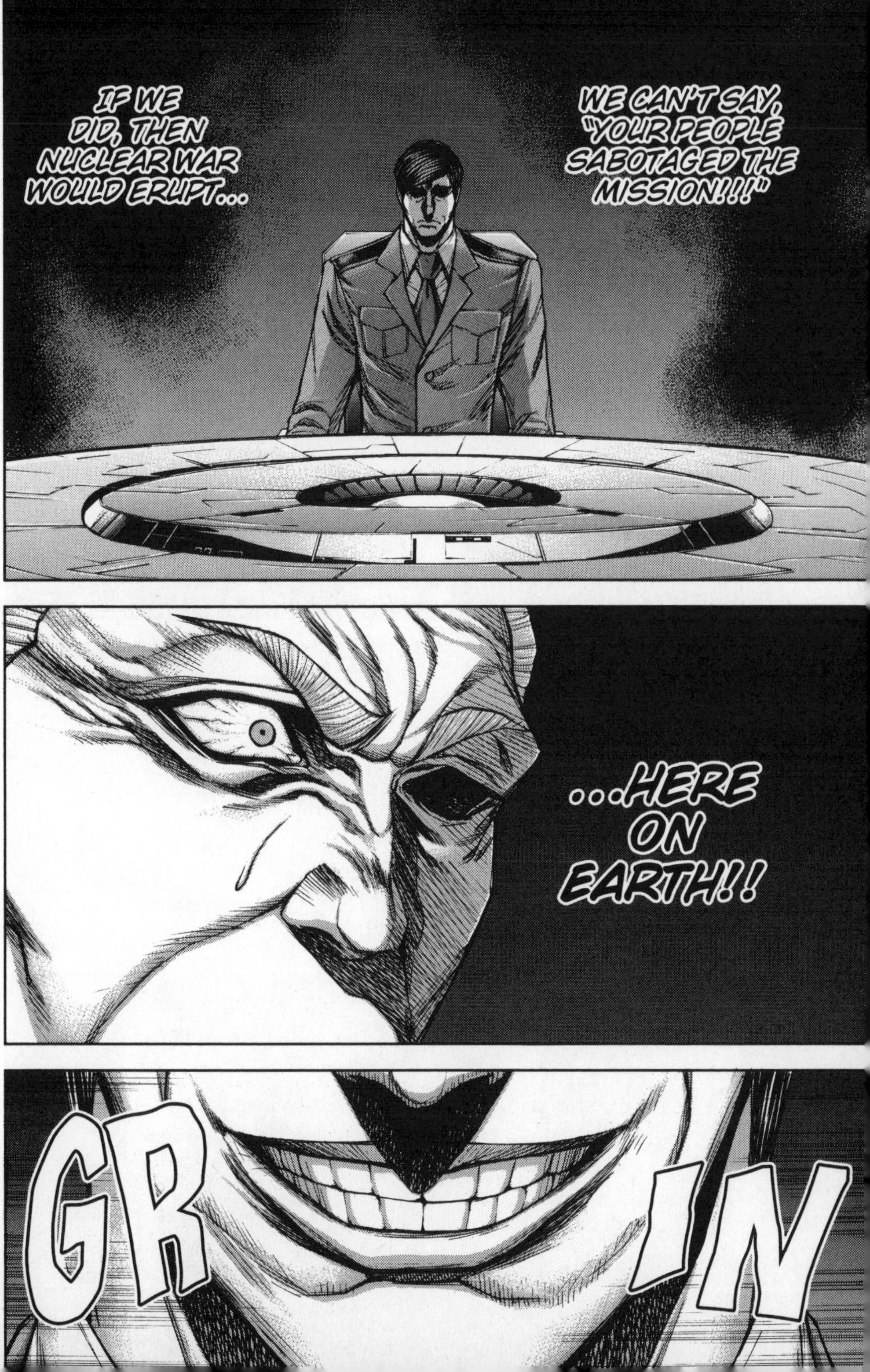
WE CAN'T SAY, "YOUR PEOPLE SABOTAGED THE MISSION!!!"
IF WE DID, THEN NUCLEAR WAR WOULD ERUPT...
...HERE ON EARTH!!
GR IN

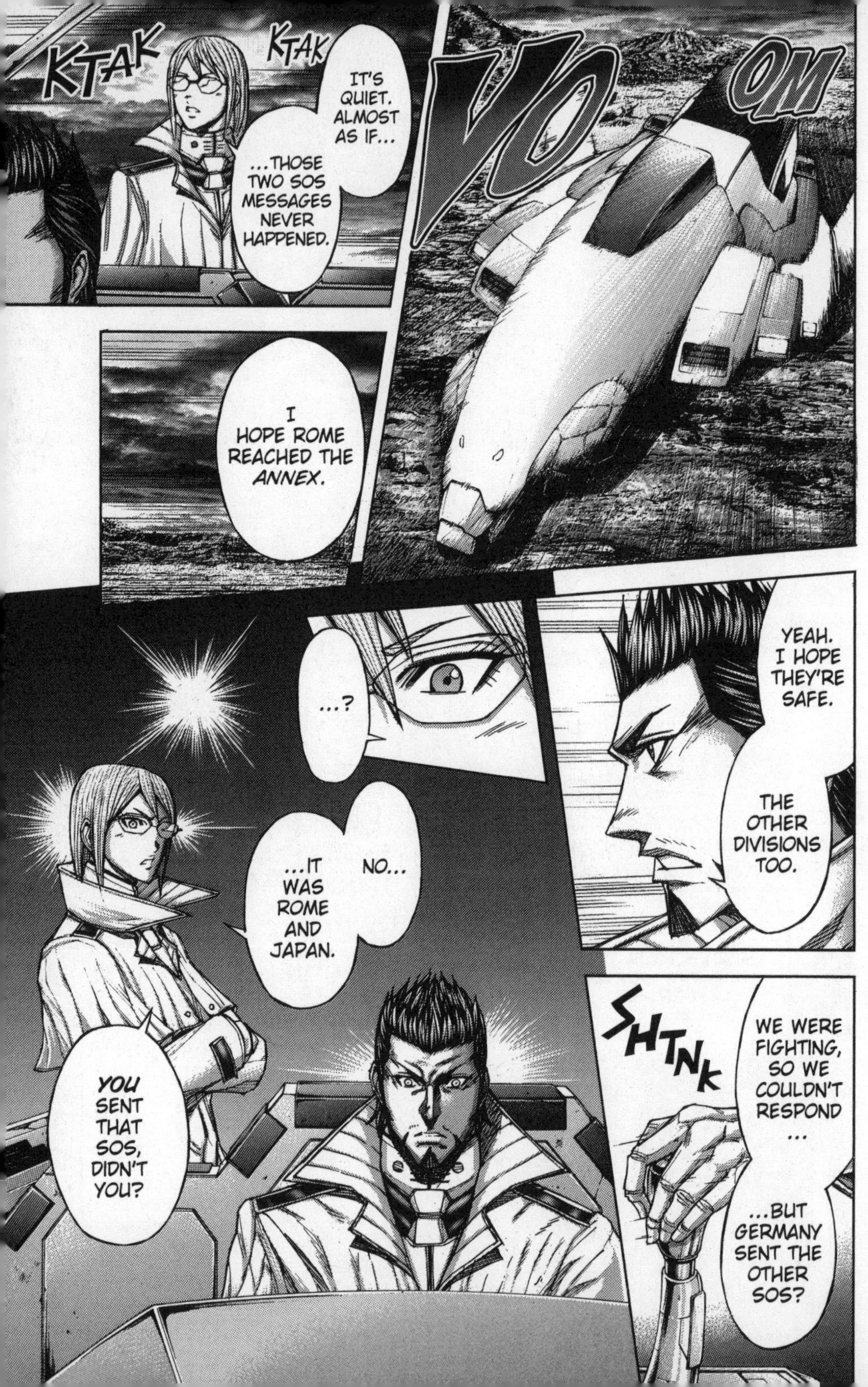
VOOM
KTAK KTAK
IT'S QUIET. ALMOST AS IF...
...THOSE TWO SOS MESSAGES NEVER HAPPENED.
I HOPE ROME REACHED THE *ANNEX*.
YEAH. I HOPE THEY'RE SAFE.
THE OTHER DIVISIONS TOO.
...?
NO...
...IT WAS ROME AND JAPAN.
SHTNK
WE WERE FIGHTING, SO WE COULDN'T RESPOND...
...BUT GERMANY SENT THE OTHER SOS?
YOU SENT THAT SOS, DIDN'T YOU?

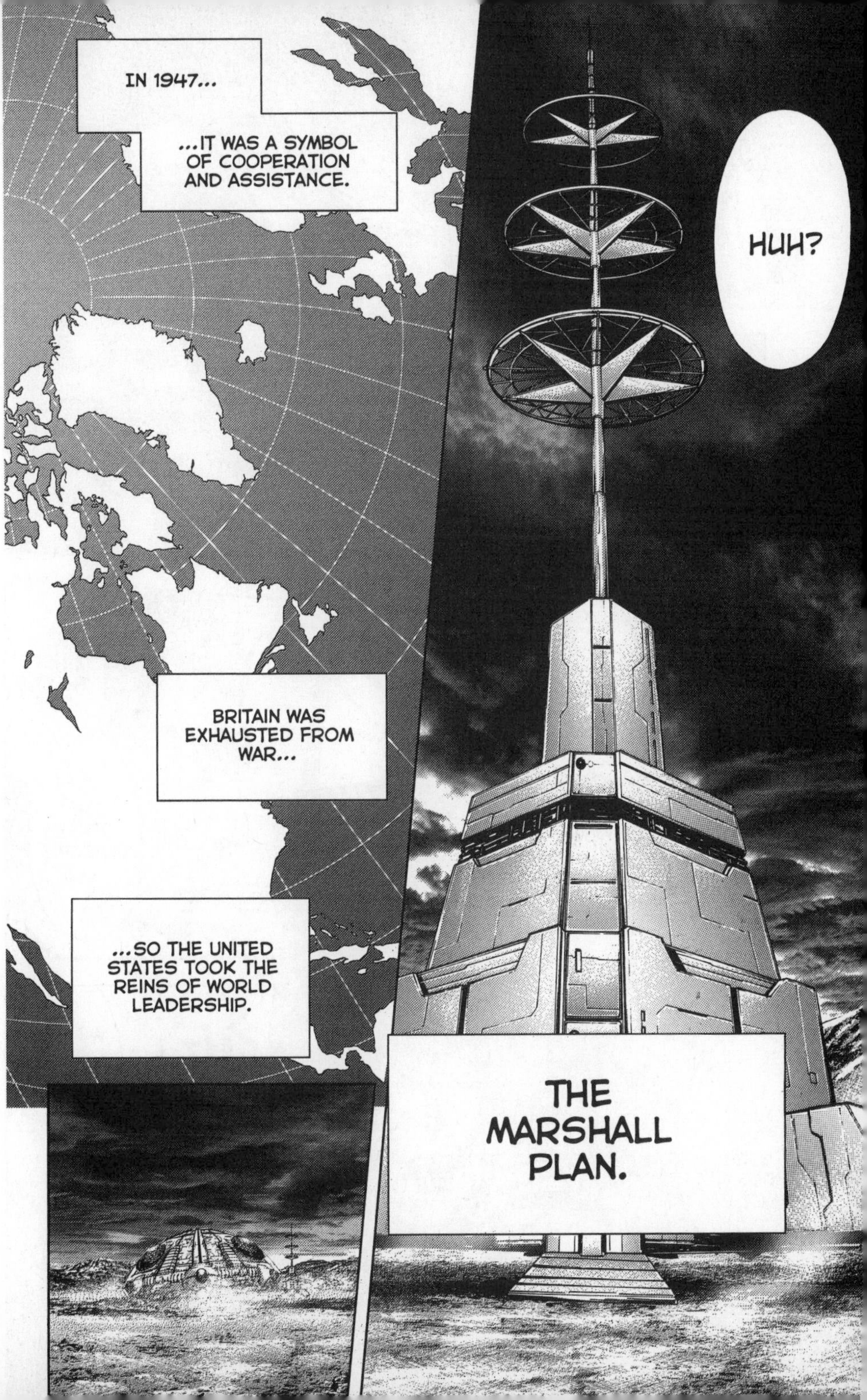
HUH?
THE MARSHALL PLAN.
IN 1947...
...IT WAS A SYMBOL OF COOPERATION AND ASSISTANCE.
BRITAIN WAS EXHAUSTED FROM WAR...
...SO THE UNITED STATES TOOK THE REINS OF WORLD LEADERSHIP.

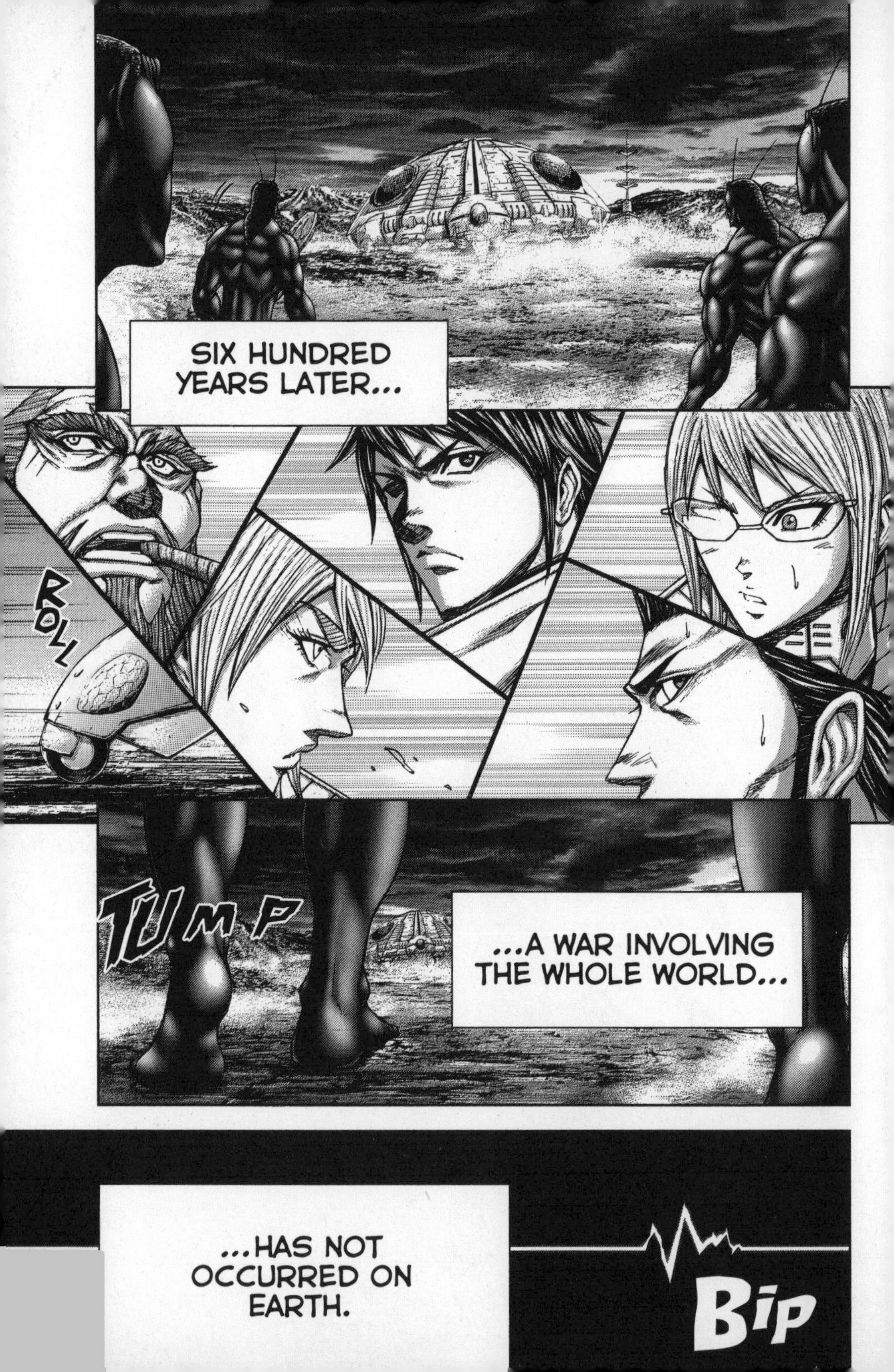
SIX HUNDRED YEARS LATER...
ROLL
...A WAR INVOLVING THE WHOLE WORLD...
TUMP
...HAS NOT OCCURRED ON EARTH.
Bip

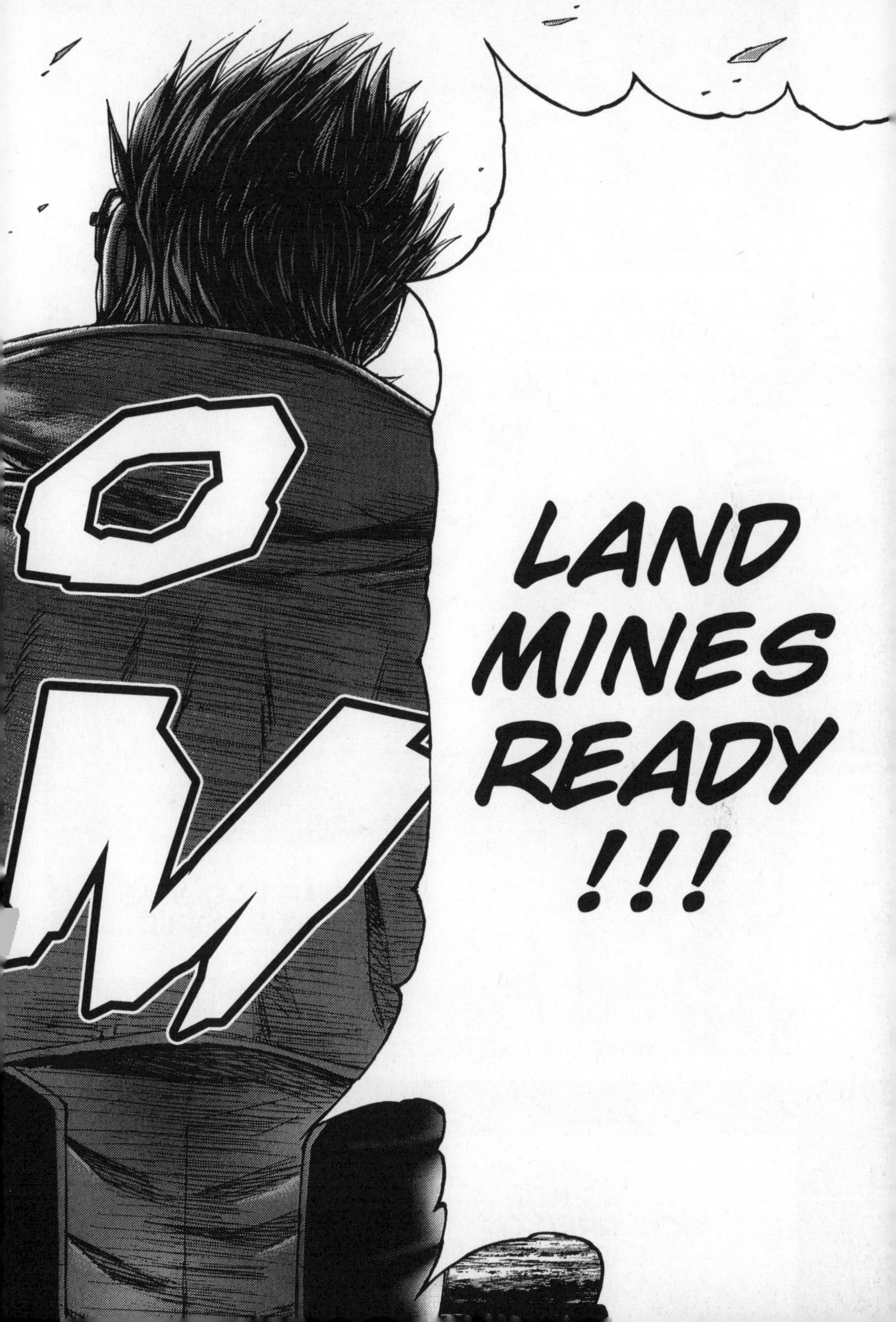
LAND MINES READY !!!

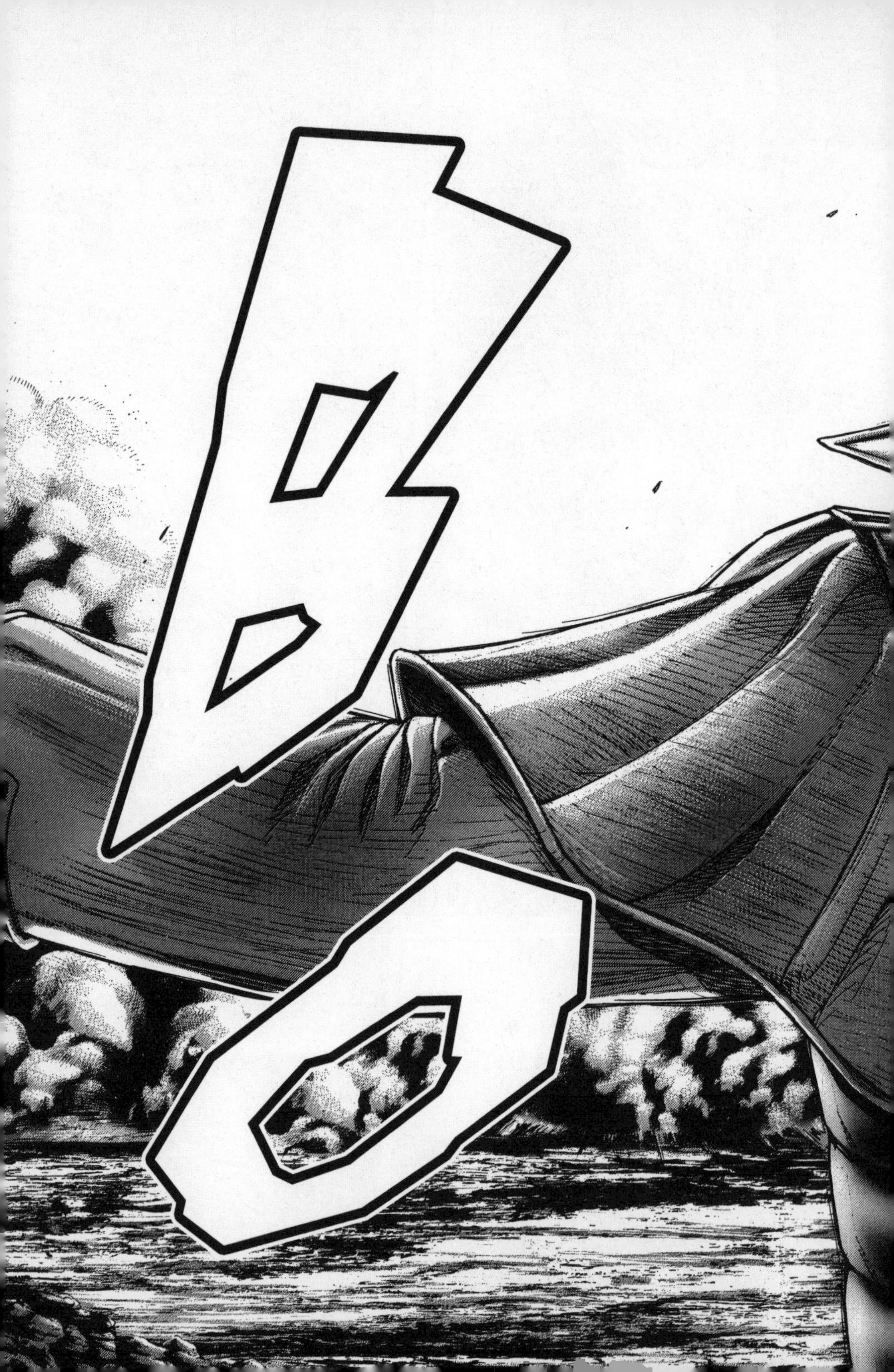

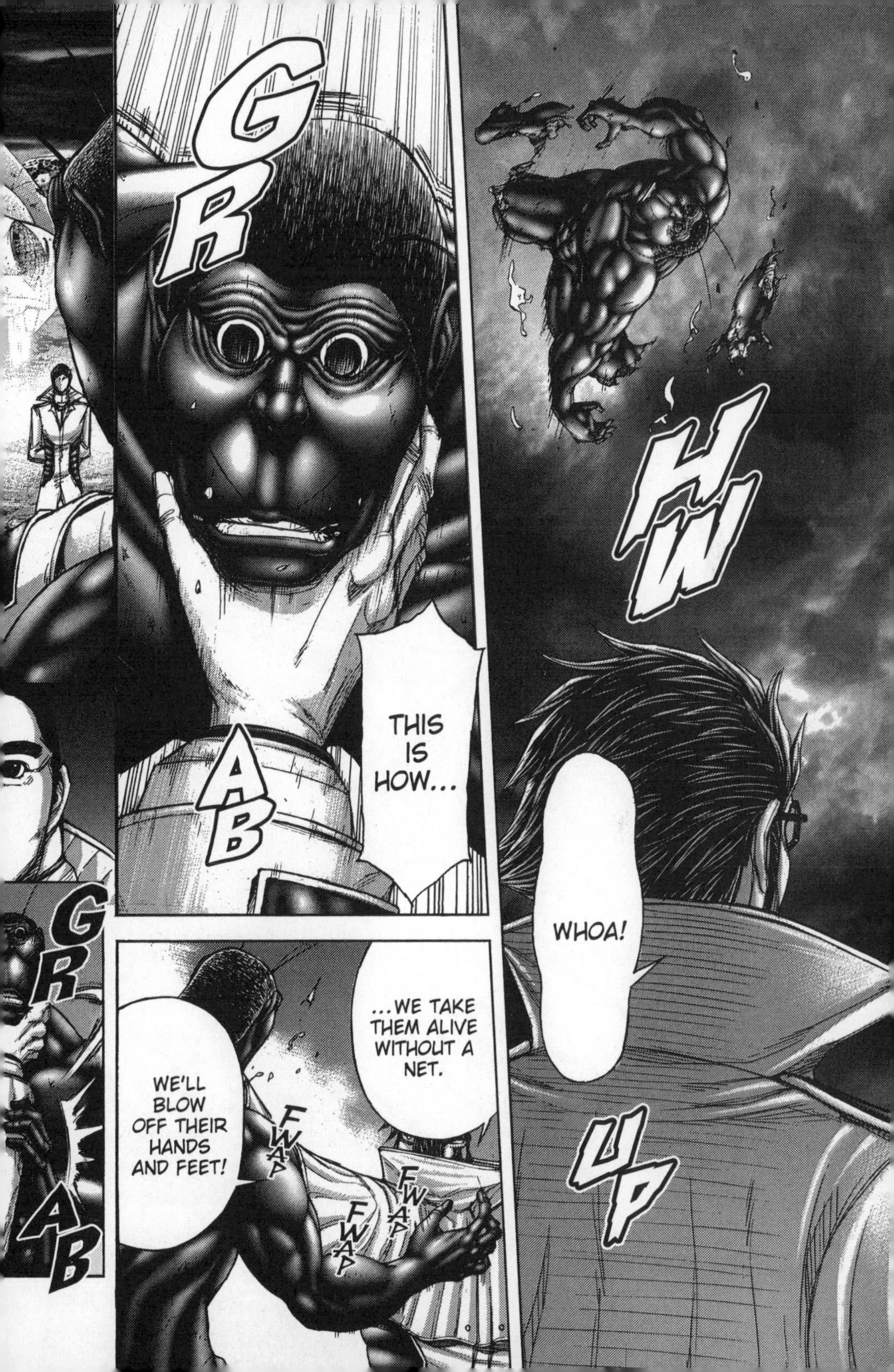
HW
WHOA!
UP
GR
AB
THIS IS HOW...
...WE TAKE THEM ALIVE WITHOUT A NET.
WE'LL BLOW OFF THEIR HANDS AND FEET!
FWAP
FWAP
FWAP
GR
AB

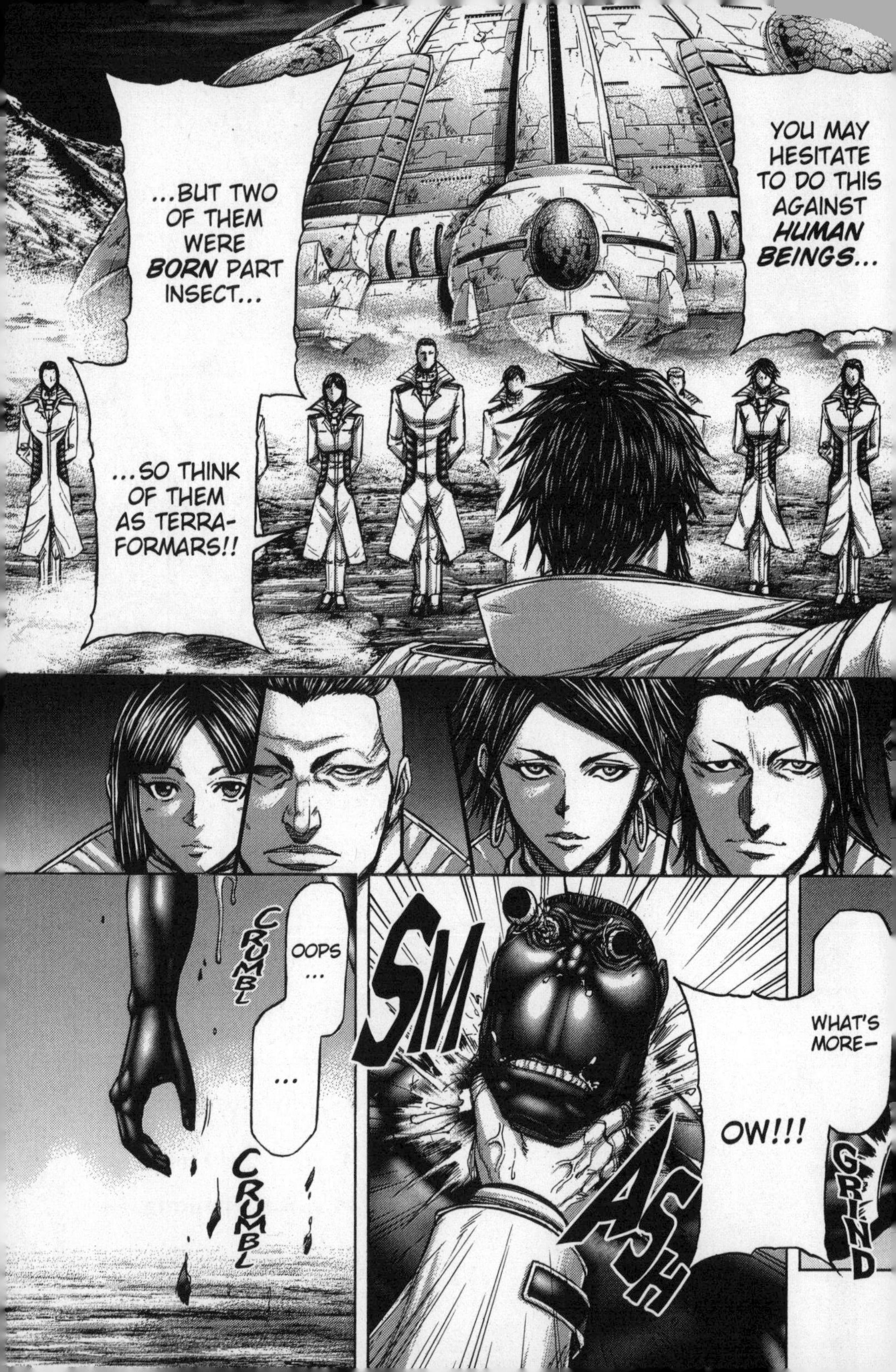
YOU MAY HESITATE TO DO THIS AGAINST HUMAN BEINGS...
...BUT TWO OF THEM WERE BORN PART INSECT...
...SO THINK OF THEM AS TERRA-FORMARS!!
WHAT'S MORE—
SMASH
OW!!!
GRIND
OOPS ...
...
CRUMBL
CRUMBL

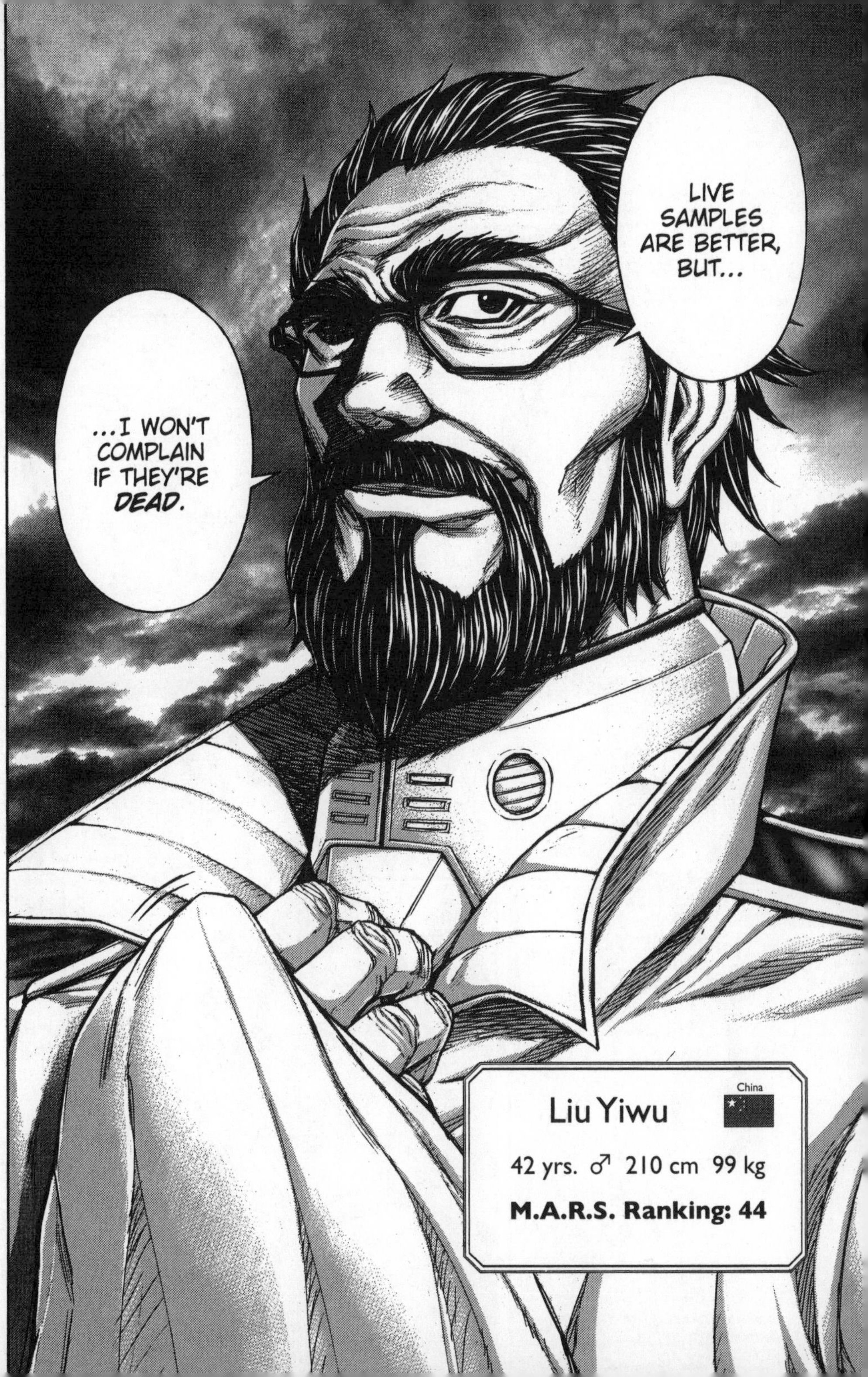
LIVE SAMPLES ARE BETTER, BUT...
...I WON'T COMPLAIN IF THEY'RE *DEAD*.
China
Liu Yiwu
42 yrs. ♂ 210 cm 99 kg
M.A.R.S. Ranking: 44

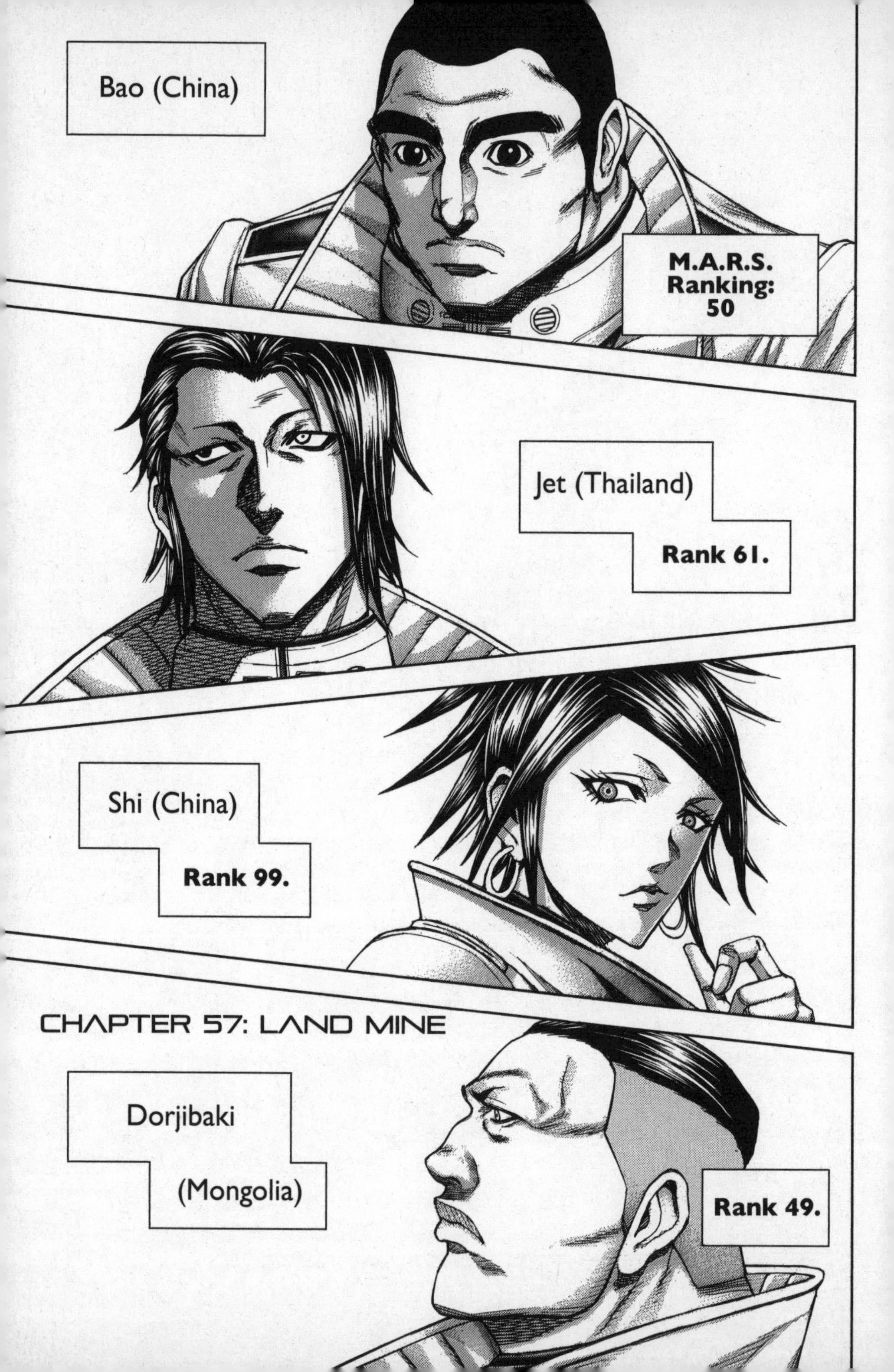

Bao (China)
M.A.R.S. Ranking: 50
Jet (Thailand)
Rank 61.
Shi (China)
Rank 99.
CHAPTER 57: LAND MINE
Dorjibaki (Mongolia)
Rank 49.

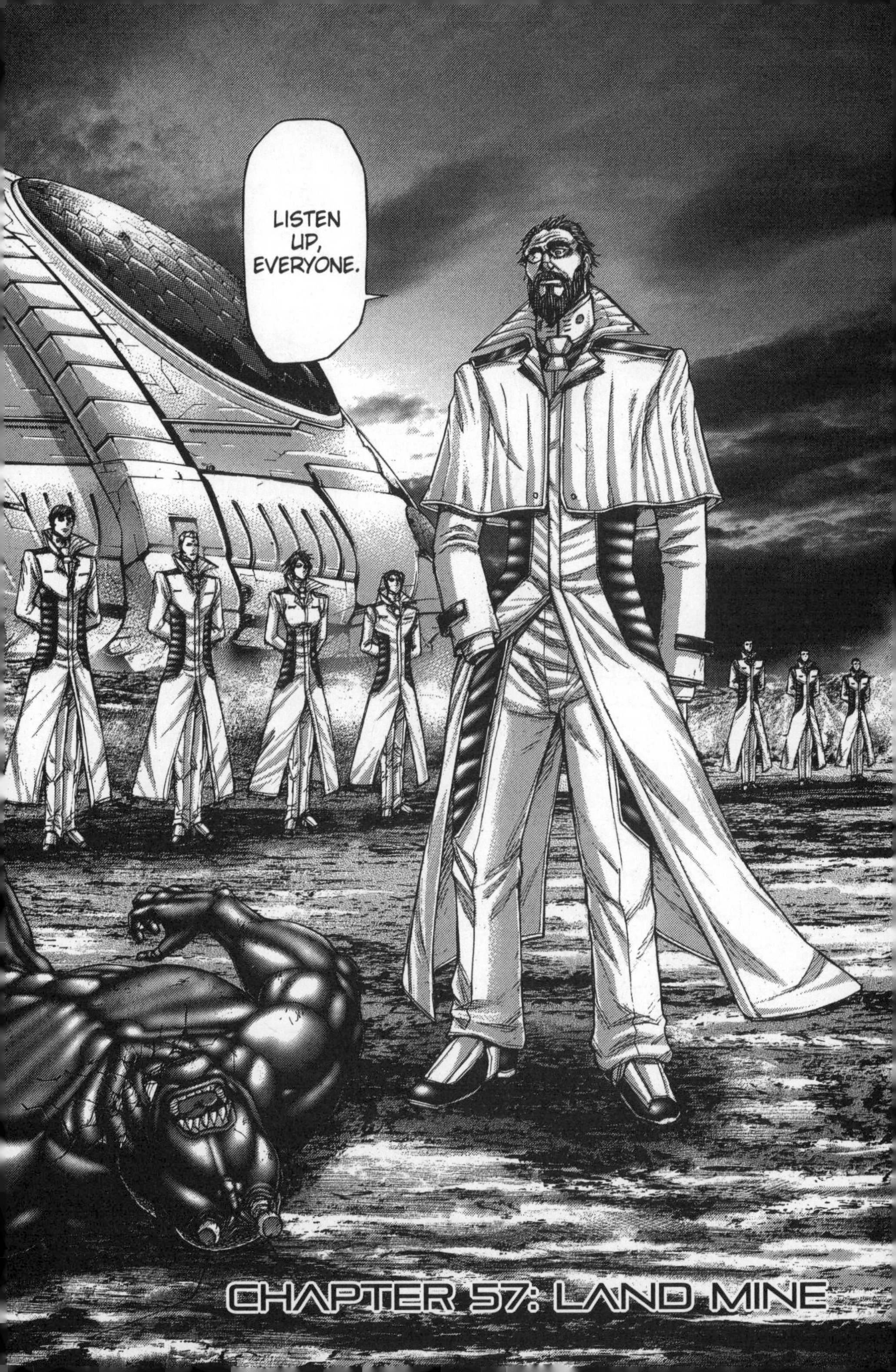
LISTEN UP, EVERYONE.
CHAPTER 57: LAND MINE

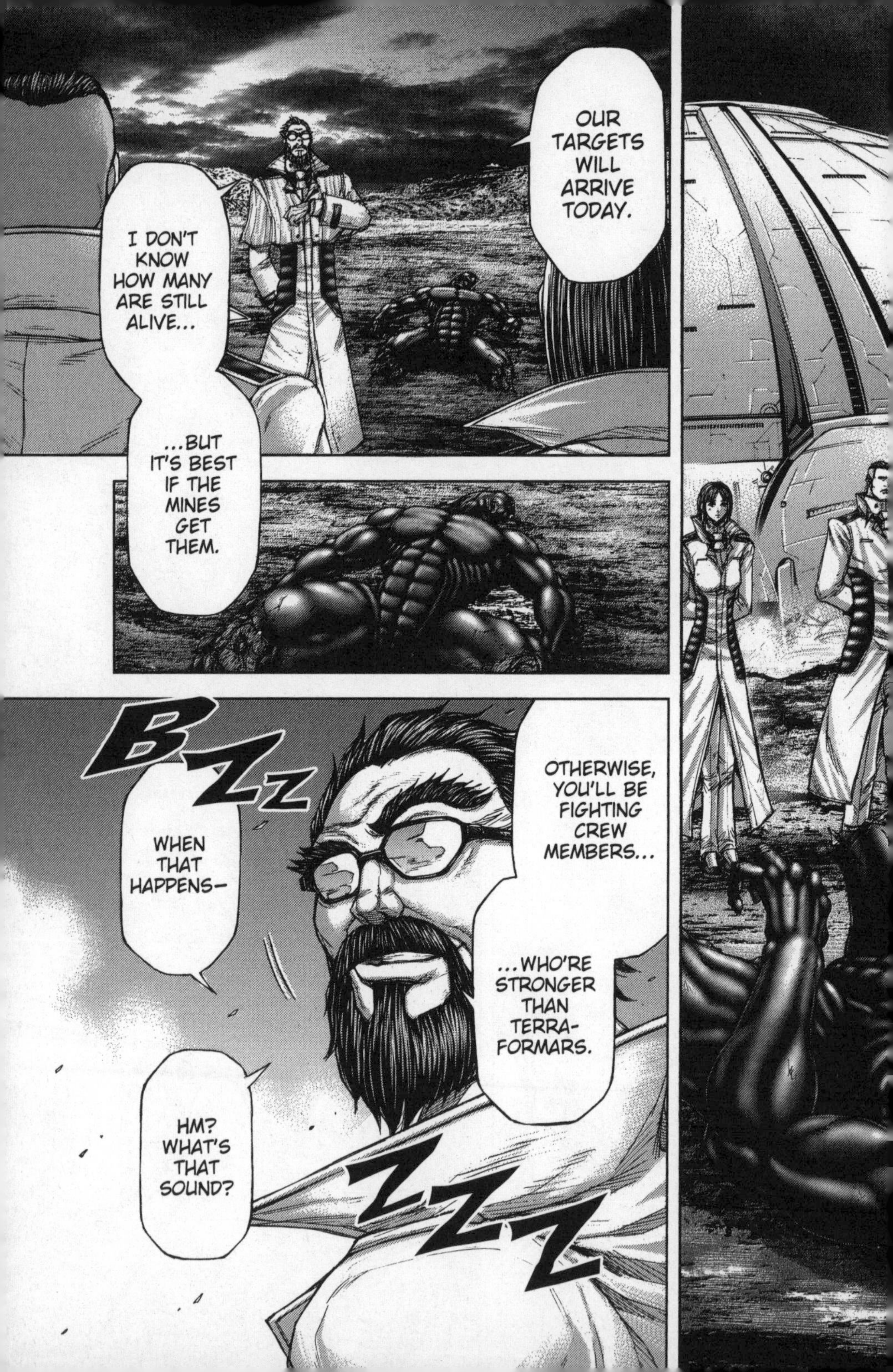
OUR TARGETS WILL ARRIVE TODAY.
I DON'T KNOW HOW MANY ARE STILL ALIVE...
...BUT IT'S BEST IF THE MINES GET THEM.
OTHERWISE, YOU'LL BE FIGHTING CREW MEMBERS...
...WHO'RE STRONGER THAN TERRA-FORMARS.
BZZ
WHEN THAT HAPPENS—
HM? WHAT'S THAT SOUND?
ZZZ

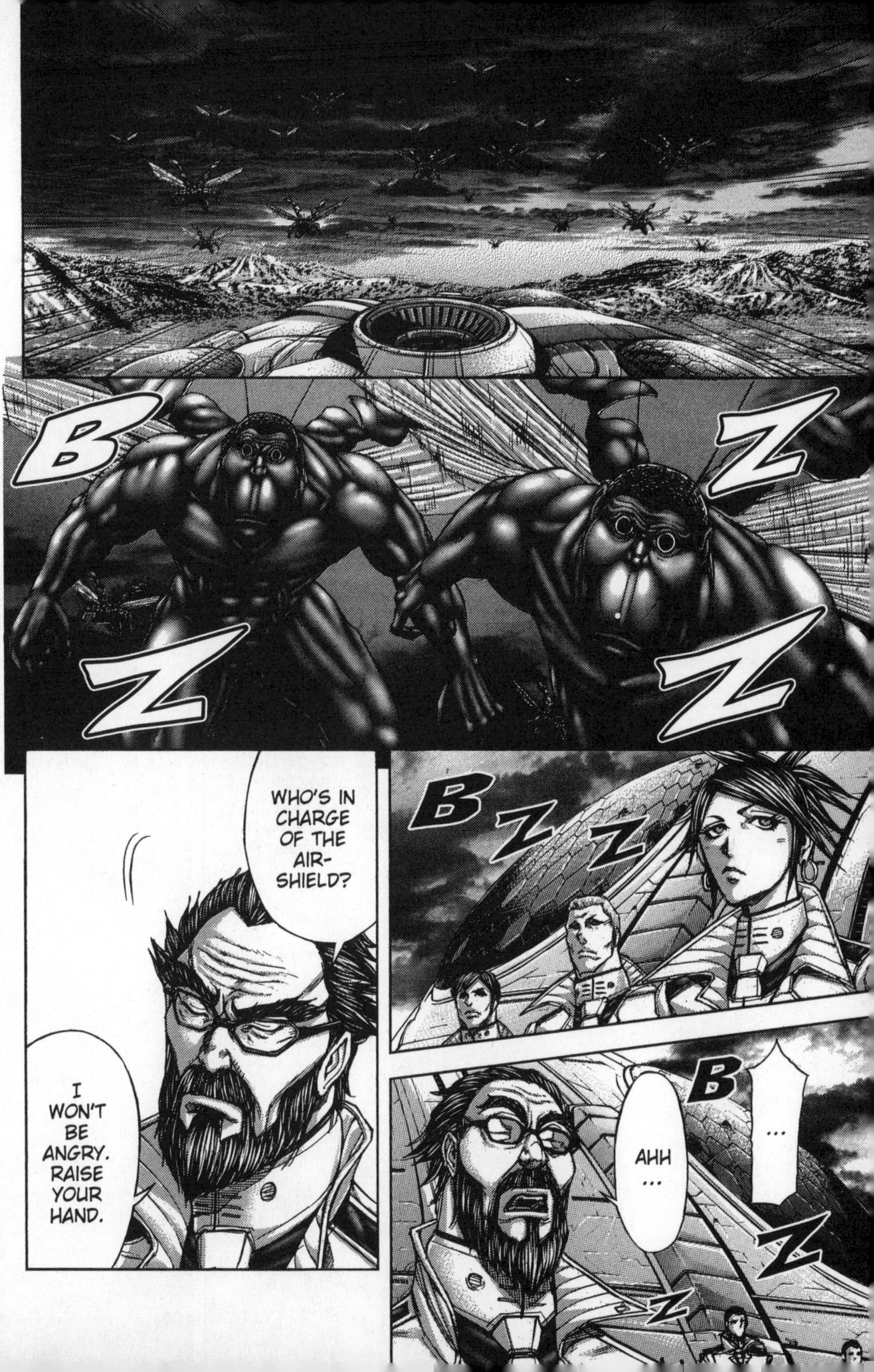
BZZZ
BZZ
AHH ...
...
BZZ
WHO'S IN CHARGE OF THE AIR-SHIELD?
I WON'T BE ANGRY. RAISE YOUR HAND.

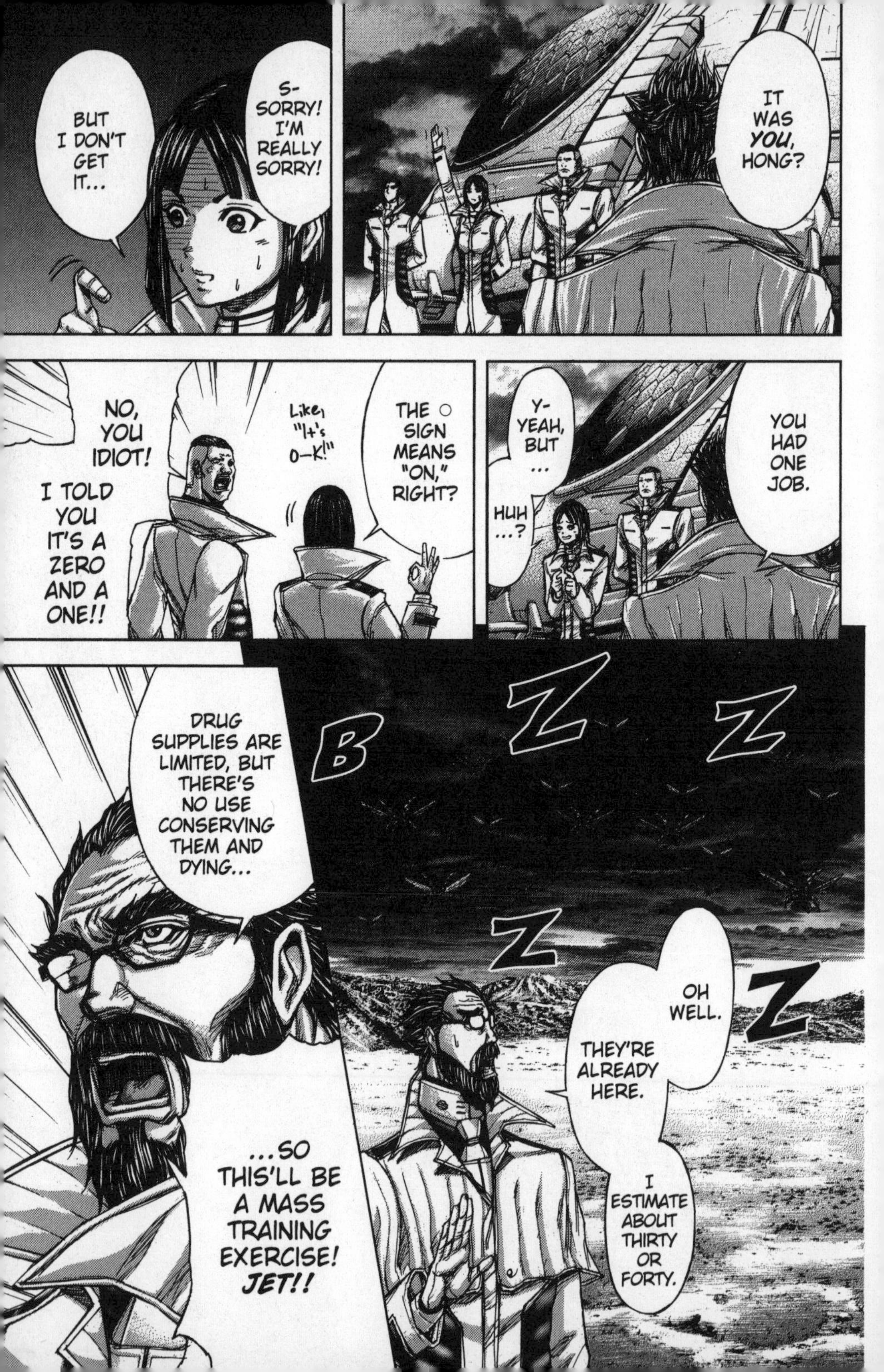
IT WAS *YOU*, HONG?
S-SORRY! I'M REALLY SORRY!
BUT I DON'T GET IT...
YOU HAD ONE JOB.
Y-YEAH, BUT ...
HUH ...?
THE ○ SIGN MEANS "ON," RIGHT?
Like, "It's O-K!"
NO, YOU IDIOT!
I TOLD YOU IT'S A ZERO AND A ONE!!
BZZZZ
OH WELL.
THEY'RE ALREADY HERE.
I ESTIMATE ABOUT THIRTY OR FORTY.
DRUG SUPPLIES ARE LIMITED, BUT THERE'S NO USE CONSERVING THEM AND DYING...
...SO THIS'LL BE A MASS TRAINING EXERCISE! *JET!!*

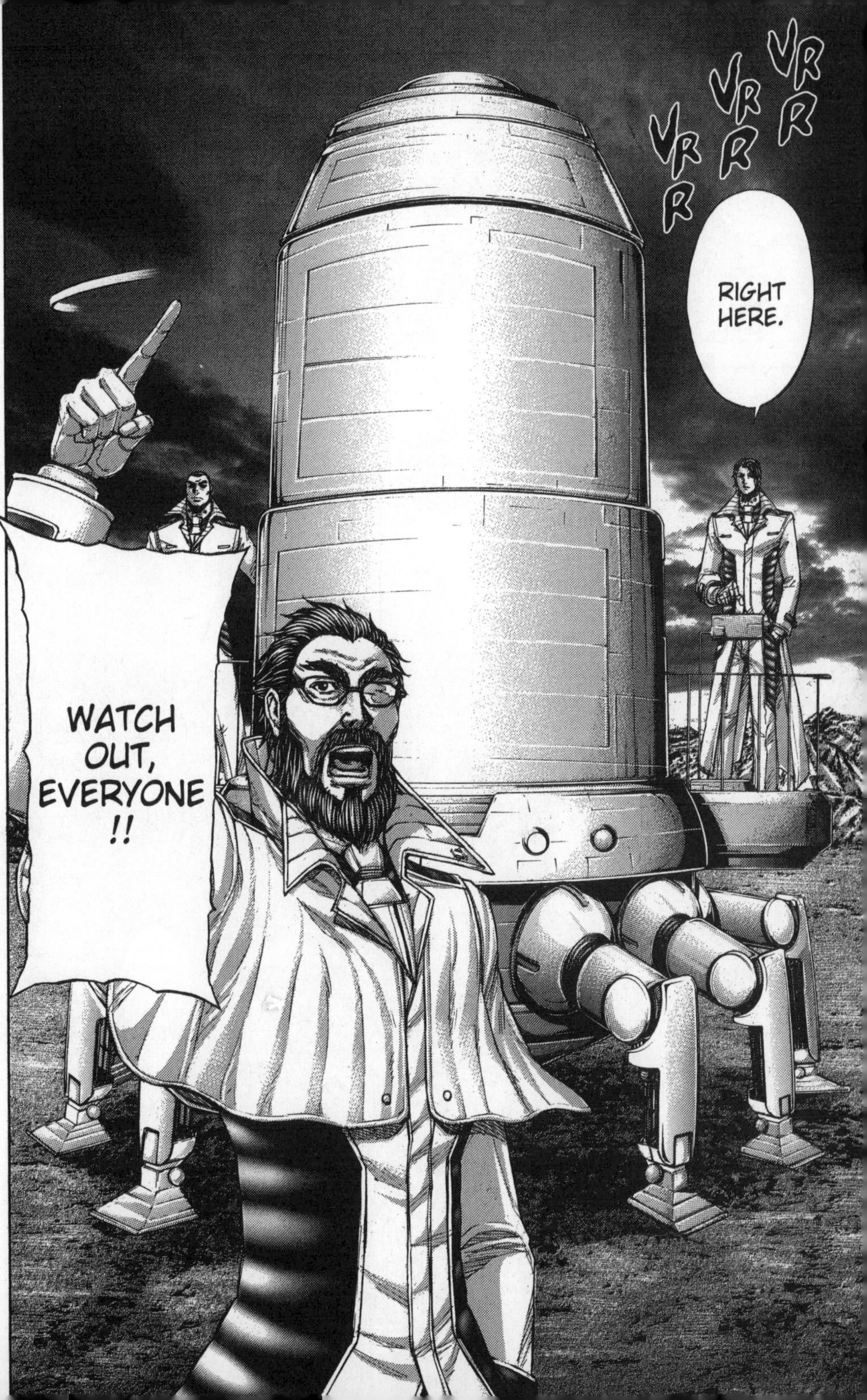
VRR VRR VRR
RIGHT HERE.
WATCH OUT, EVERYONE!!

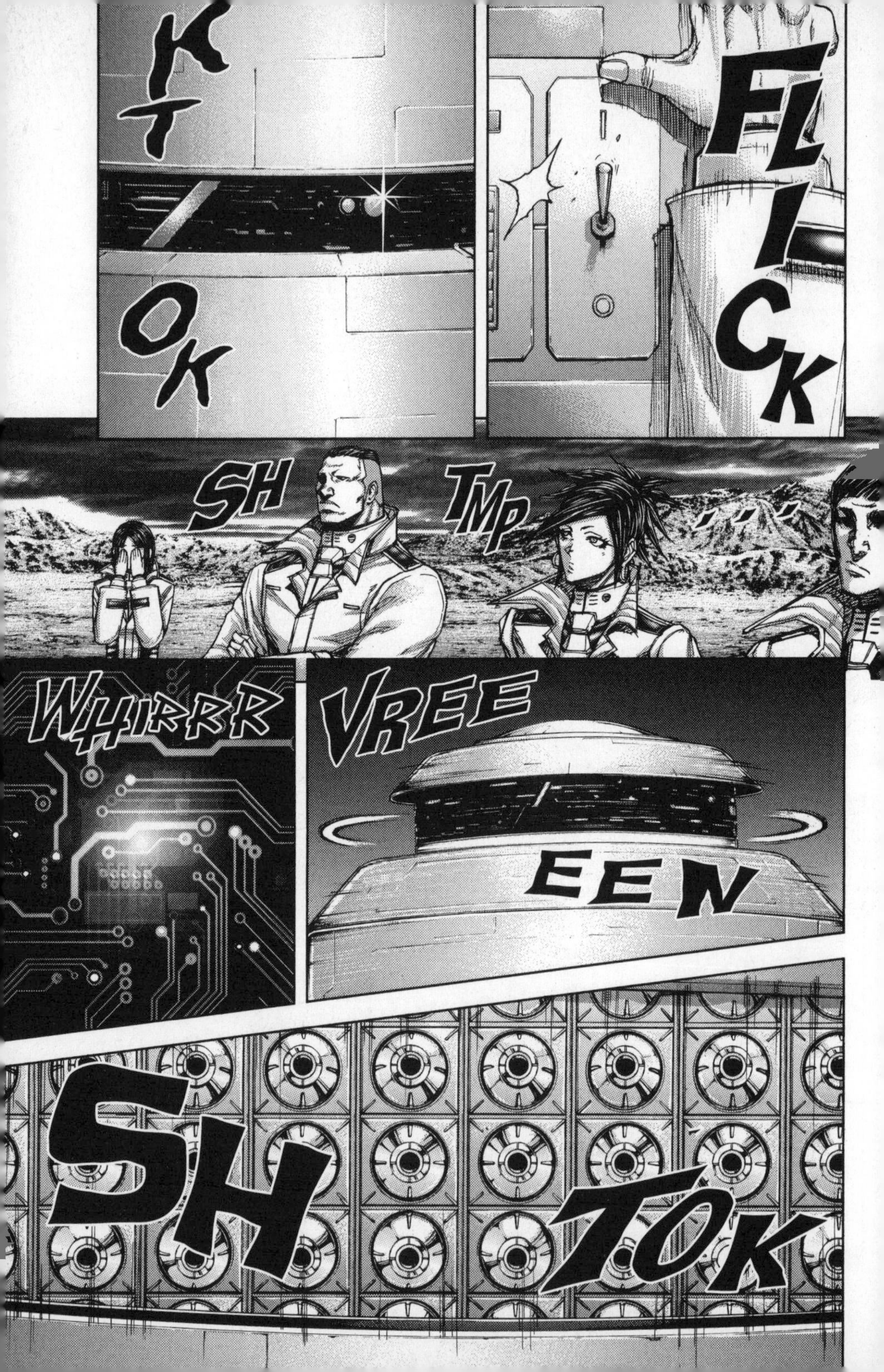
FLICK
KTOK
...
SH TMP
VREEEEN
WHIRRR
SHTOK

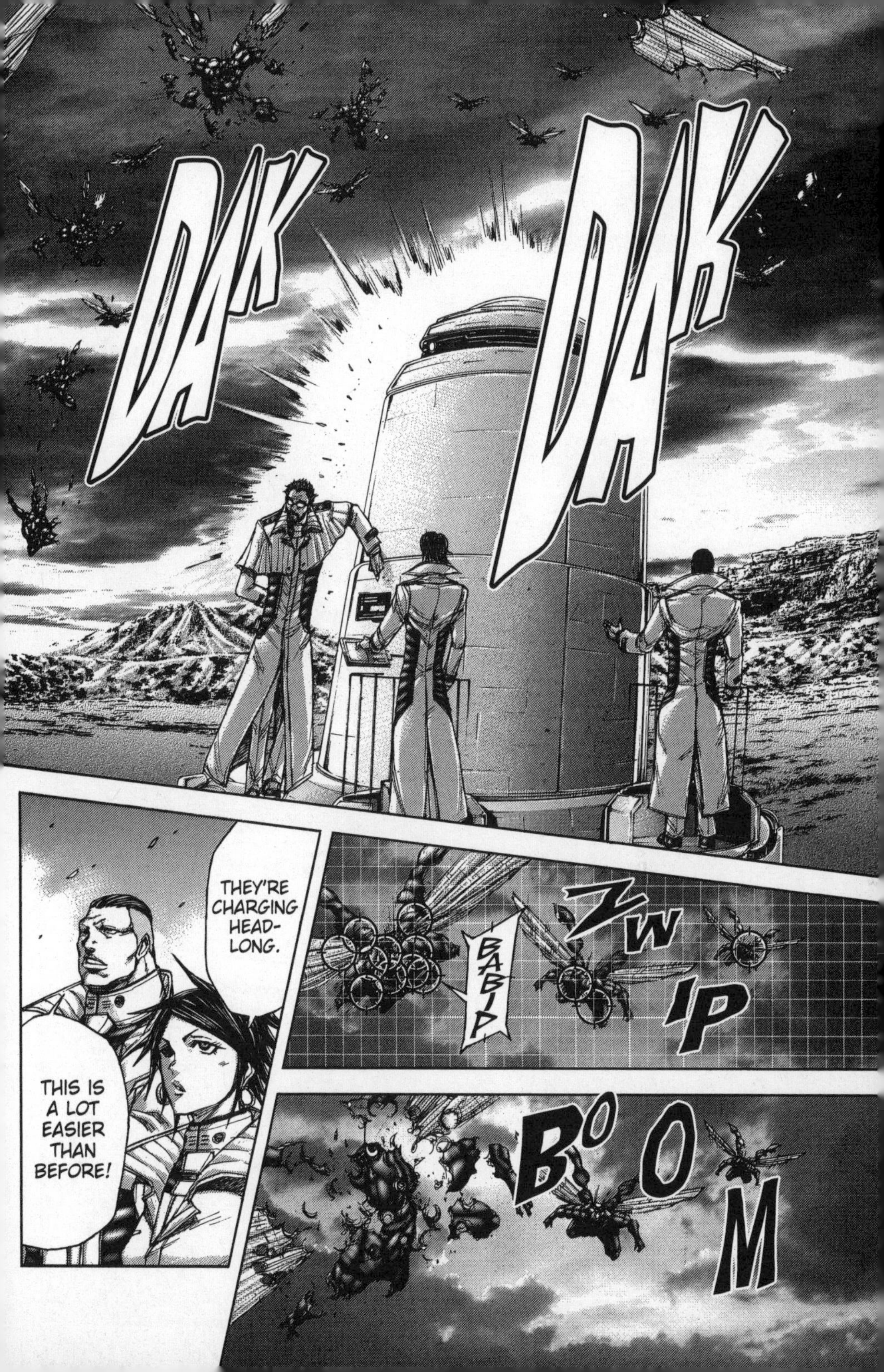
DA DAK
DA DAK
ZWIP
BABIP
BOOM
THEY'RE CHARGING HEAD-LONG.
THIS IS A LOT EASIER THAN BEFORE!

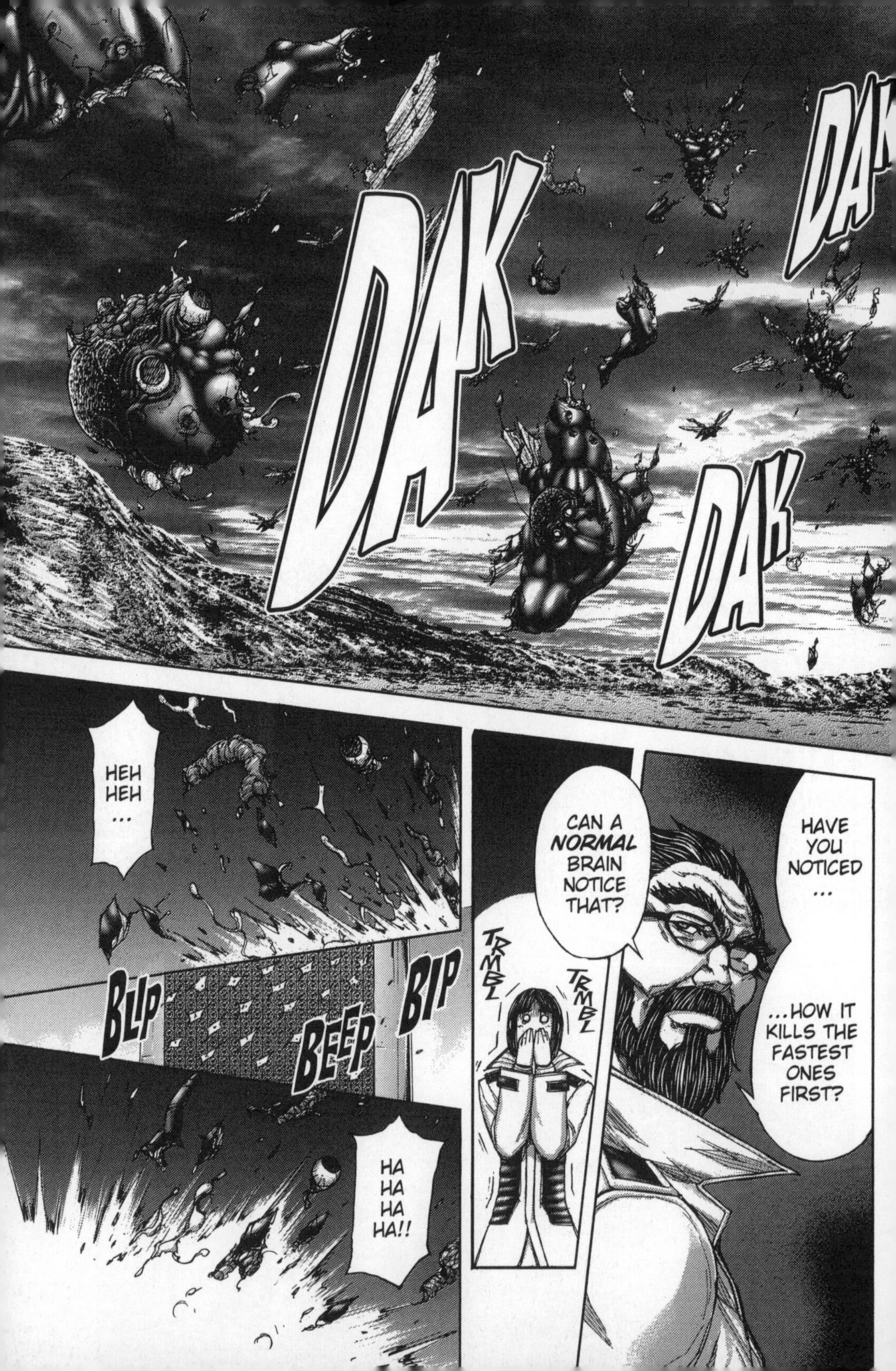
DAK
DAK
DAK
HAVE YOU NOTICED ...
...HOW IT KILLS THE FASTEST ONES FIRST?
CAN A NORMAL BRAIN NOTICE THAT?
TRMBL
TRMBL
HEH HEH ...
BIP
BEEP
BLIP
HA HA HA HA!!

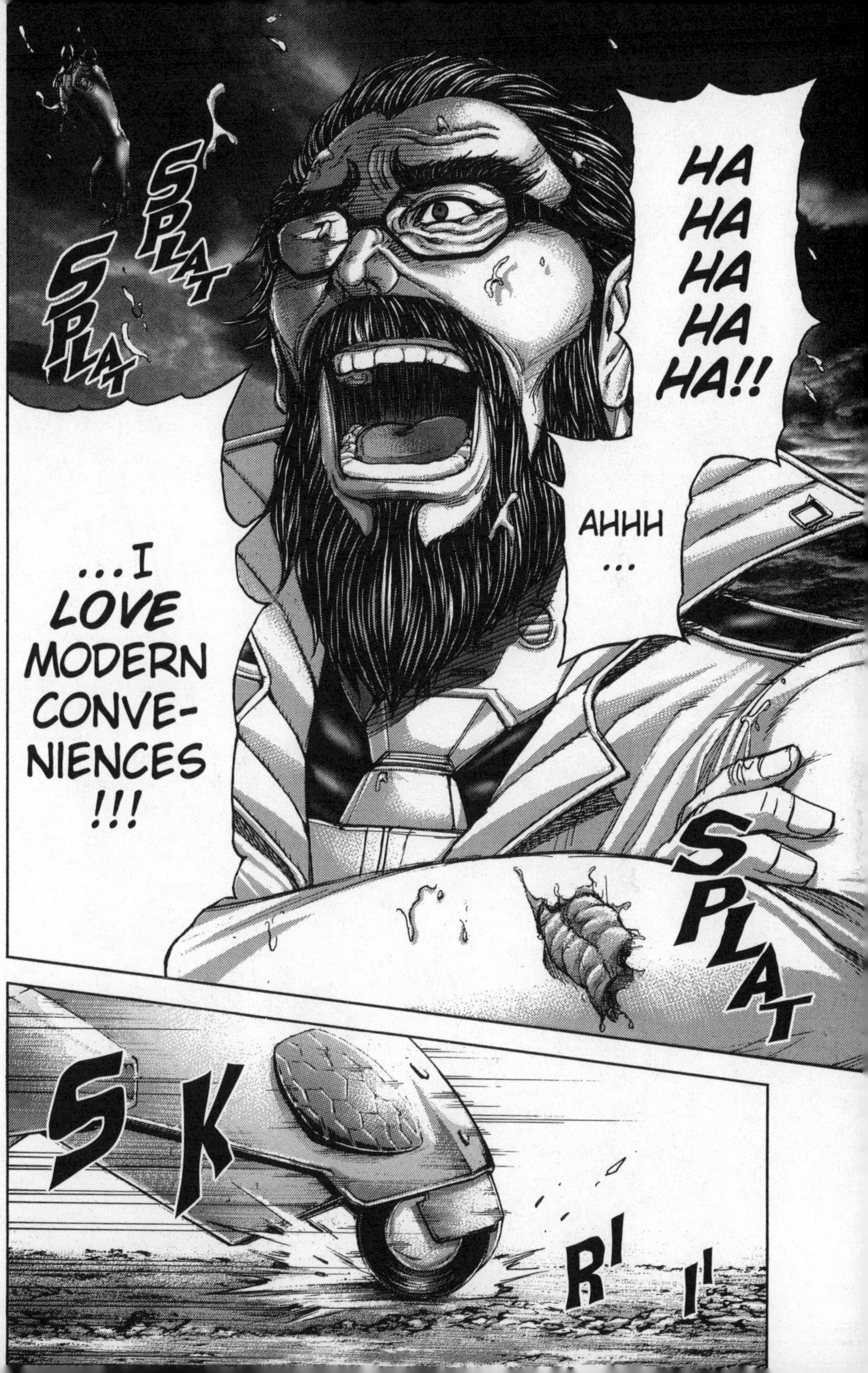
HA HA HA HA HA!!
SPLAT SPLAT
AHHH ...
...I LOVE MODERN CONVENIENCES!!!
SPLAT
SK
RII

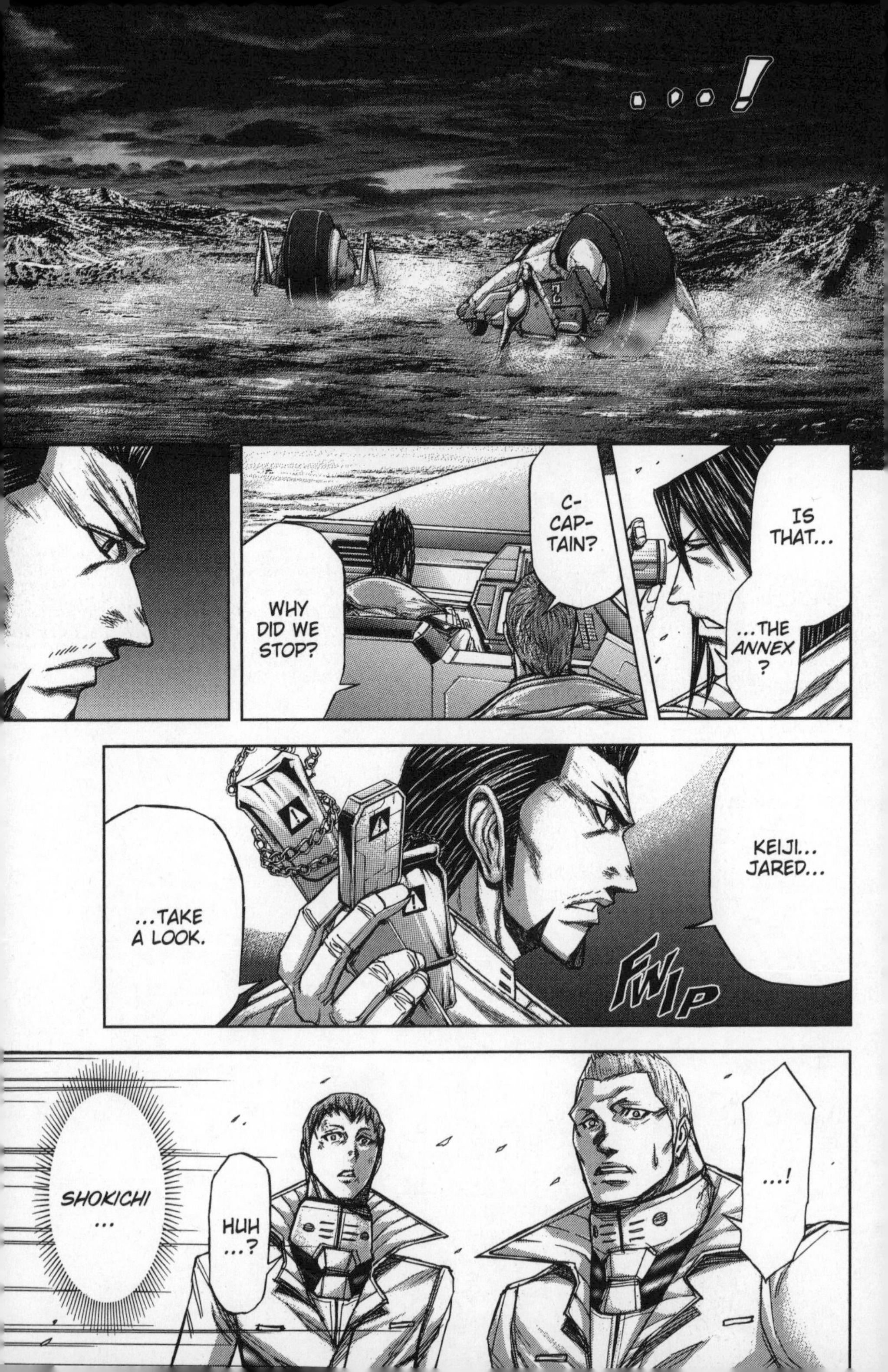
...!
IS THAT...
...THE ANNEX?
C-CAPTAIN?
WHY DID WE STOP?
KEIJI... JARED...
FWIP
...TAKE A LOOK.
...!
HUH...?
SHOKICHI...

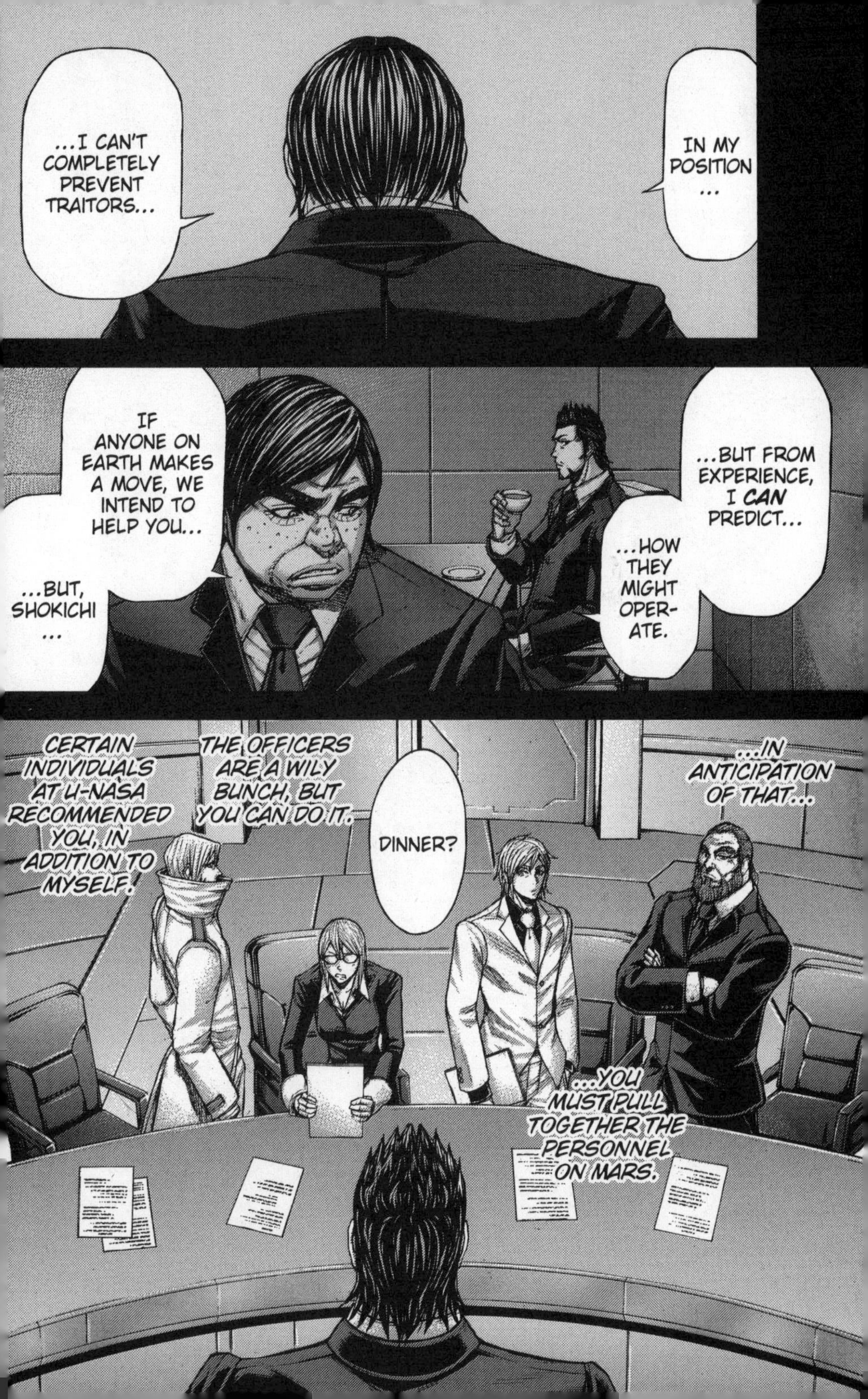
IN MY POSITION...
...I CAN'T COMPLETELY PREVENT TRAITORS...
...BUT FROM EXPERIENCE, I *CAN* PREDICT...
...HOW THEY MIGHT OPER-ATE.
IF ANYONE ON EARTH MAKES A MOVE, WE INTEND TO HELP YOU...
...BUT, SHOKICHI...
...IN ANTICIPATION OF THAT...
...YOU MUST PULL TOGETHER THE PERSONNEL ON MARS.
DINNER?
THE OFFICERS ARE A WILY BUNCH, BUT YOU CAN DO IT.
CERTAIN INDIVIDUALS AT U-NASA RECOMMENDED YOU, IN ADDITION TO MYSELF.

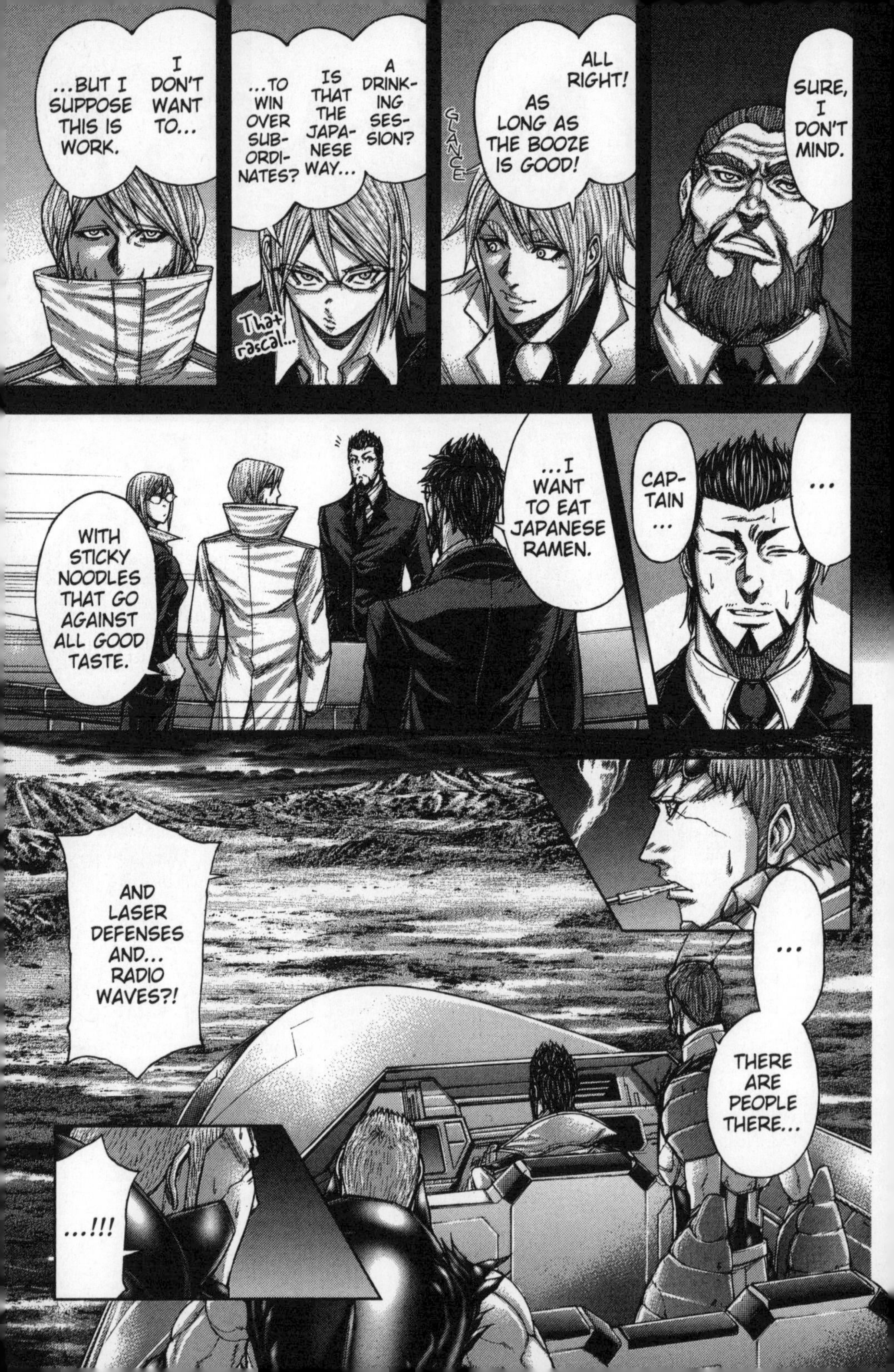
SURE, I DON'T MIND.
ALL RIGHT! AS LONG AS THE BOOZE IS GOOD!
GLANCE
A DRINKING SESSION?
IS THAT THE JAPANESE WAY...
...TO WIN OVER SUBORDINATES?
That rascal...
I DON'T WANT TO...
...BUT I SUPPOSE THIS IS WORK.
...
CAPTAIN...
...I WANT TO EAT JAPANESE RAMEN.
WITH STICKY NOODLES THAT GO AGAINST ALL GOOD TASTE.
...
THERE ARE PEOPLE THERE...
AND LASER DEFENSES AND... RADIO WAVES?!
...!!!

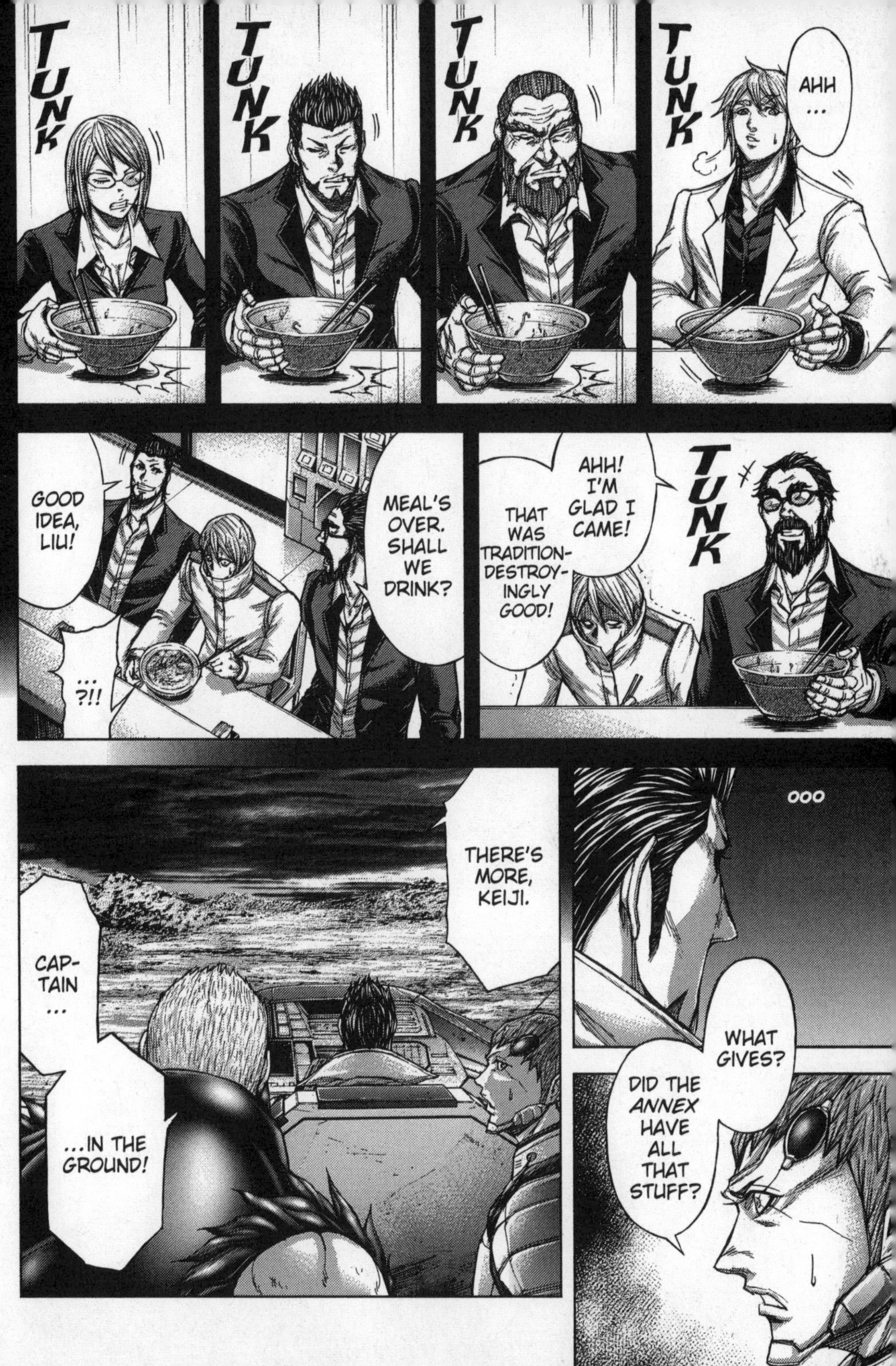
TUNK
AHH ...
TUNK
TUNK
TUNK
TUNK
AHH! I'M GLAD I CAME!
THAT WAS TRADITION-DESTROYINGLY GOOD!
MEAL'S OVER. SHALL WE DRINK?
GOOD IDEA, LIU!
... ?!!
ooo
WHAT GIVES?
DID THE *ANNEX* HAVE ALL THAT STUFF?
THERE'S MORE, KEIJI.
CAPTAIN ...
...IN THE GROUND!

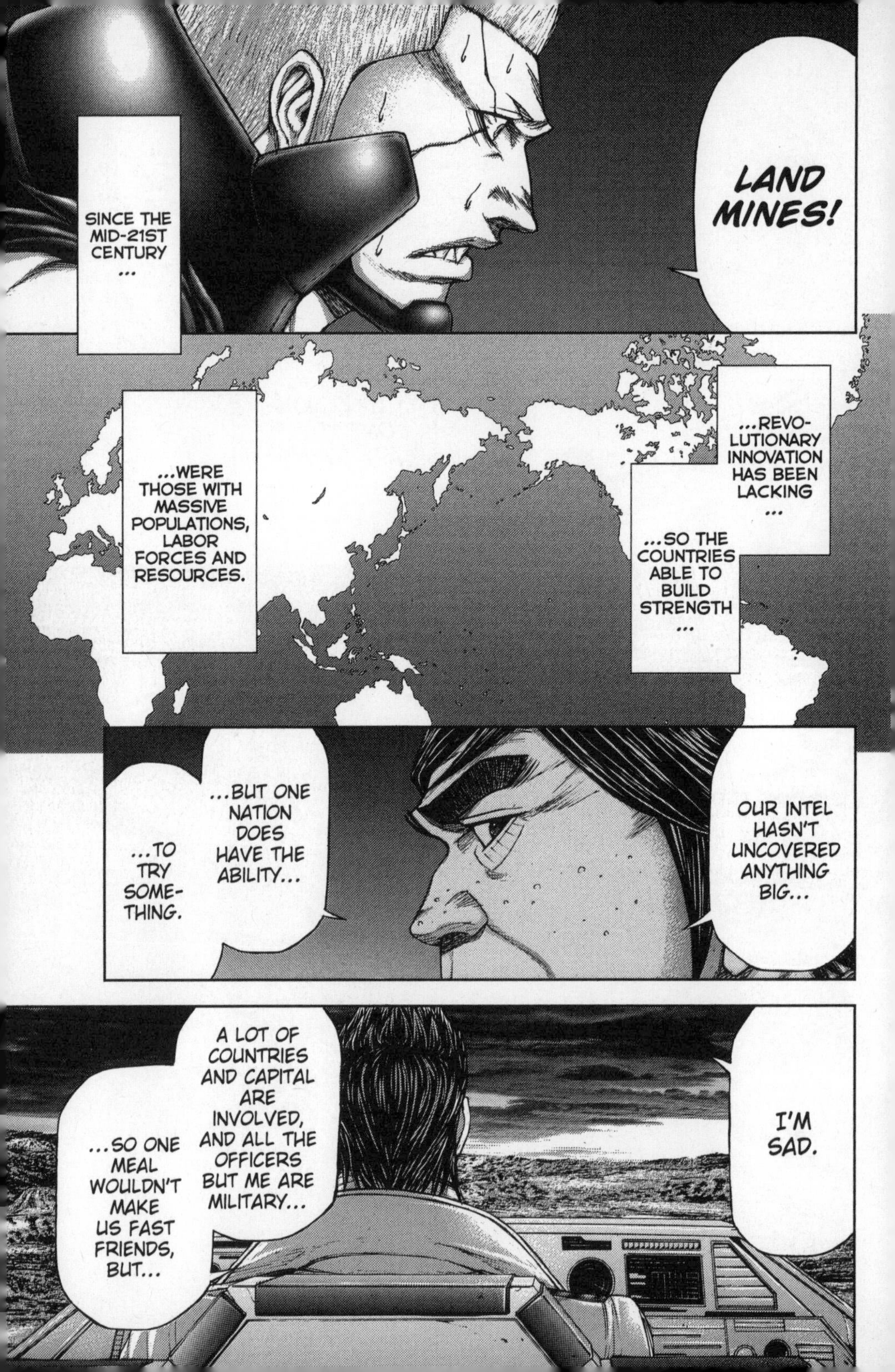
LAND MINES!
SINCE THE MID-21ST CENTURY ...
...REVO-LUTIONARY INNOVATION HAS BEEN LACKING ...
...SO THE COUNTRIES ABLE TO BUILD STRENGTH ...
...WERE THOSE WITH MASSIVE POPULATIONS, LABOR FORCES AND RESOURCES.
OUR INTEL HASN'T UNCOVERED ANYTHING BIG...
...BUT ONE NATION DOES HAVE THE ABILITY...
...TO TRY SOME-THING.
I'M SAD.
A LOT OF COUNTRIES AND CAPITAL ARE INVOLVED, AND ALL THE OFFICERS BUT ME ARE MILITARY...
...SO ONE MEAL WOULDN'T MAKE US FAST FRIENDS, BUT...

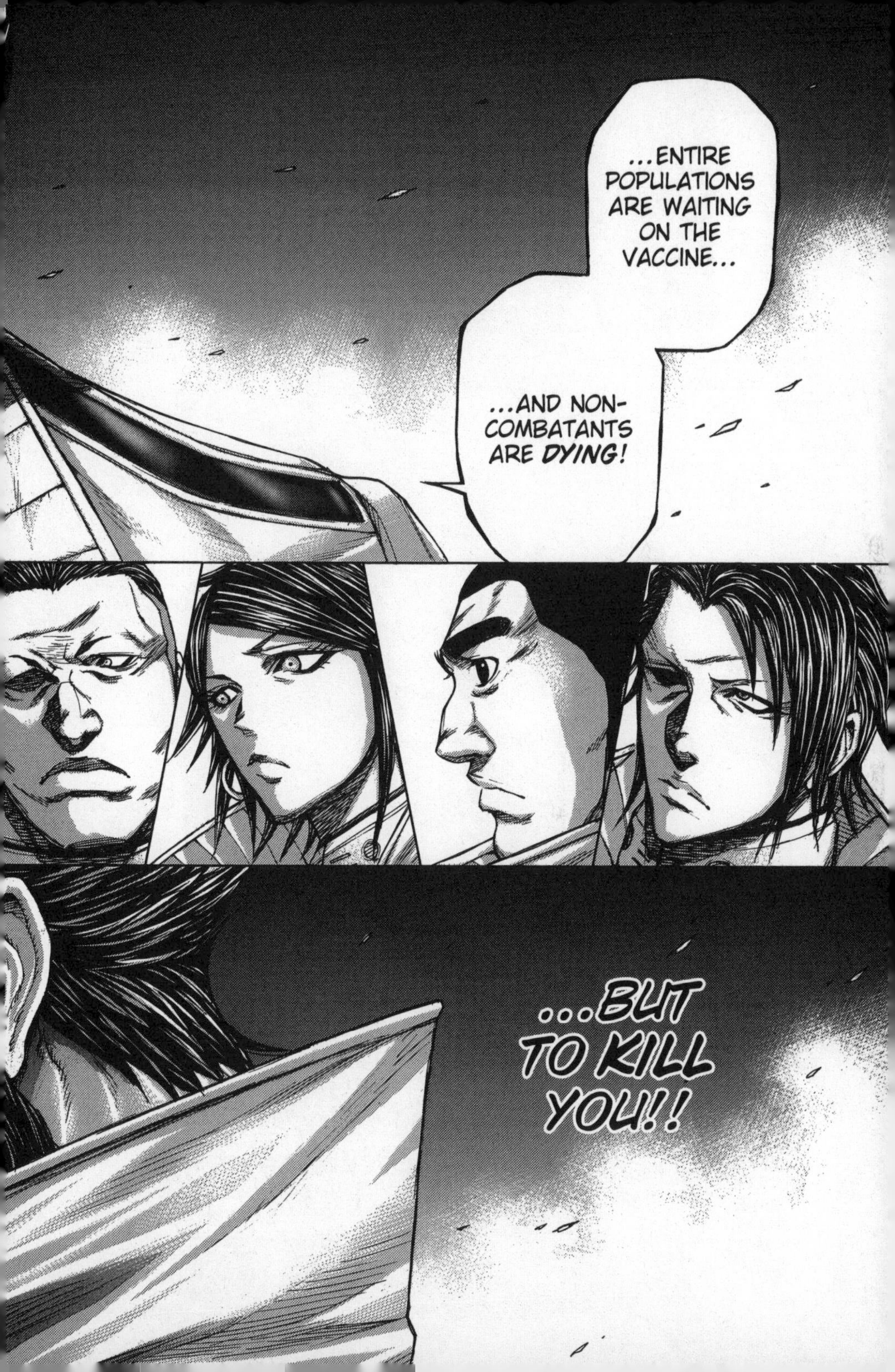
...ENTIRE POPULATIONS ARE WAITING ON THE VACCINE...
...AND NON-COMBATANTS ARE DYING!
...BUT TO KILL YOU!!

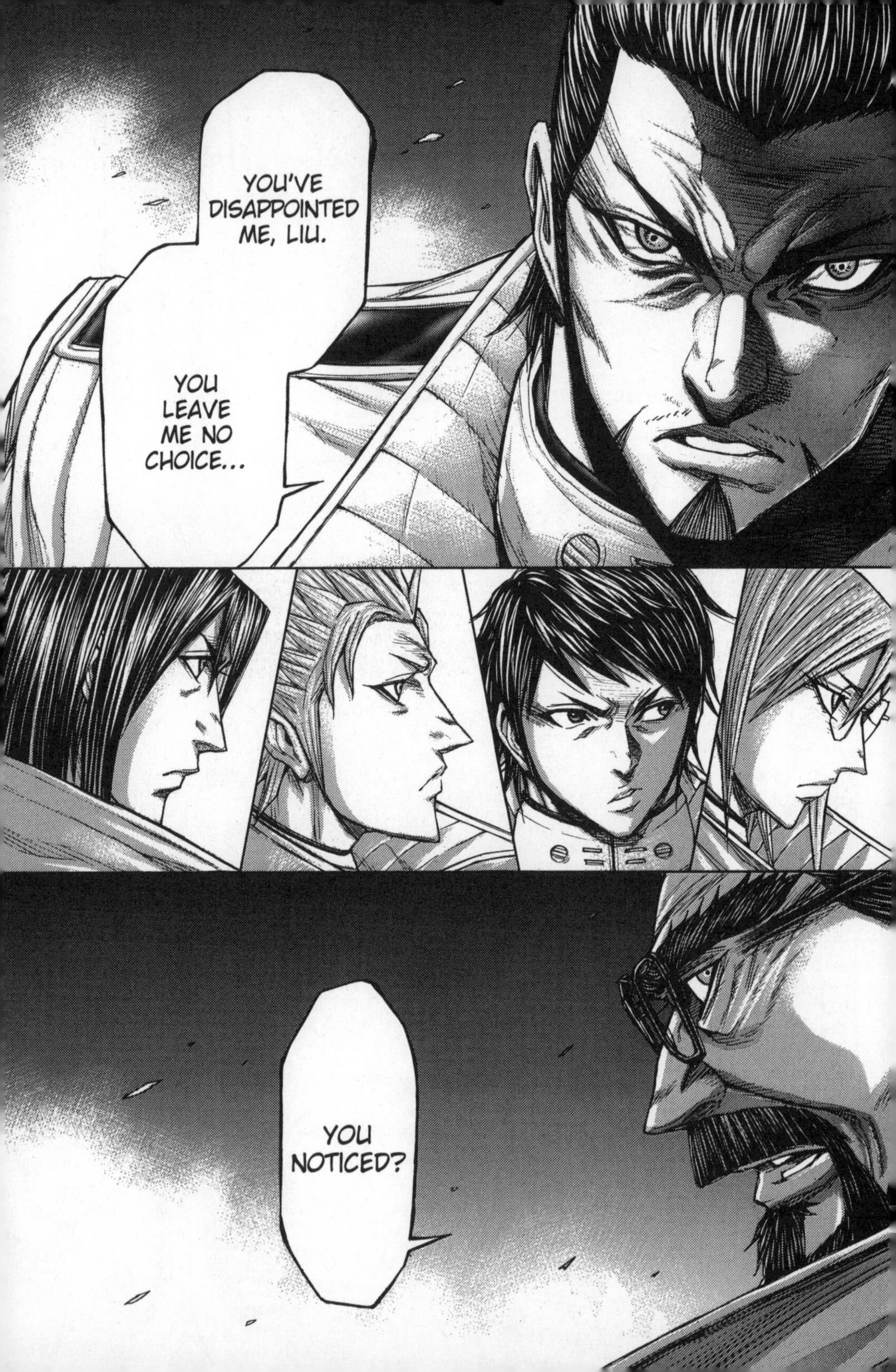
YOU'VE DISAPPOINTED ME, LIU.
YOU LEAVE ME NO CHOICE...
YOU NOTICED?

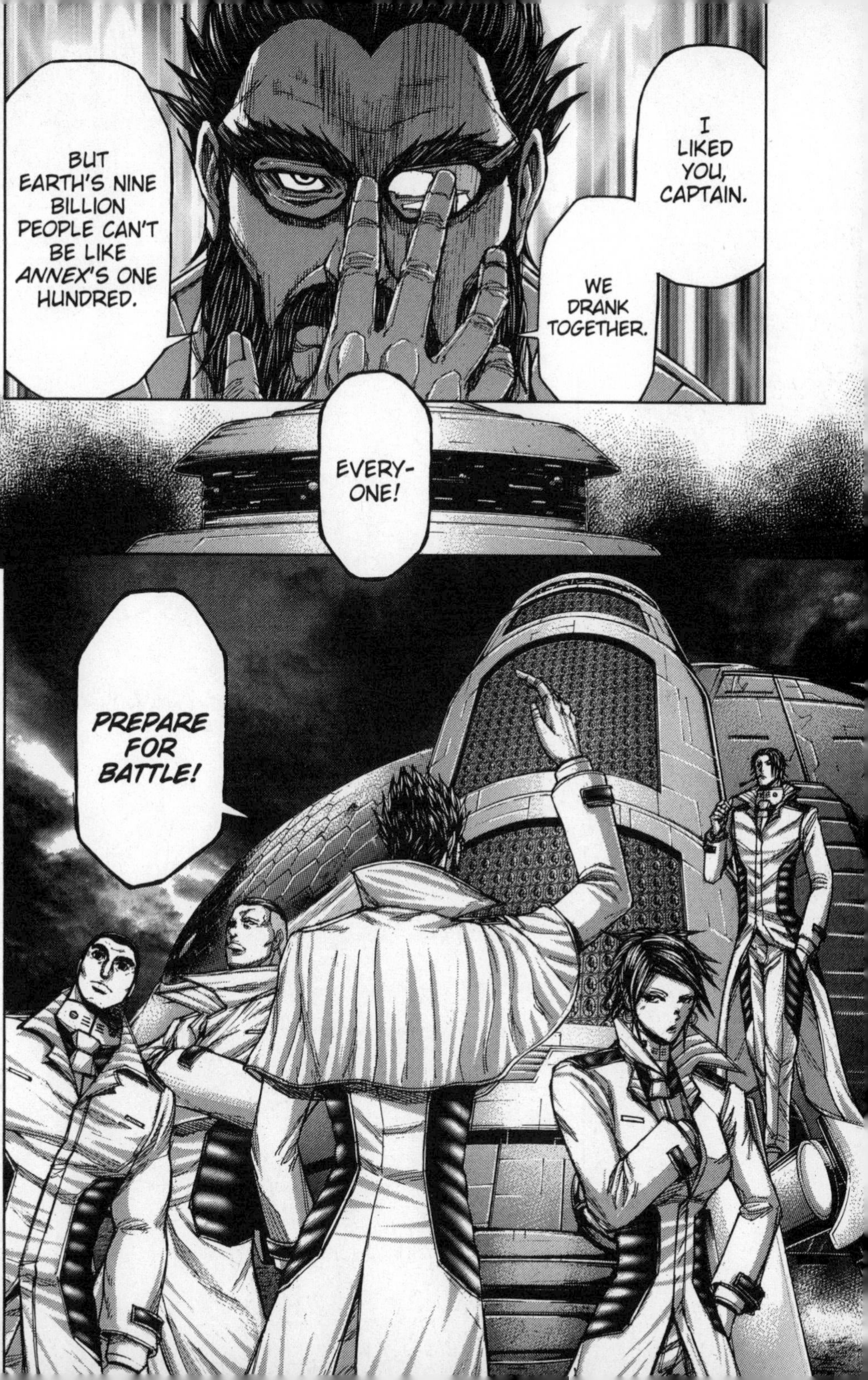
I LIKED YOU, CAPTAIN.
WE DRANK TOGETHER.
BUT EARTH'S NINE BILLION PEOPLE CAN'T BE LIKE *ANNEX'S* ONE HUNDRED.
EVERY-ONE!
PREPARE FOR BATTLE!

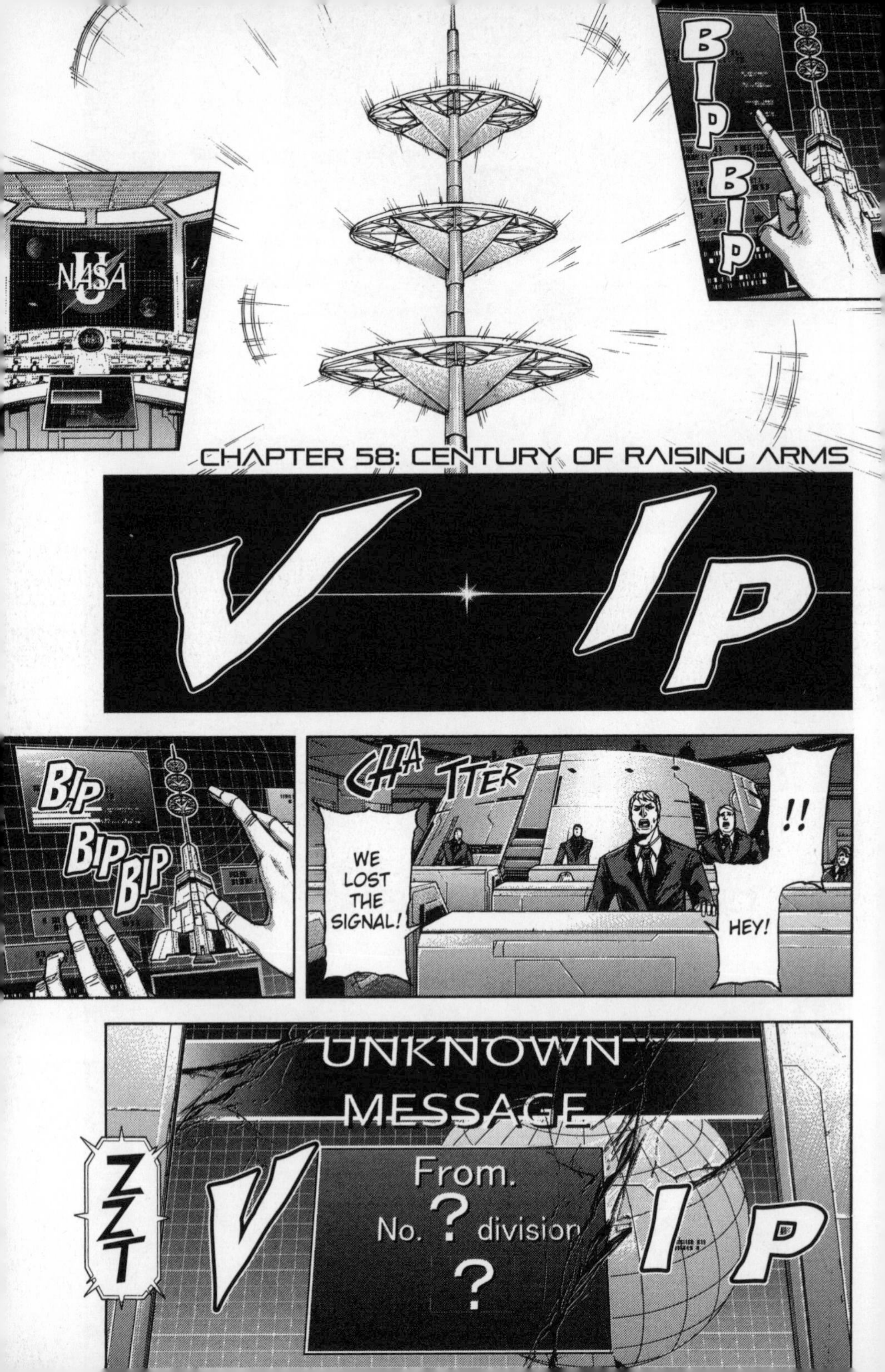
BIP
BIP
BIP
NASA
CHAPTER 58: CENTURY OF RAISING ARMS
V-IP
CHATTER
!!
HEY!
WE LOST THE SIGNAL!
BIP
BIP BIP
UNKNOWN MESSAGE
From.
No. ? division
?
V IP
ZZT

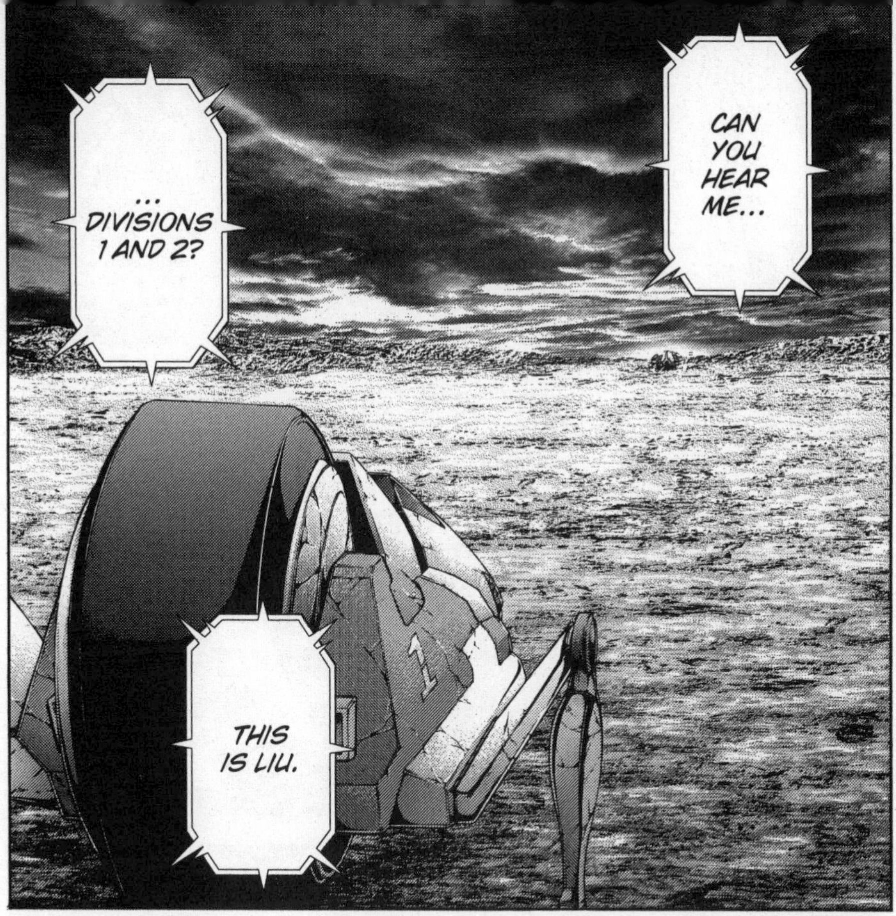
CAN YOU HEAR ME...
...DIVISIONS 1 AND 2?
THIS IS LIU.

CHAPTER 58: CENTURY OF RAISING ARMS

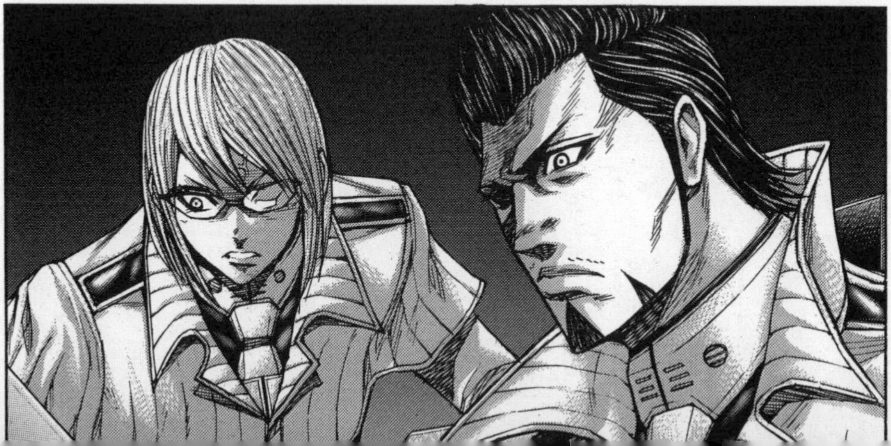

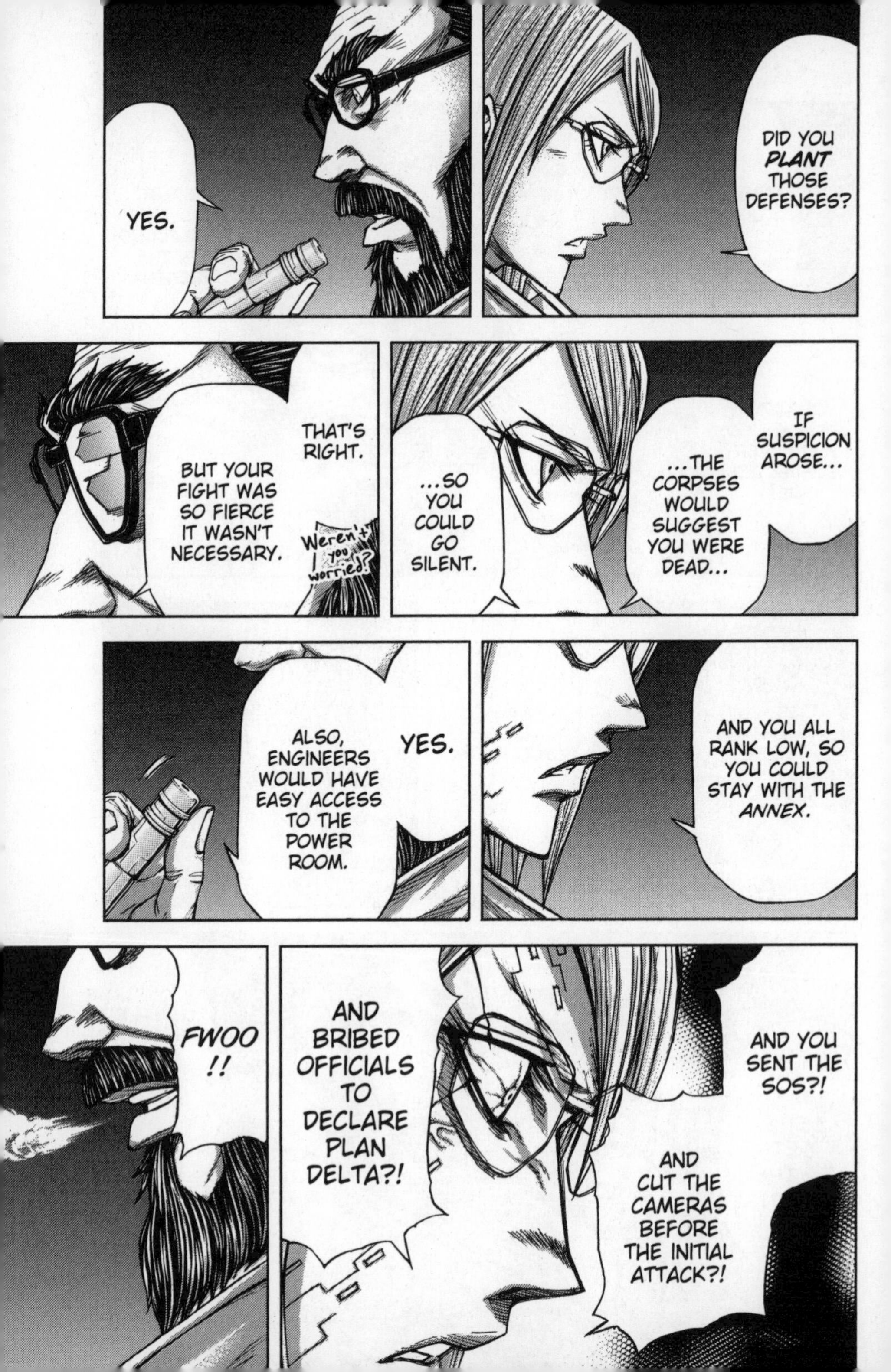
DID YOU PLANT THOSE DEFENSES?
YES.
IF SUSPICION AROSE...
...THE CORPSES WOULD SUGGEST YOU WERE DEAD...
...SO YOU COULD GO SILENT.
THAT'S RIGHT.
Weren't you worried?
BUT YOUR FIGHT WAS SO FIERCE IT WASN'T NECESSARY.
AND YOU ALL RANK LOW, SO YOU COULD STAY WITH THE ANNEX.
YES.
ALSO, ENGINEERS WOULD HAVE EASY ACCESS TO THE POWER ROOM.
AND YOU SENT THE SOS?!
AND CUT THE CAMERAS BEFORE THE INITIAL ATTACK?!
AND BRIBED OFFICIALS TO DECLARE PLAN DELTA?!
FWOO!!

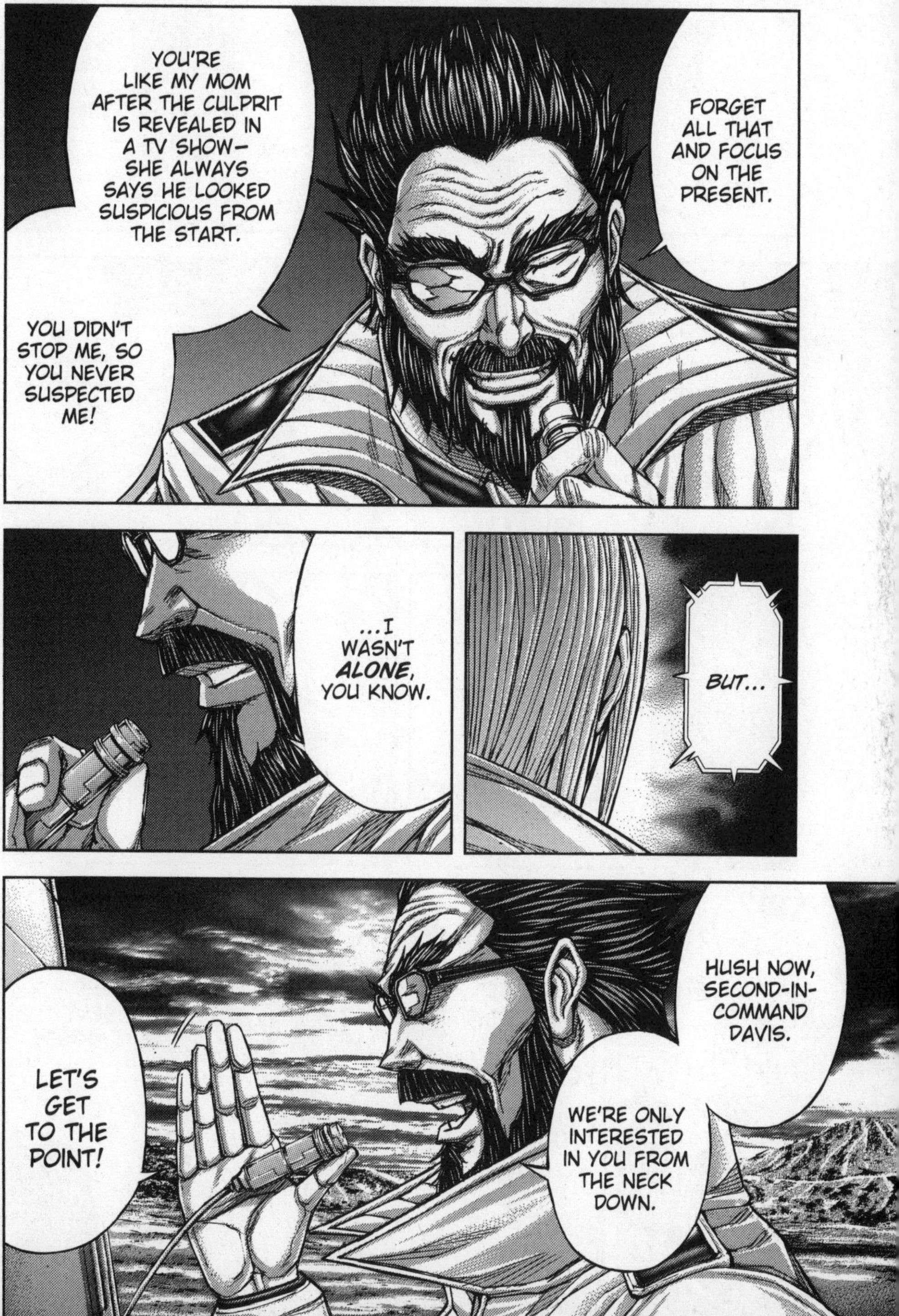
FORGET ALL THAT AND FOCUS ON THE PRESENT.
YOU'RE LIKE MY MOM AFTER THE CULPRIT IS REVEALED IN A TV SHOW—SHE ALWAYS SAYS HE LOOKED SUSPICIOUS FROM THE START.
YOU DIDN'T STOP ME, SO YOU NEVER SUSPECTED ME!
BUT...
...I WASN'T *ALONE*, YOU KNOW.
HUSH NOW, SECOND-IN-COMMAND DAVIS.
WE'RE ONLY INTERESTED IN YOU FROM THE NECK DOWN.
LET'S GET TO THE POINT!

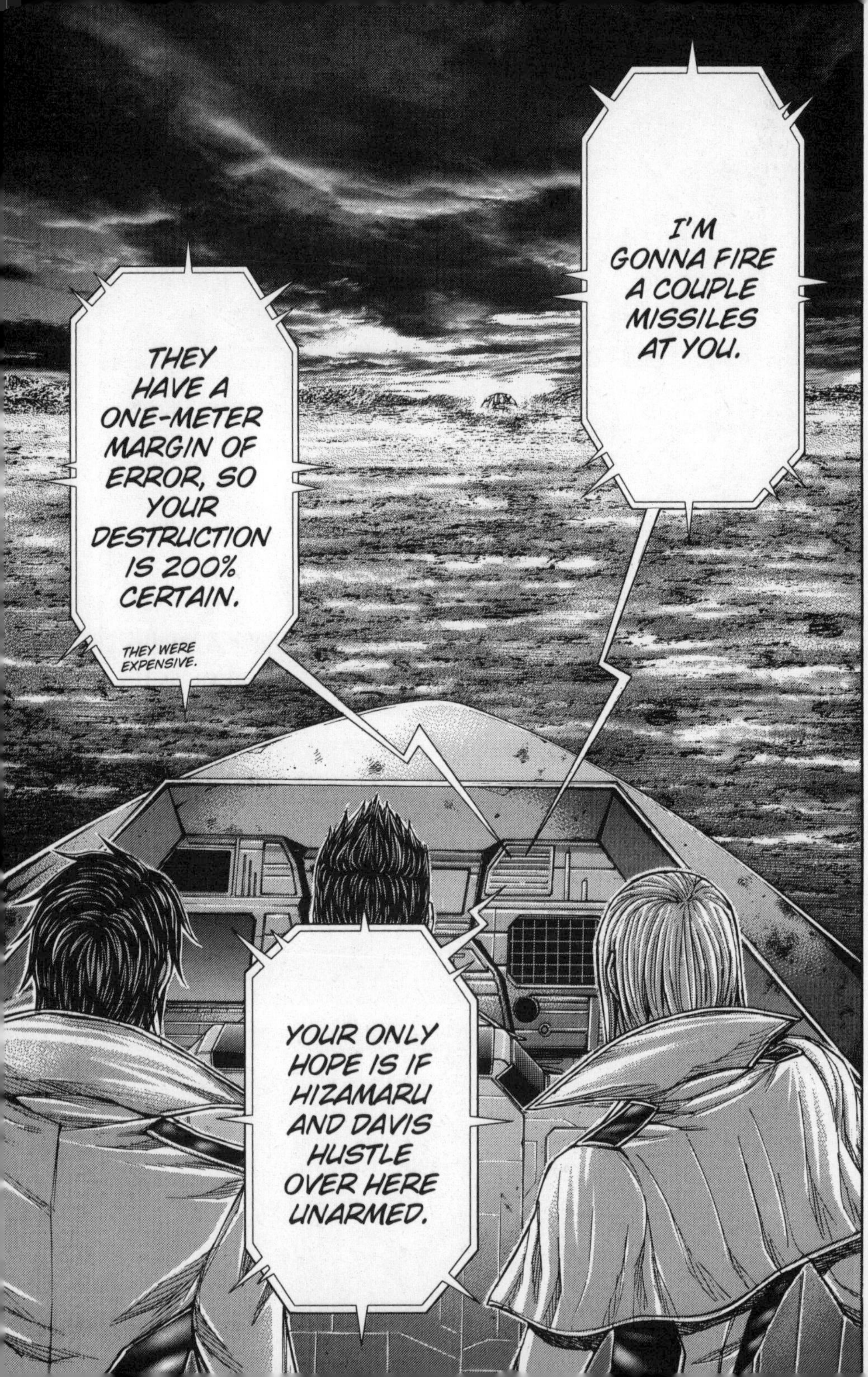
I'M GONNA FIRE A COUPLE MISSILES AT YOU.
THEY HAVE A ONE-METER MARGIN OF ERROR, SO YOUR DESTRUCTION IS 200% CERTAIN.
THEY WERE EXPENSIVE.
YOUR ONLY HOPE IS IF HIZAMARU AND DAVIS HUSTLE OVER HERE UNARMED.

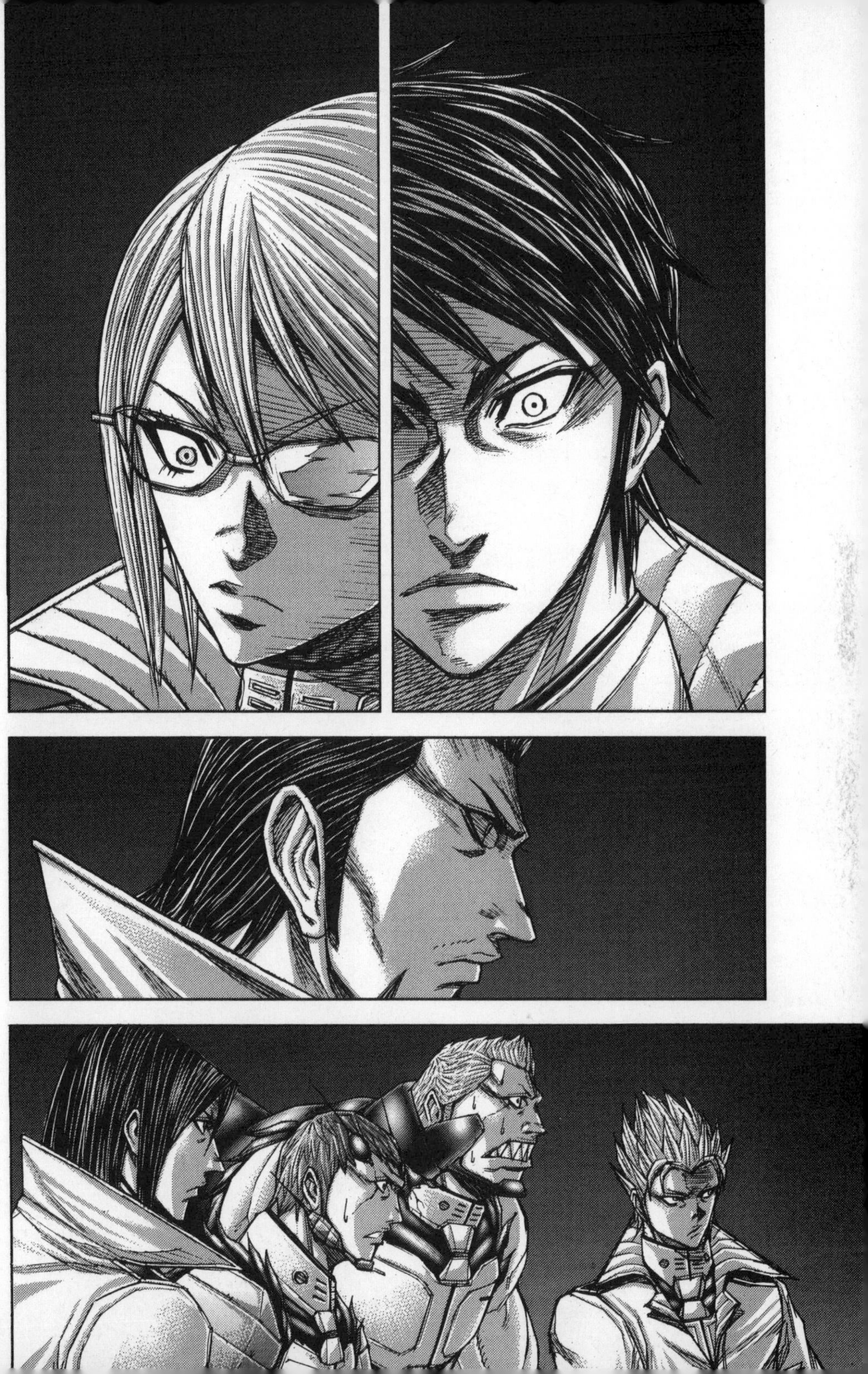

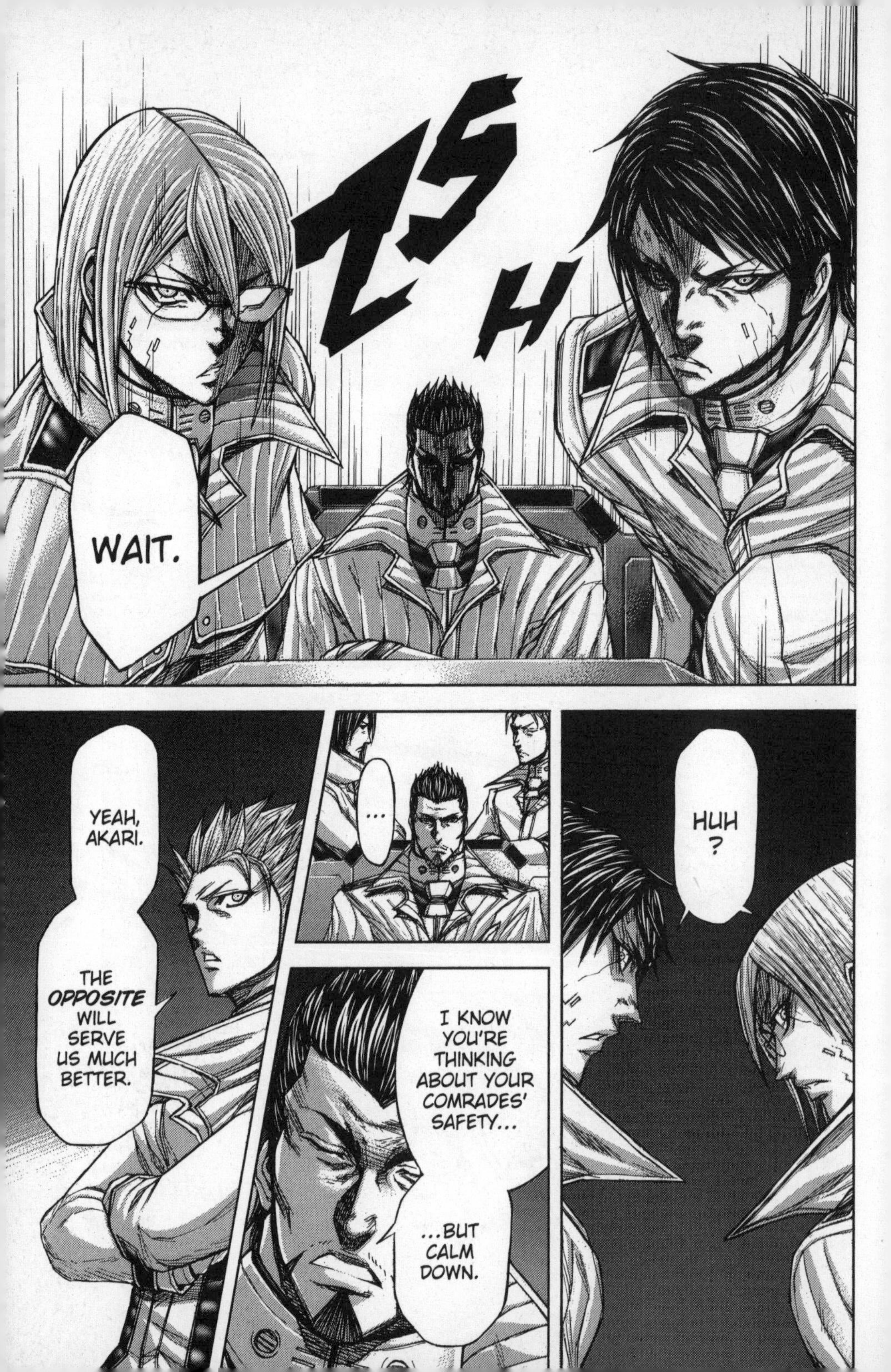
ZSH
WAIT.
HUH ?
...
I KNOW YOU'RE THINKING ABOUT YOUR COMRADES' SAFETY...
...BUT CALM DOWN.
YEAH, AKARI.
THE *OPPOSITE* WILL SERVE US MUCH BETTER.

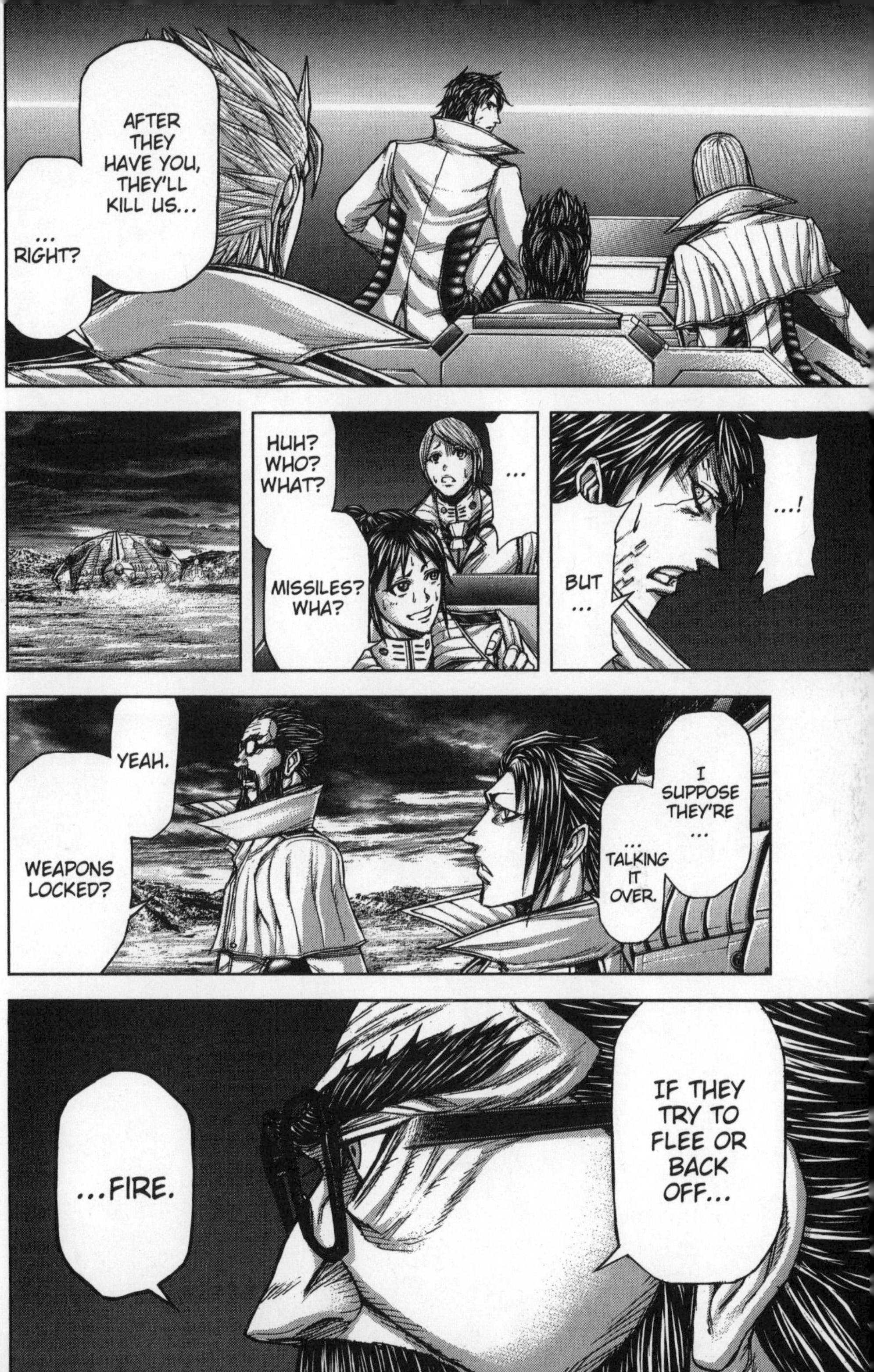
AFTER THEY HAVE YOU, THEY'LL KILL US...
...RIGHT?
...!
BUT ...
...
HUH? WHO? WHAT?
MISSILES? WHA?
I SUPPOSE THEY'RE ...
... TALKING IT OVER.
YEAH.
WEAPONS LOCKED?
IF THEY TRY TO FLEE OR BACK OFF...
...FIRE.

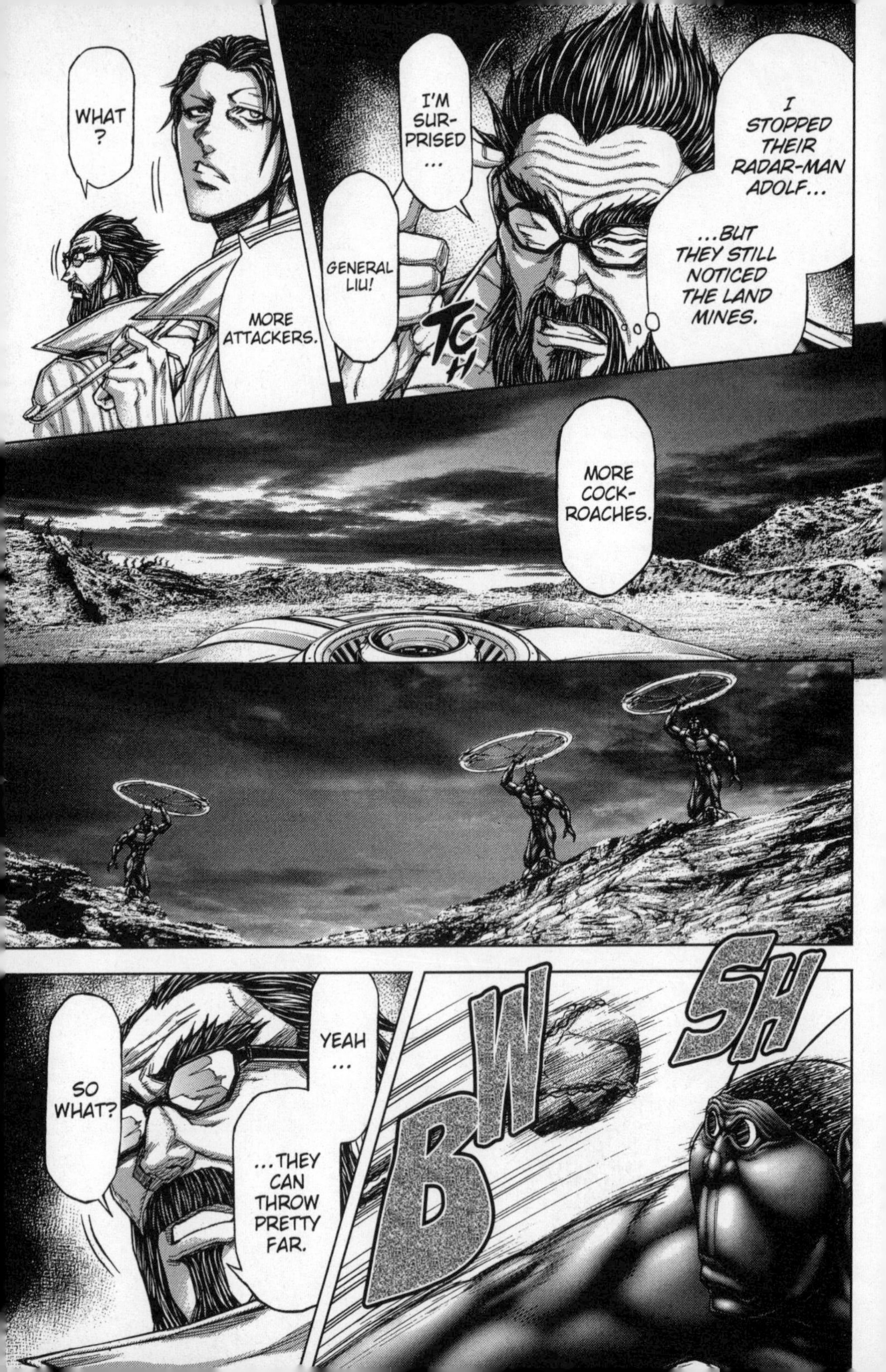
I STOPPED THEIR RADAR-MAN ADOLF...
...BUT THEY STILL NOTICED THE LAND MINES.
I'M SUR-PRISED...
GENERAL LIU!
TCH
MORE ATTACKERS.
WHAT?
MORE COCK-ROACHES.
BWSH
YEAH...
...THEY CAN THROW PRETTY FAR.
SO WHAT?

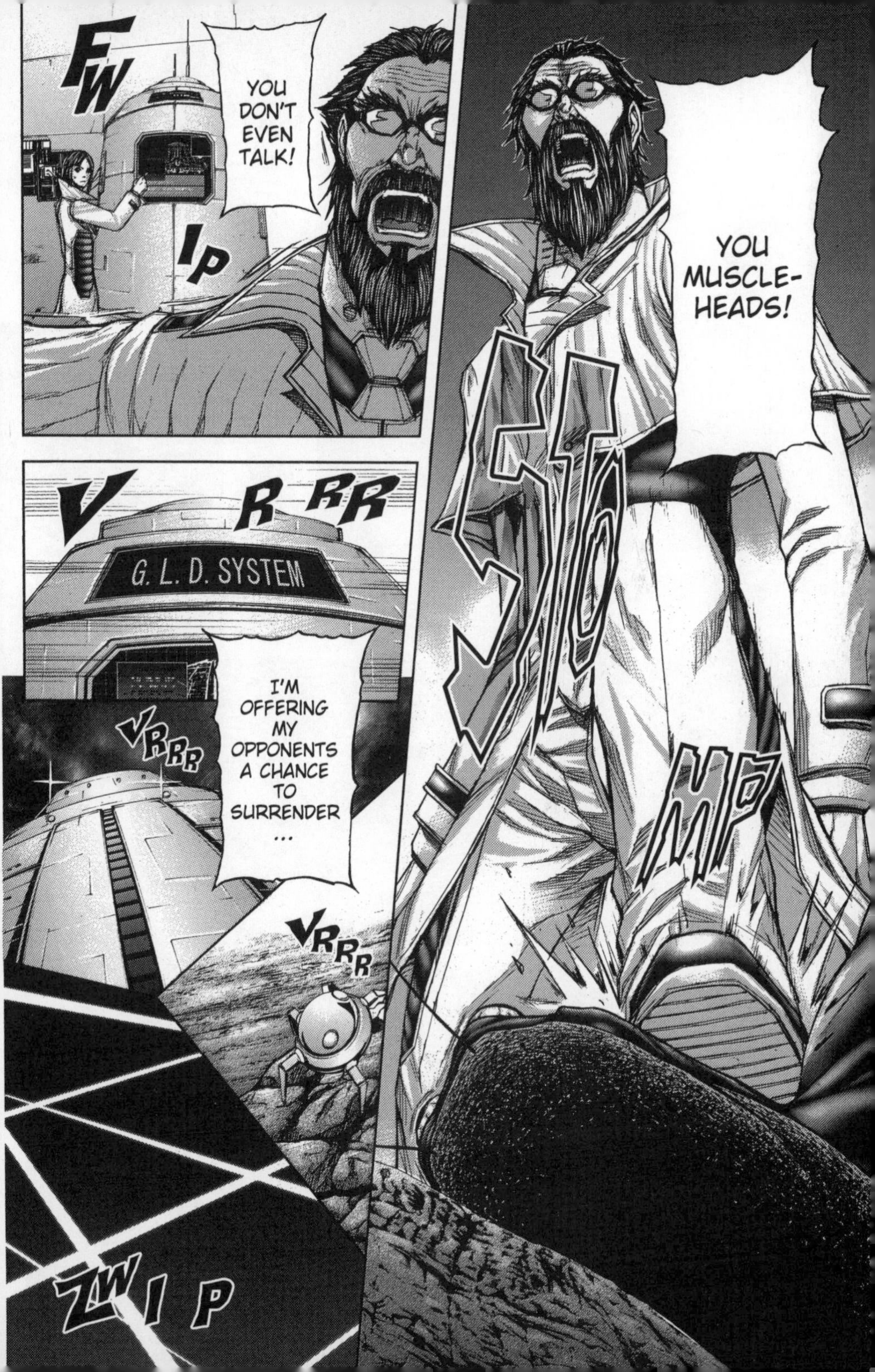
YOU MUSCLE-HEADS!
STOMP
FWIP
YOU DON'T EVEN TALK!
VRRR
G. L. D. SYSTEM
I'M OFFERING MY OPPONENTS A CHANCE TO SURRENDER...
VRRR
VRRR
ZWIP

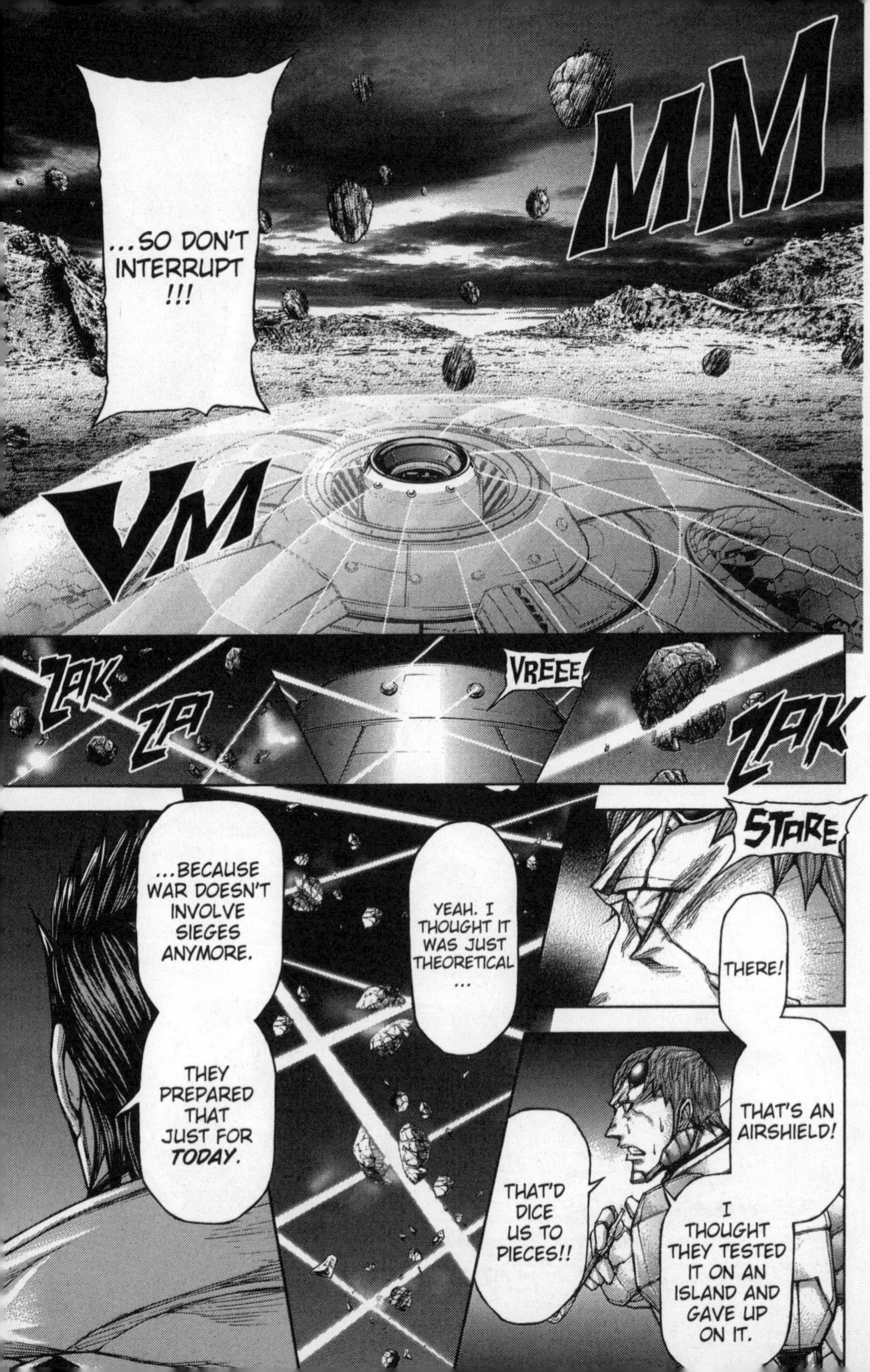
MM
...SO DON'T INTERRUPT !!!
VM
ZAK
VREEE
ZAK
ZA
STARE
THERE!
THAT'S AN AIRSHIELD!
I THOUGHT THEY TESTED IT ON AN ISLAND AND GAVE UP ON IT.
THAT'D DICE US TO PIECES!!
YEAH. I THOUGHT IT WAS JUST THEORETICAL...
...BECAUSE WAR DOESN'T INVOLVE SIEGES ANYMORE.
THEY PREPARED THAT JUST FOR *TODAY*.

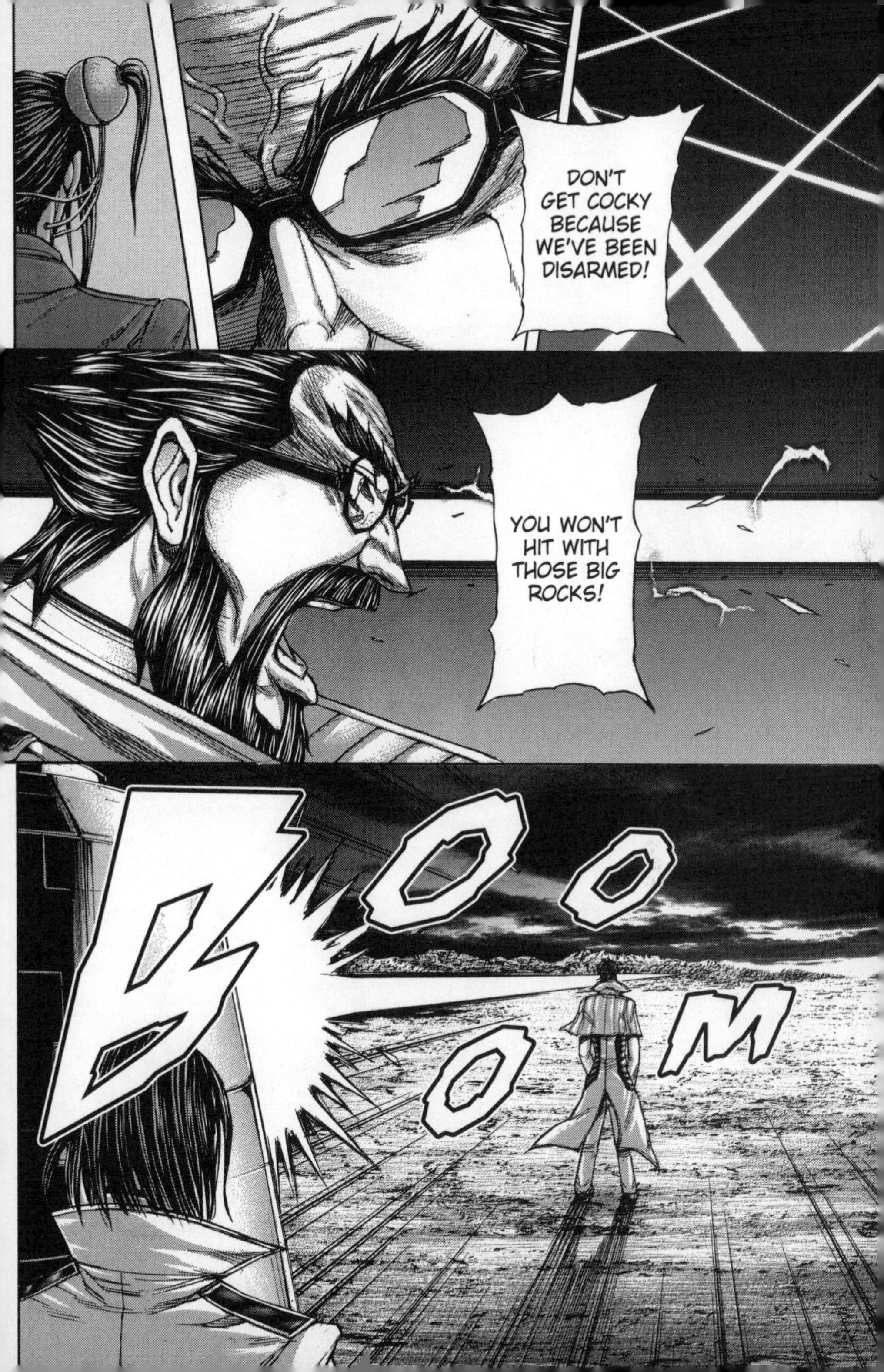
DON'T GET COCKY BECAUSE WE'VE BEEN DISARMED!
YOU WON'T HIT WITH THOSE BIG ROCKS!
BOOOOM

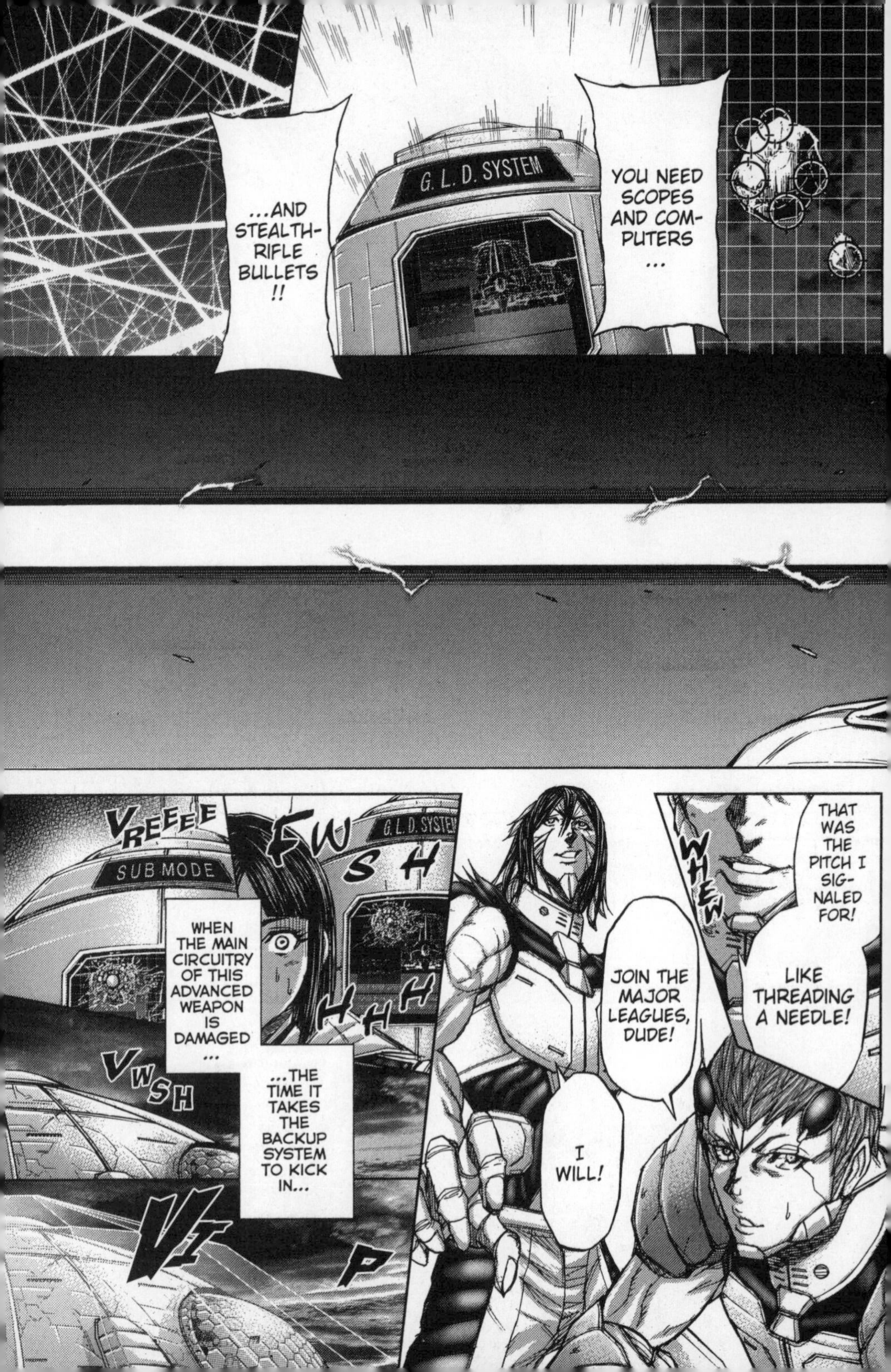
YOU NEED SCOPES AND COM- PUTERS ...
G. L. D. SYSTEM
...AND STEALTH- RIFLE BULLETS !!
WHEW
THAT WAS THE PITCH I SIG- NALED FOR!
LIKE THREADING A NEEDLE!
JOIN THE MAJOR LEAGUES, DUDE!
I WILL!
G. L. D. SYSTEM
FWSHHHH
VREEEE
SUB MODE
WHEN THE MAIN CIRCUITRY OF THIS ADVANCED WEAPON IS DAMAGED ...
VWSH
...THE TIME IT TAKES THE BACKUP SYSTEM TO KICK IN...
VIP

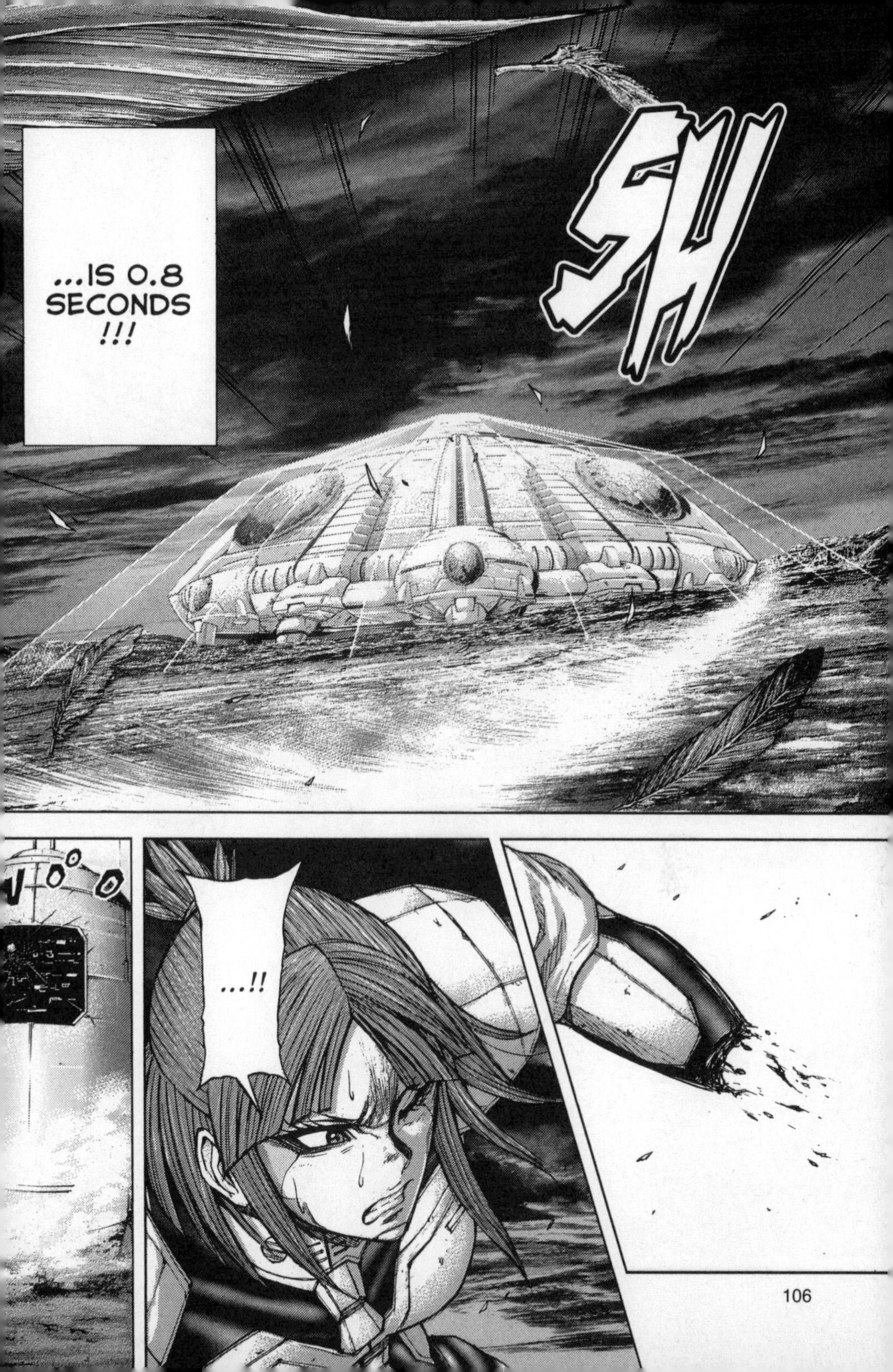
SH
...IS 0.8 SECONDS !!!
...!!
VOOO

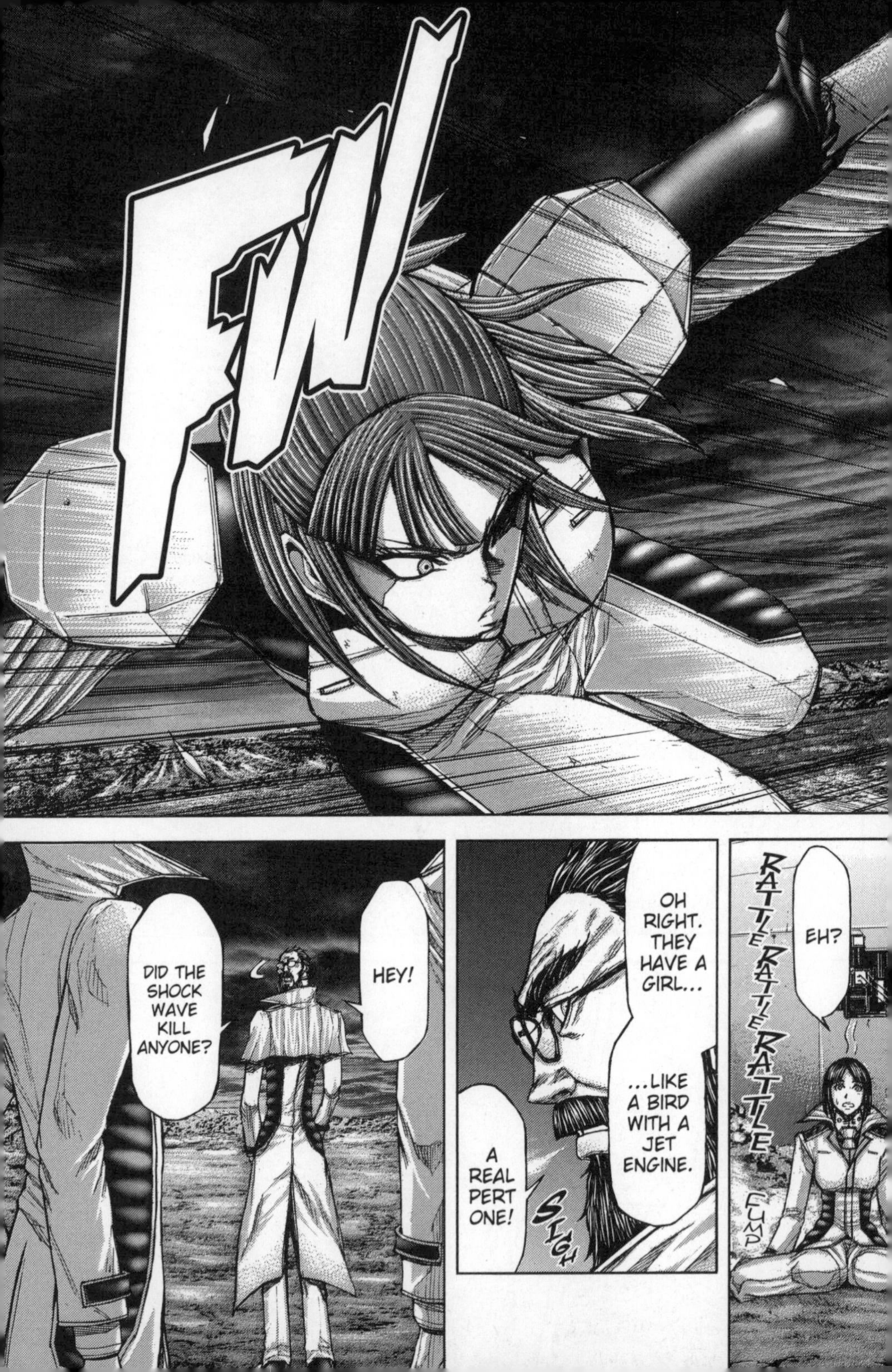
FW
RATTLE RATTLE RATTLE
EH?
FUMP
OH RIGHT. THEY HAVE A GIRL...
...LIKE A BIRD WITH A JET ENGINE.
A REAL PERT ONE!
SIGH
HEY!
DID THE SHOCK WAVE KILL ANYONE?

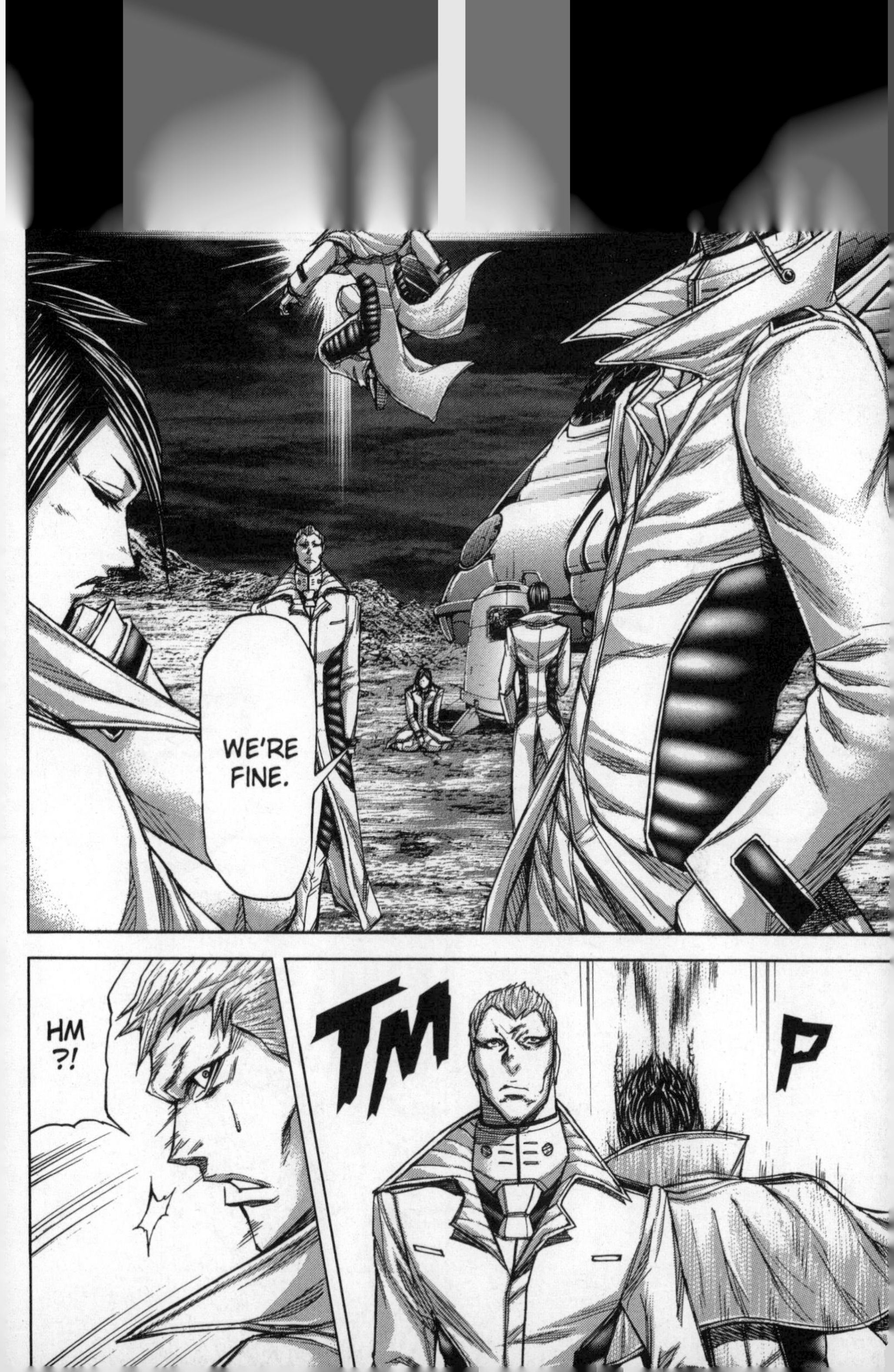
WE'RE FINE.
TM
P
HM ?!

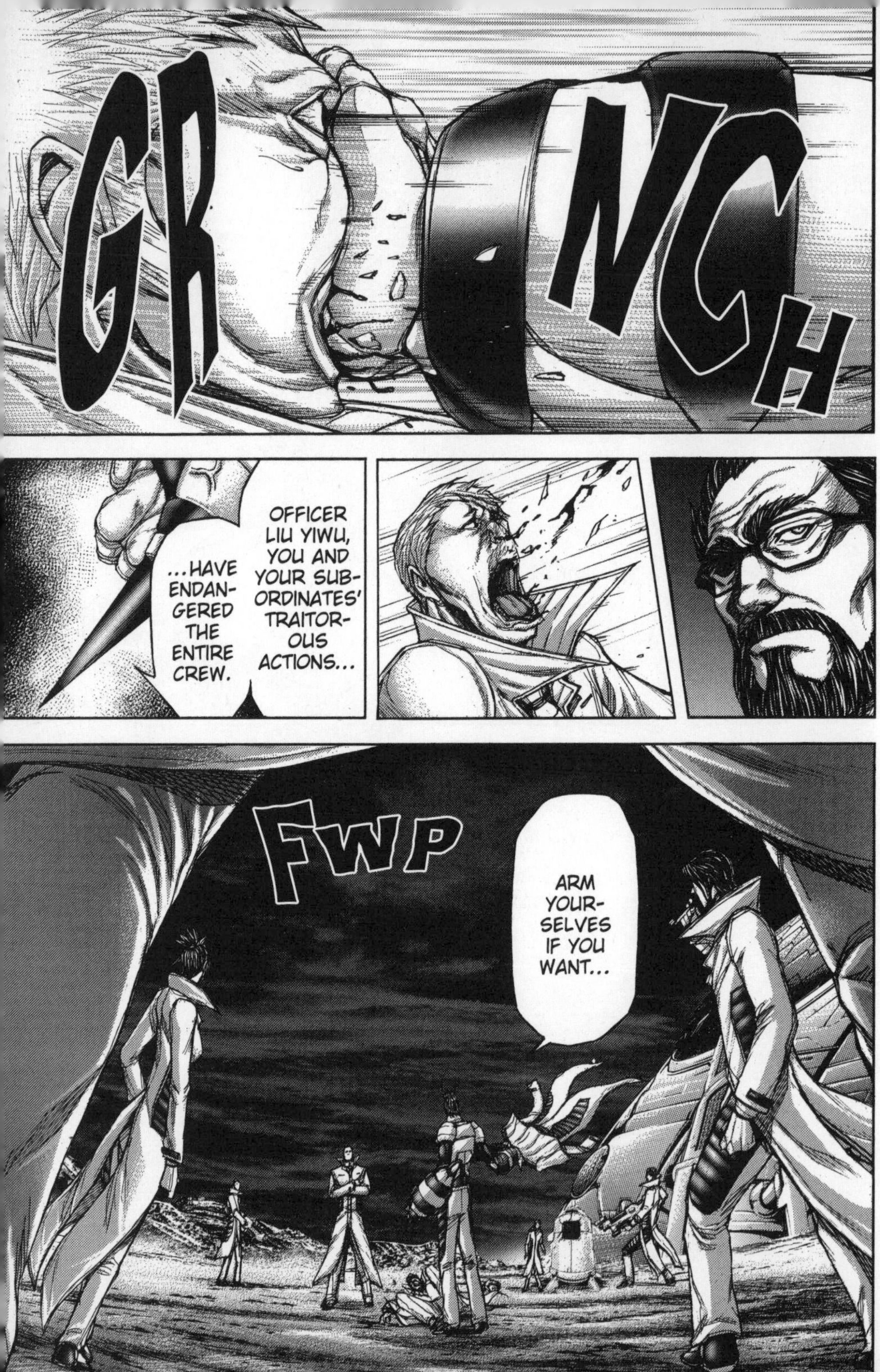
GRNCH
OFFICER LIU YIWU, YOU AND YOUR SUBORDINATES' TRAITOROUS ACTIONS...
...HAVE ENDANGERED THE ENTIRE CREW.
ARM YOURSELVES IF YOU WANT...
FWP

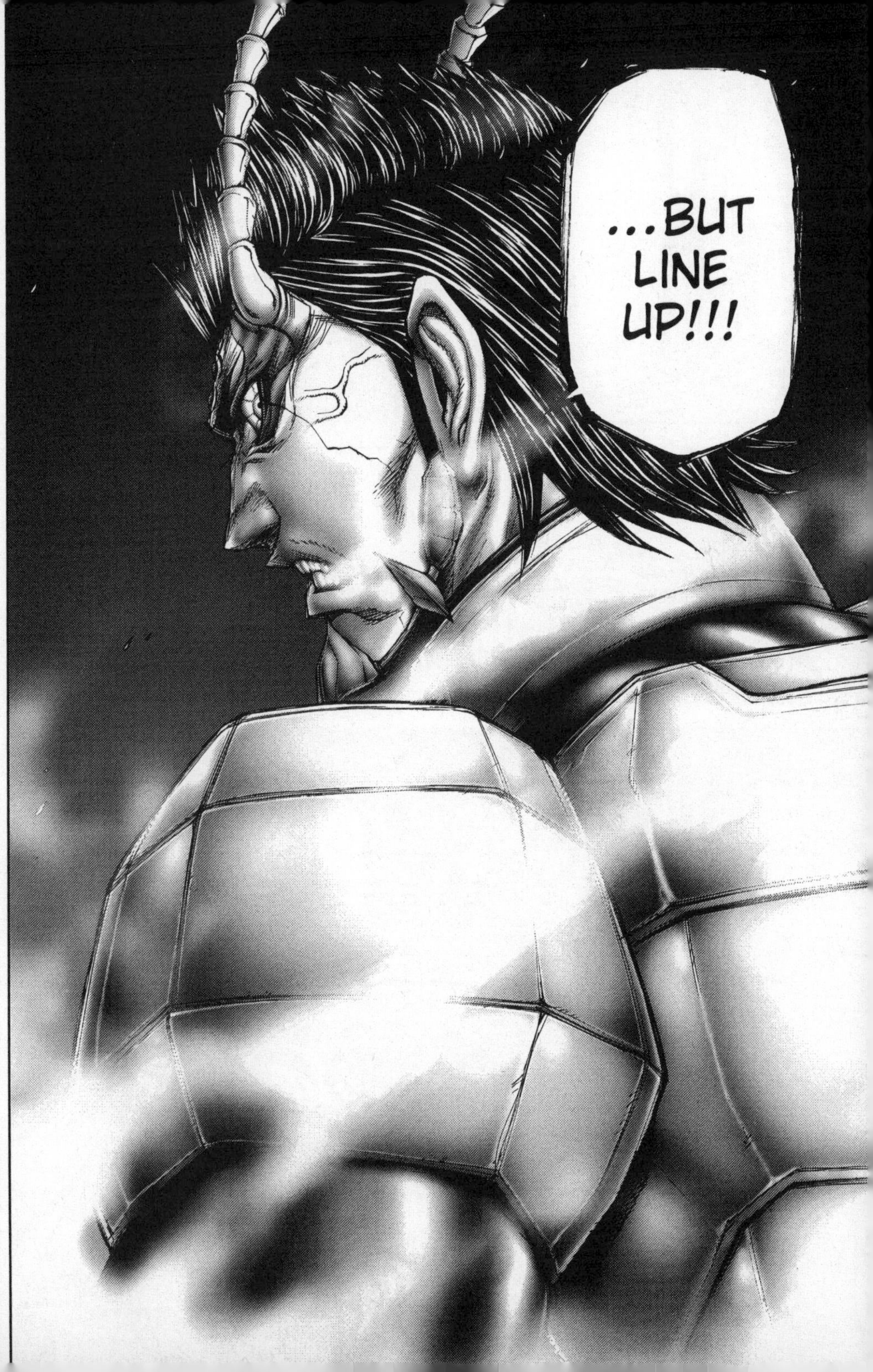
...BUT LINE UP!!!

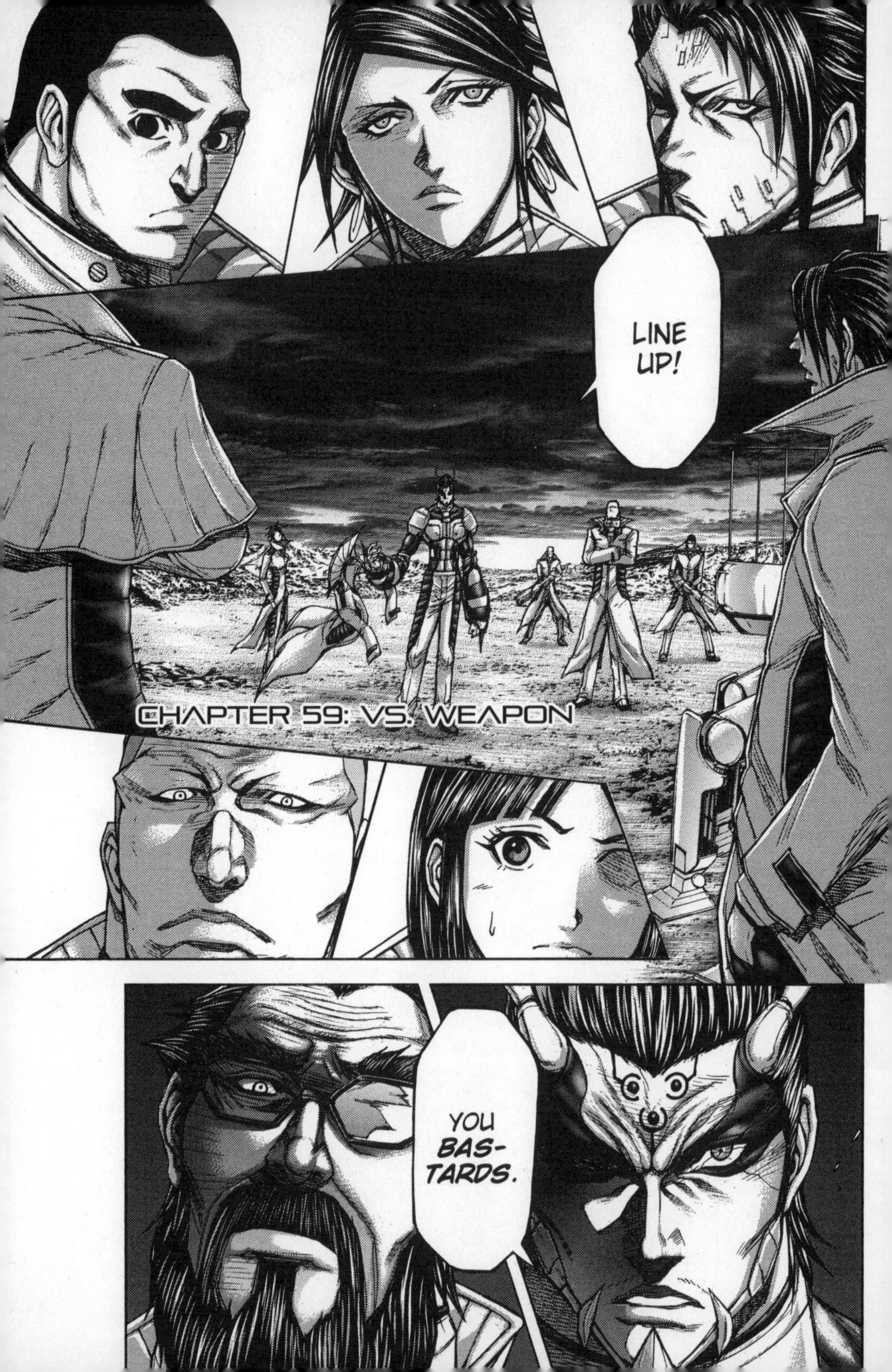
LINE UP!
CHAPTER 59: VS. WEAPON
YOU BAS-TARDS.

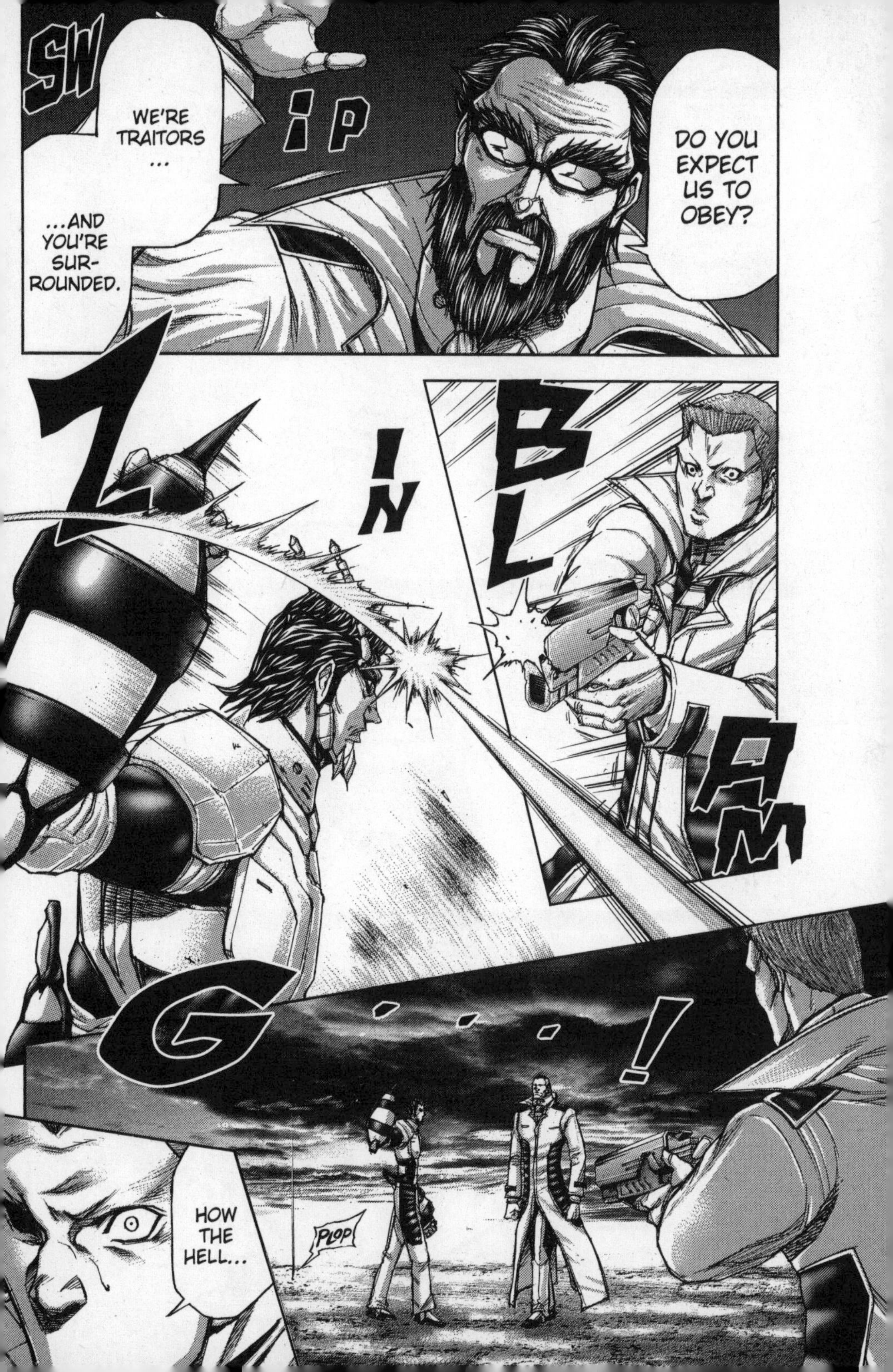
DO YOU EXPECT US TO OBEY?
SWIP
WE'RE TRAITORS ...
...AND YOU'RE SUR-ROUNDED.
BLAM
ZING
G...!
HOW THE HELL...
PLOP

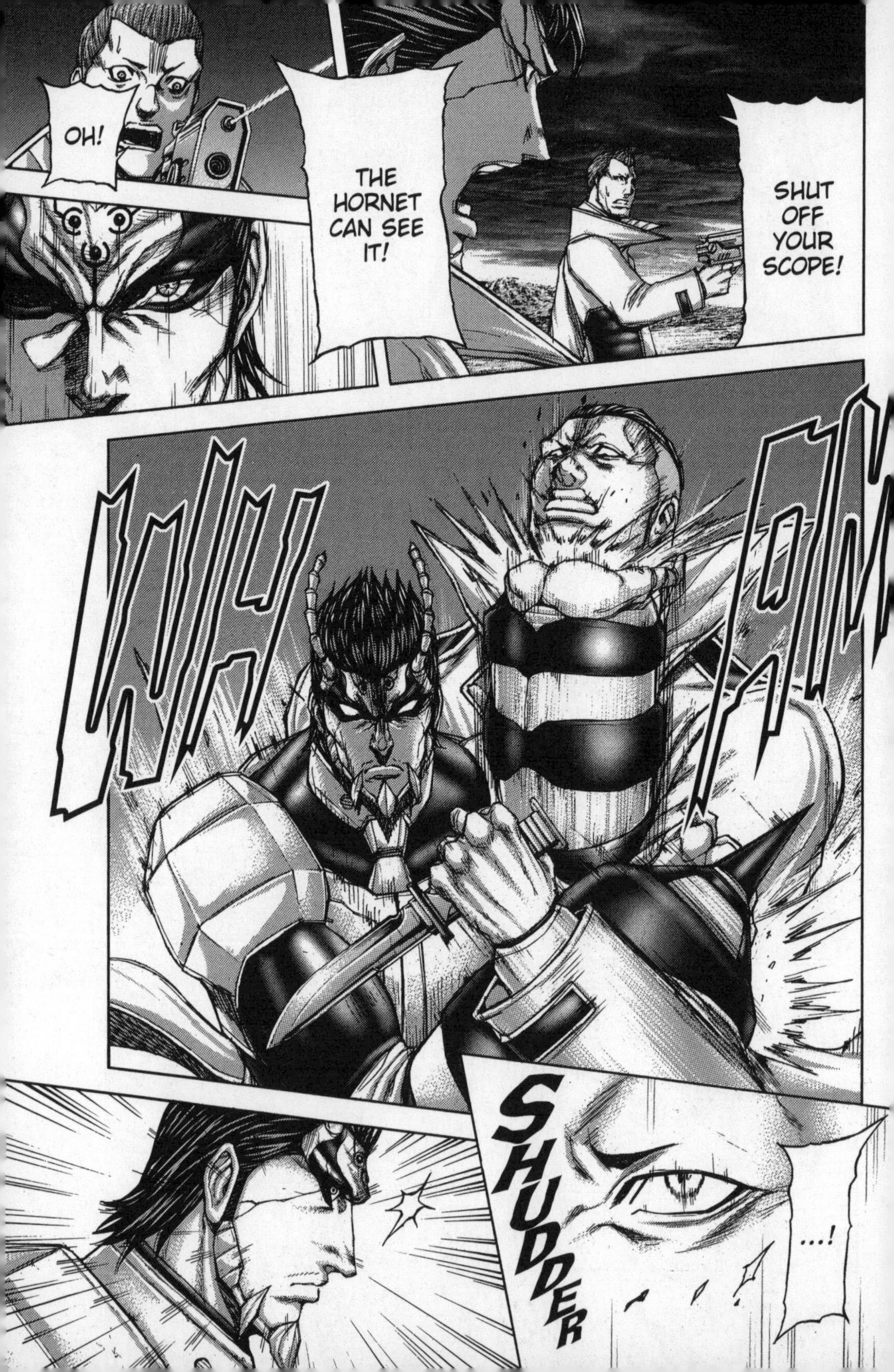
SHUT OFF YOUR SCOPE!
THE HORNET CAN SEE IT!
OH!
SHUDDER
...!

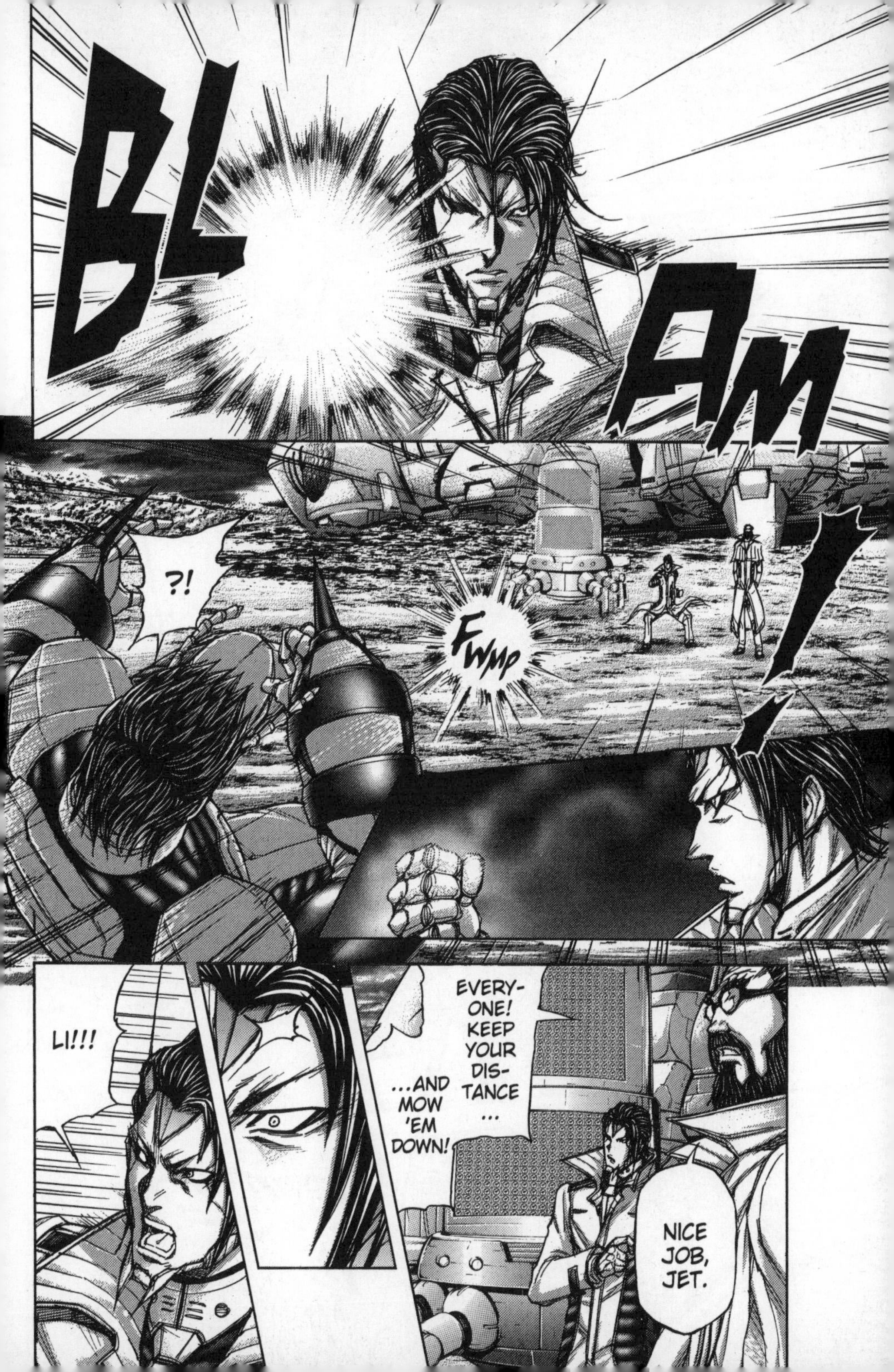
BLAM!
FWMP
?!
EVERY-ONE! KEEP YOUR DIS-TANCE ...
...AND MOW 'EM DOWN!
NICE JOB, JET.
LI!!!

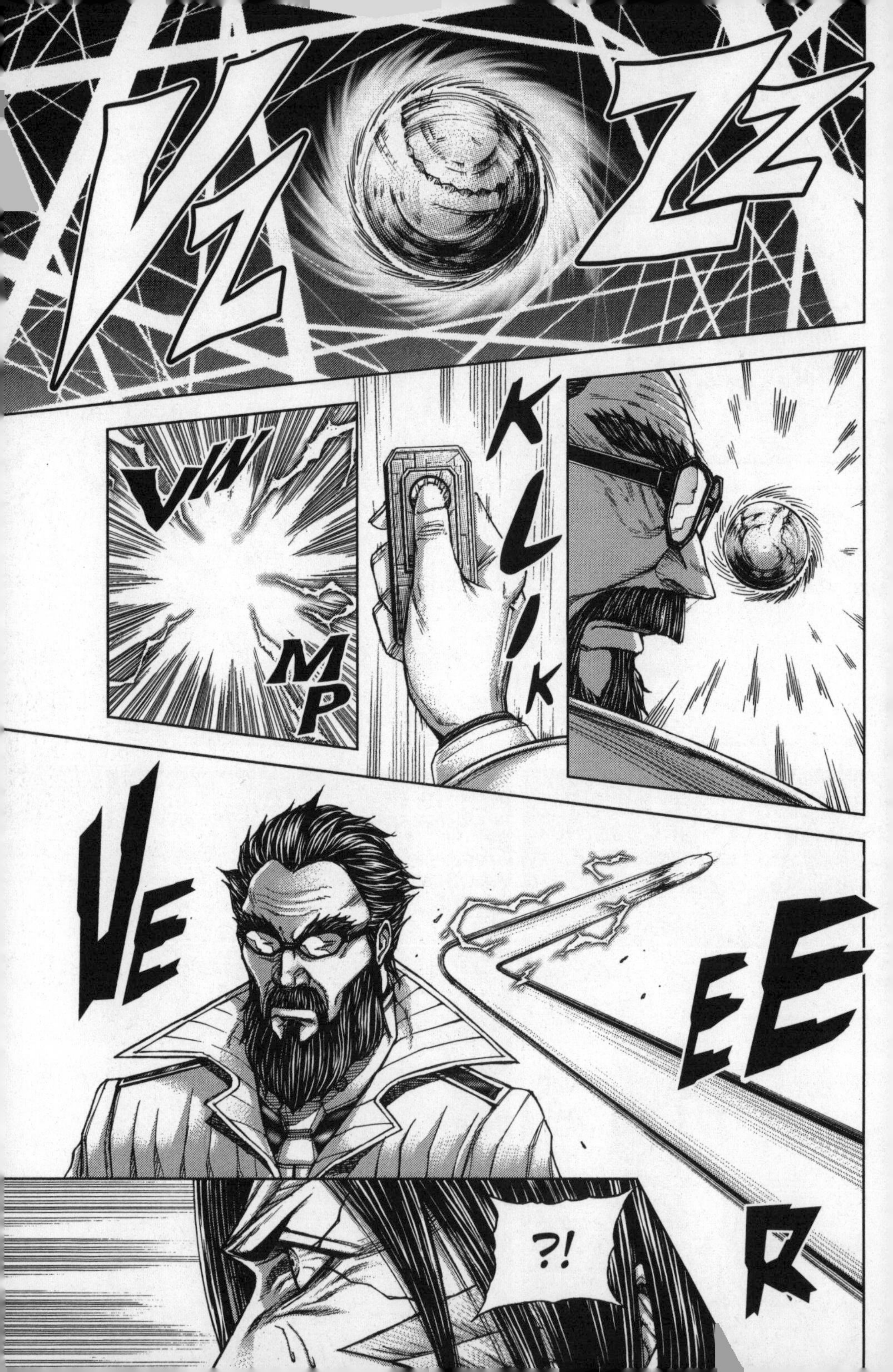
VZZZ
KLIK
VWMP
VEEER
?!

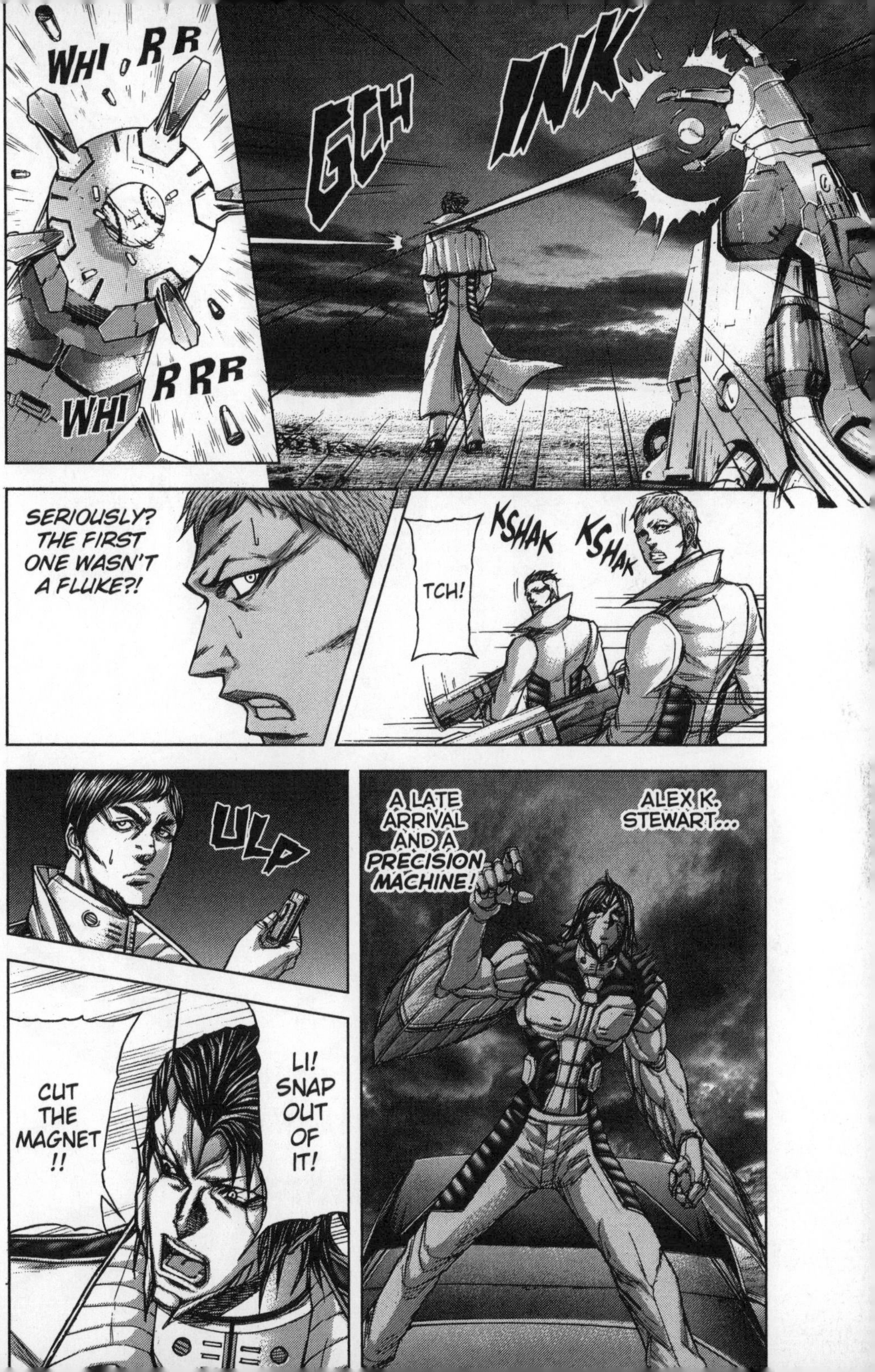
GCH INK
WHI RR
WHI RRR
KSHAK KSHAK
TCH!
SERIOUSLY? THE FIRST ONE WASN'T A FLUKE?!
ALEX K. STEWART...
A LATE ARRIVAL AND A PRECISION MACHINE!
ULP
LI! SNAP OUT OF IT!
CUT THE MAGNET!!

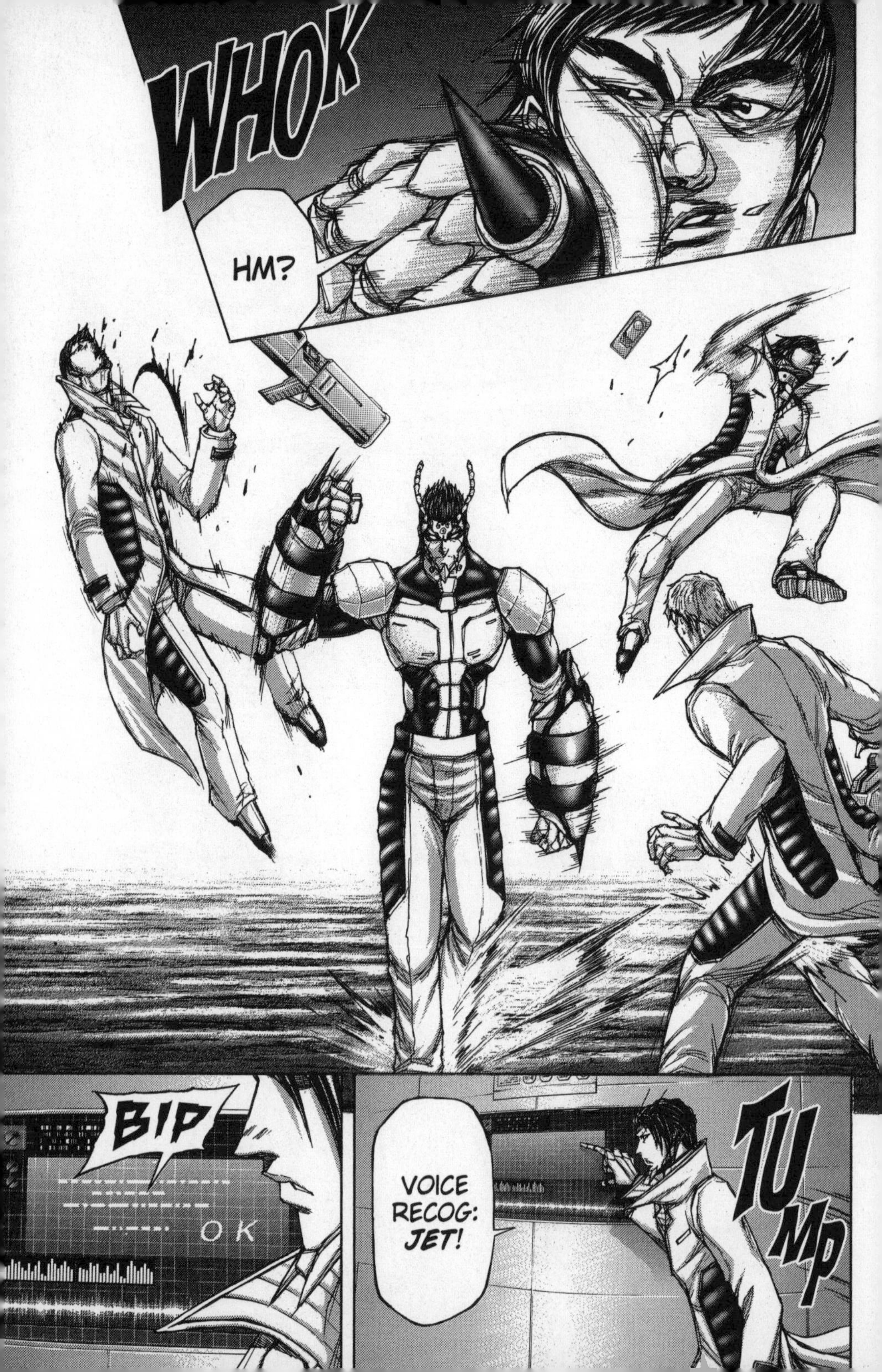
WHOK
HM?
TUMP
VOICE RECOG: JET!
BIP
OK

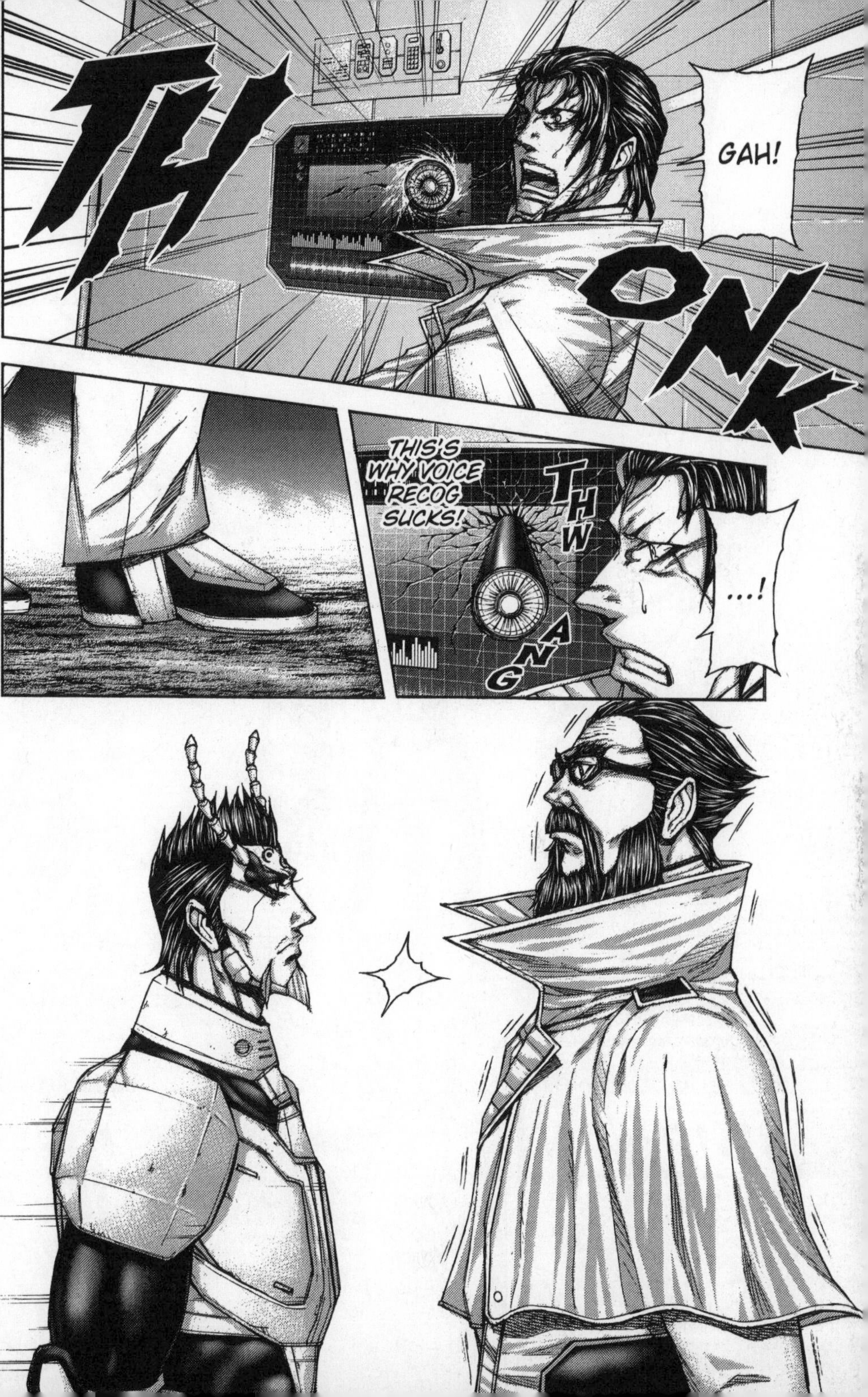
GAH!
THONK
...!
THWANG
THIS'S WHY VOICE RECOG SUCKS!

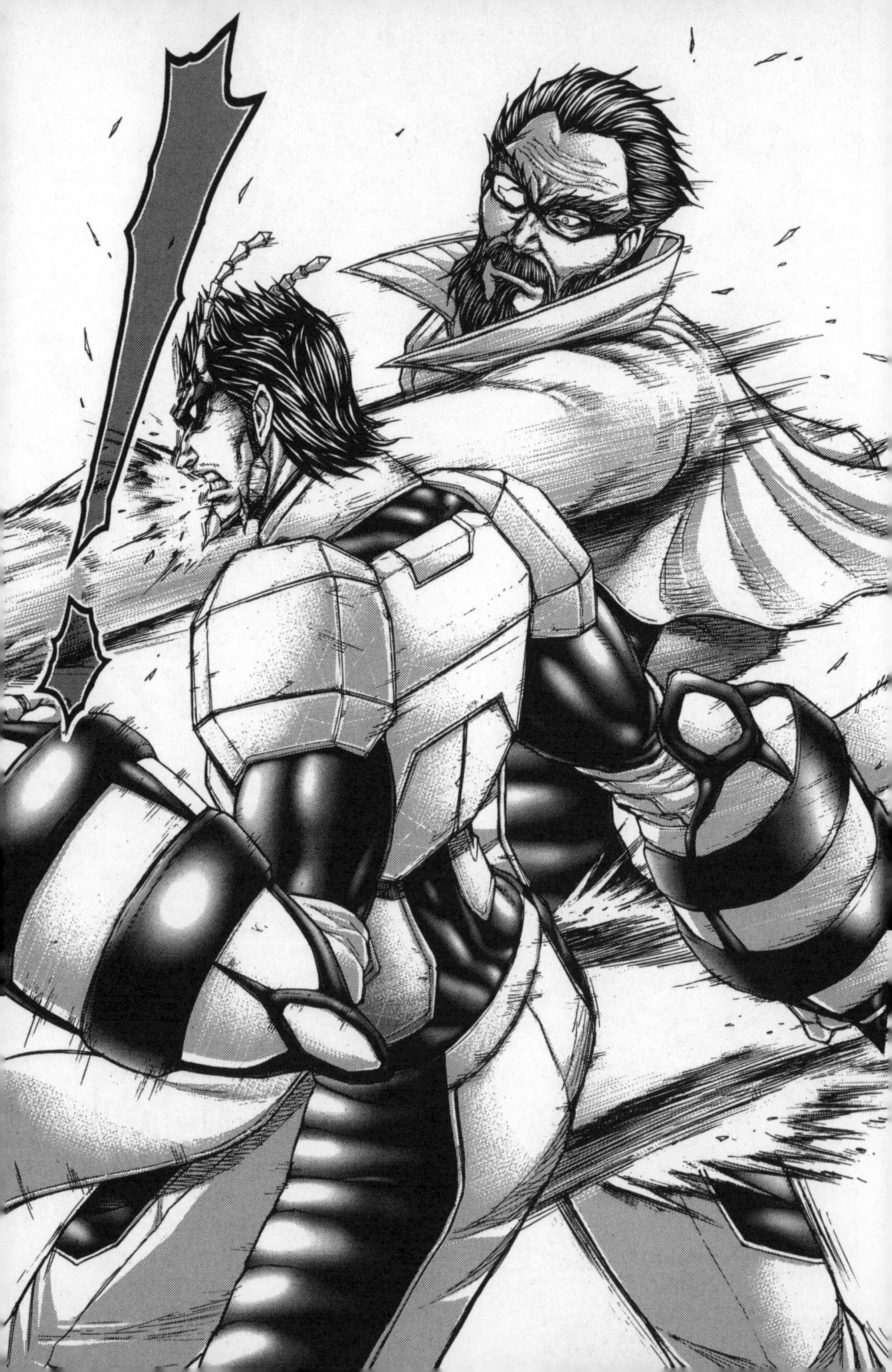

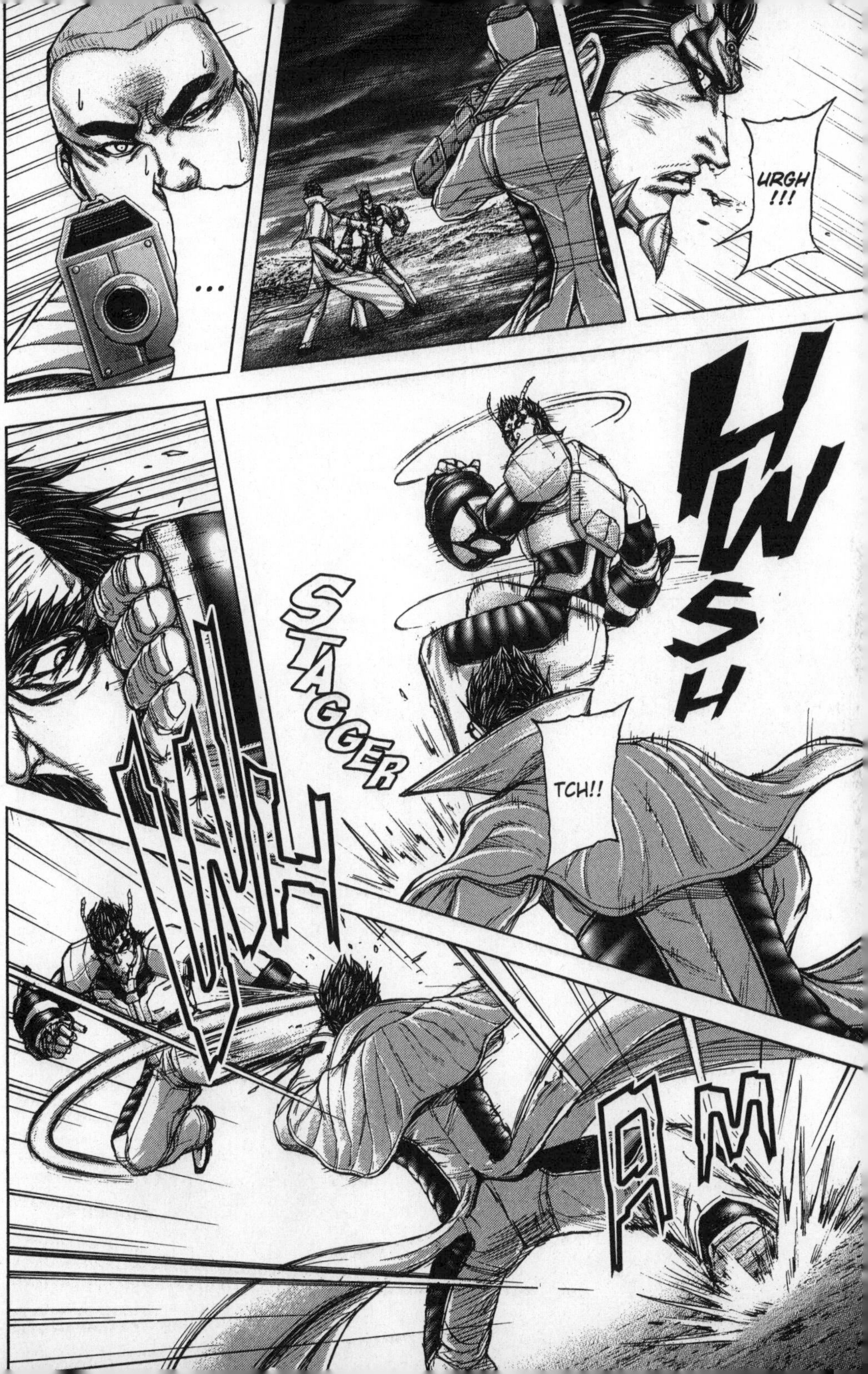
URGH!!!
...
HWWSH
STAGGER
TCH!!

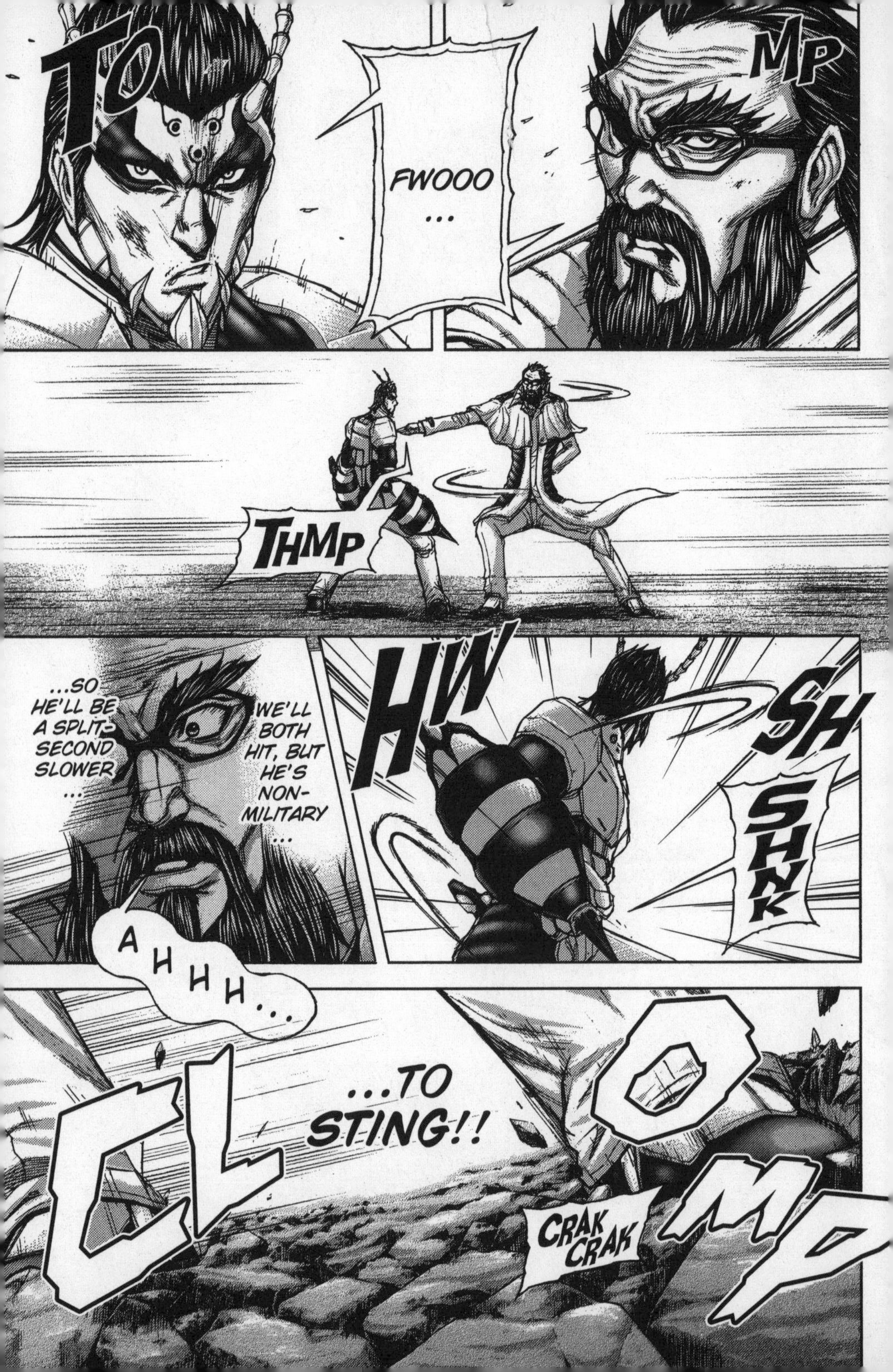
MP
FWOOO ...
TO
THMP
SH
SHNK
HW
WE'LL BOTH HIT, BUT HE'S NON-MILITARY ...
...SO HE'LL BE A SPLIT-SECOND SLOWER ...
AHHH...
OMP
CRAK CRAK
...TO STING!!
CL

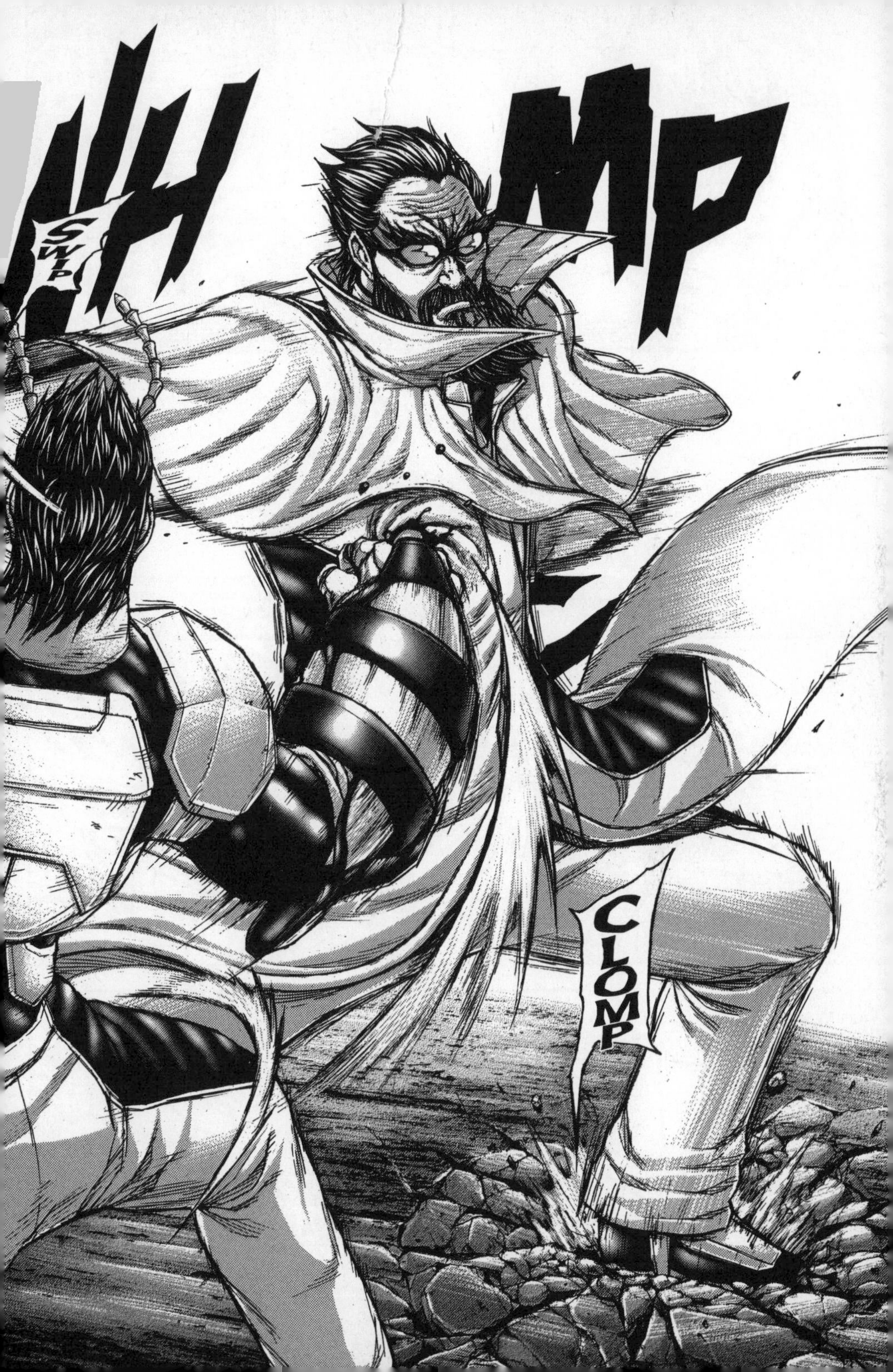
SWIP
CLOMP

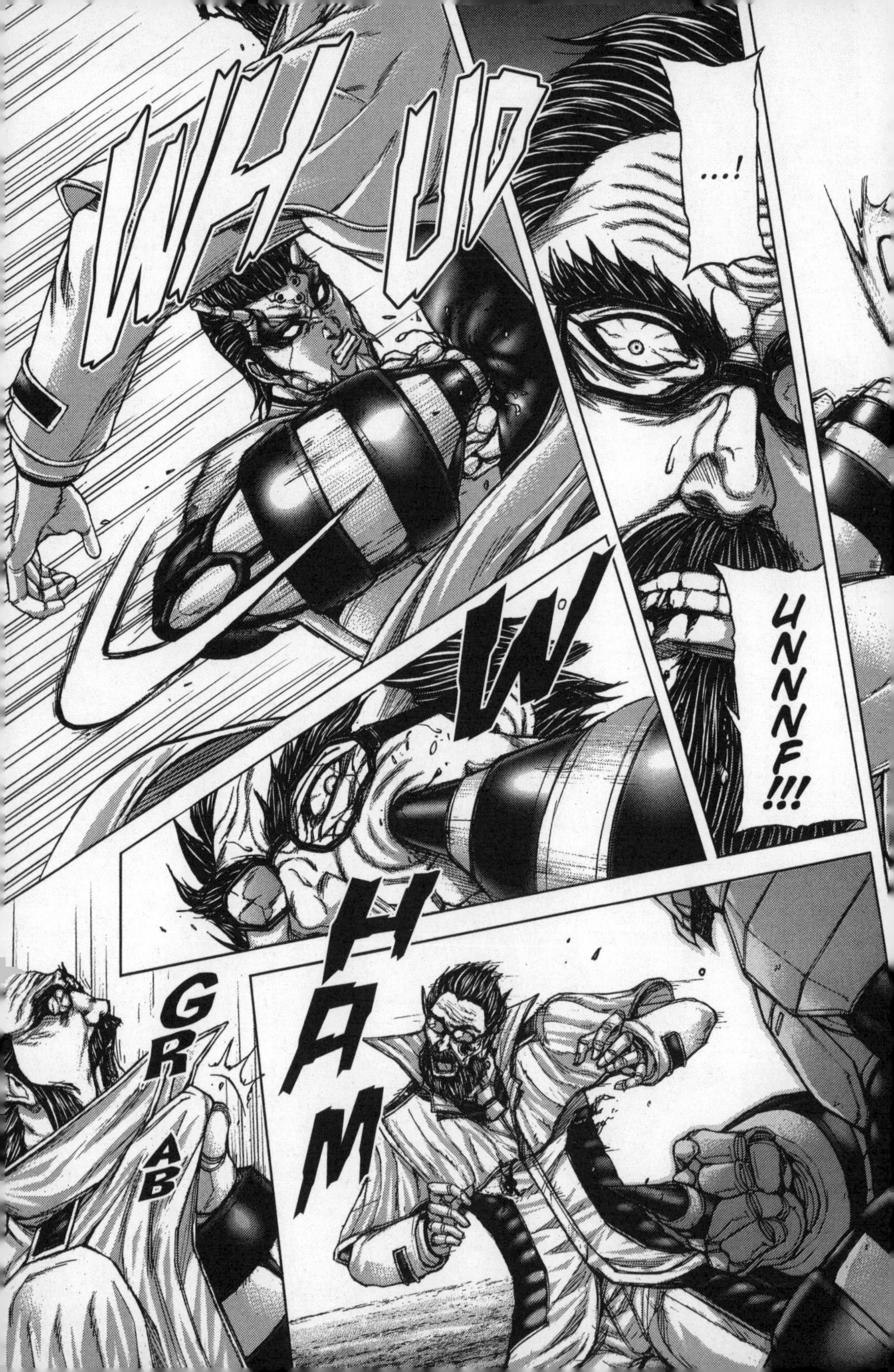
WHUD
...!
UNNNF!!!
WHAM
GRAB

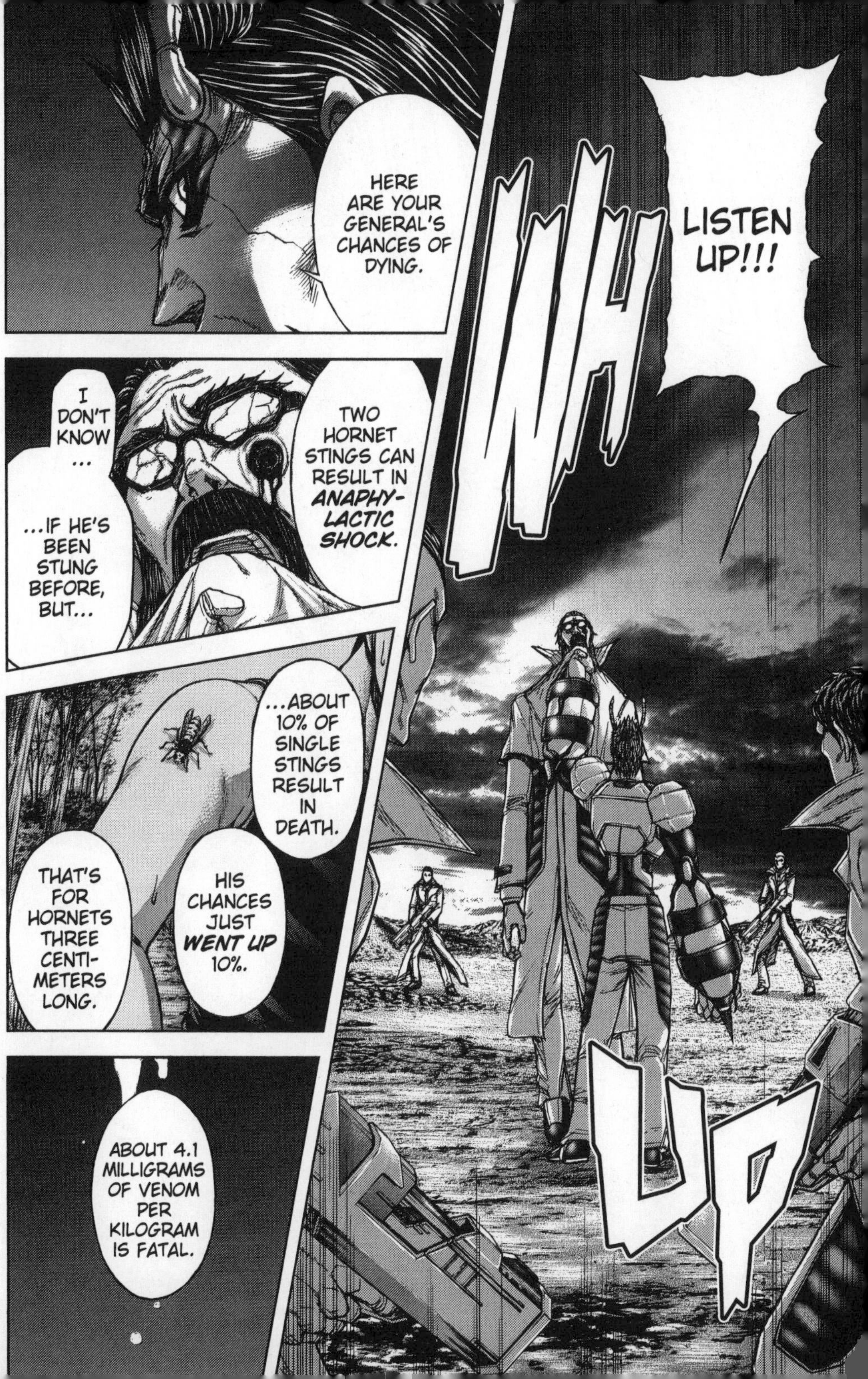
LISTEN UP!!!
WHH
UP
HERE ARE YOUR GENERAL'S CHANCES OF DYING.
TWO HORNET STINGS CAN RESULT IN *ANAPHY-LACTIC SHOCK*.
I DON'T KNOW ...
...IF HE'S BEEN STUNG BEFORE, BUT...
...ABOUT 10% OF SINGLE STINGS RESULT IN DEATH.
HIS CHANCES JUST *WENT UP* 10%.
THAT'S FOR HORNETS THREE CENTI-METERS LONG.
ABOUT 4.1 MILLIGRAMS OF VENOM PER KILOGRAM IS FATAL.

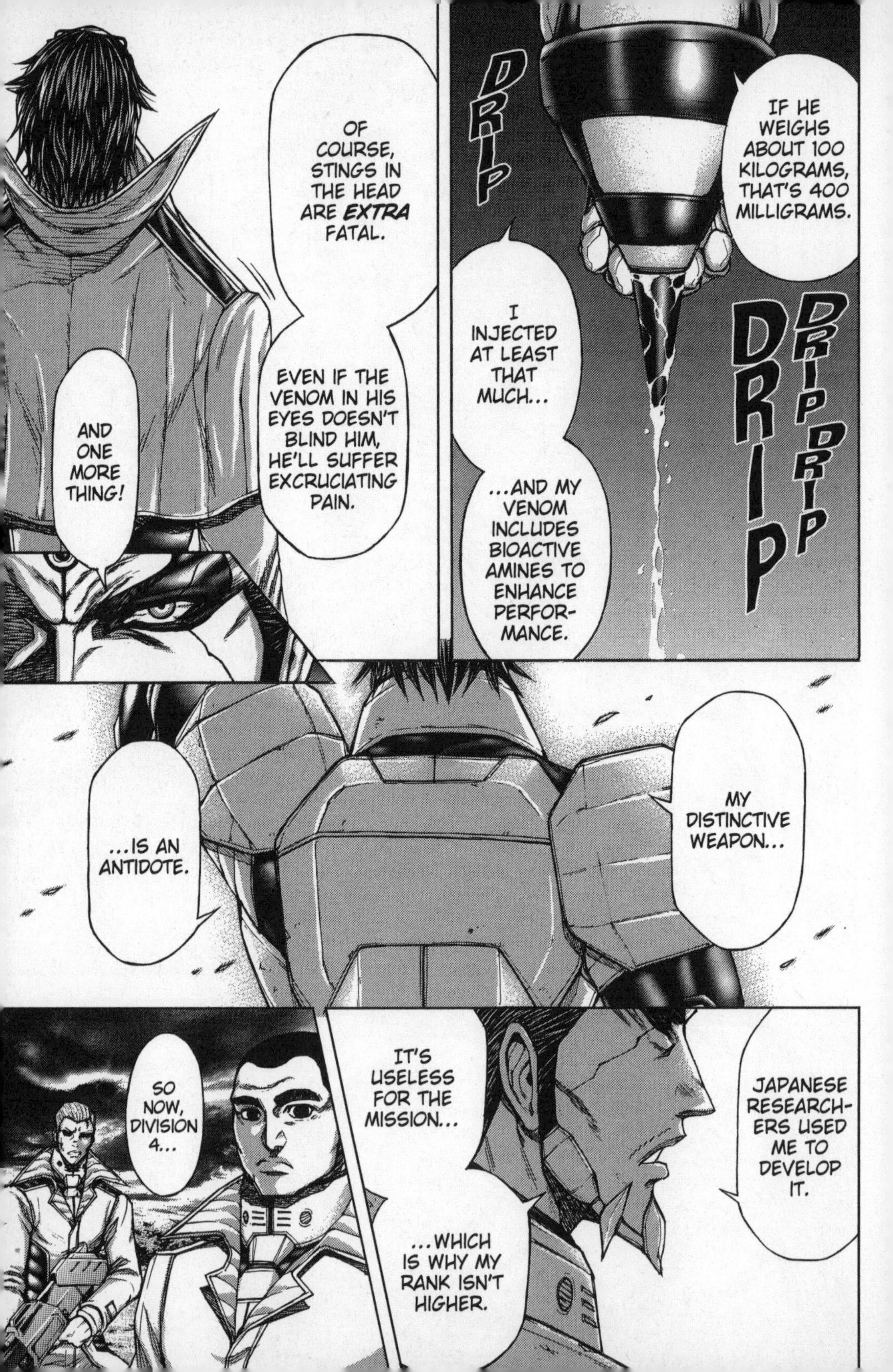
IF HE WEIGHS ABOUT 100 KILOGRAMS, THAT'S 400 MILLIGRAMS.
DRIP
DRIP DRIP DRIP
DRIP
I INJECTED AT LEAST THAT MUCH...
...AND MY VENOM INCLUDES BIOACTIVE AMINES TO ENHANCE PERFORMANCE.
OF COURSE, STINGS IN THE HEAD ARE EXTRA FATAL.
EVEN IF THE VENOM IN HIS EYES DOESN'T BLIND HIM, HE'LL SUFFER EXCRUCIATING PAIN.
AND ONE MORE THING!
MY DISTINCTIVE WEAPON...
...IS AN ANTIDOTE.
JAPANESE RESEARCHERS USED ME TO DEVELOP IT.
IT'S USELESS FOR THE MISSION...
...WHICH IS WHY MY RANK ISN'T HIGHER.
SO NOW, DIVISION 4...

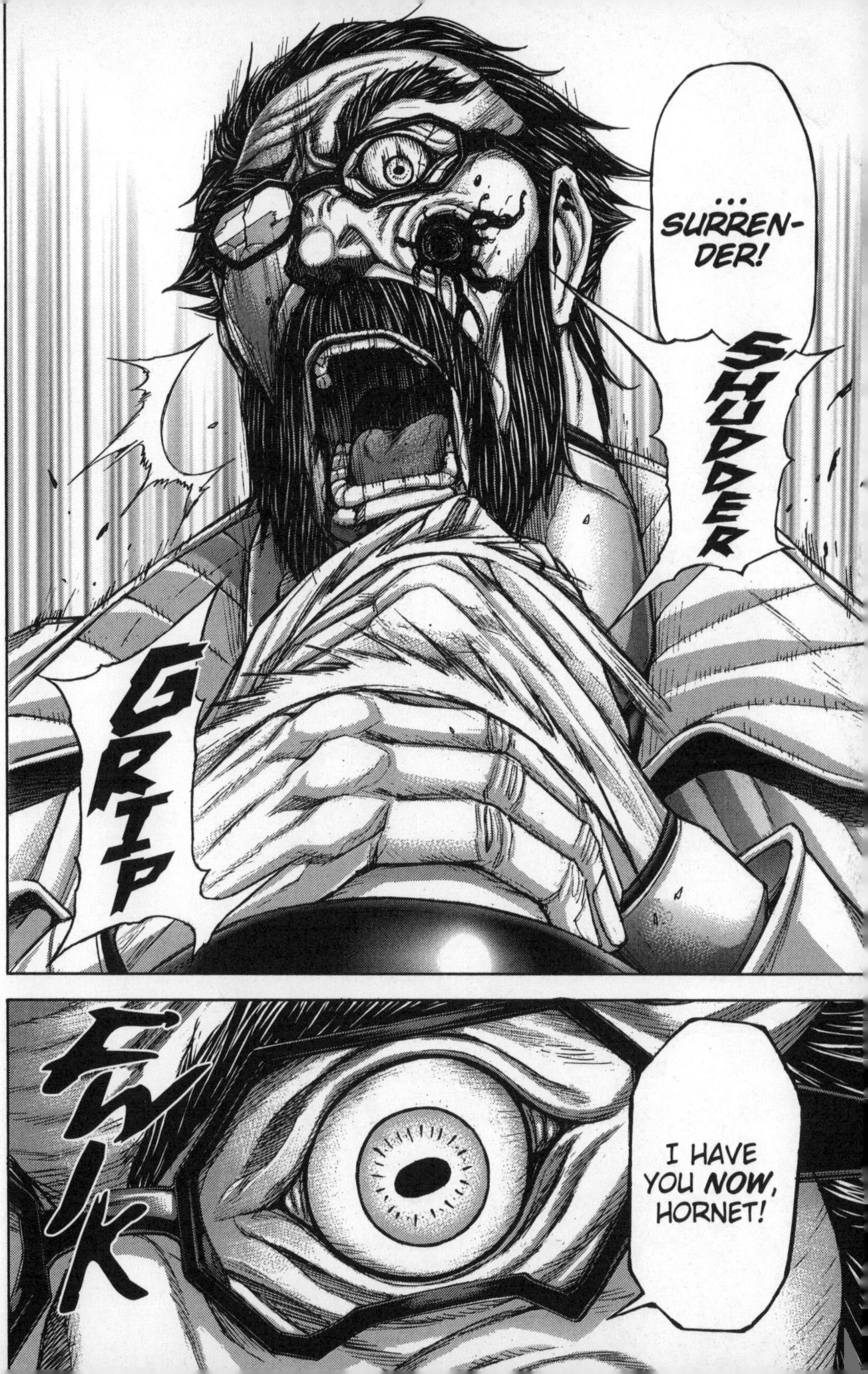
...SURREN-DER!
SHUDDER
GRIP
I HAVE YOU NOW, HORNET!
FWIK

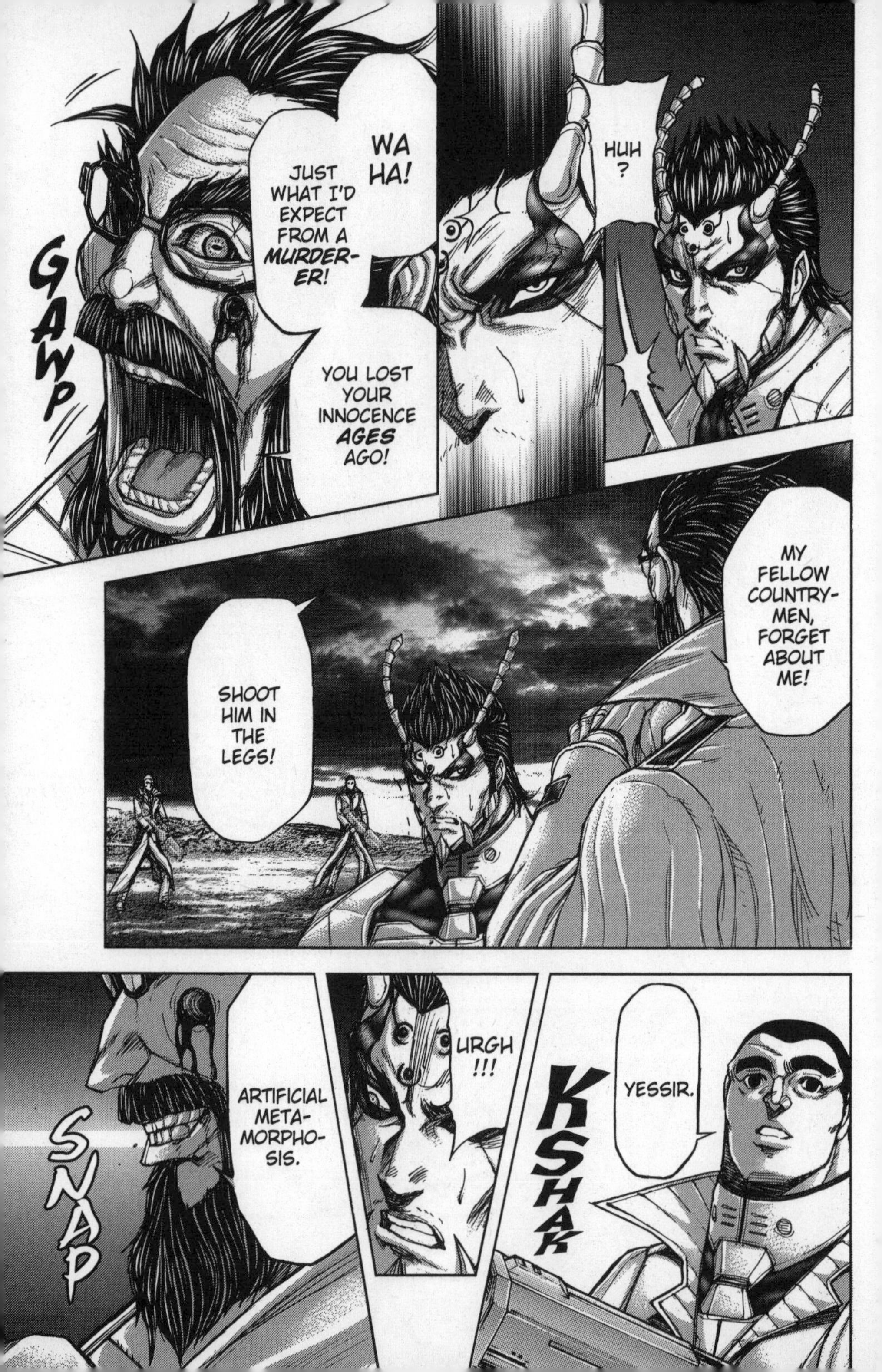
HUH ?
WA HA!
JUST WHAT I'D EXPECT FROM A MURDERER!
YOU LOST YOUR INNOCENCE AGES AGO!
GAWP
MY FELLOW COUNTRYMEN, FORGET ABOUT ME!
SHOOT HIM IN THE LEGS!
YESSIR.
KSHAK
URGH !!!
ARTIFICIAL METAMORPHOSIS.
SNAP

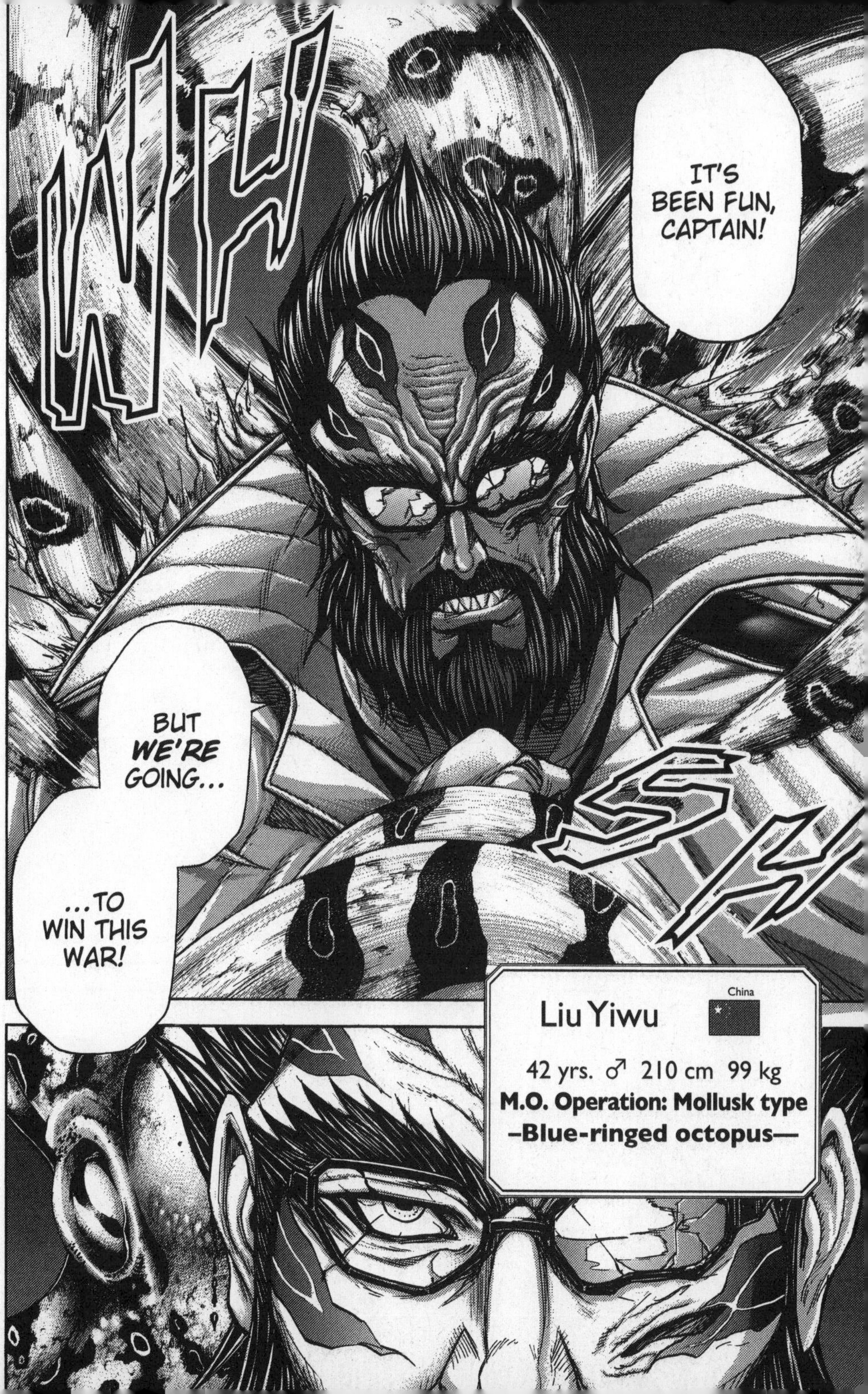
IT'S BEEN FUN, CAPTAIN!
BUT *WE'RE* GOING...
...TO WIN THIS WAR!
China
Liu Yiwu
42 yrs. ♂ 210 cm 99 kg
M.O. Operation: Mollusk type
–Blue-ringed octopus–

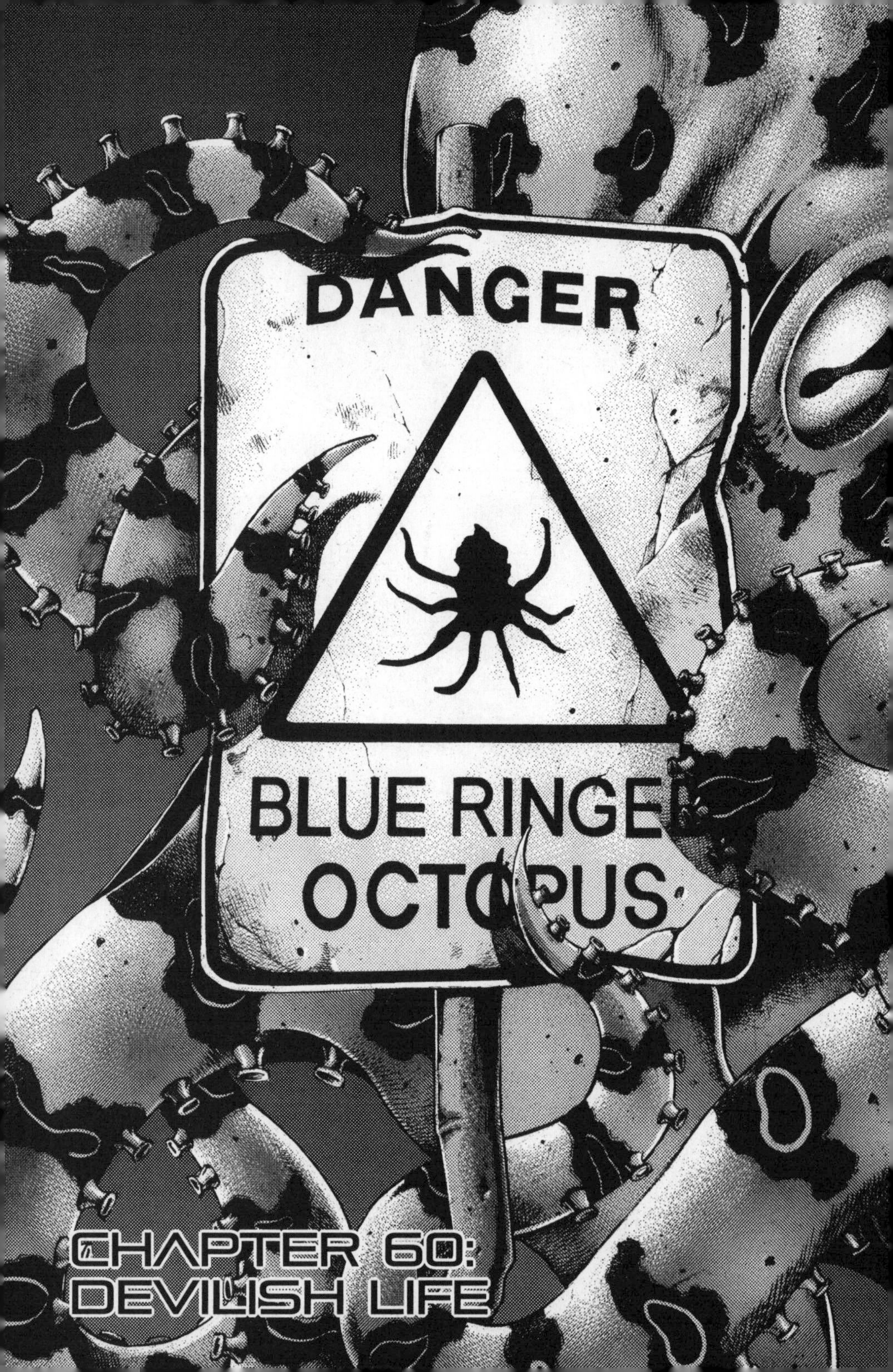
DANGER
BLUE RINGED
OCTOPUS

CHAPTER 60: DEVILISH LIFE

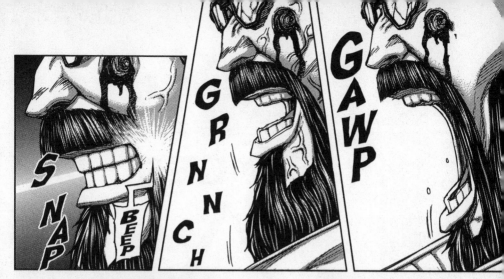

SNAP

BEEP

GRNNCH

GAWP

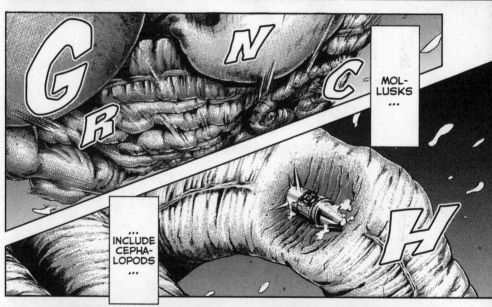

GRNNCH

MOL-LUSKS...

...INCLUDE CEPHA-LOPODS...

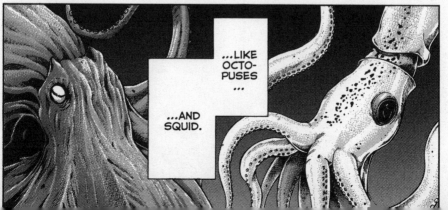

...LIKE OCTO-PUSES...

...AND SQUID.

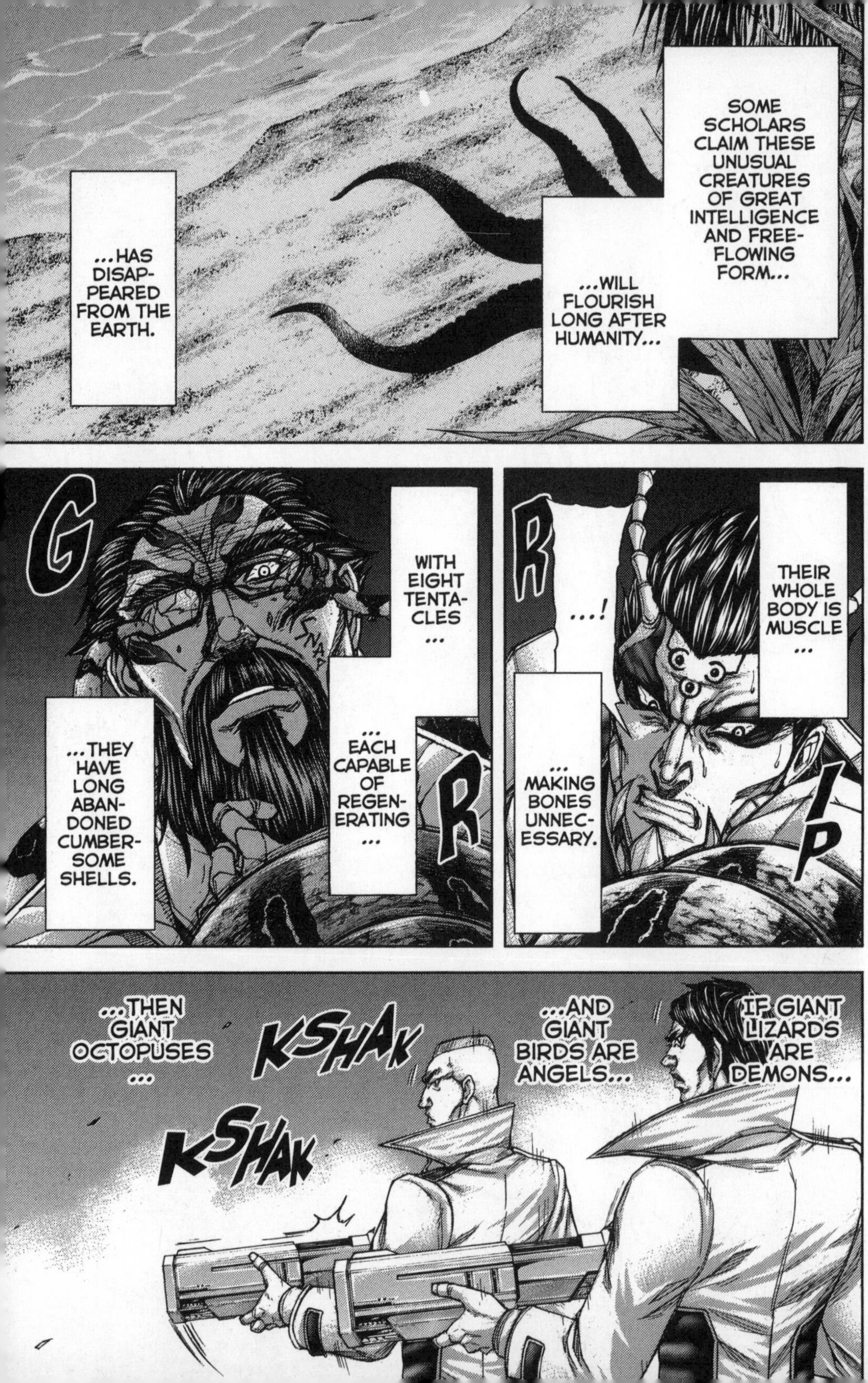
SOME SCHOLARS CLAIM THESE UNUSUAL CREATURES OF GREAT INTELLIGENCE AND FREE-FLOWING FORM...
...WILL FLOURISH LONG AFTER HUMANITY...
...HAS DISAPPEARED FROM THE EARTH.
R
THEIR WHOLE BODY IS MUSCLE...
...!
...MAKING BONES UNNECESSARY.
IP
G
WITH EIGHT TENTACLES...
...EACH CAPABLE OF REGENERATING...
...THEY HAVE LONG ABANDONED CUMBERSOME SHELLS.
R
IF GIANT LIZARDS ARE DEMONS...
...AND GIANT BIRDS ARE ANGELS...
KSHAK
...THEN GIANT OCTOPUSES...
KSHAK

DIXON, JOHN ADAMS (AUTHORS), TAKAFUMI MATSUI (EDITOR), AKIKO TSUCHIYA (TRANSLATOR), DIAMOND, INC., 2004

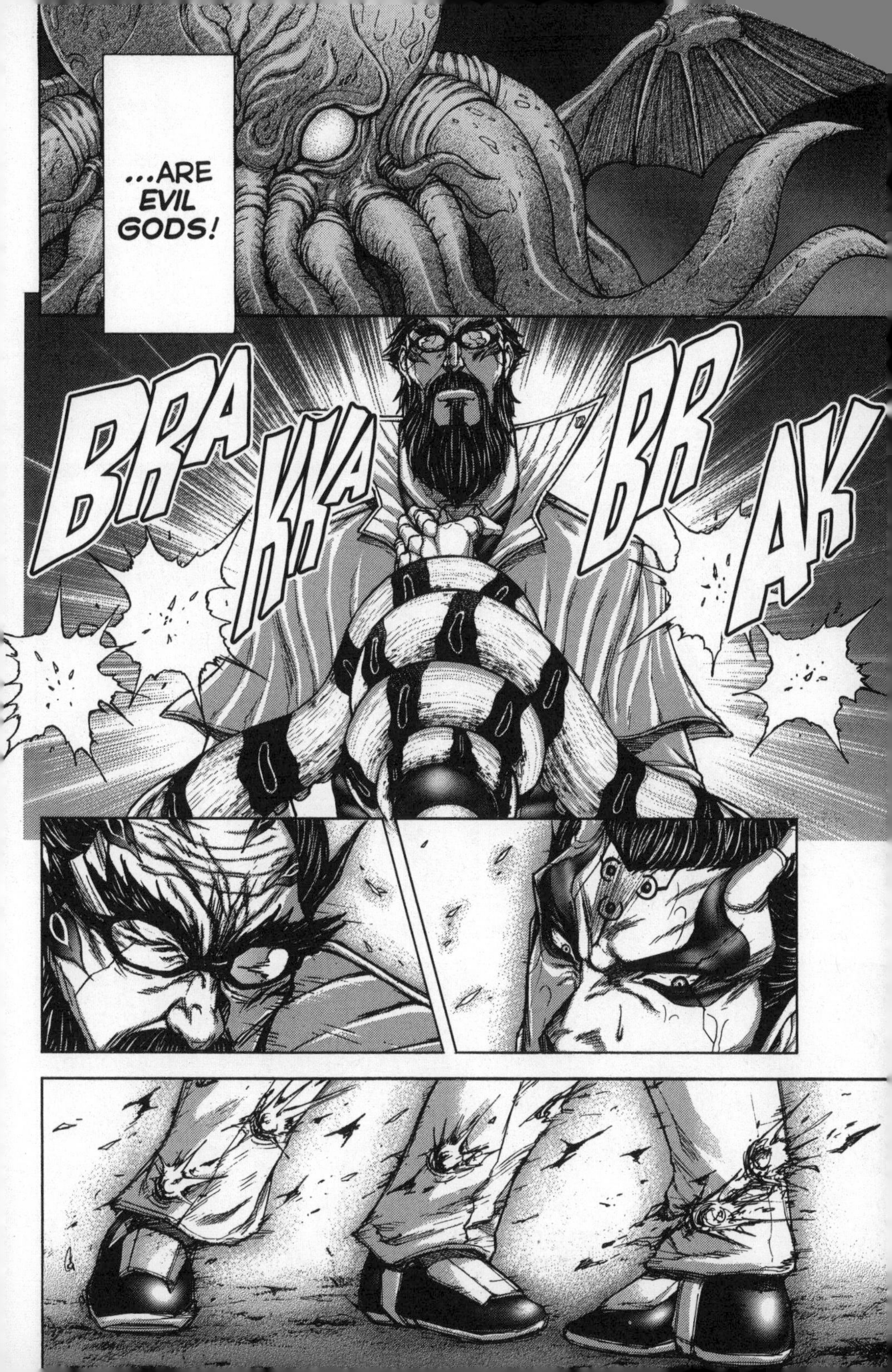
...ARE EVIL GODS!
BRAKKA
BRRAK

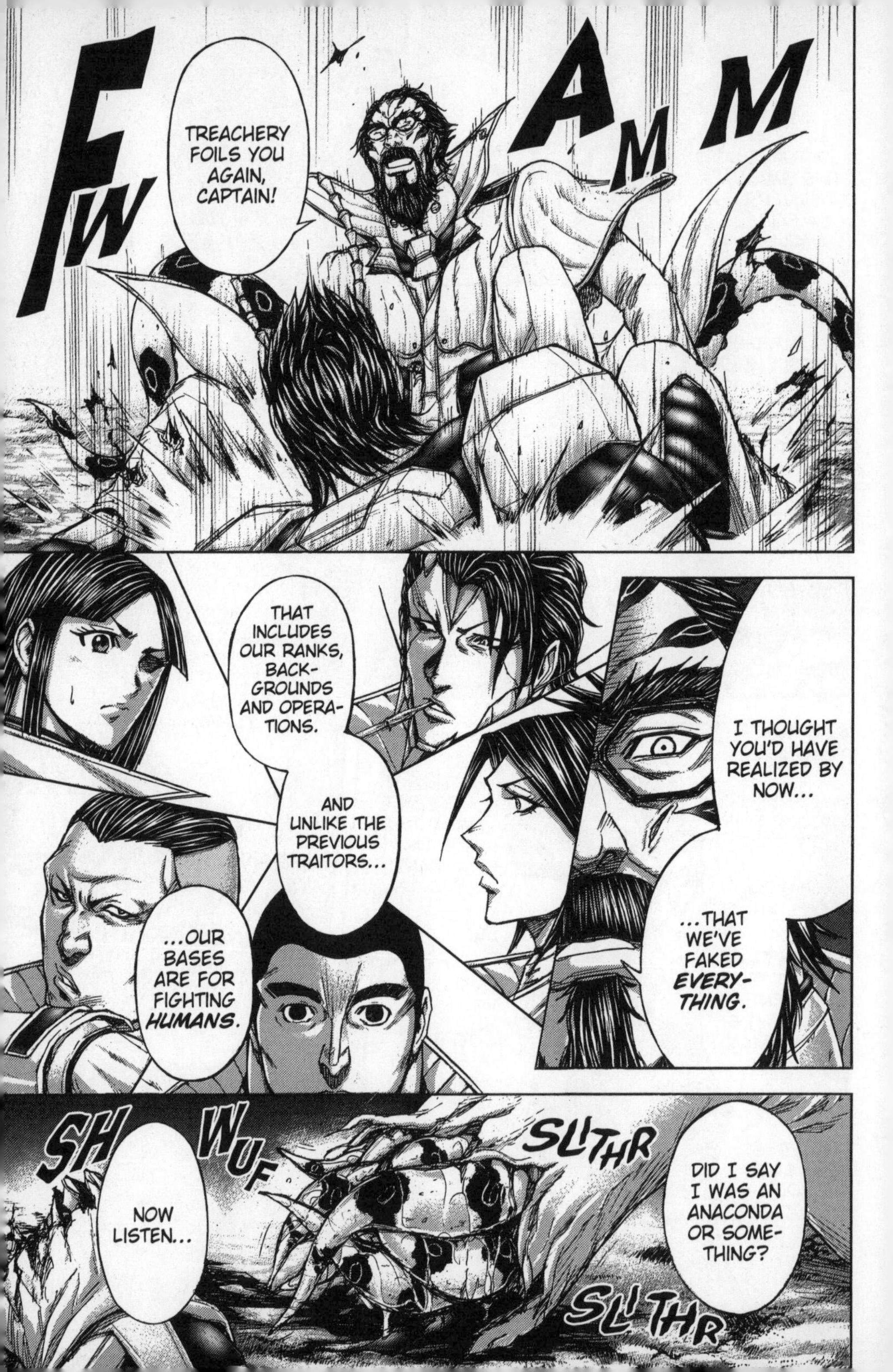
FWAMM
TREACHERY FOILS YOU AGAIN, CAPTAIN!
I THOUGHT YOU'D HAVE REALIZED BY NOW...
...THAT WE'VE FAKED *EVERYTHING*.
THAT INCLUDES OUR RANKS, BACKGROUNDS AND OPERATIONS.
AND UNLIKE THE PREVIOUS TRAITORS...
...OUR BASES ARE FOR FIGHTING *HUMANS*.
SLITHR
DID I SAY I WAS AN ANACONDA OR SOMETHING?
SH WUF
NOW LISTEN...
SLITHR

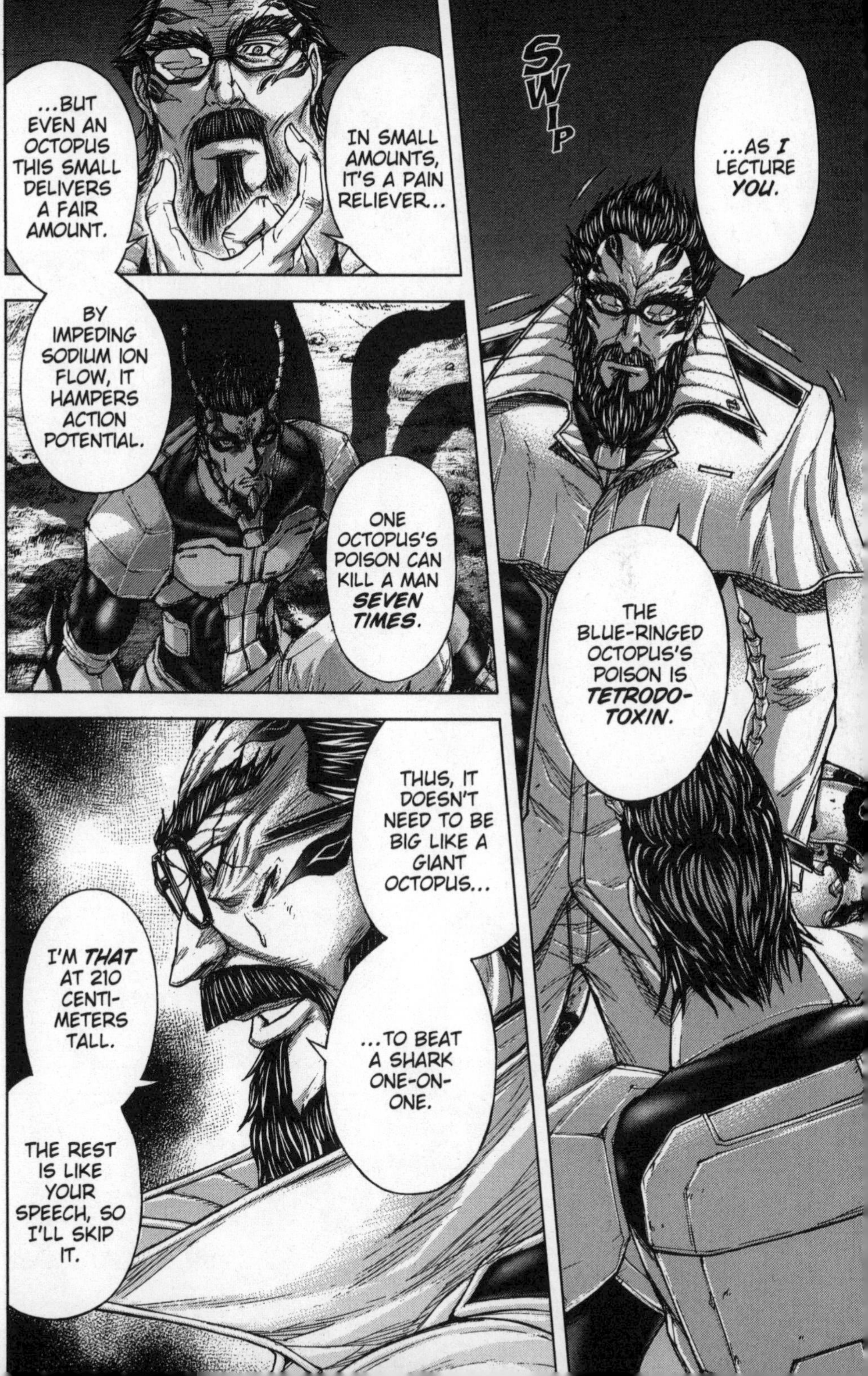
SWIP
...AS *I* LECTURE *YOU*.
THE BLUE-RINGED OCTOPUS'S POISON IS ***TETRODO-TOXIN***.
IN SMALL AMOUNTS, IT'S A PAIN RELIEVER...
...BUT EVEN AN OCTOPUS THIS SMALL DELIVERS A FAIR AMOUNT.
BY IMPEDING SODIUM ION FLOW, IT HAMPERS ACTION POTENTIAL.
ONE OCTOPUS'S POISON CAN KILL A MAN ***SEVEN TIMES***.
THUS, IT DOESN'T NEED TO BE BIG LIKE A GIANT OCTOPUS...
...TO BEAT A SHARK ONE-ON-ONE.
I'M ***THAT*** AT 210 CENTI-METERS TALL.
THE REST IS LIKE YOUR SPEECH, SO I'LL SKIP IT.

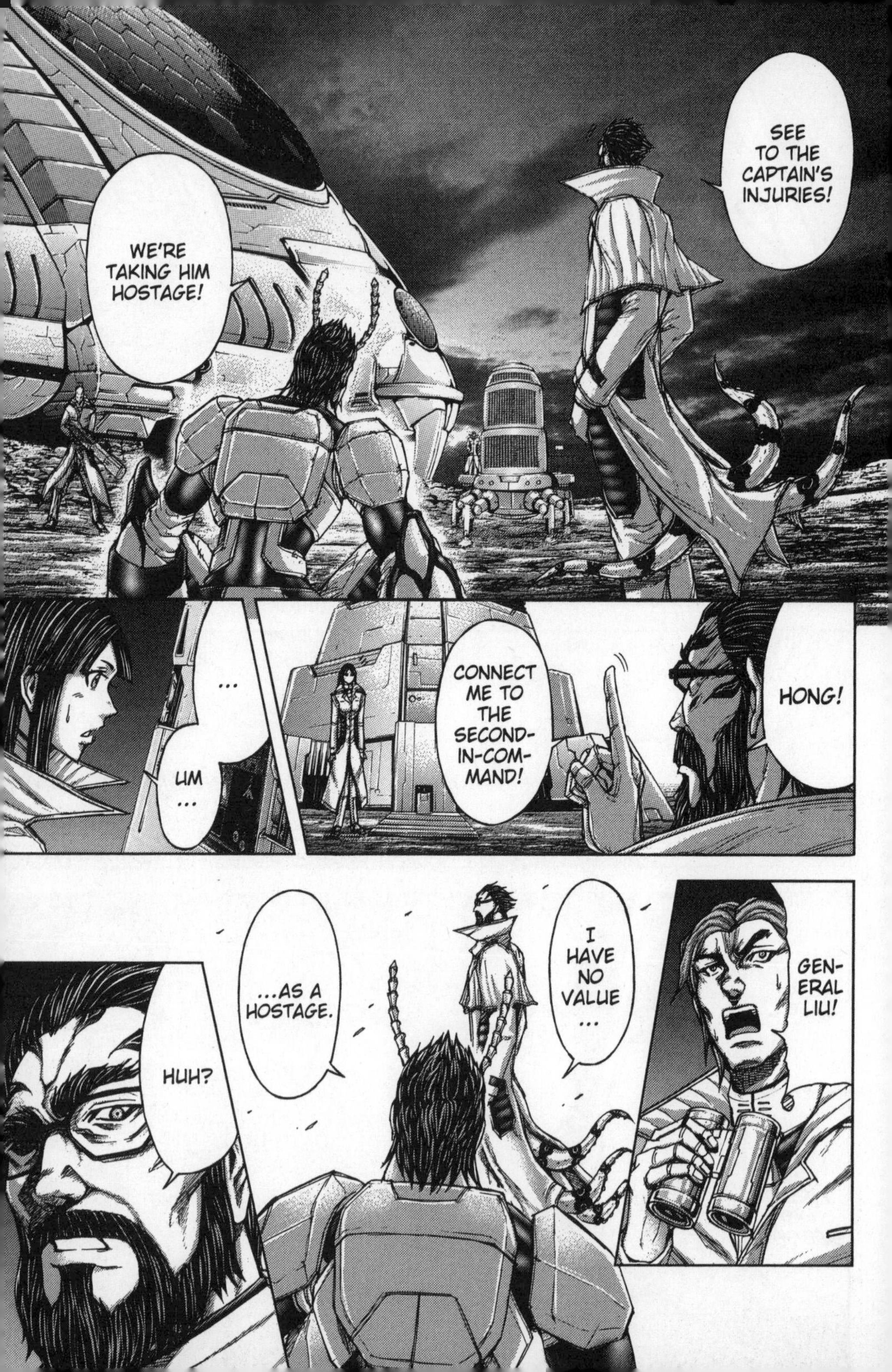
SEE TO THE CAPTAIN'S INJURIES!
WE'RE TAKING HIM HOSTAGE!
HONG!
CONNECT ME TO THE SECOND-IN-COMMAND!
...
UM ...
GEN-ERAL LIU!
I HAVE NO VALUE ...
...AS A HOSTAGE.
HUH?

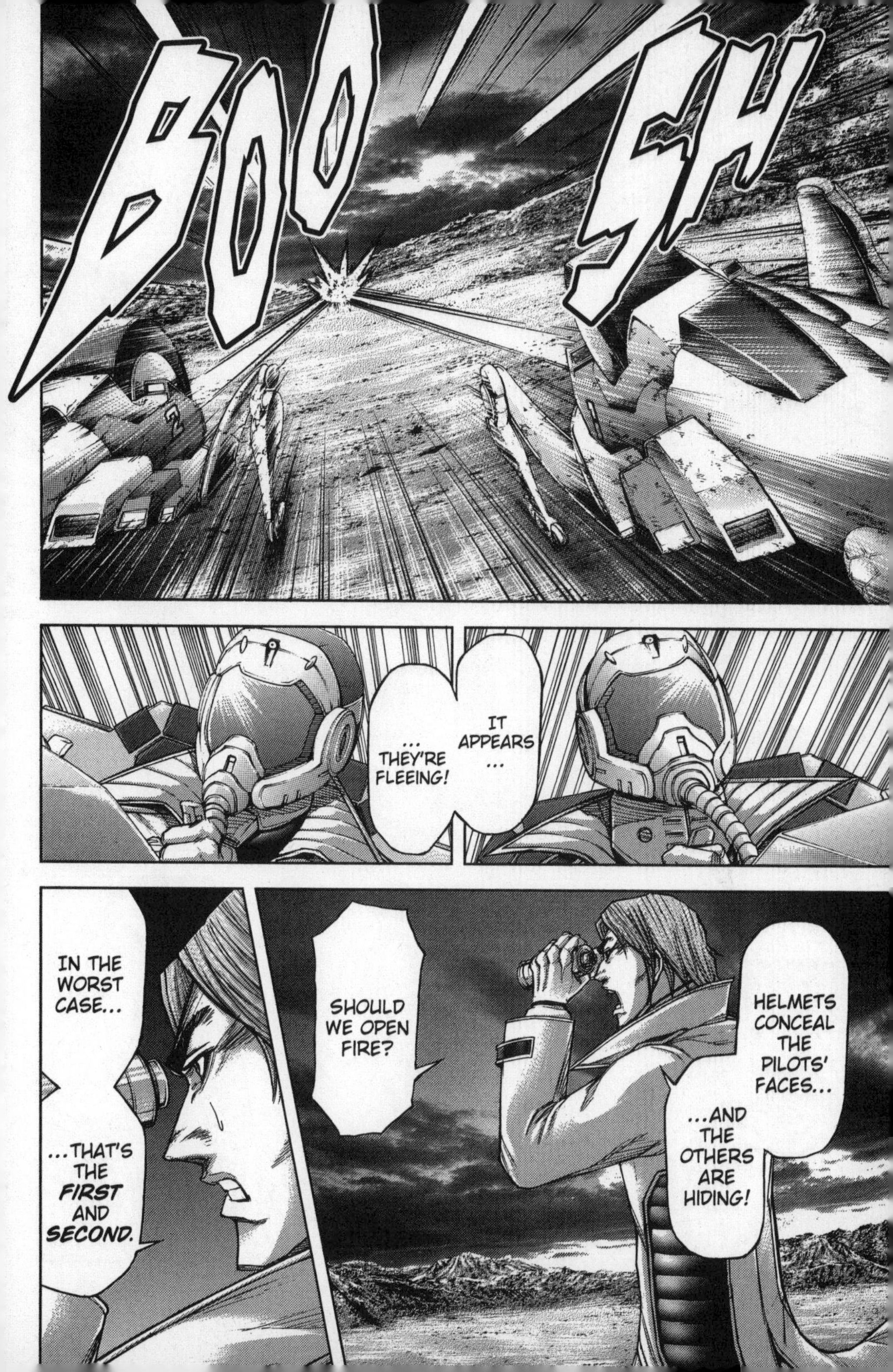
BOOSH
IT APPEARS... ...THEY'RE FLEEING!
HELMETS CONCEAL THE PILOTS' FACES...
...AND THE OTHERS ARE HIDING!
SHOULD WE OPEN FIRE?
IN THE WORST CASE...
...THAT'S THE *FIRST* AND *SECOND*.

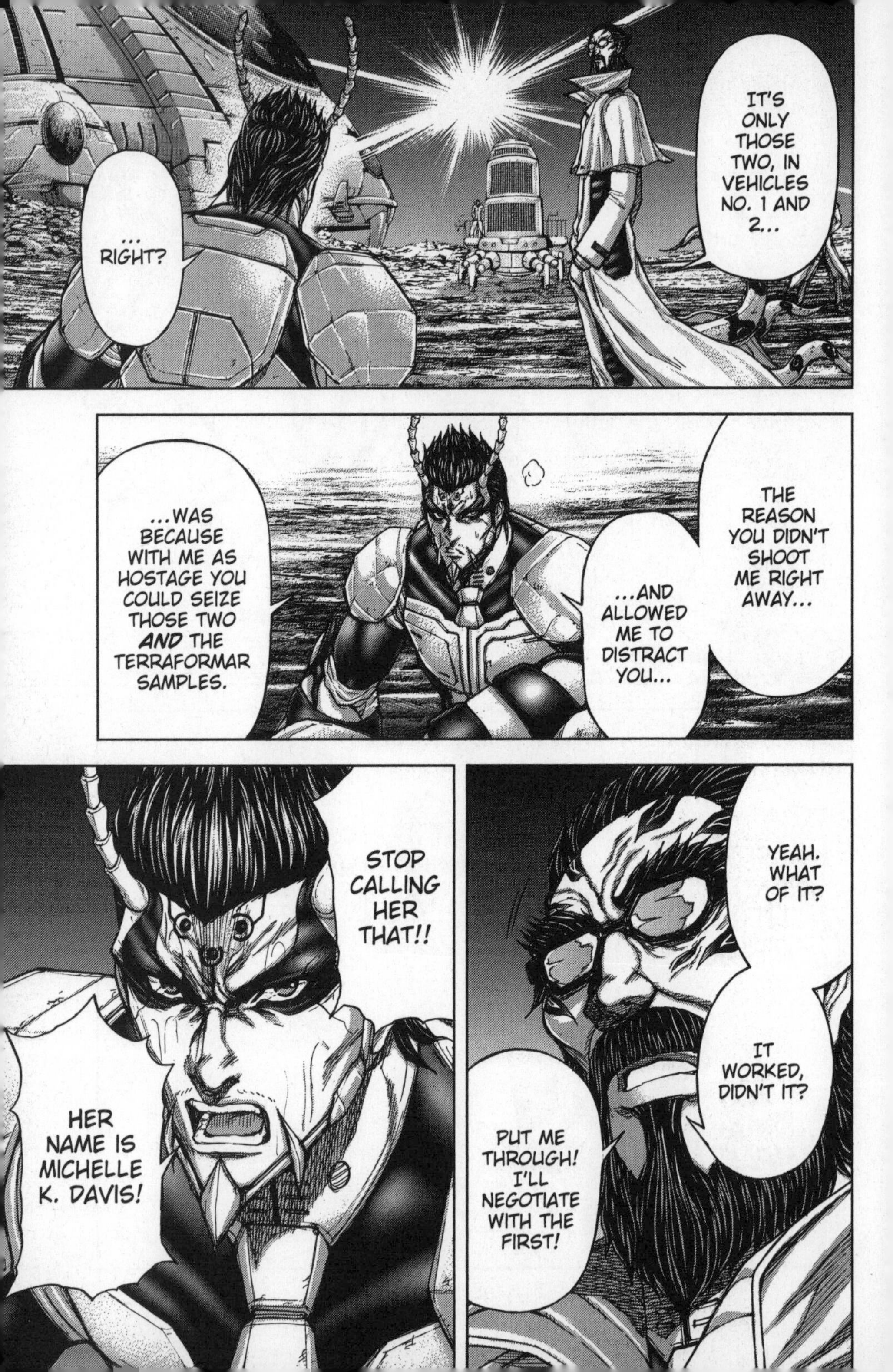
IT'S ONLY THOSE TWO, IN VEHICLES NO. 1 AND 2...
...RIGHT?
THE REASON YOU DIDN'T SHOOT ME RIGHT AWAY...
...AND ALLOWED ME TO DISTRACT YOU...
...WAS BECAUSE WITH ME AS HOSTAGE YOU COULD SEIZE THOSE TWO *AND* THE TERRAFORMAR SAMPLES.
YEAH. WHAT OF IT?
IT WORKED, DIDN'T IT?
PUT ME THROUGH! I'LL NEGOTIATE WITH THE FIRST!
STOP CALLING HER THAT!!
HER NAME IS MICHELLE K. DAVIS!

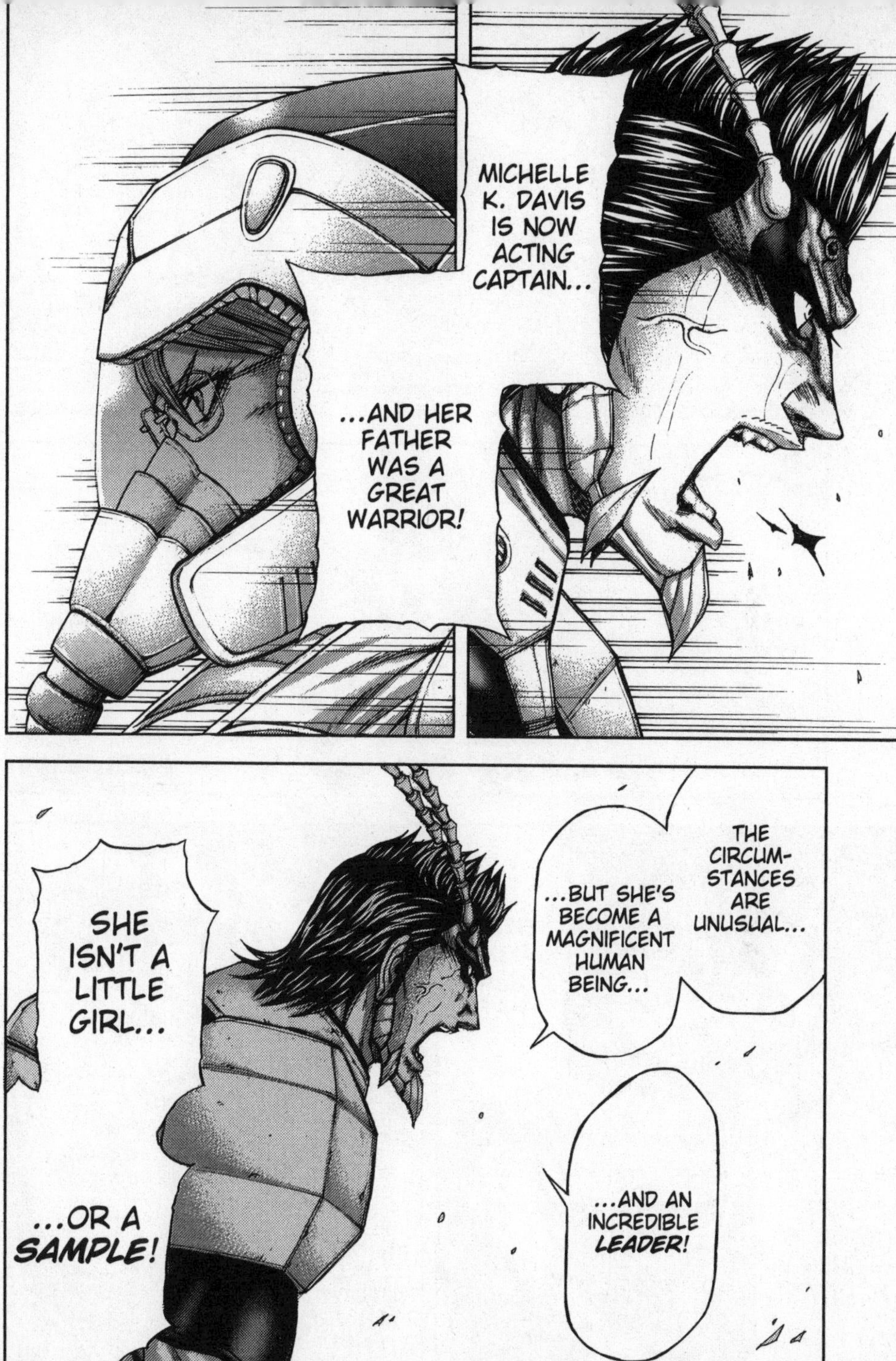
MICHELLE K. DAVIS IS NOW ACTING CAPTAIN...
...AND HER FATHER WAS A GREAT WARRIOR!
THE CIRCUM-STANCES ARE UNUSUAL...
...BUT SHE'S BECOME A MAGNIFICENT HUMAN BEING...
...AND AN INCREDIBLE *LEADER*!
SHE ISN'T A LITTLE GIRL...
...OR A *SAMPLE*!

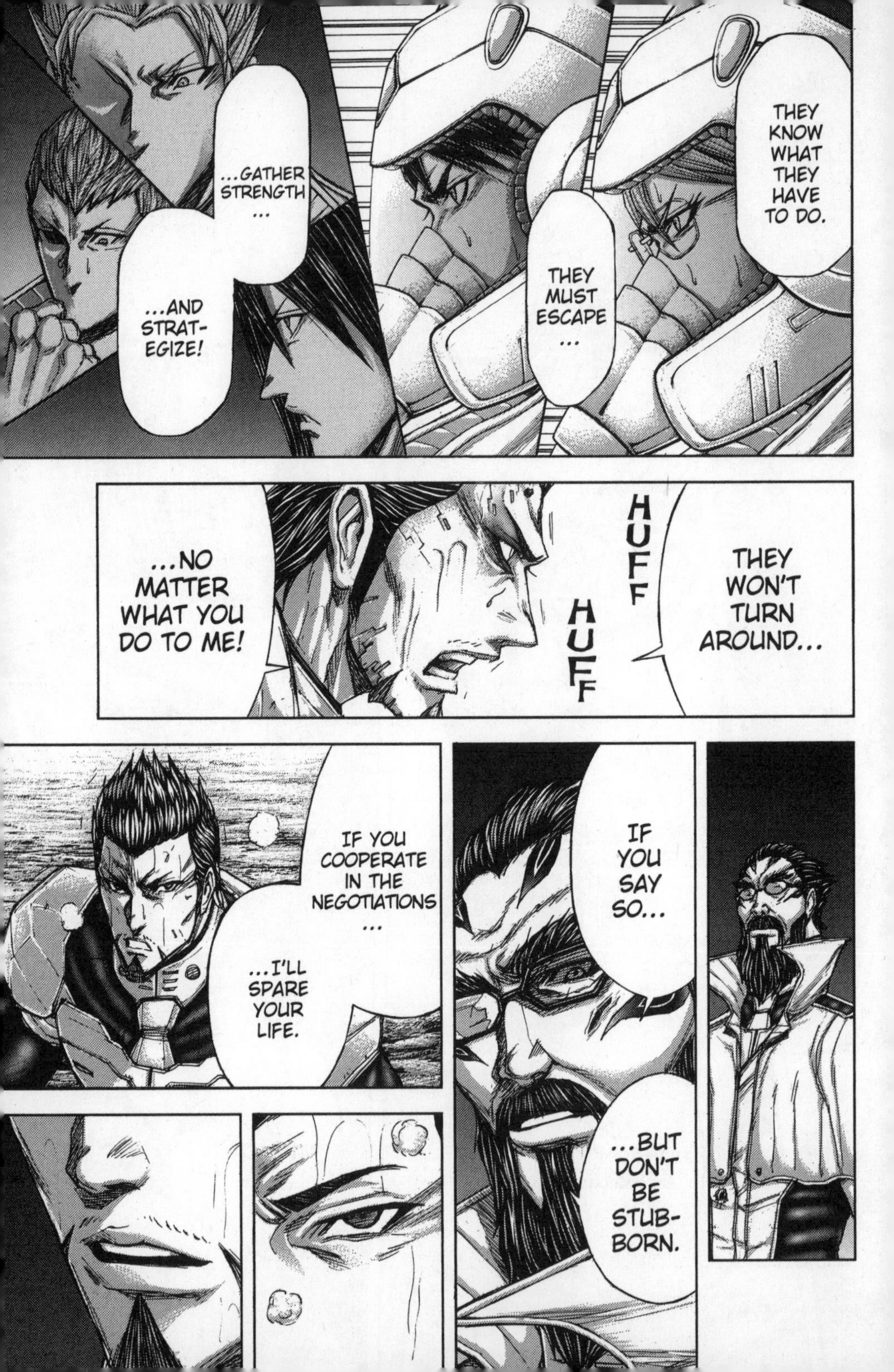
THEY KNOW WHAT THEY HAVE TO DO.
THEY MUST ESCAPE...
...GATHER STRENGTH...
...AND STRAT-EGIZE!
THEY WON'T TURN AROUND...
HUFF
HUFF
...NO MATTER WHAT YOU DO TO ME!
IF YOU SAY SO...
...BUT DON'T BE STUB-BORN.
IF YOU COOPERATE IN THE NEGOTIATIONS...
...I'LL SPARE YOUR LIFE.

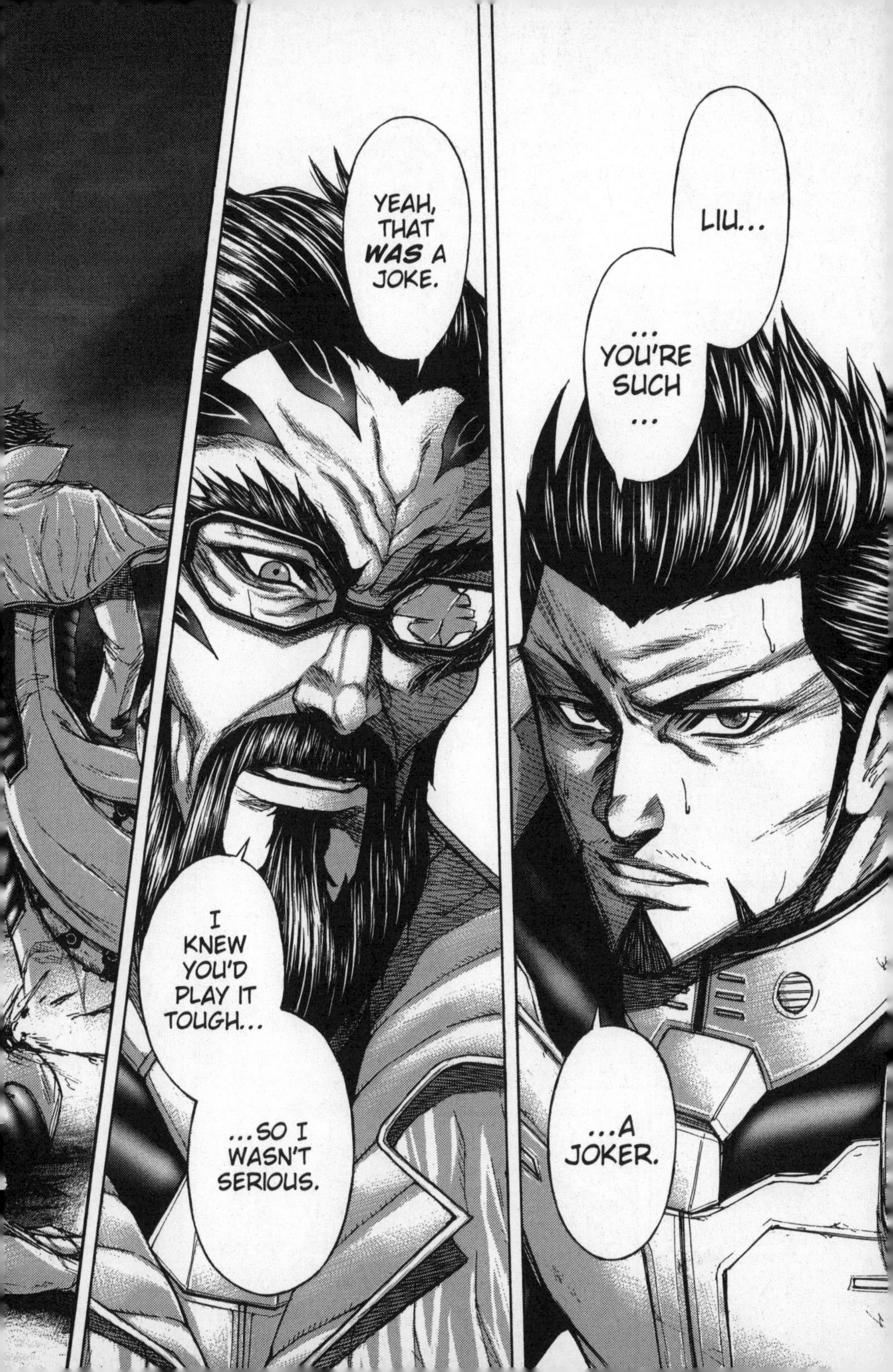
LIU...
...YOU'RE SUCH...
...A JOKER.
YEAH, THAT *WAS* A JOKE.
I KNEW YOU'D PLAY IT TOUGH...
...SO I WASN'T SERIOUS.

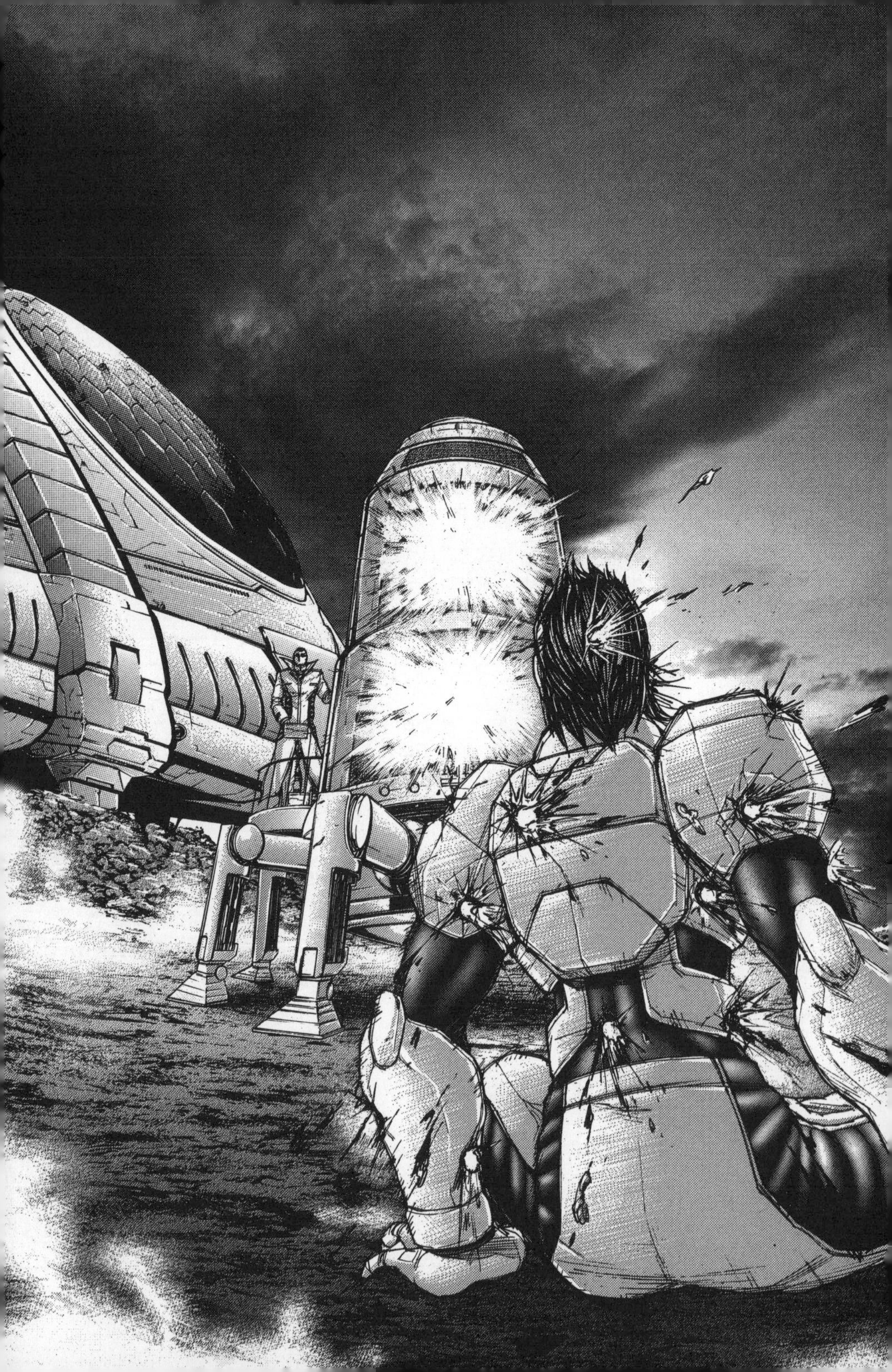

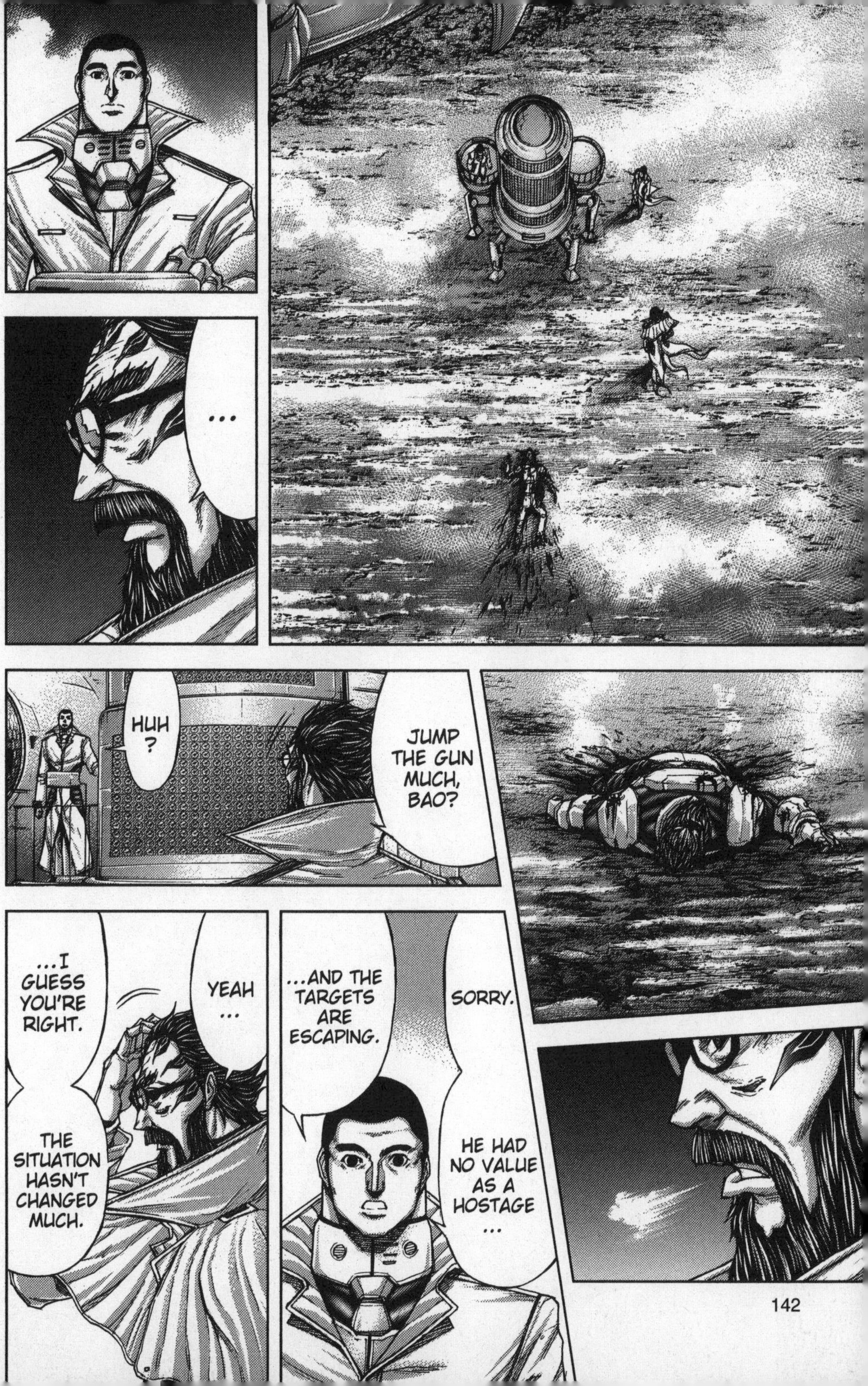
...
JUMP THE GUN MUCH, BAO?
HUH ?
SORRY.
HE HAD NO VALUE AS A HOSTAGE ...
...AND THE TARGETS ARE ESCAPING.
YEAH ...
...I GUESS YOU'RE RIGHT.
THE SITUATION HASN'T CHANGED MUCH.

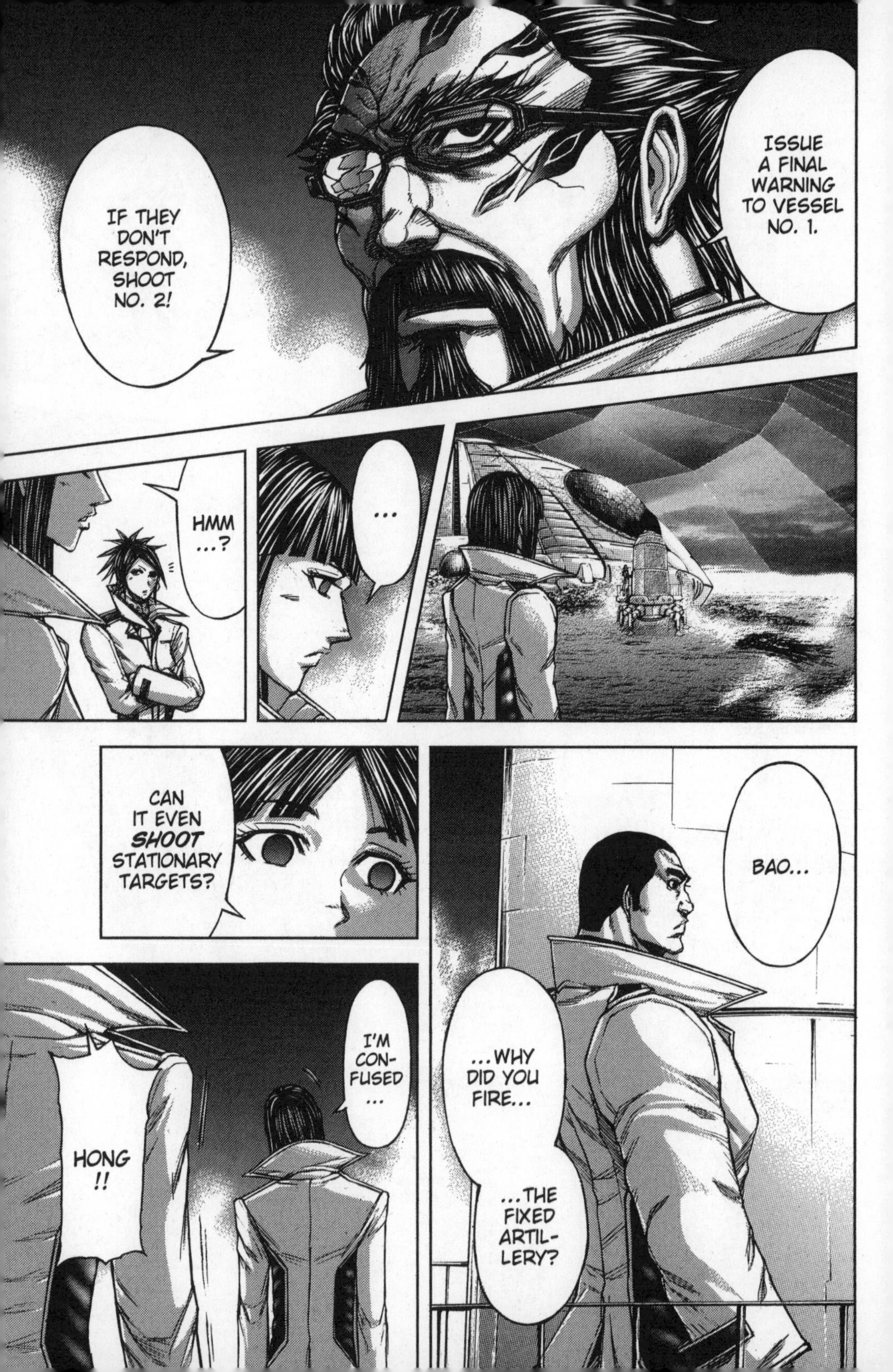
ISSUE A FINAL WARNING TO VESSEL NO. 1.
IF THEY DON'T RESPOND, SHOOT NO. 2!
...
HMM ...?
BAO...
...WHY DID YOU FIRE...
...THE FIXED ARTIL-LERY?
CAN IT EVEN *SHOOT* STATIONARY TARGETS?
I'M CON-FUSED ...
HONG !!

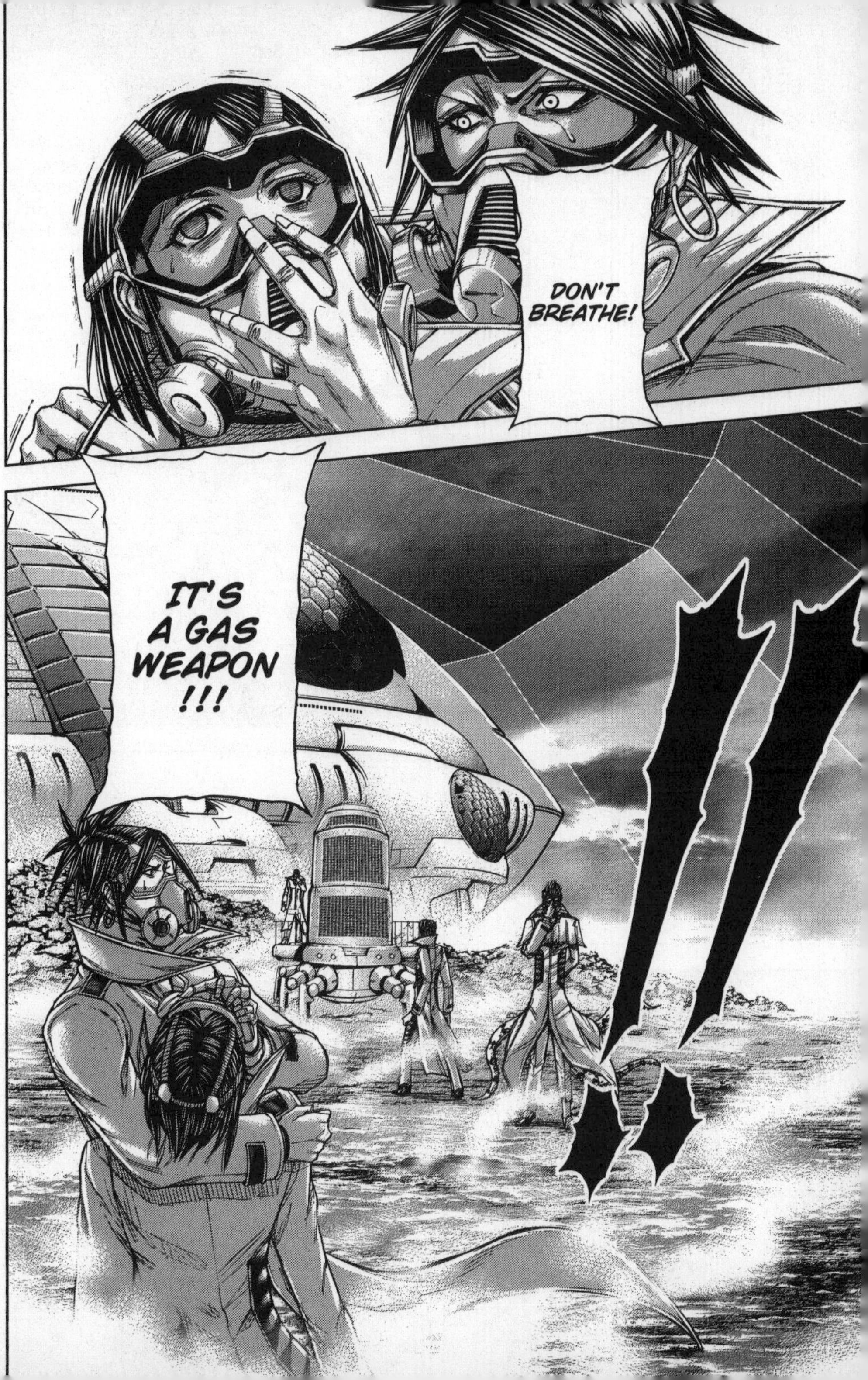
DON'T BREATHE!
IT'S A GAS WEAPON !!!

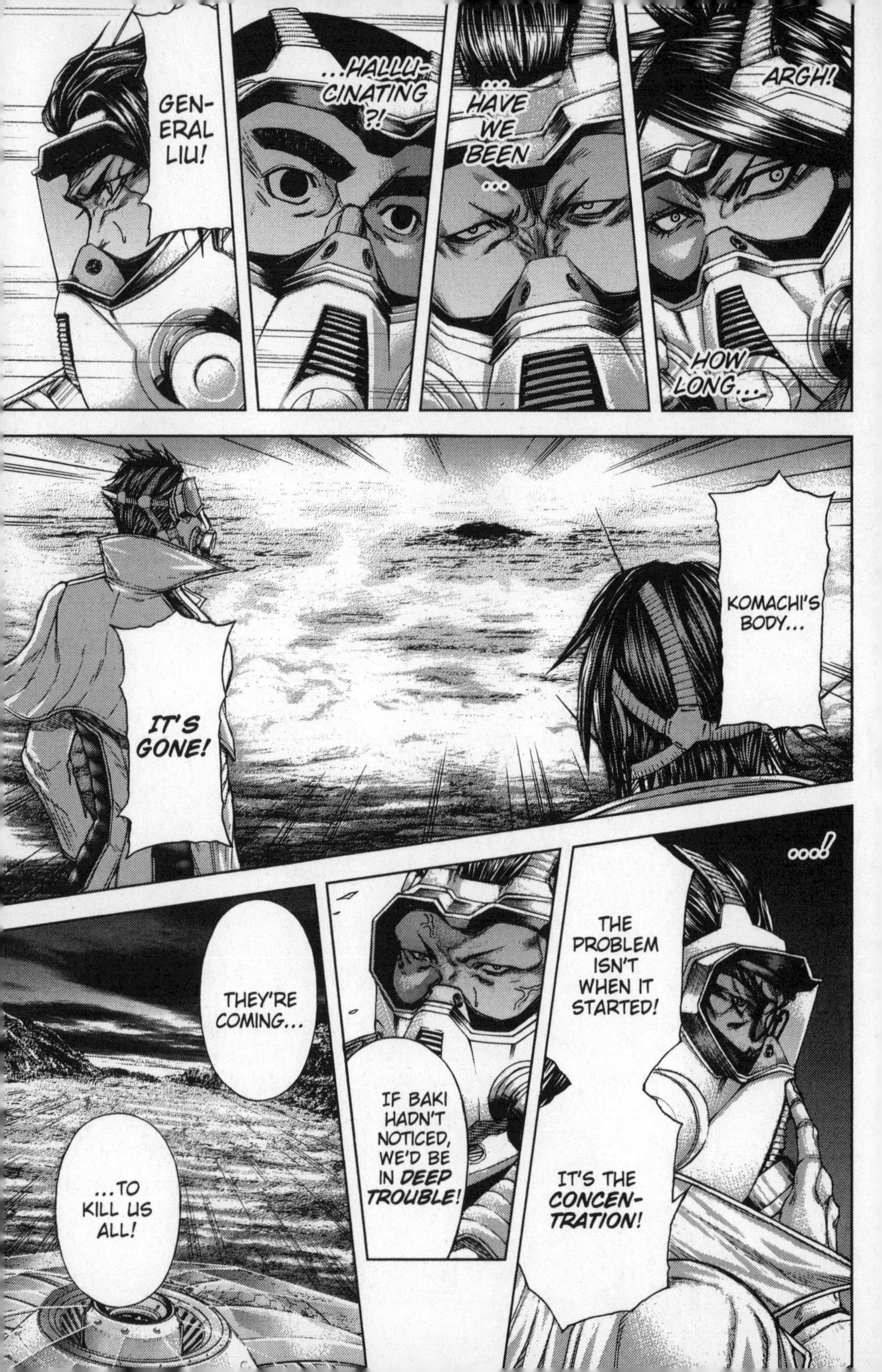
ARGH!
HOW LONG...
...HAVE WE BEEN...
...HALLUCINATING?!
GENERAL LIU!
KOMACHI'S BODY...
IT'S GONE!
...!
THE PROBLEM ISN'T WHEN IT STARTED!
IT'S THE CONCENTRATION!
IF BAKI HADN'T NOTICED, WE'D BE IN DEEP TROUBLE!
THEY'RE COMING...
...TO KILL US ALL!

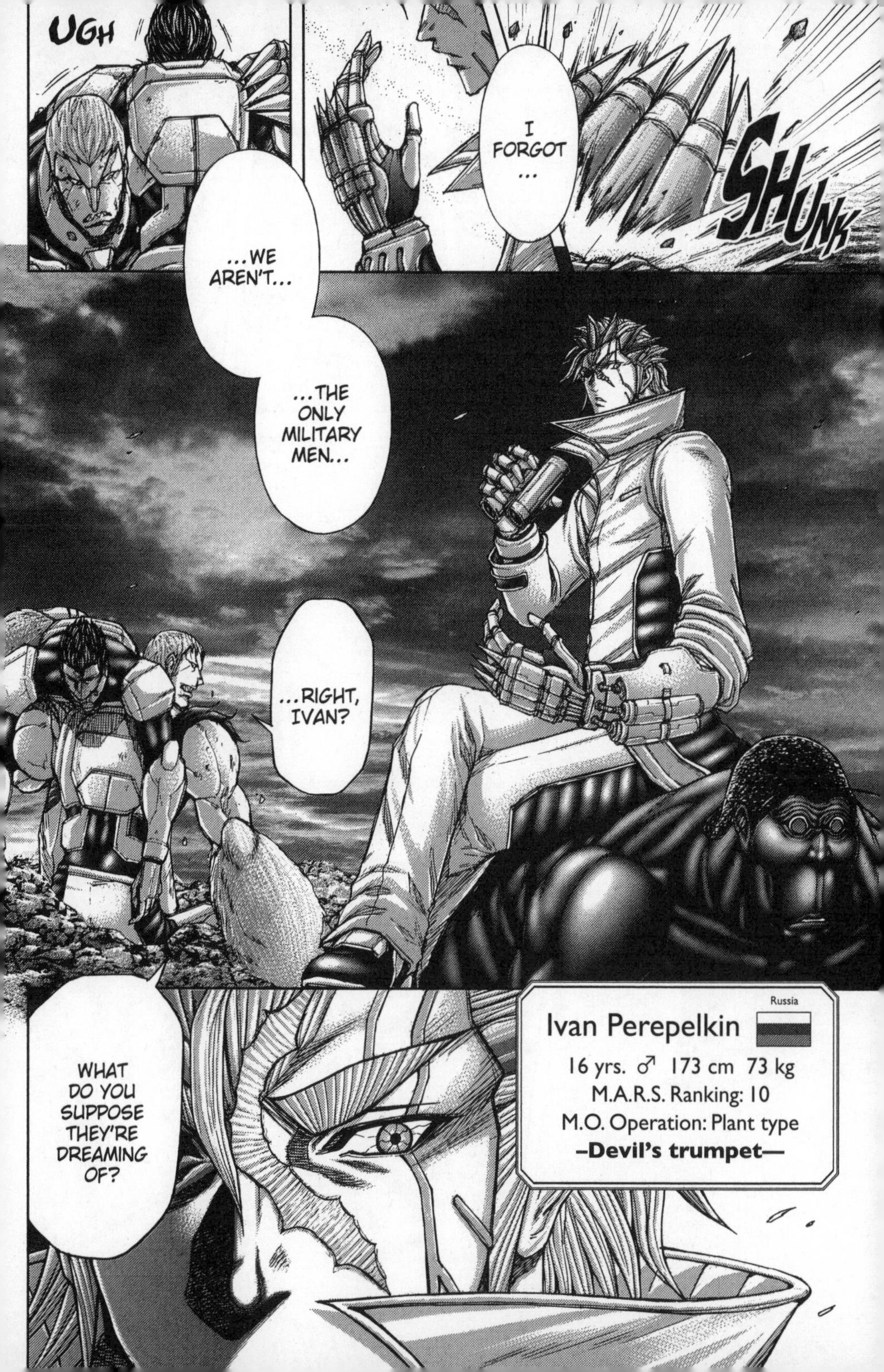
SHUNK
I FORGOT...
UGH
...WE AREN'T...
...THE ONLY MILITARY MEN...
...RIGHT, IVAN?
Russia
Ivan Perepelkin
16 yrs. ♂ 173 cm 73 kg
M.A.R.S. Ranking: 10
M.O. Operation: Plant type
–Devil's trumpet—
WHAT DO YOU SUPPOSE THEY'RE DREAMING OF?

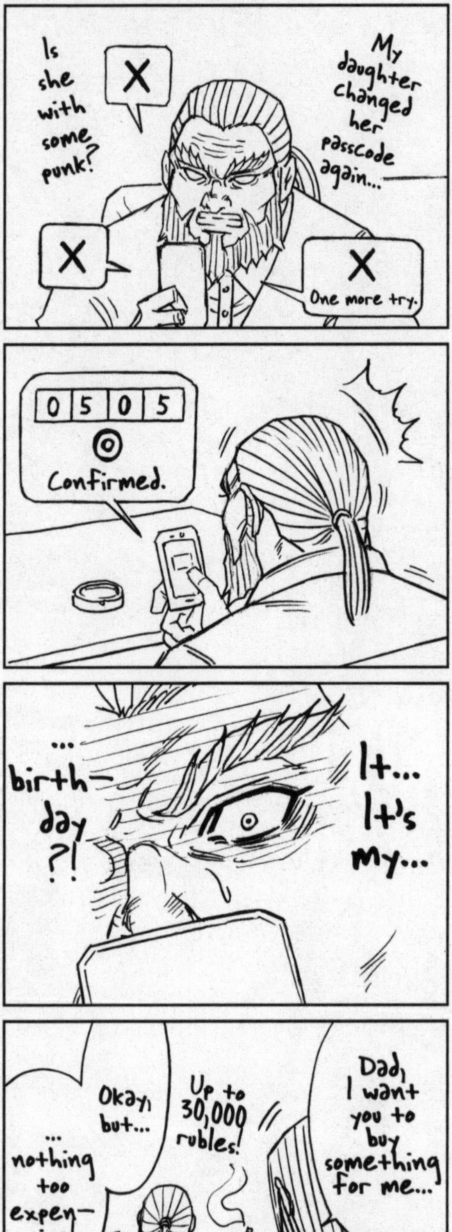
My daughter changed her passcode again...
X
Is she with some punk?
X
One more try.
X
0505
Confirmed.
It... It's my...
...birth-day?!
Dad, I want you to buy something for me...
Up to 30,000 rubles!
Okay, but...
... nothing too expen-sive!

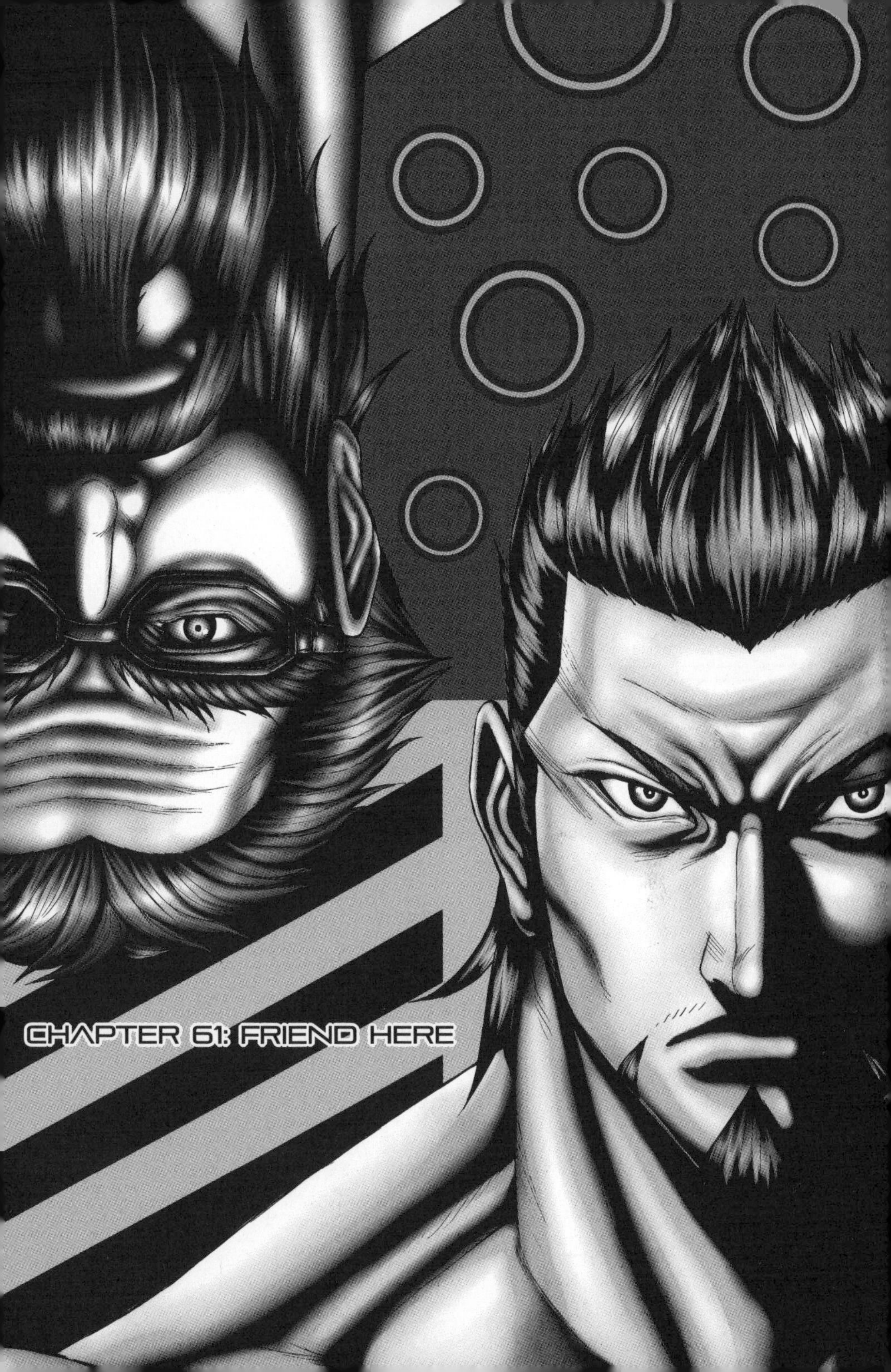
CHAPTER 61: FRIEND HERE

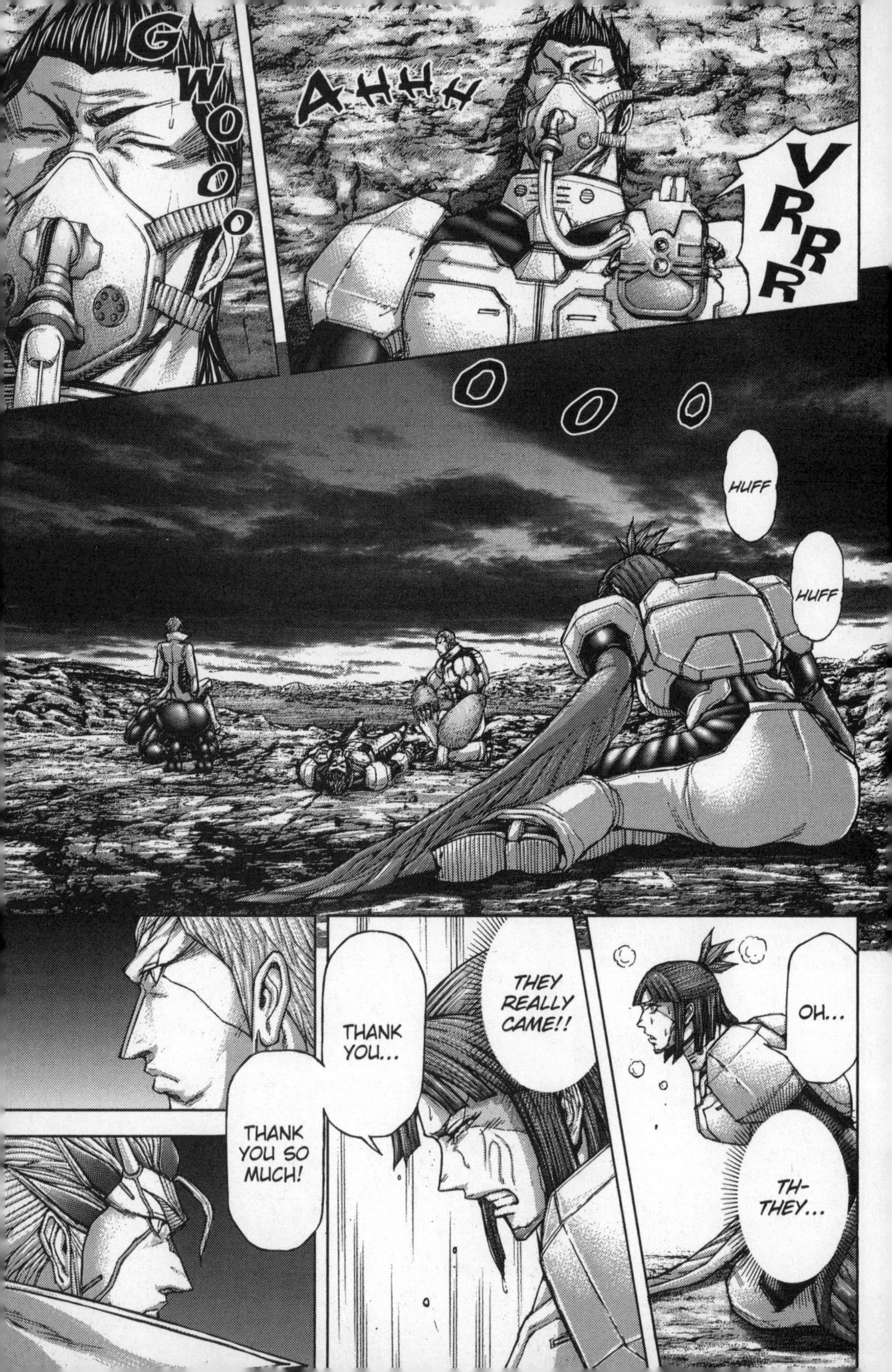
VRRR
AHHH
GWOOOO
OOO
HUFF
HUFF
OH...
TH- THEY...
THEY REALLY CAME!!
THANK YOU...
THANK YOU SO MUCH!

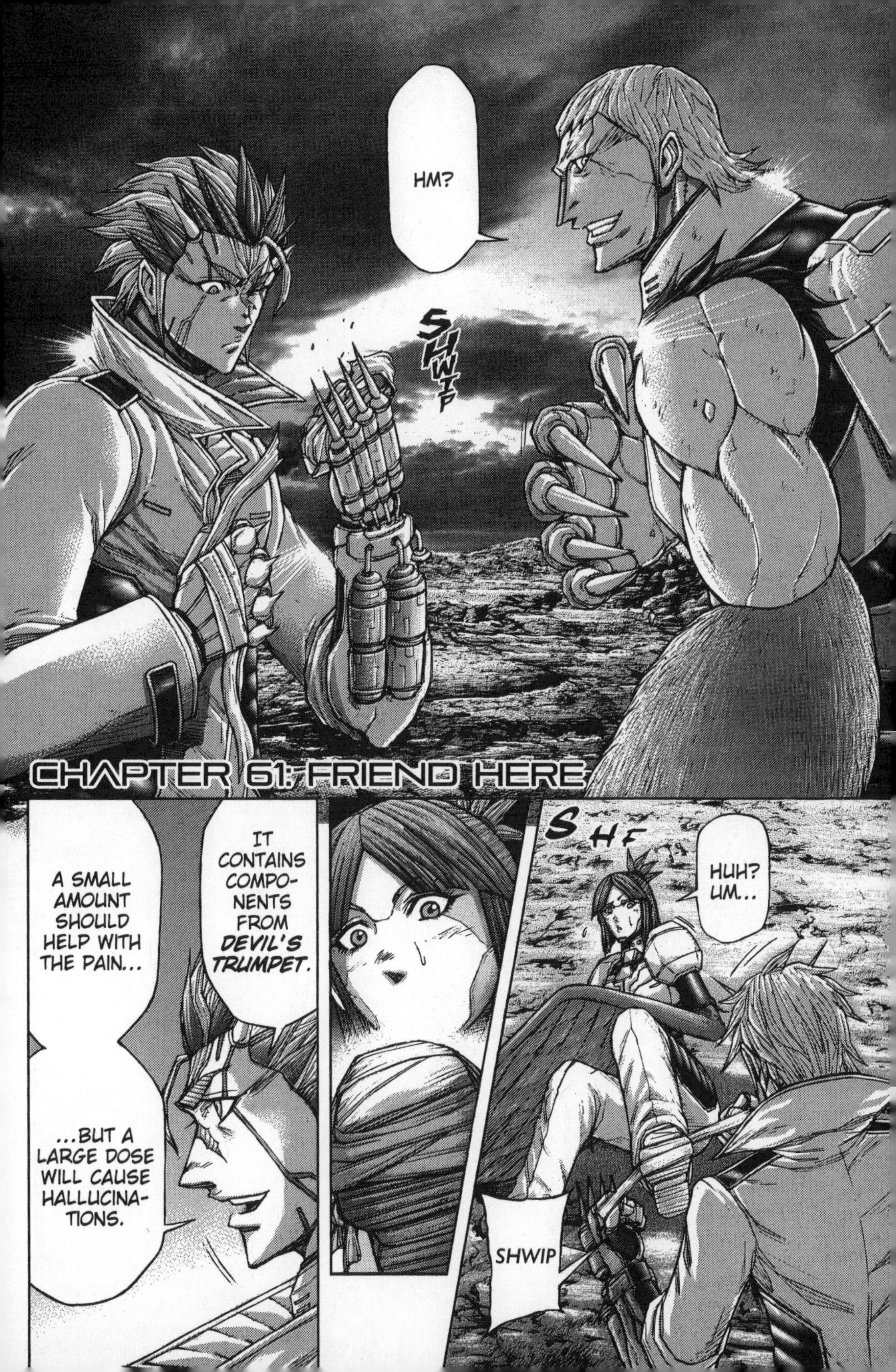
HM?
SHWIP
CHAPTER 61: FRIEND HERE
SHF
HUH? UM...
SHWIP
IT CONTAINS COMPONENTS FROM *DEVIL'S TRUMPET*.
A SMALL AMOUNT SHOULD HELP WITH THE PAIN...
...BUT A LARGE DOSE WILL CAUSE HALLUCINATIONS.

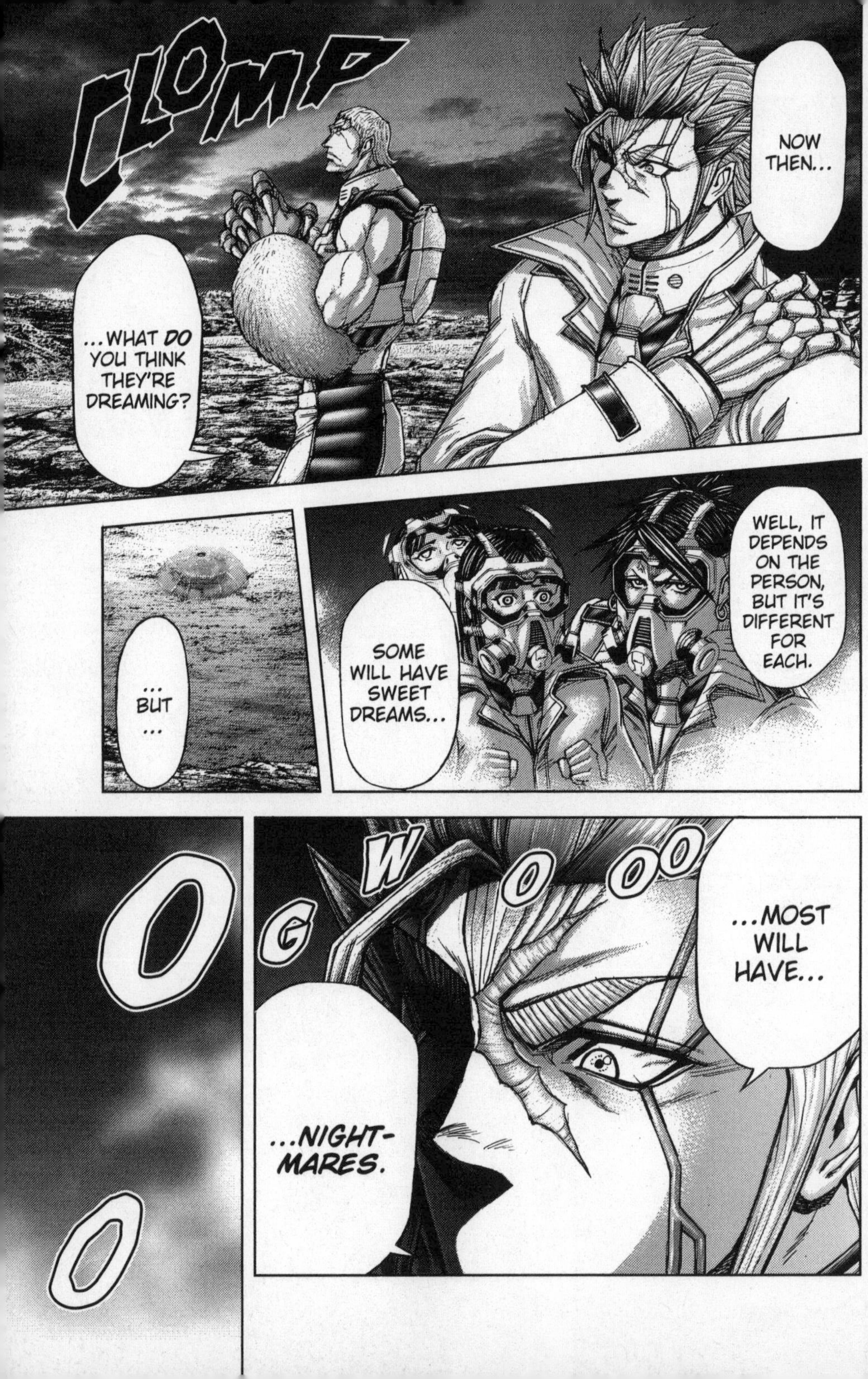
CLOMP
NOW THEN...
...WHAT DO YOU THINK THEY'RE DREAMING?
WELL, IT DEPENDS ON THE PERSON, BUT IT'S DIFFERENT FOR EACH.
SOME WILL HAVE SWEET DREAMS...
...BUT...
GWOOO
...MOST WILL HAVE...
...NIGHT-MARES.
OO

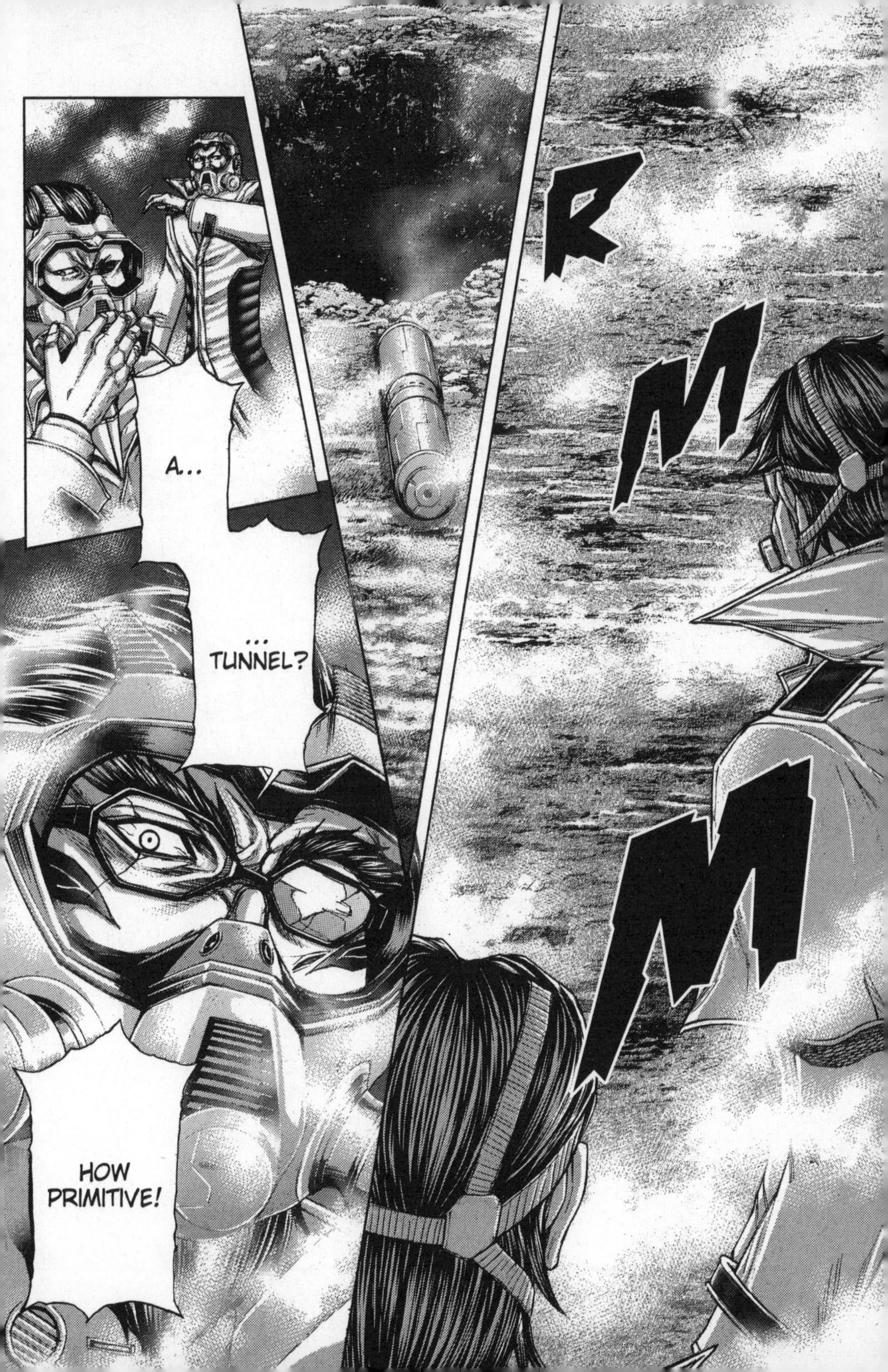
RMM
A...
...TUNNEL?
HOW PRIMITIVE!

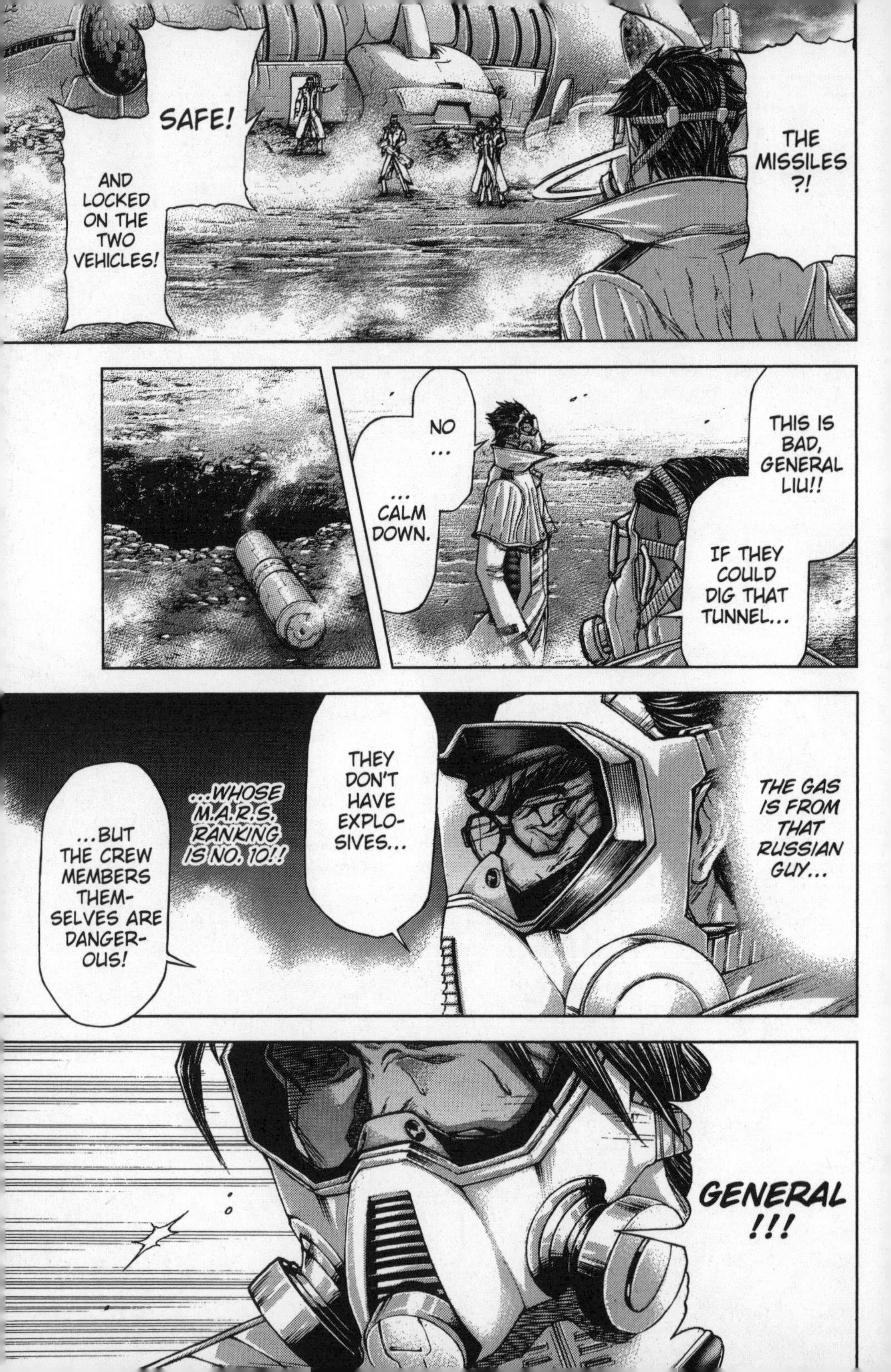
THE MISSILES ?!
SAFE!
AND LOCKED ON THE TWO VEHICLES!
THIS IS BAD, GENERAL LIU!!
IF THEY COULD DIG THAT TUNNEL...
NO ... ... CALM DOWN.
THE GAS IS FROM THAT RUSSIAN GUY...
THEY DON'T HAVE EXPLOSIVES...
...WHOSE M.A.R.S. RANKING IS NO. 10!!
...BUT THE CREW MEMBERS THEMSELVES ARE DANGEROUS!
GENERAL !!!

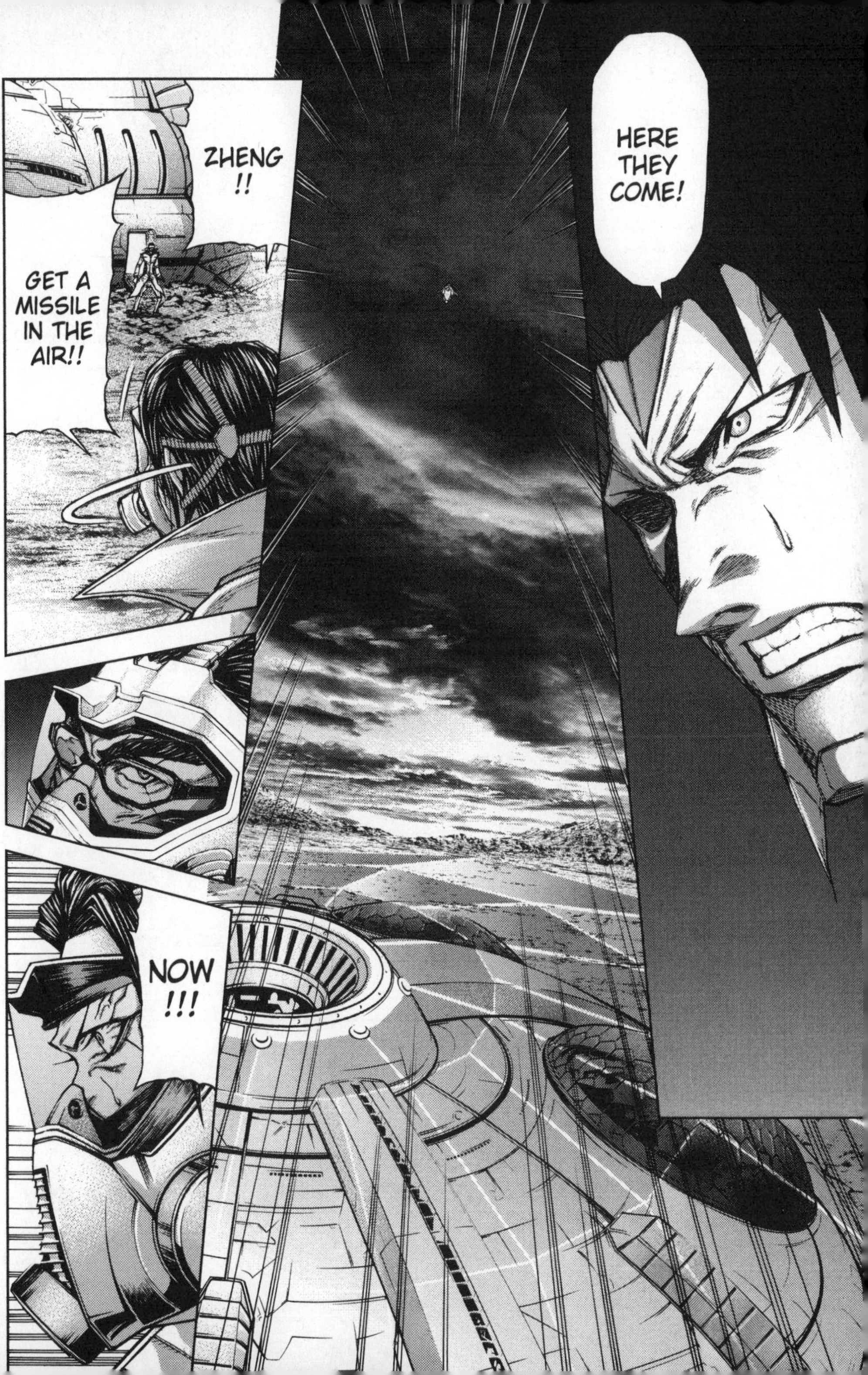
HERE THEY COME!
ZHENG !!
GET A MISSILE IN THE AIR!!
NOW !!!

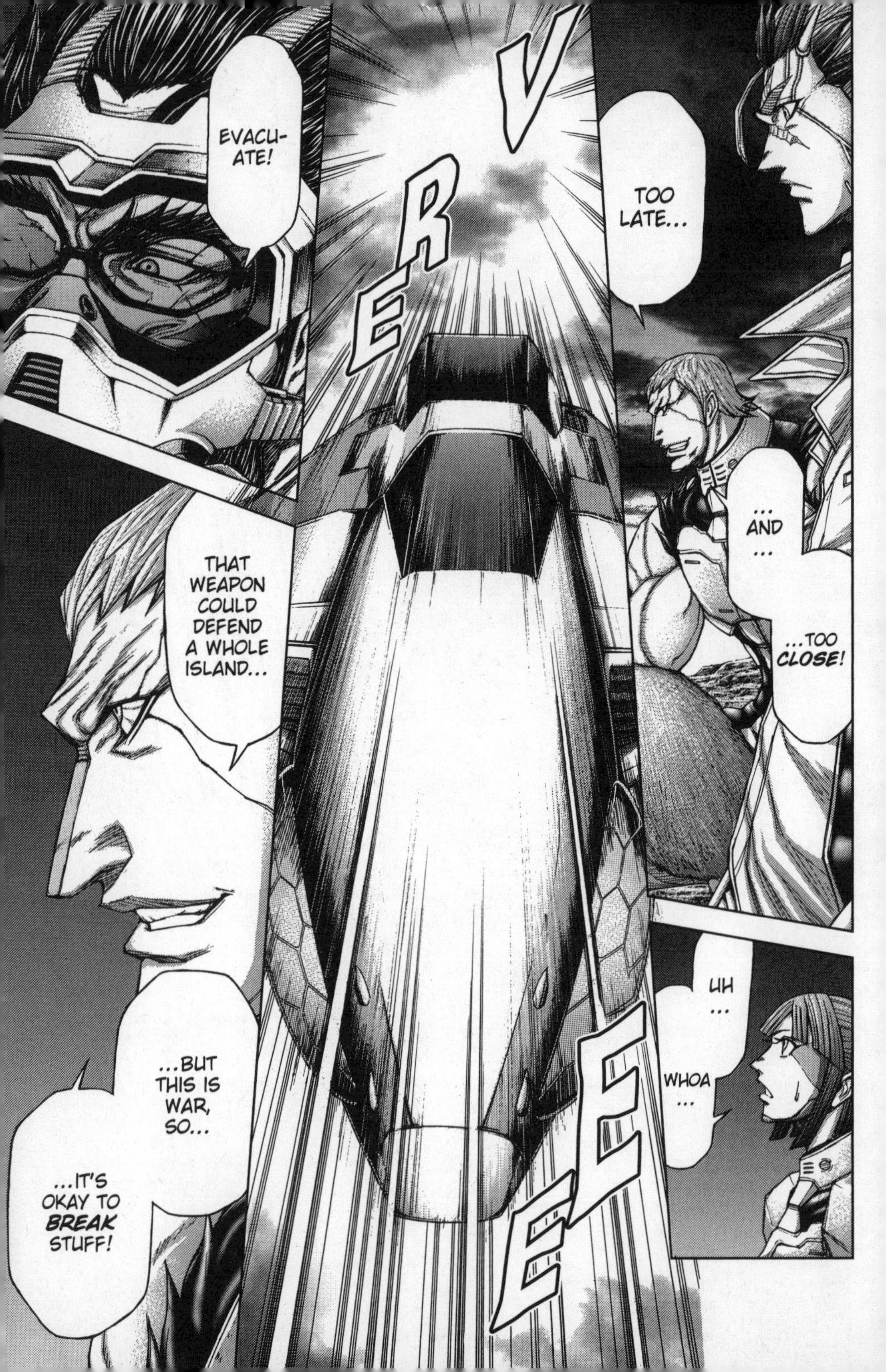
TOO LATE...
... AND ...
...TOO CLOSE!
UH ...
WHOA ...
VREEE
EVACUATE!
THAT WEAPON COULD DEFEND A WHOLE ISLAND...
...BUT THIS IS WAR, SO...
...IT'S OKAY TO BREAK STUFF!

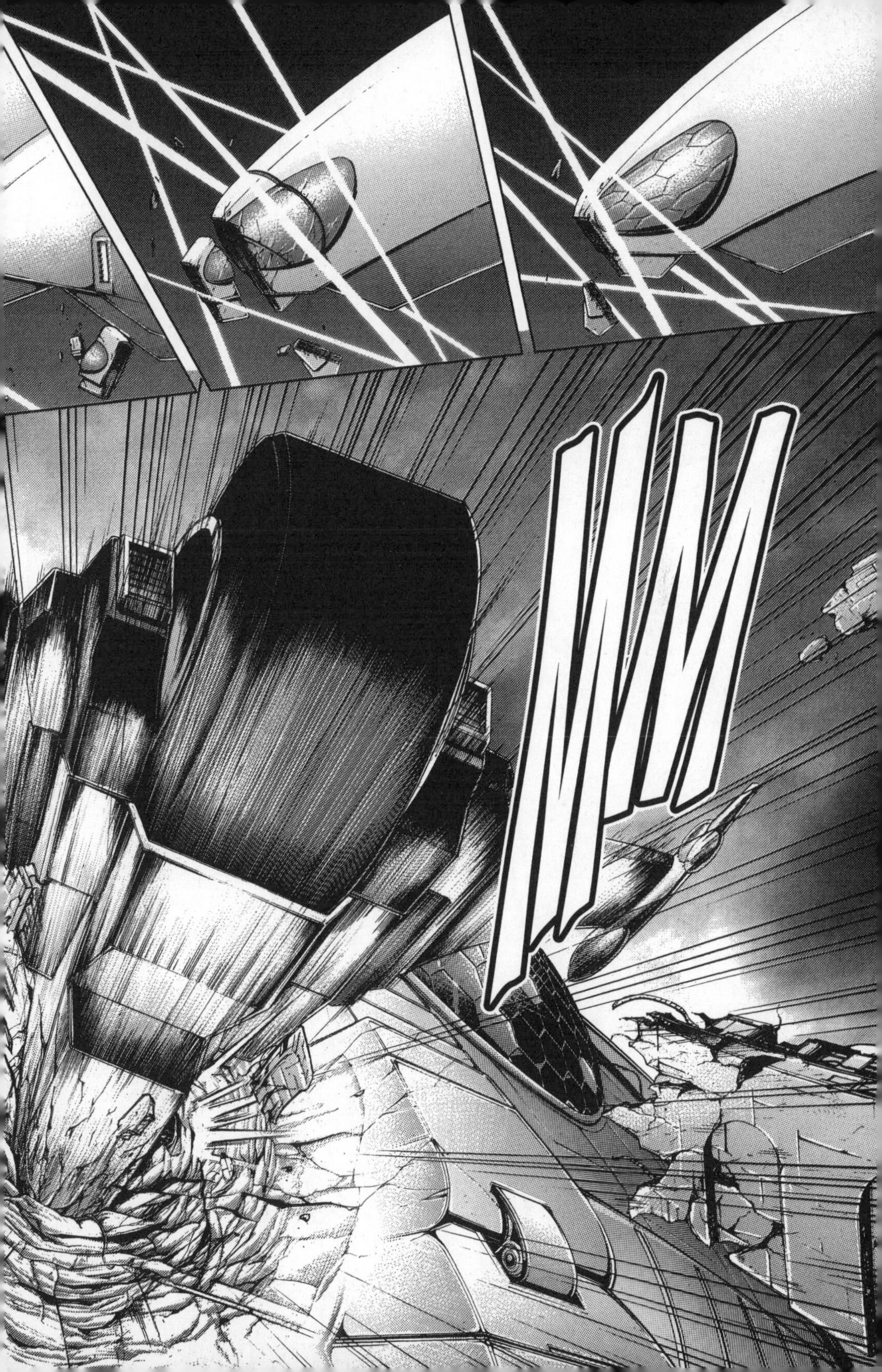

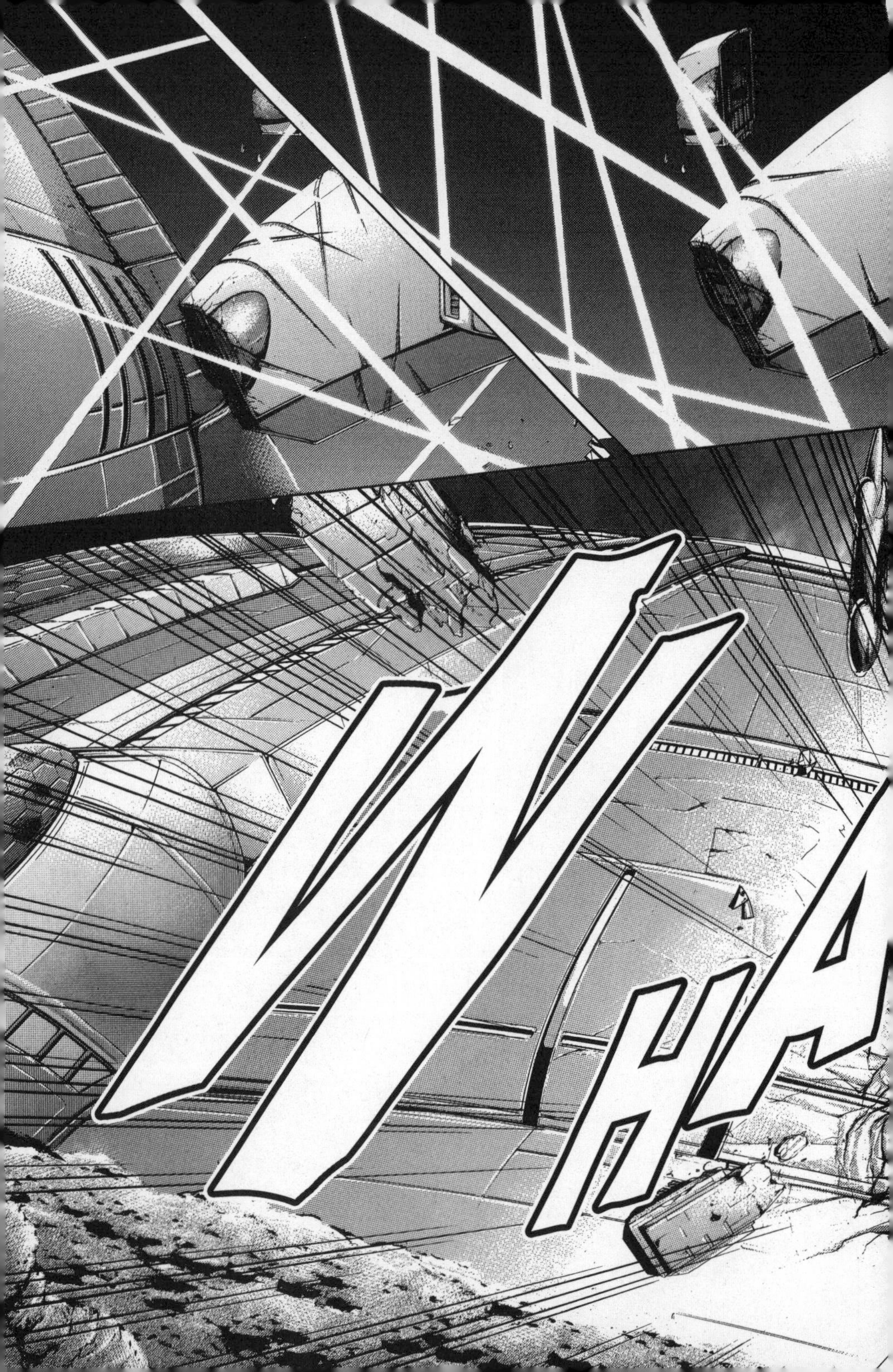
WHA

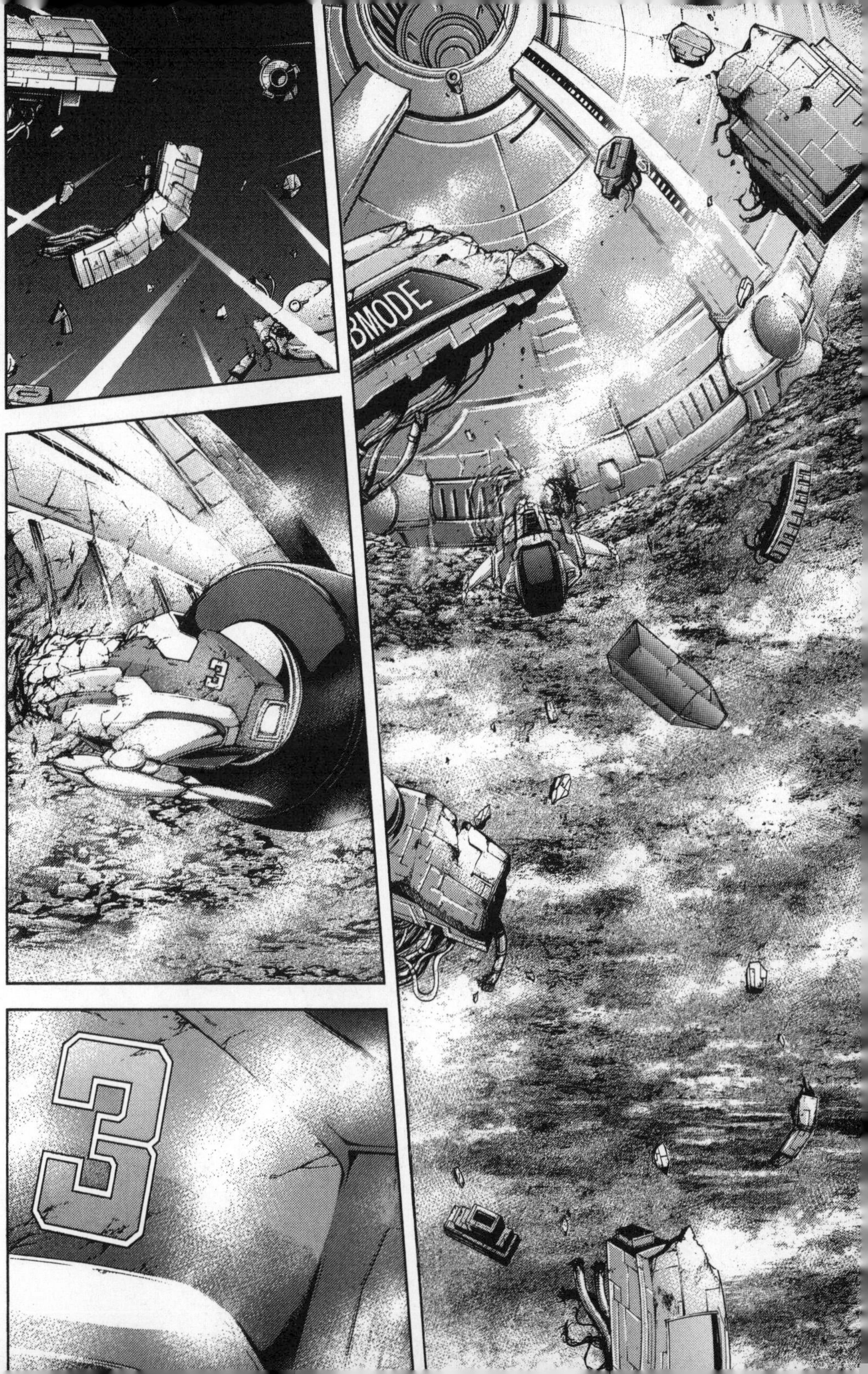
BMODE
3
3

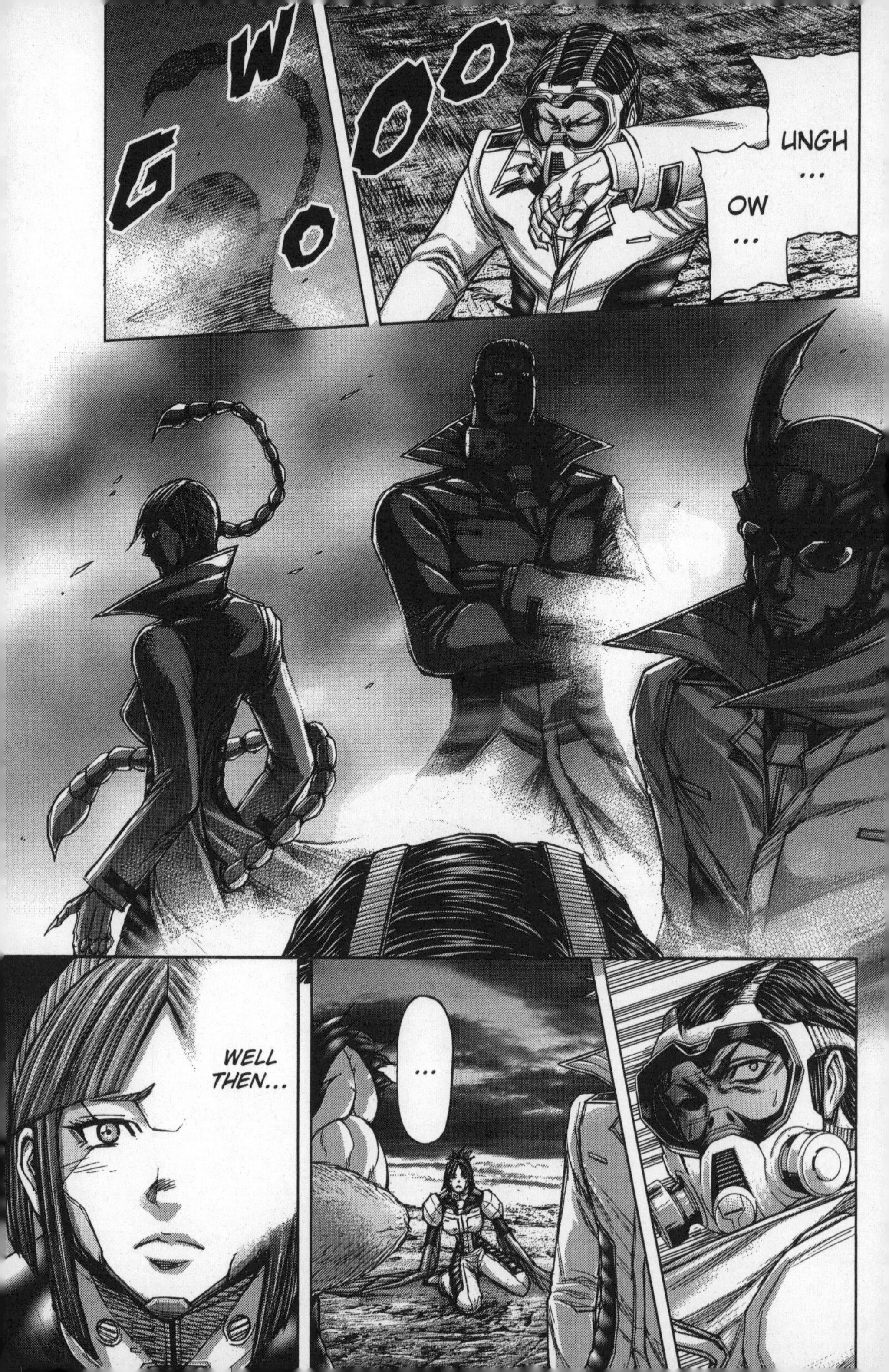
UNGH ...
OW ...
GWOOOO
...
WELL THEN...

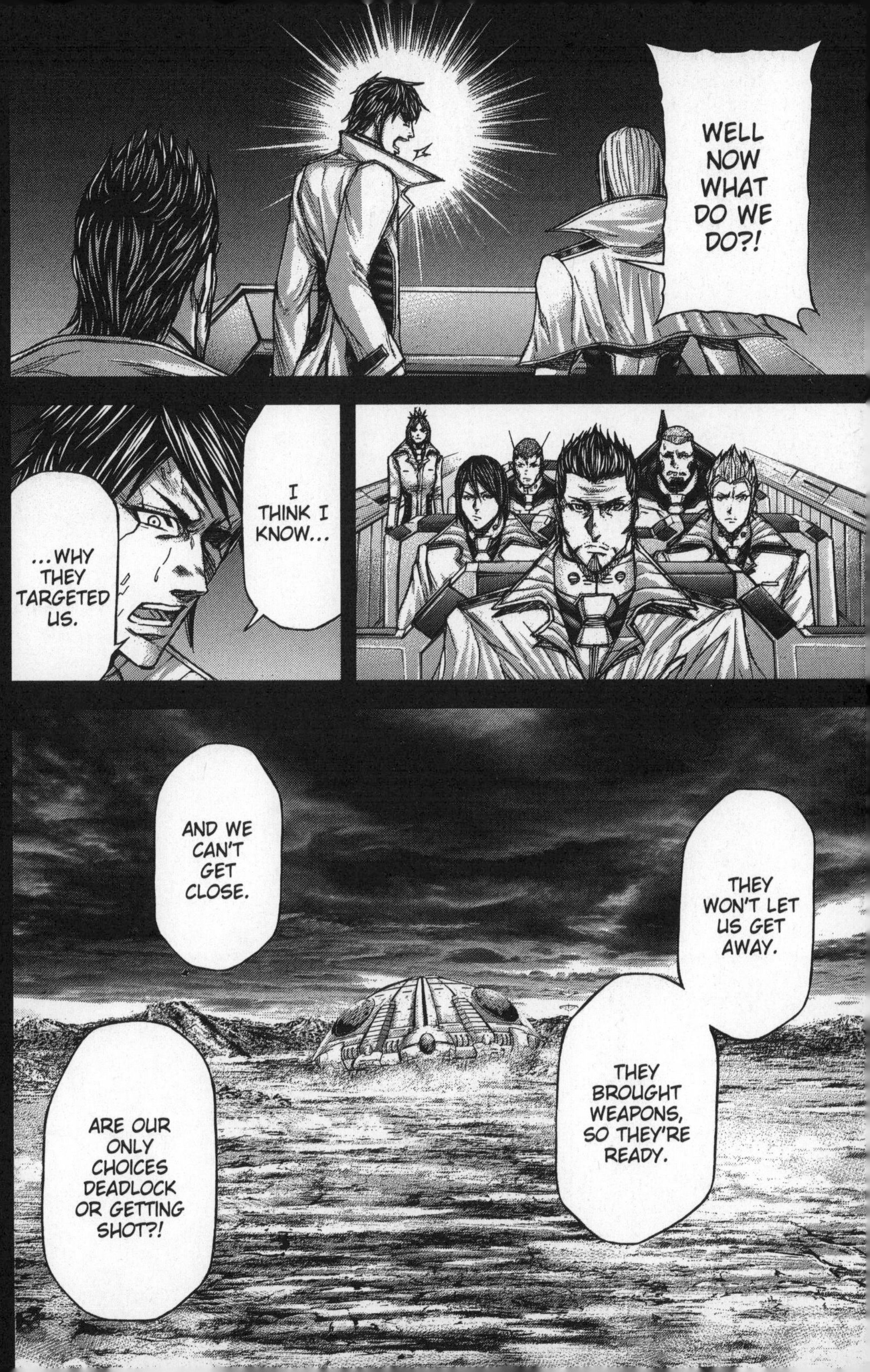
WELL NOW WHAT DO WE DO?!
I THINK I KNOW...
...WHY THEY TARGETED US.
THEY WON'T LET US GET AWAY.
AND WE CAN'T GET CLOSE.
THEY BROUGHT WEAPONS, SO THEY'RE READY.
ARE OUR ONLY CHOICES DEADLOCK OR GETTING SHOT?!

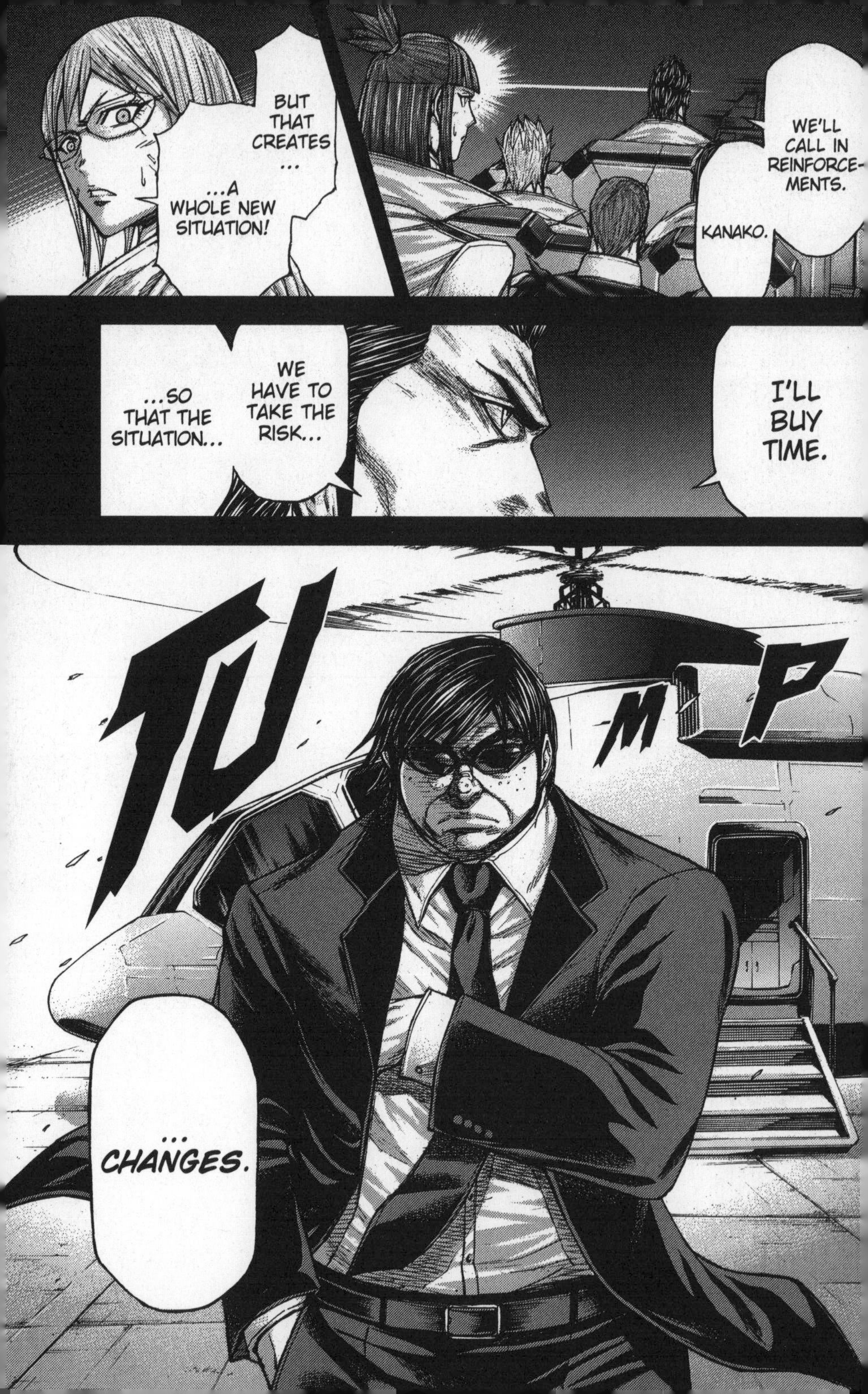

WE'LL CALL IN REINFORCE-MENTS.
KANAKO.
BUT THAT CREATES...
...A WHOLE NEW SITUATION!
I'LL BUY TIME.
WE HAVE TO TAKE THE RISK...
...SO THAT THE SITUATION...
TUMP
...CHANGES.

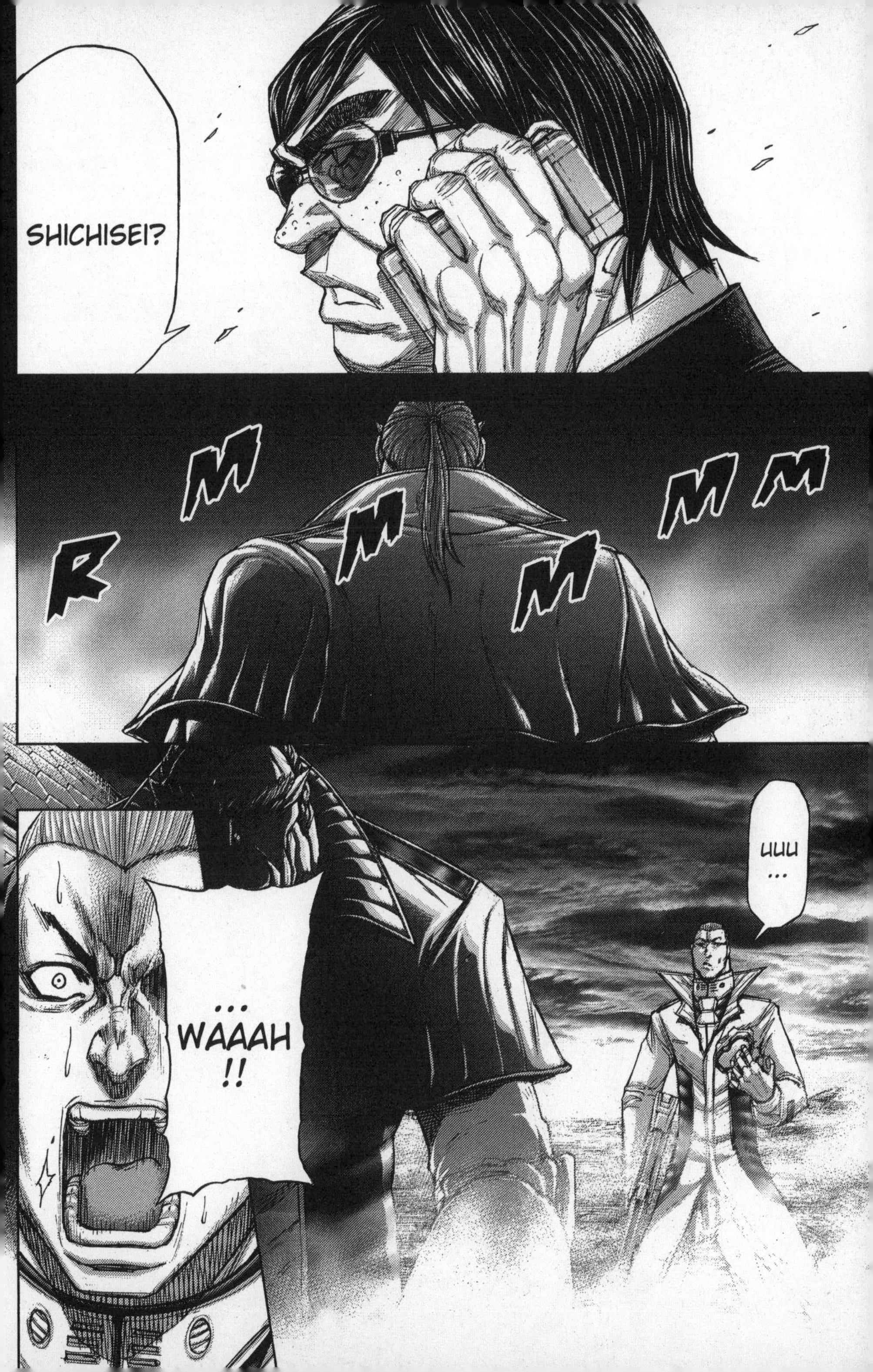
SHICHISEI?
RMMMMM
UUU ...
... WAAAH !!

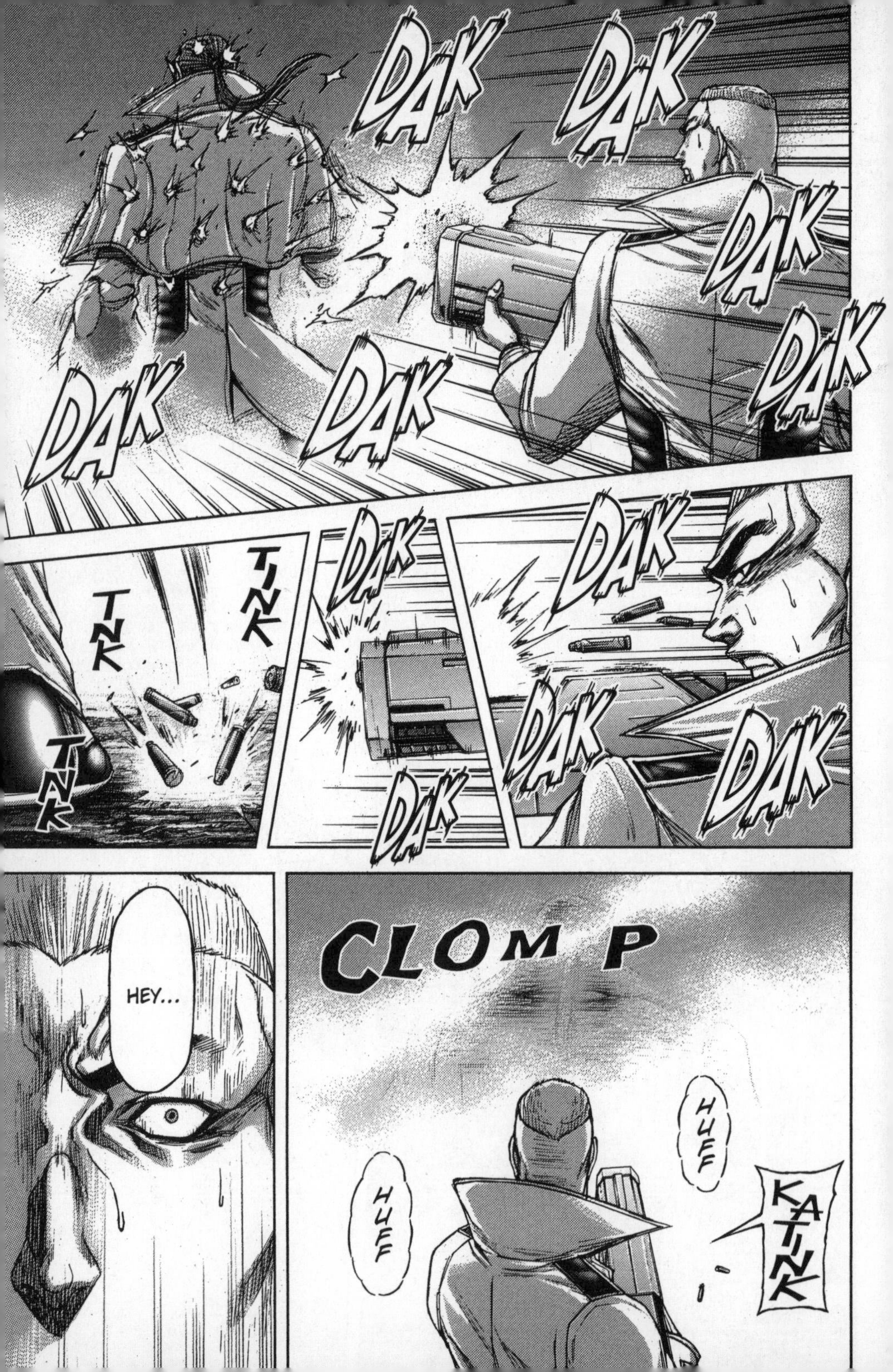
DAK
DAK
DAK
DAK
DAK
DAK
DAK
DAK
DAK
DAK
DAK
TINK
TNK
TNK
CLOMP
HUFF
KATINK
HUFF
HEY...

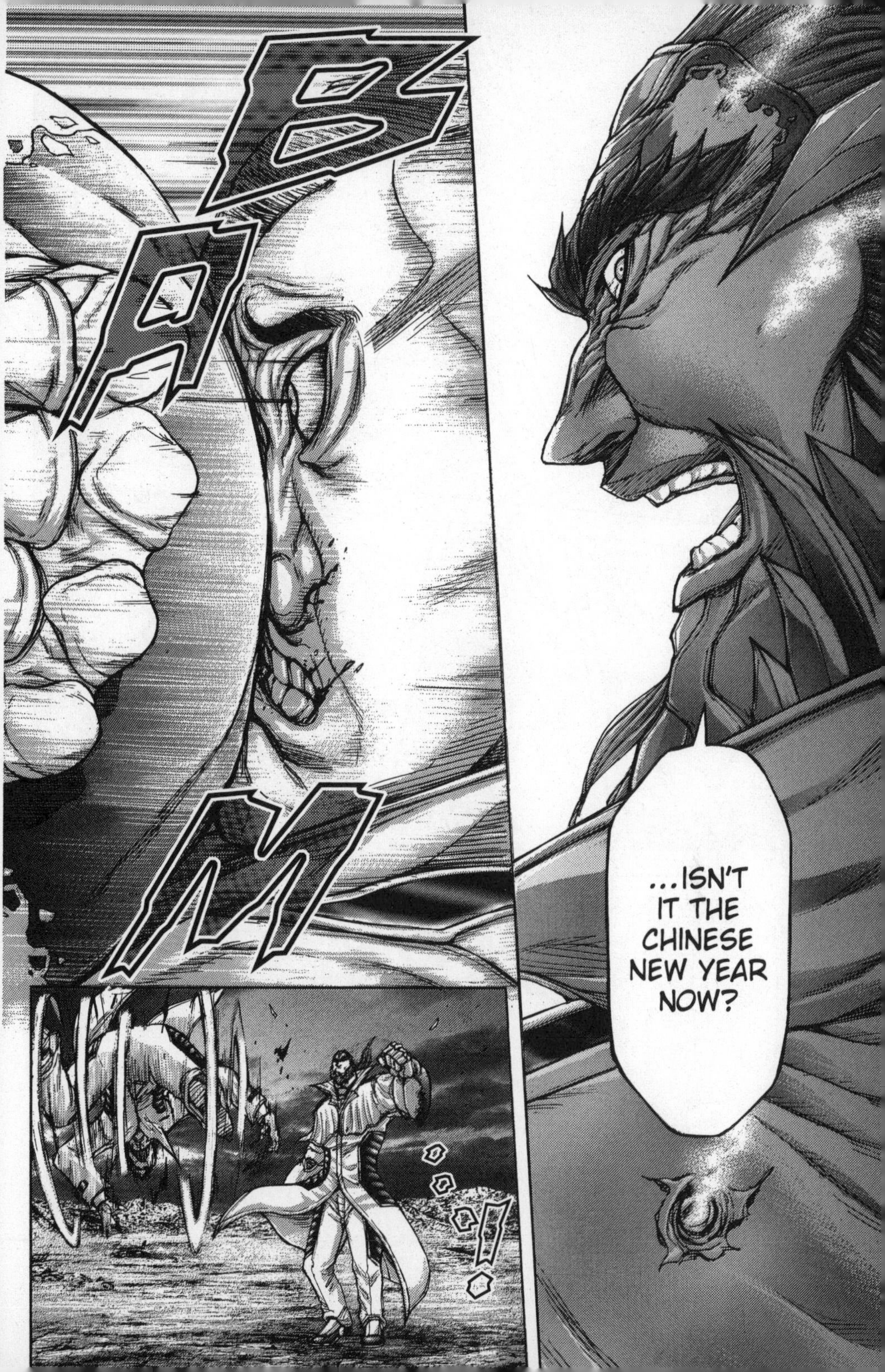
...ISN'T IT THE CHINESE NEW YEAR NOW?
BAM

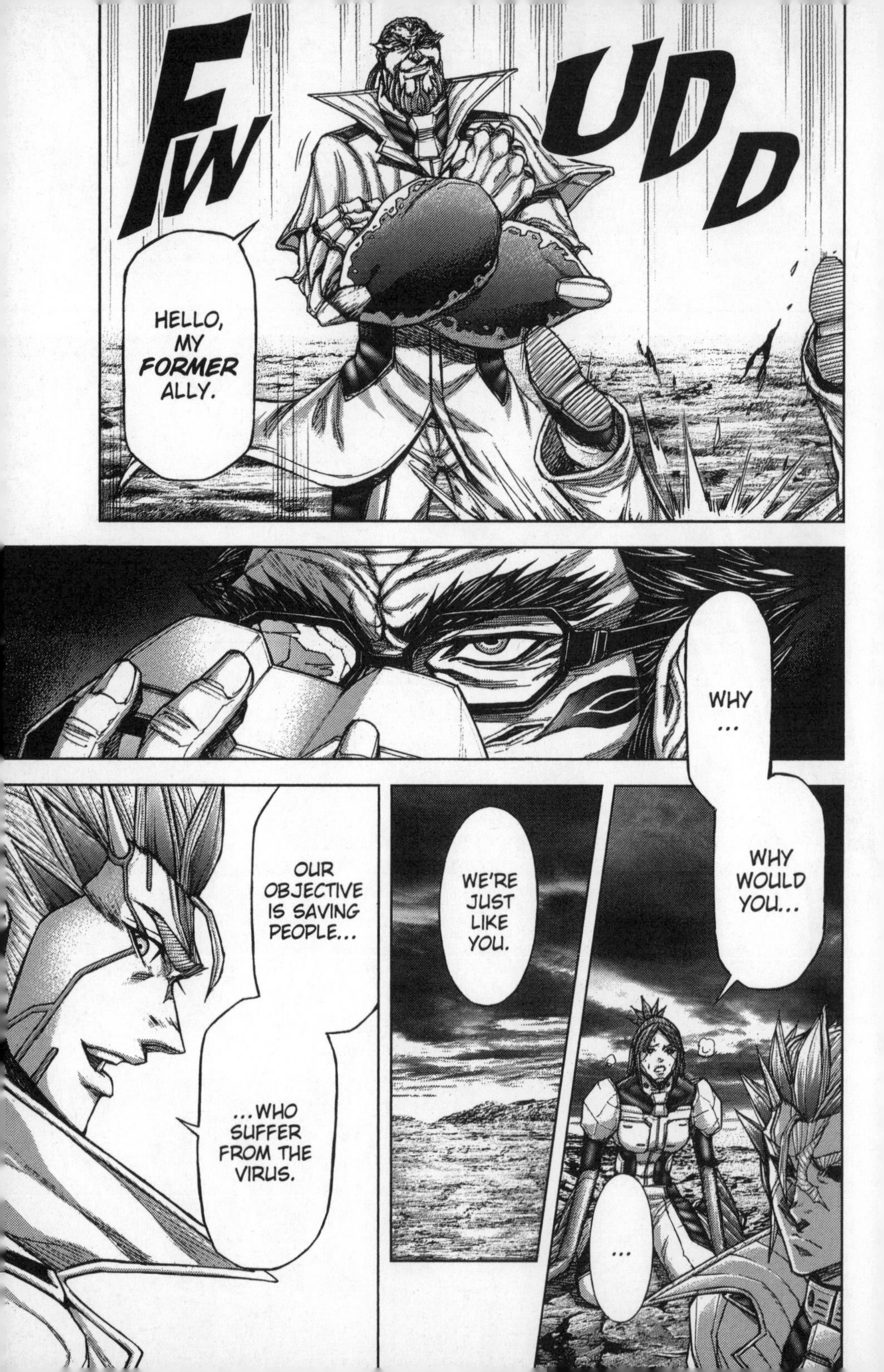
FWUDD
HELLO, MY FORMER ALLY.
WHY...
WHY WOULD YOU...
...
WE'RE JUST LIKE YOU.
OUR OBJECTIVE IS SAVING PEOPLE...
...WHO SUFFER FROM THE VIRUS.

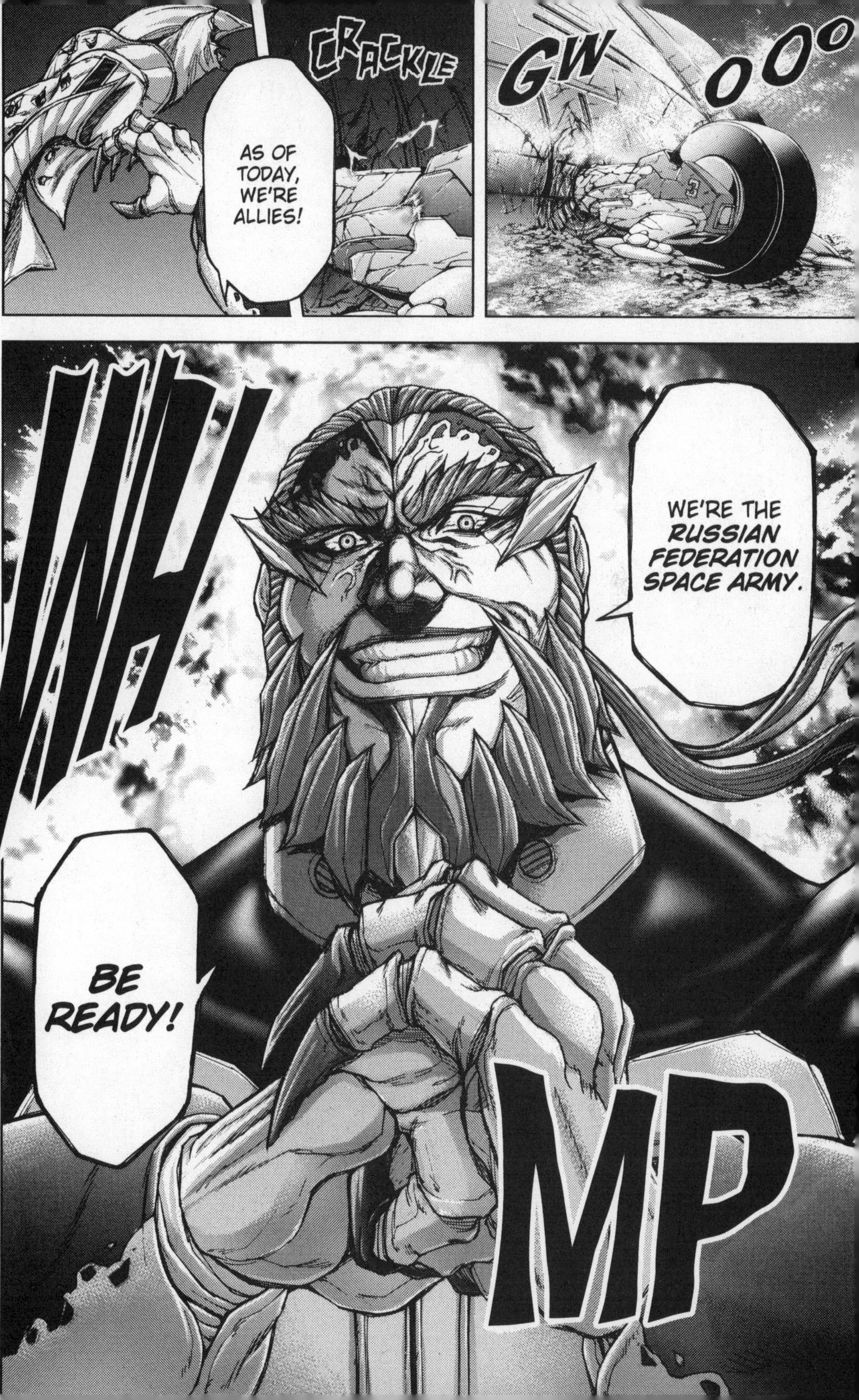
GWOOO
CRACKLE
AS OF TODAY, WE'RE ALLIES!
WE'RE THE RUSSIAN FEDERATION SPACE ARMY.
BE READY!
MP

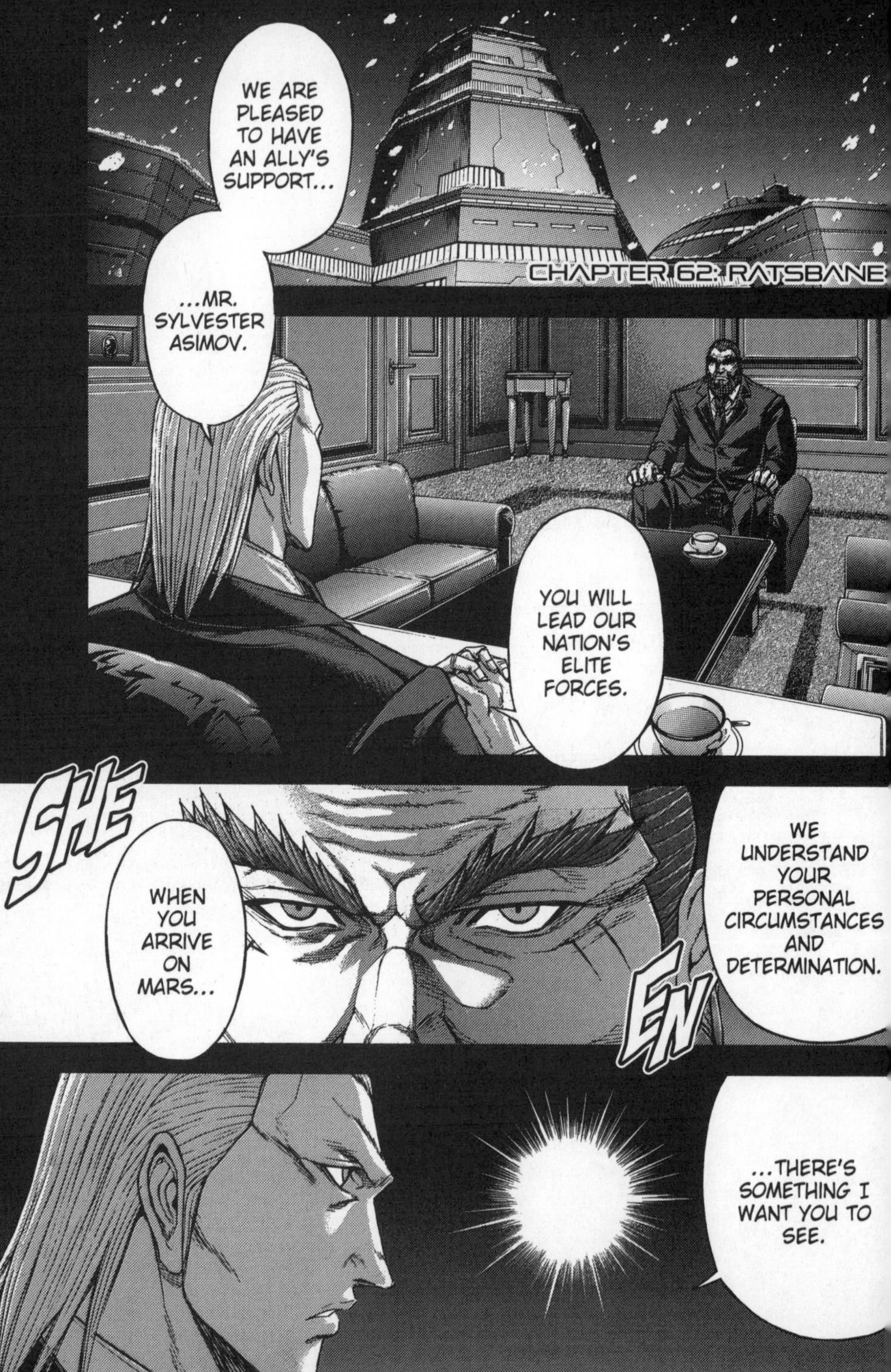
CHAPTER 62: RATSBANE
WE ARE PLEASED TO HAVE AN ALLY'S SUPPORT...
...MR. SYLVESTER ASIMOV.
YOU WILL LEAD OUR NATION'S ELITE FORCES.
WE UNDERSTAND YOUR PERSONAL CIRCUMSTANCES AND DETERMINATION.
EN
WHEN YOU ARRIVE ON MARS...
SHE
...THERE'S SOMETHING I WANT YOU TO SEE.

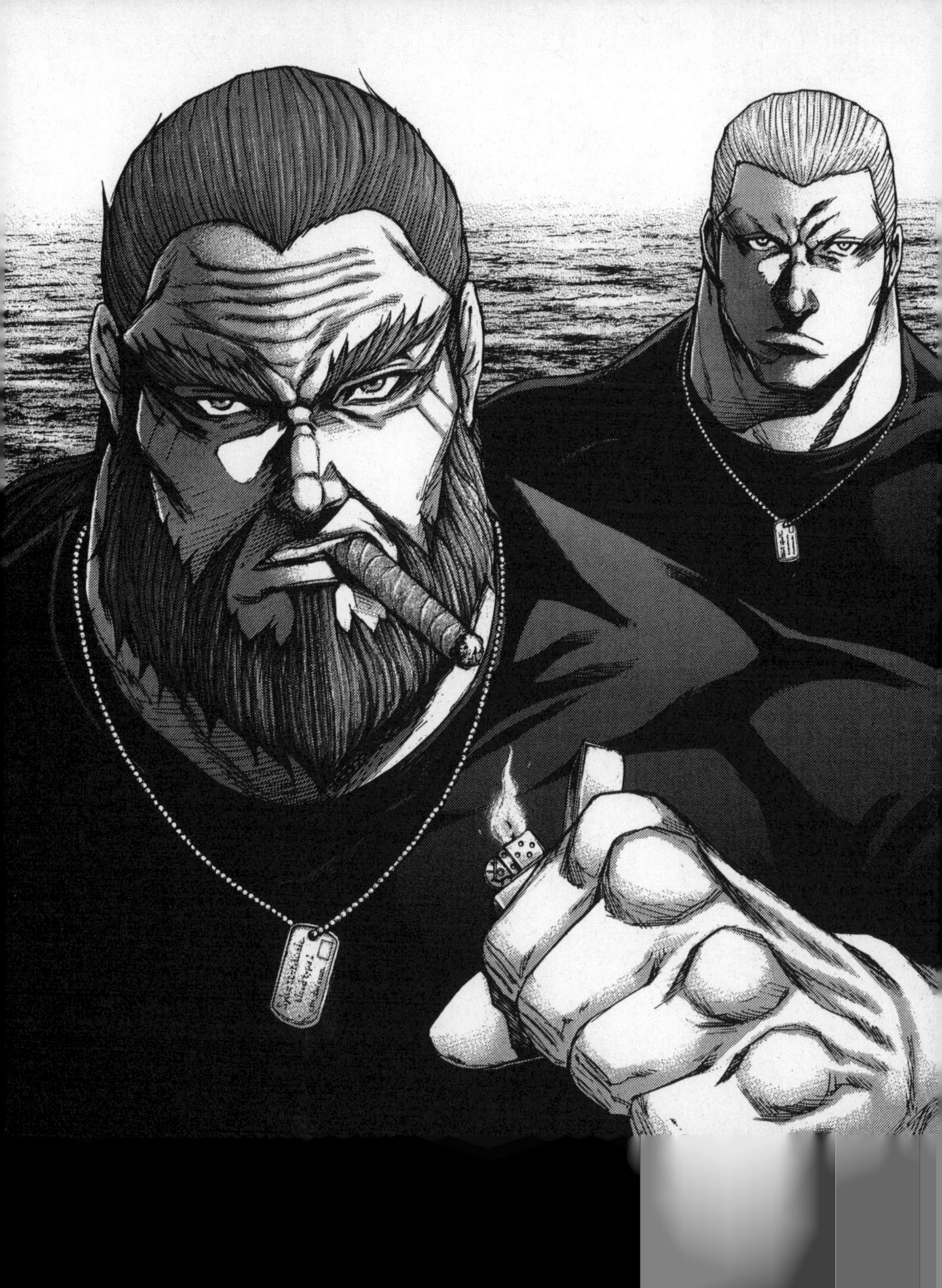

CHAPTER 62: RATSBANE

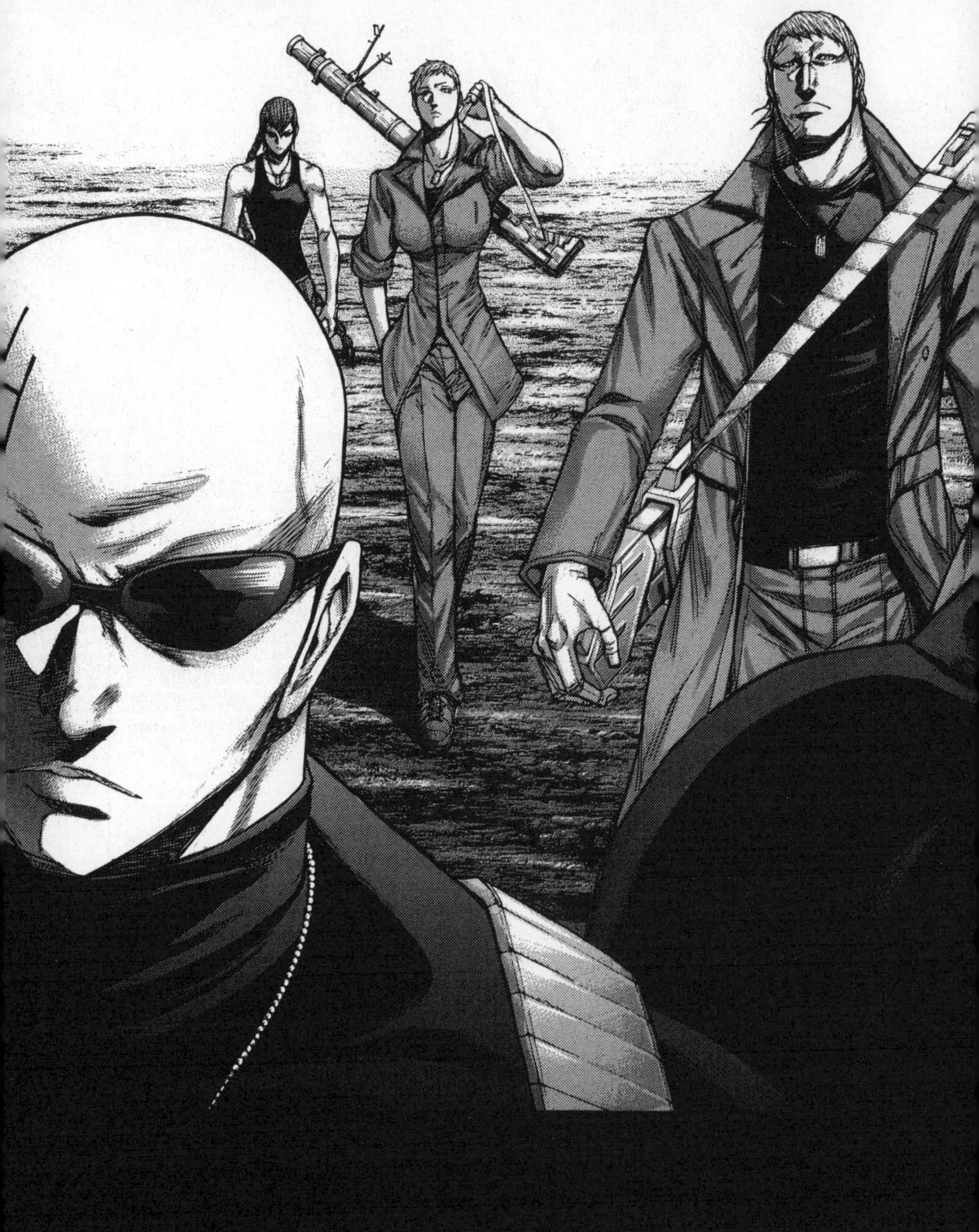

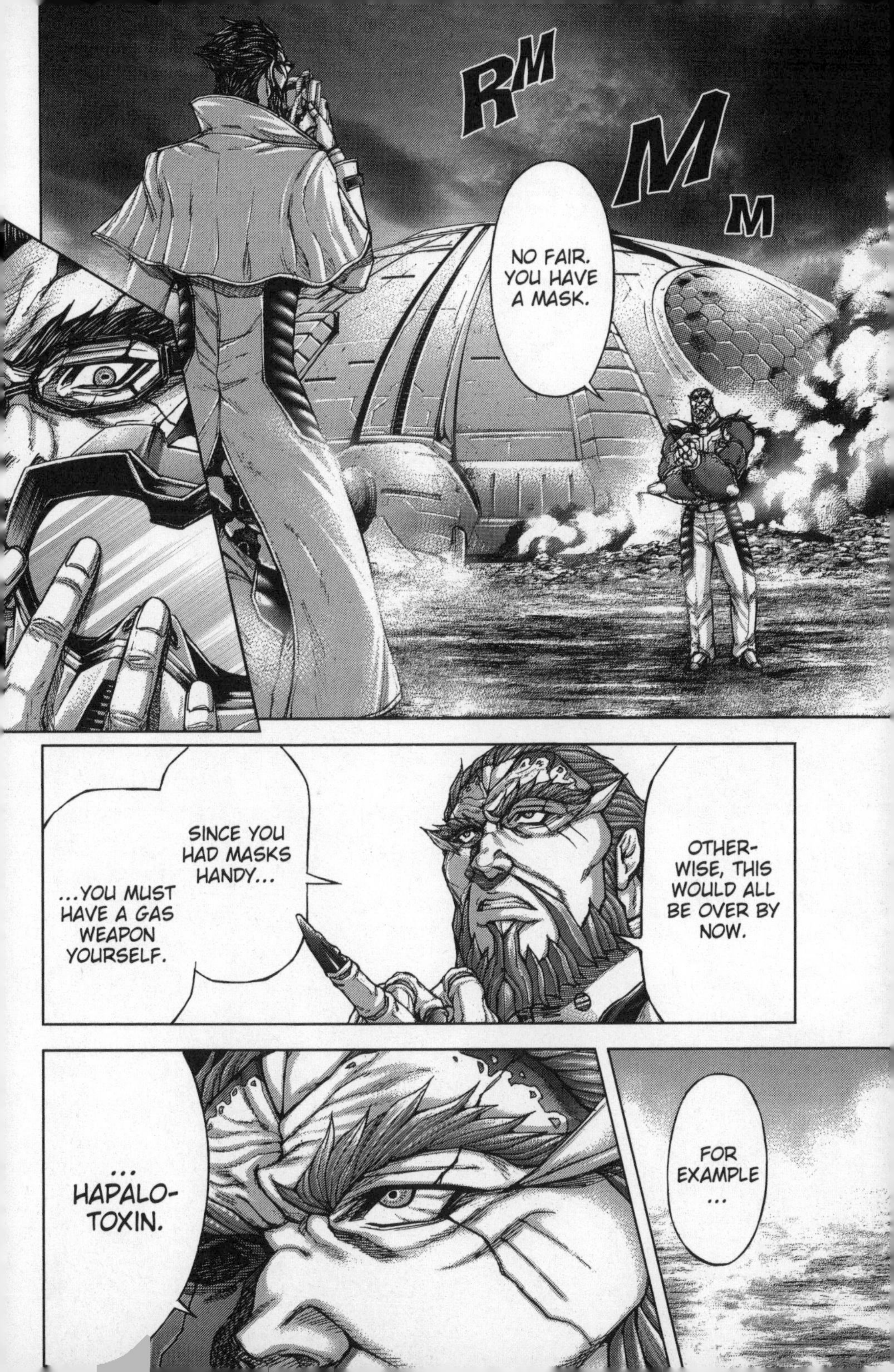
RMMM
NO FAIR. YOU HAVE A MASK.
OTHER-WISE, THIS WOULD ALL BE OVER BY NOW.
SINCE YOU HAD MASKS HANDY...
...YOU MUST HAVE A GAS WEAPON YOURSELF.
FOR EXAMPLE ...
... HAPALO-TOXIN.

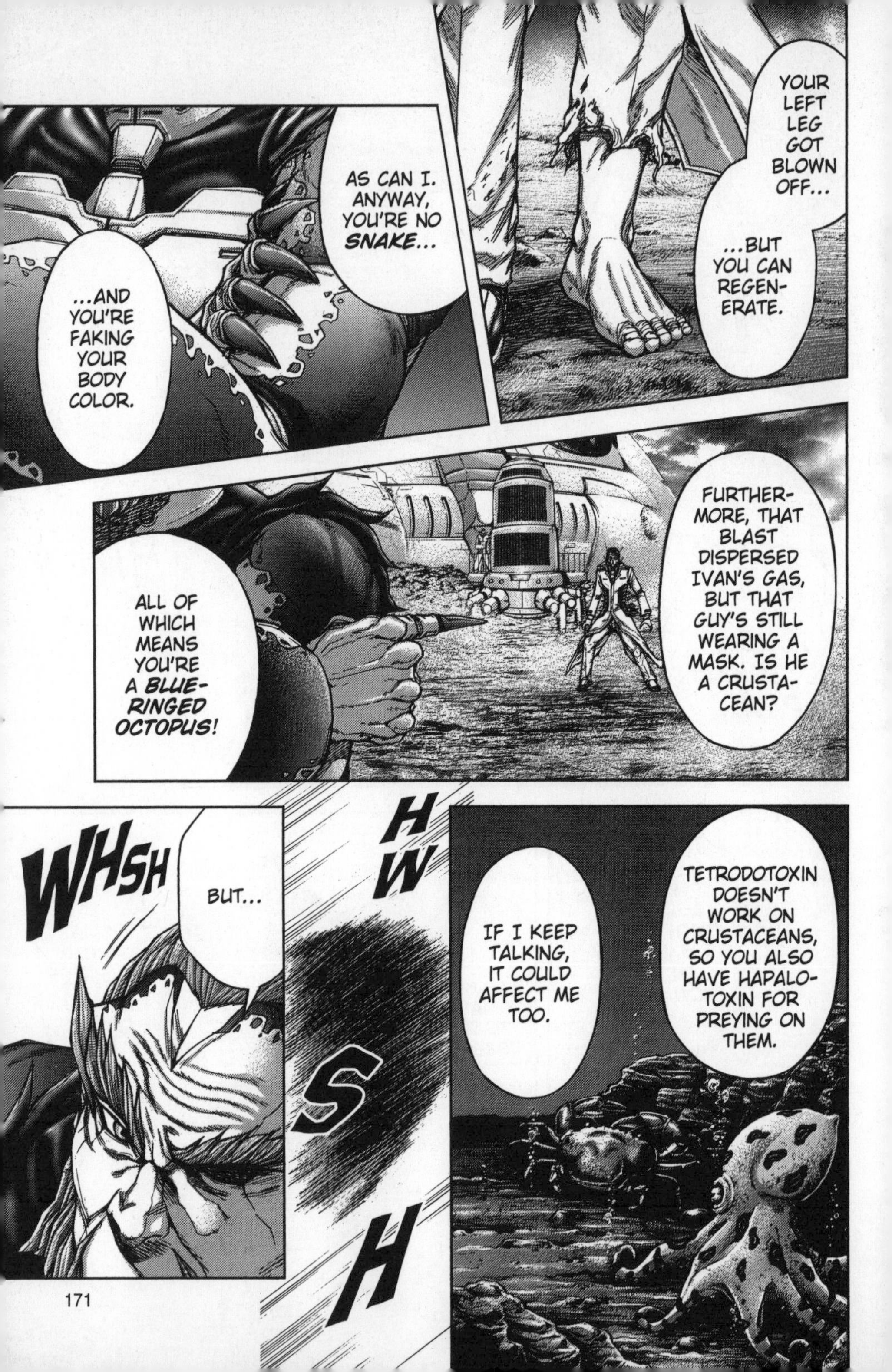
YOUR LEFT LEG GOT BLOWN OFF...
...BUT YOU CAN REGENERATE.
AS CAN I. ANYWAY, YOU'RE NO SNAKE...
...AND YOU'RE FAKING YOUR BODY COLOR.
FURTHERMORE, THAT BLAST DISPERSED IVAN'S GAS, BUT THAT GUY'S STILL WEARING A MASK. IS HE A CRUSTACEAN?
ALL OF WHICH MEANS YOU'RE A BLUE-RINGED OCTOPUS!
TETRODOTOXIN DOESN'T WORK ON CRUSTACEANS, SO YOU ALSO HAVE HAPALOTOXIN FOR PREYING ON THEM.
IF I KEEP TALKING, IT COULD AFFECT ME TOO.
HWSH
BUT...
WHSH

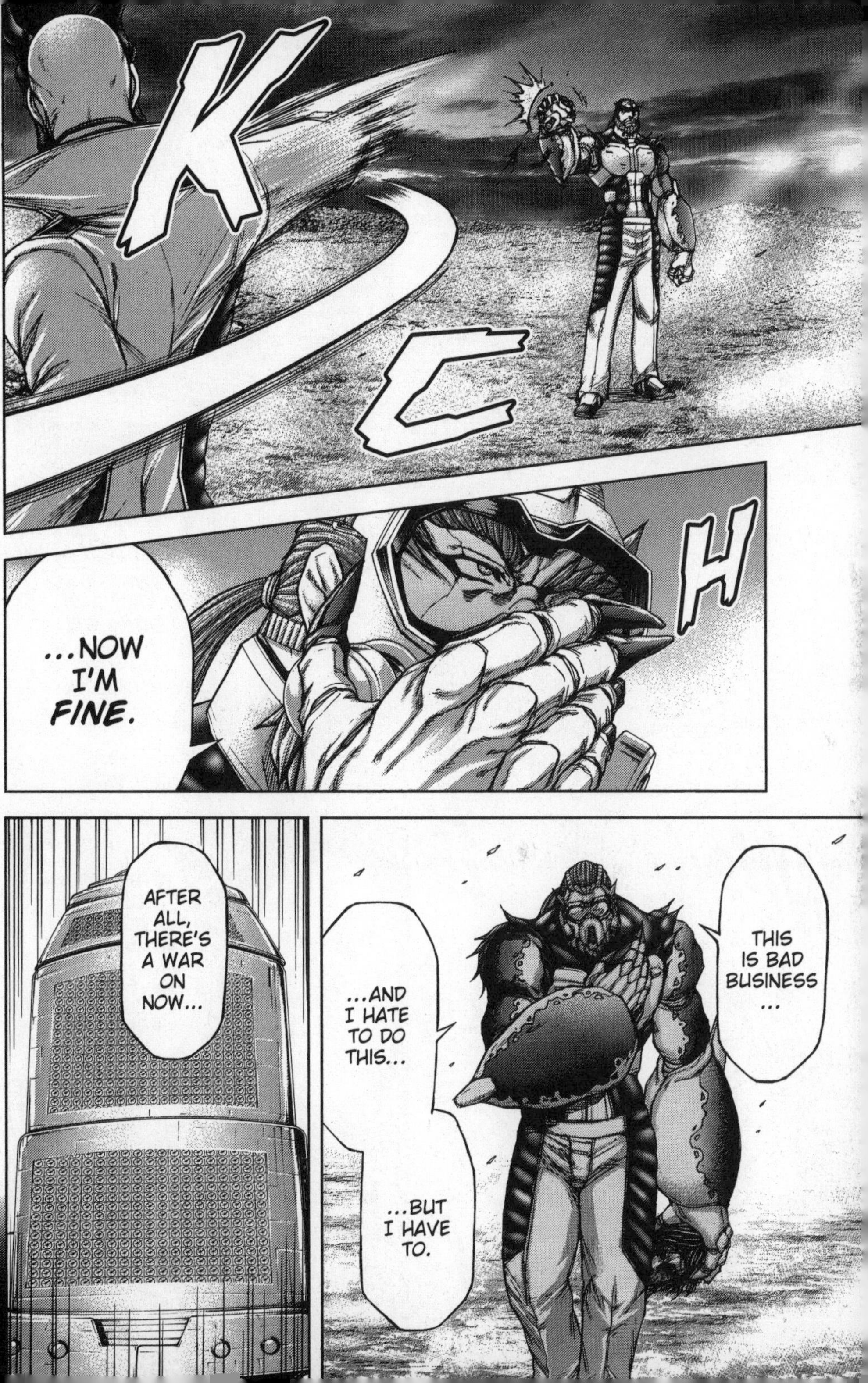
KCH
...NOW I'M FINE.
THIS IS BAD BUSINESS ...
...AND I HATE TO DO THIS...
...BUT I HAVE TO.
AFTER ALL, THERE'S A WAR ON NOW...

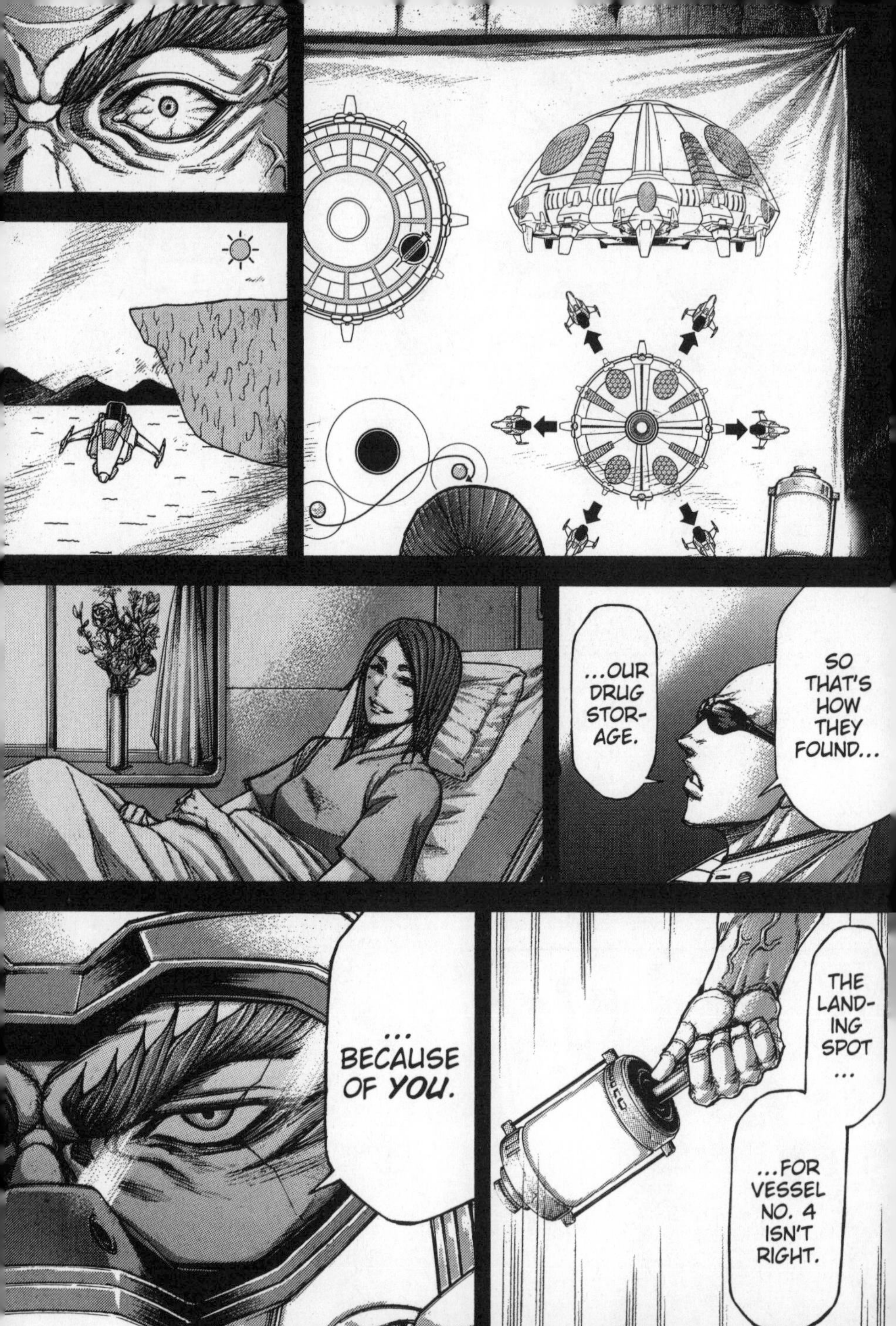
SO THAT'S HOW THEY FOUND...
...OUR DRUG STOR-AGE.
THE LAND-ING SPOT...
...FOR VESSEL NO. 4 ISN'T RIGHT.
...BECAUSE OF YOU.

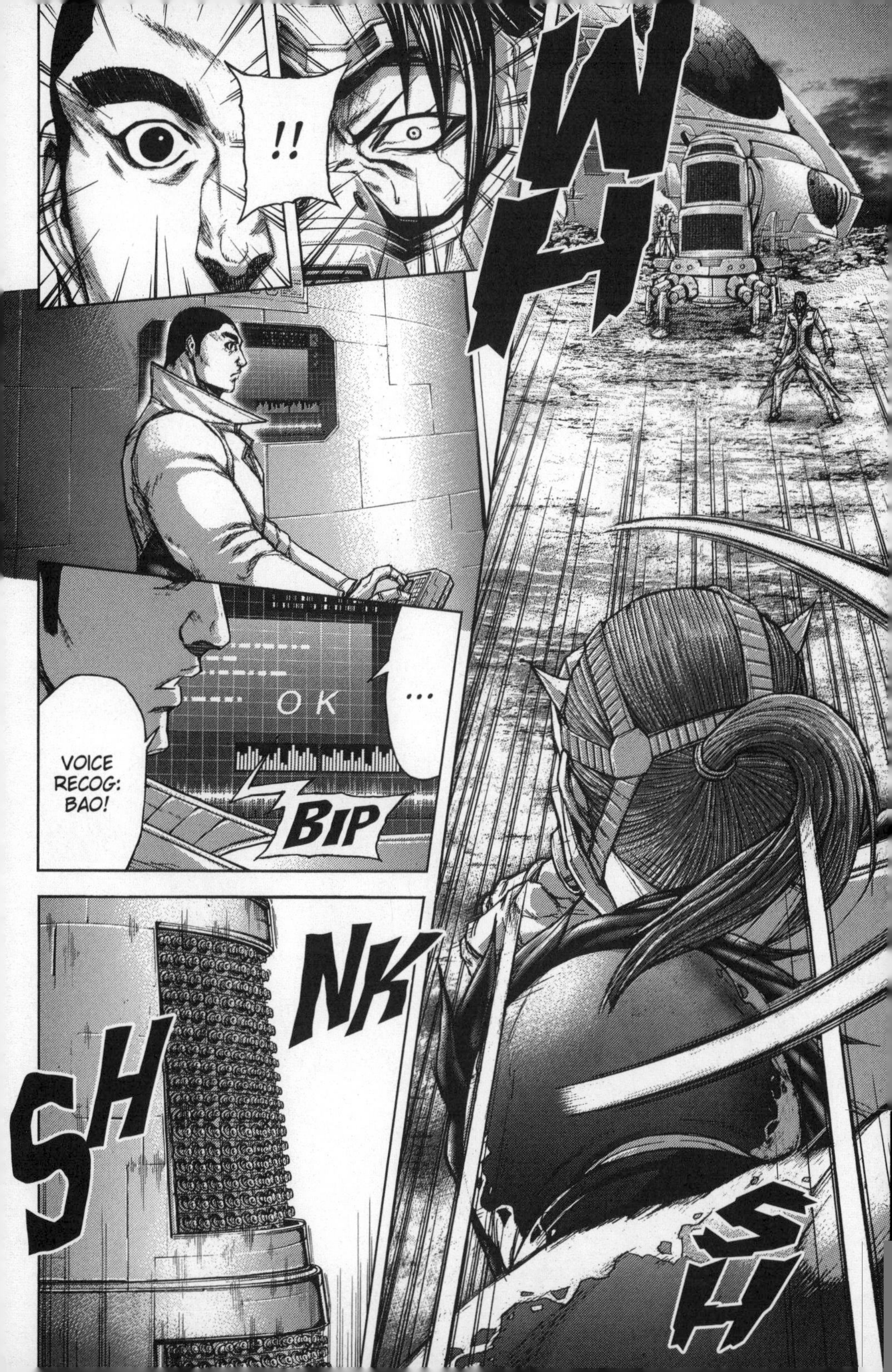
SH
!!
...
OK
VOICE RECOG: BAO!
BIP
SH
NK

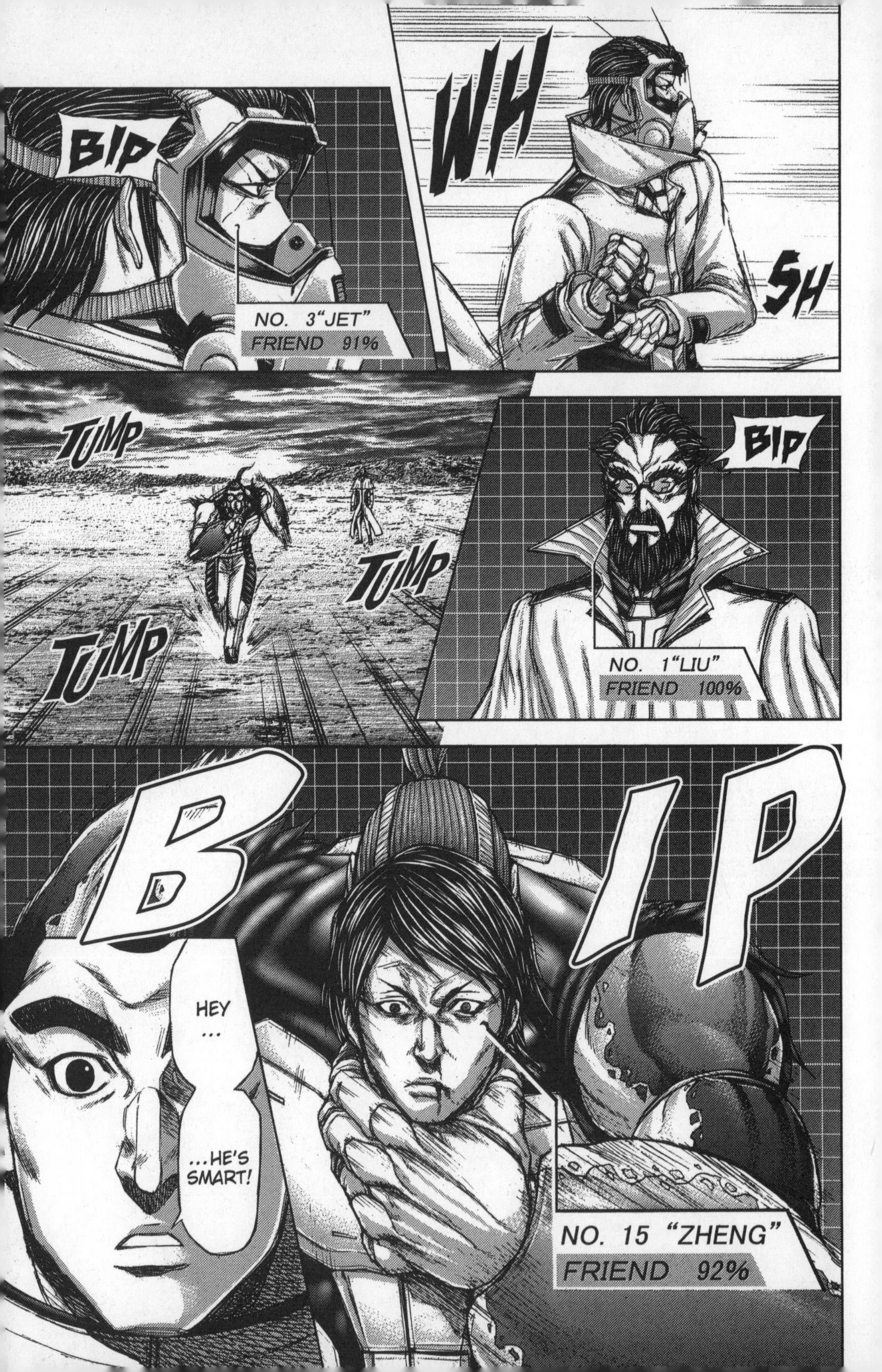
WH
SH
BIP
NO. 3 "JET"
FRIEND 91%
BIP
NO. 1 "LIU"
FRIEND 100%
TUMP
TUMP
TUMP
BIP
HEY
...
...HE'S SMART!
NO. 15 "ZHENG"
FRIEND 92%

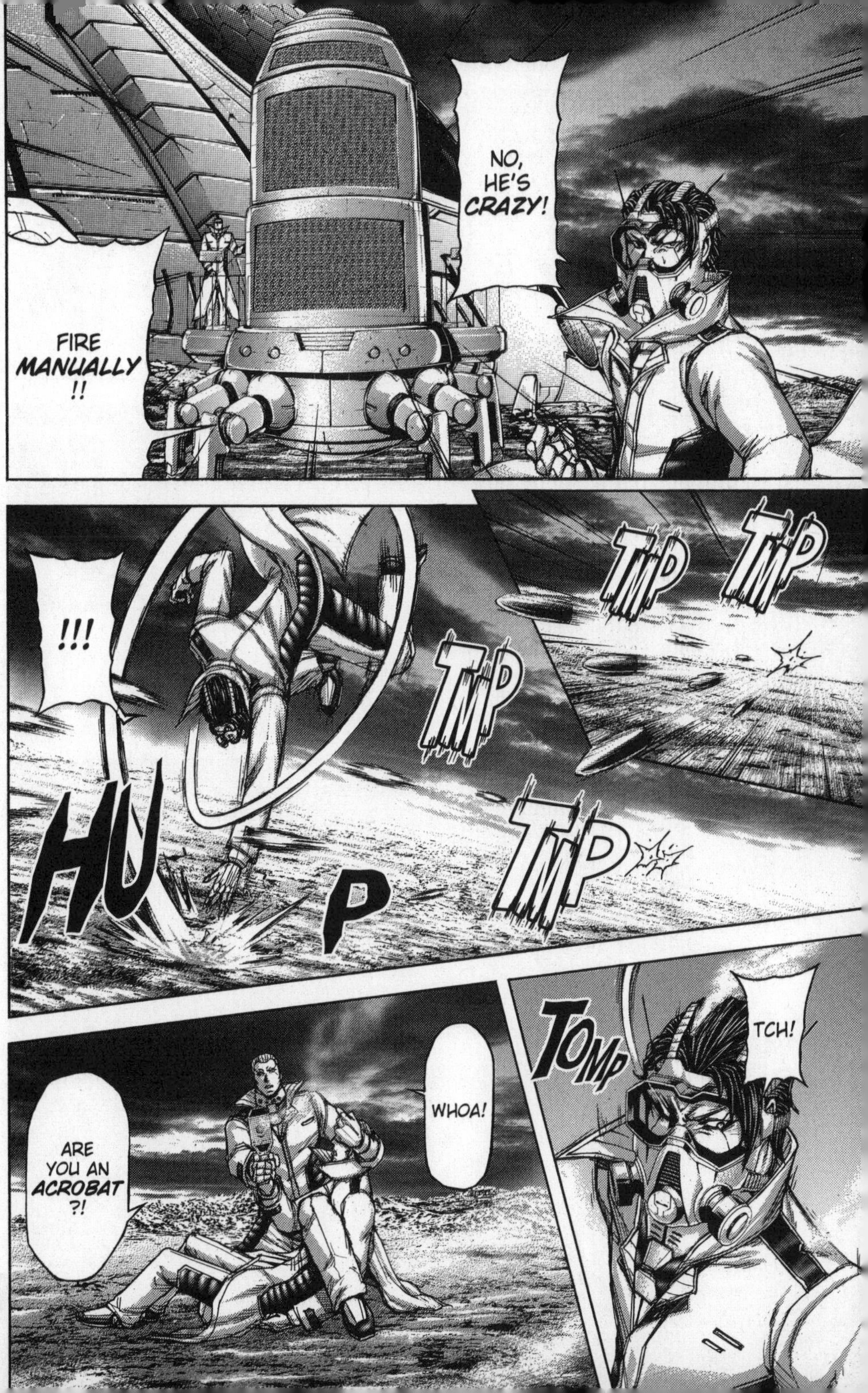

NO, HE'S CRAZY!
FIRE MANUALLY!!
TMP TMP
!!!
TMP
TMP
HUP
TCH!
TOMP
WHOA!
ARE YOU AN ACROBAT?!

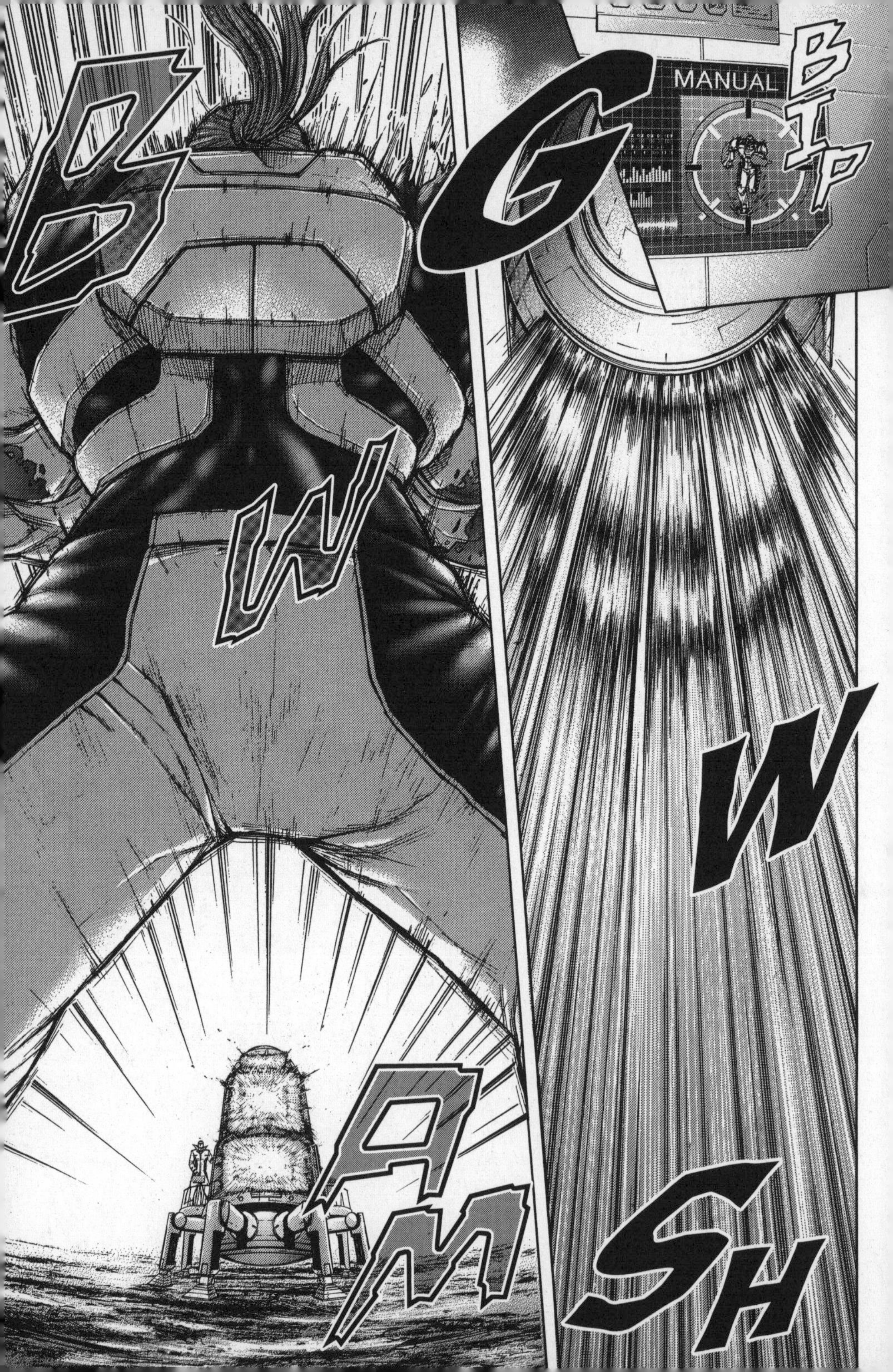
MANUAL
BIP
G
WSH
BWAM

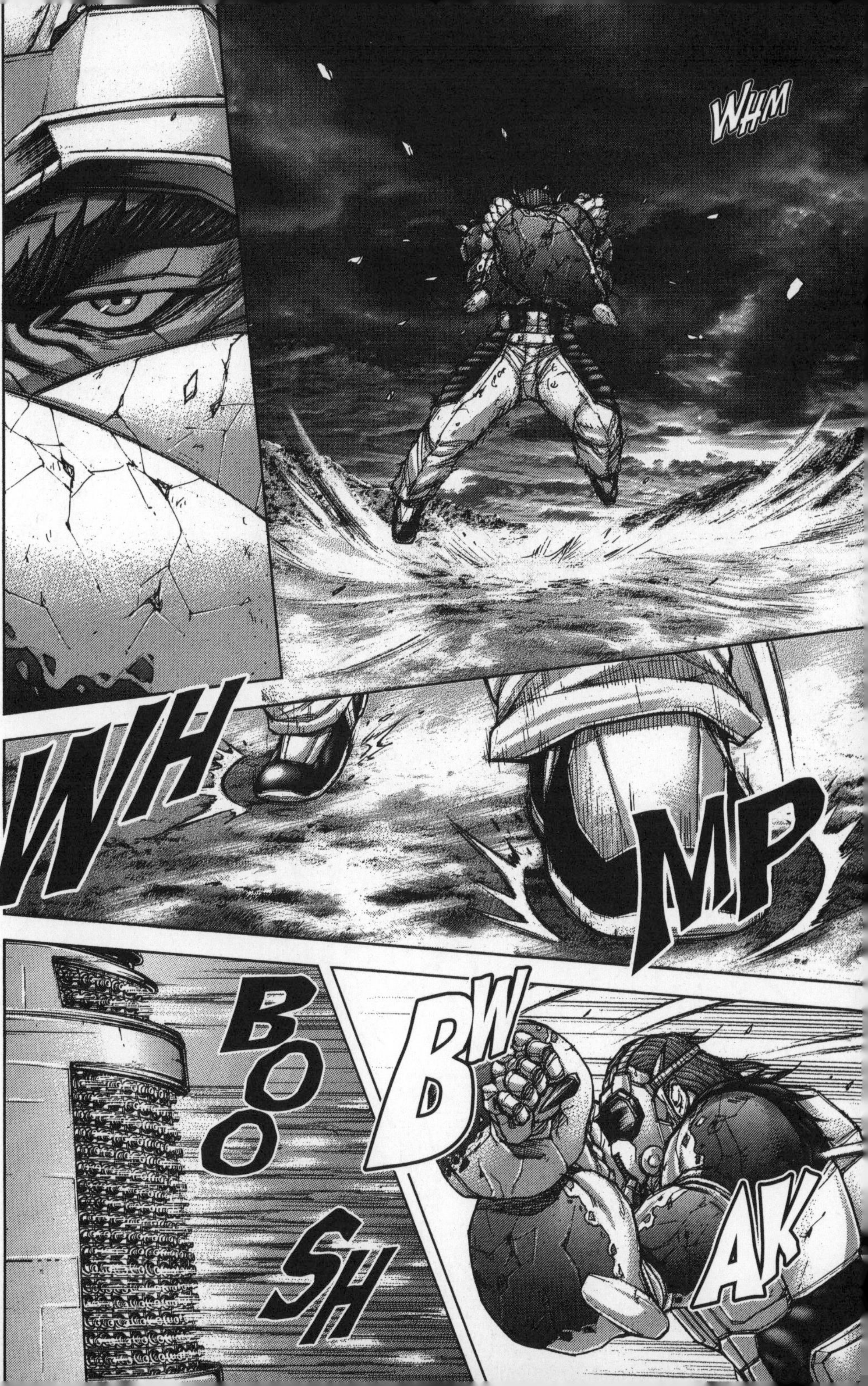
WHM
WH
UMP
BW
AK
BOO
SH

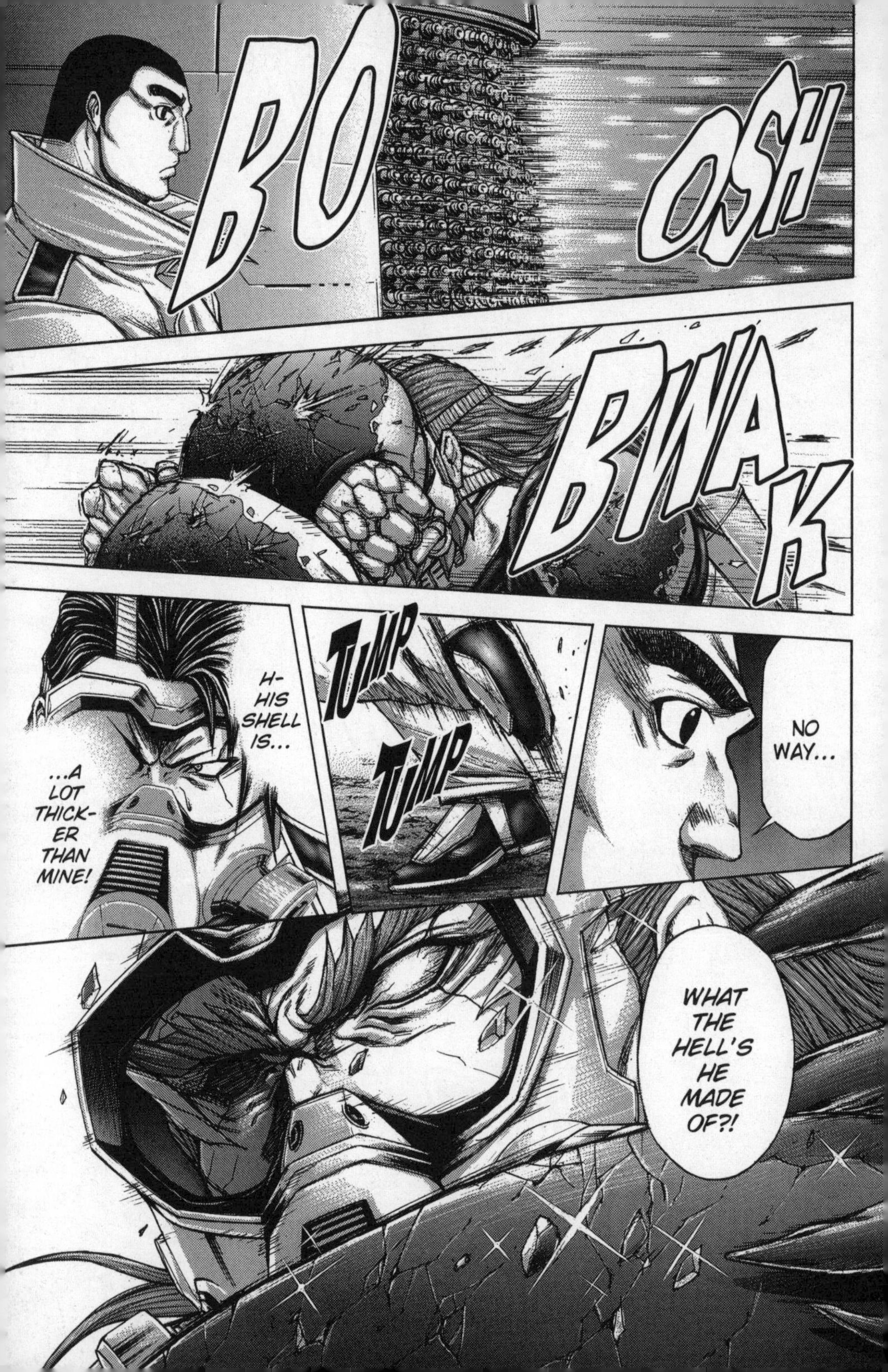
BOOSH
BWAK
NO WAY...
TUMP
TUMP
H-HIS SHELL IS...
...A LOT THICKER THAN MINE!
WHAT THE HELL'S HE MADE OF?!

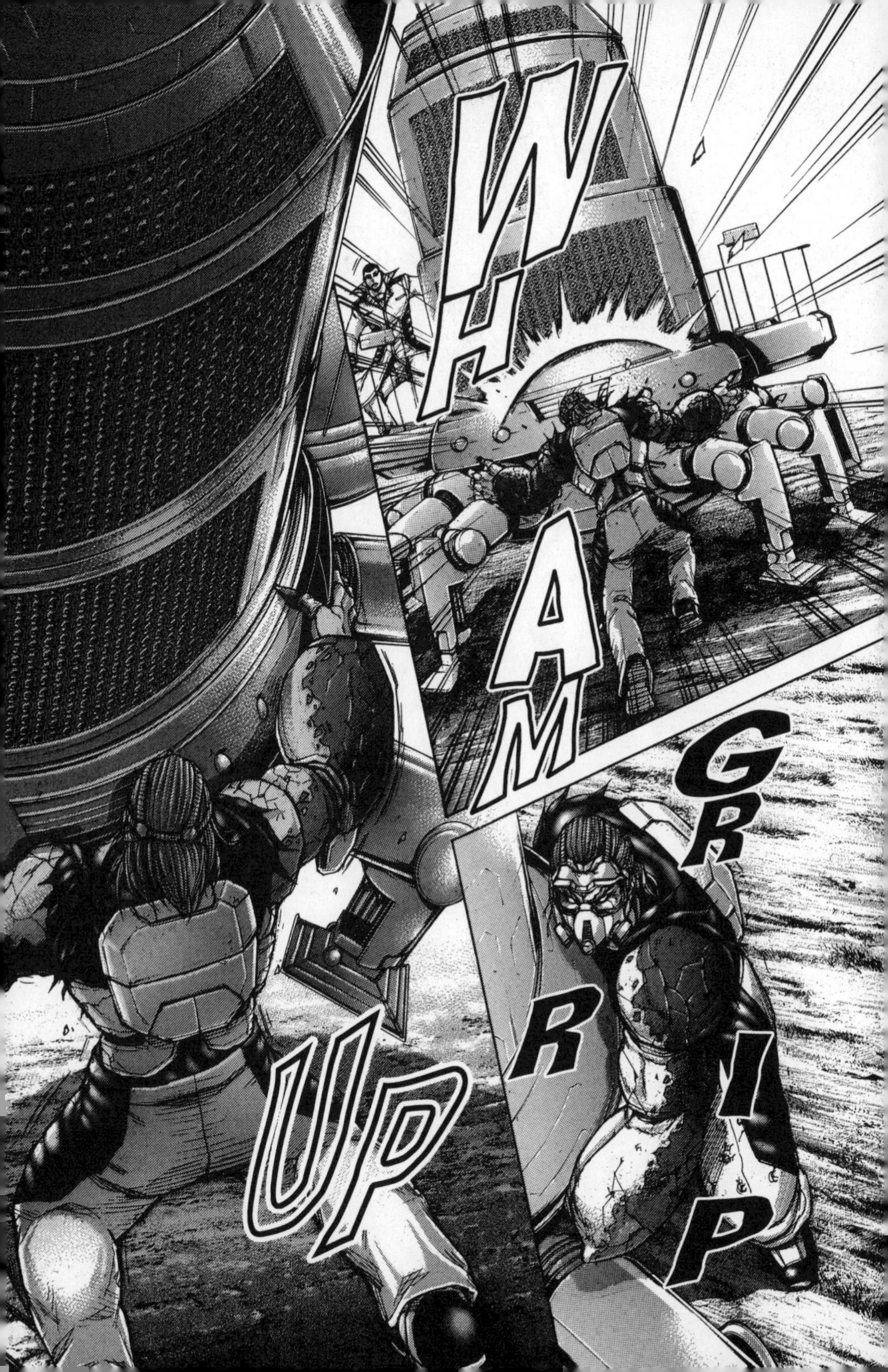
WHAM
GRIP
UP

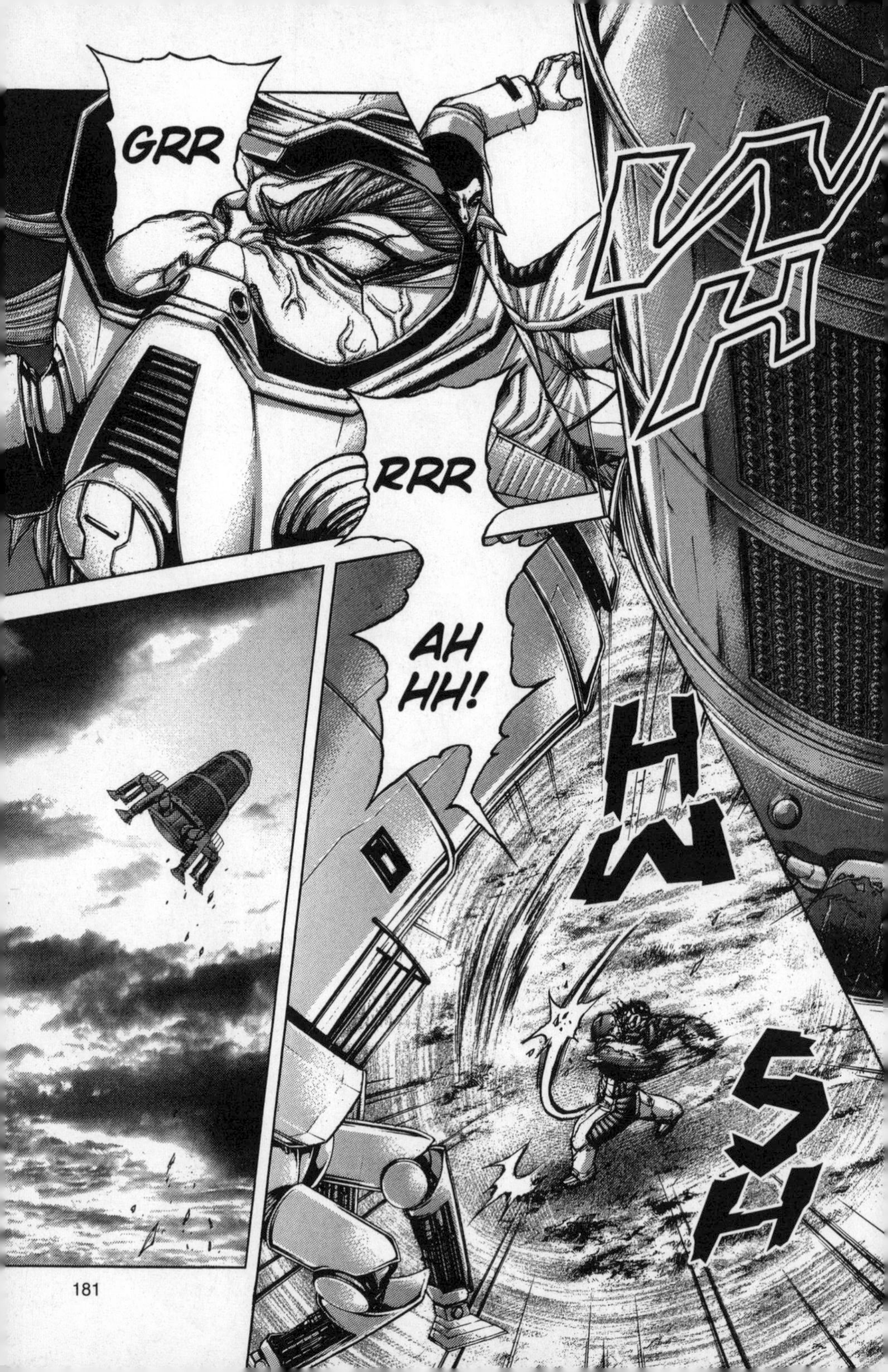
GRR
RRR
AH HH!

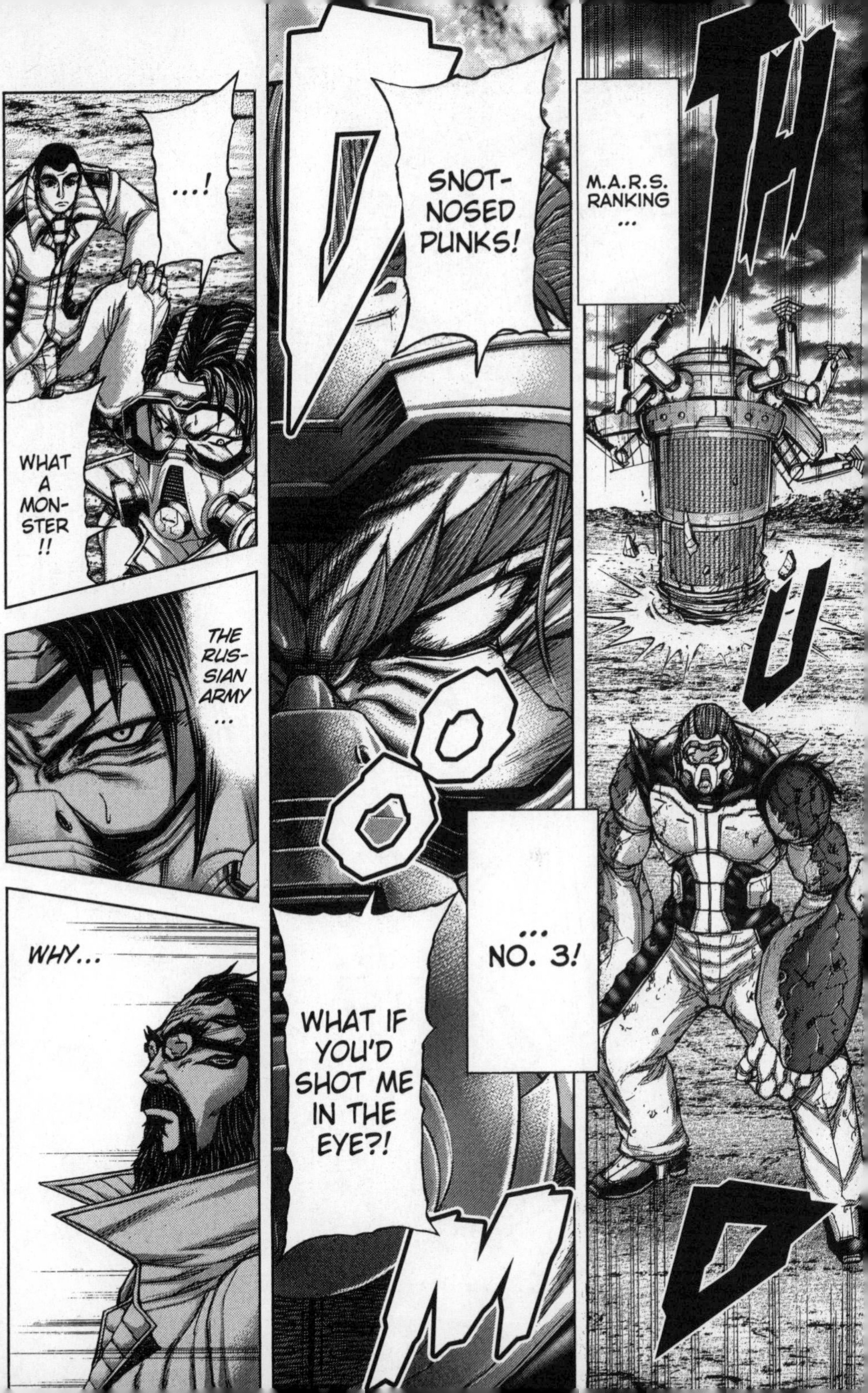
M.A.R.S. RANKING ...
THUD
... NO. 3!
SNOT-NOSED PUNKS!
DOOM
WHAT IF YOU'D SHOT ME IN THE EYE?!
...!
WHAT A MONSTER !!
THE RUSSIAN ARMY ...
WHY...

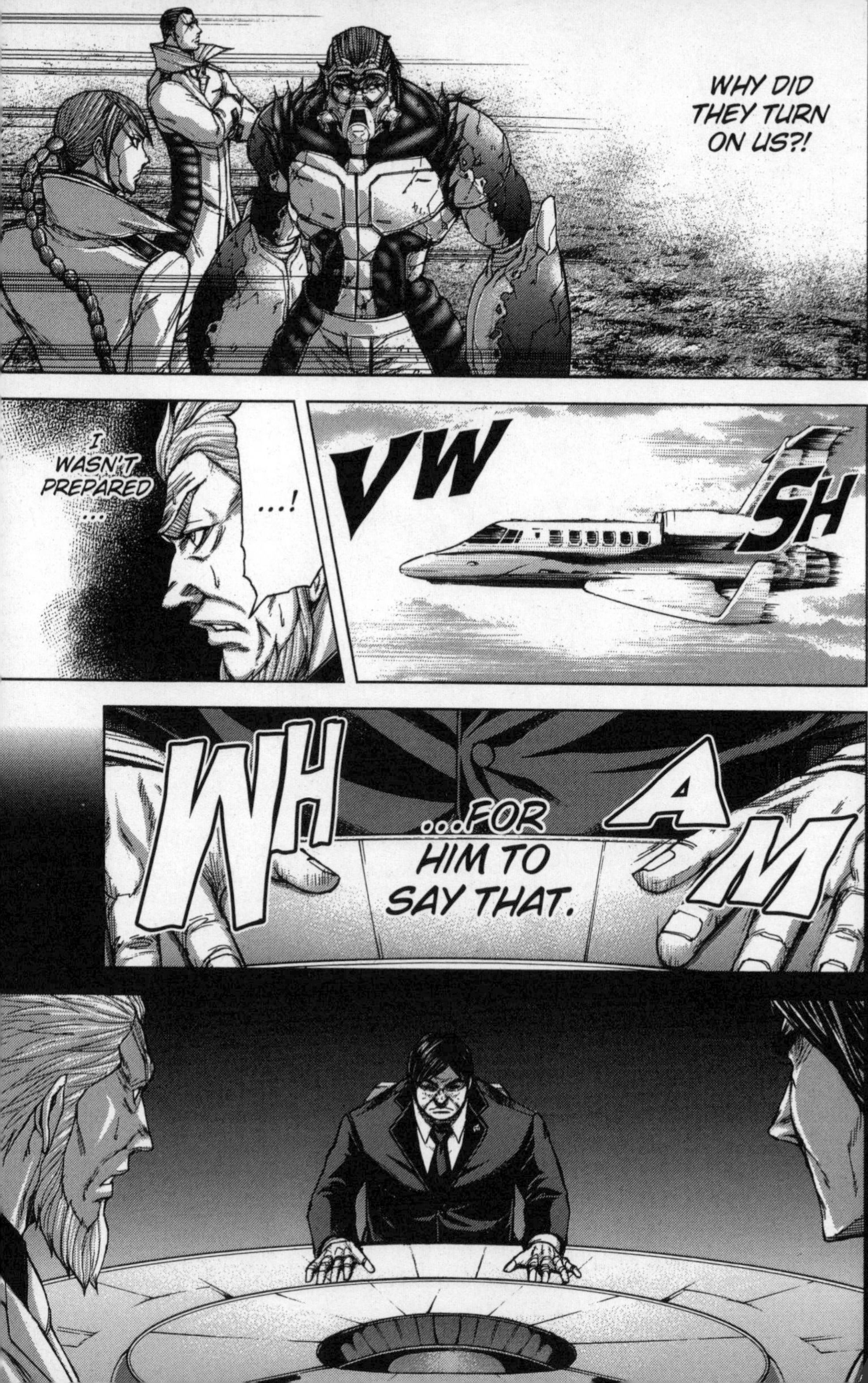
WHY DID THEY TURN ON US?!
VW
SH
...!
I WASN'T PREPARED ...
WH
A
M
...FOR HIM TO SAY THAT.

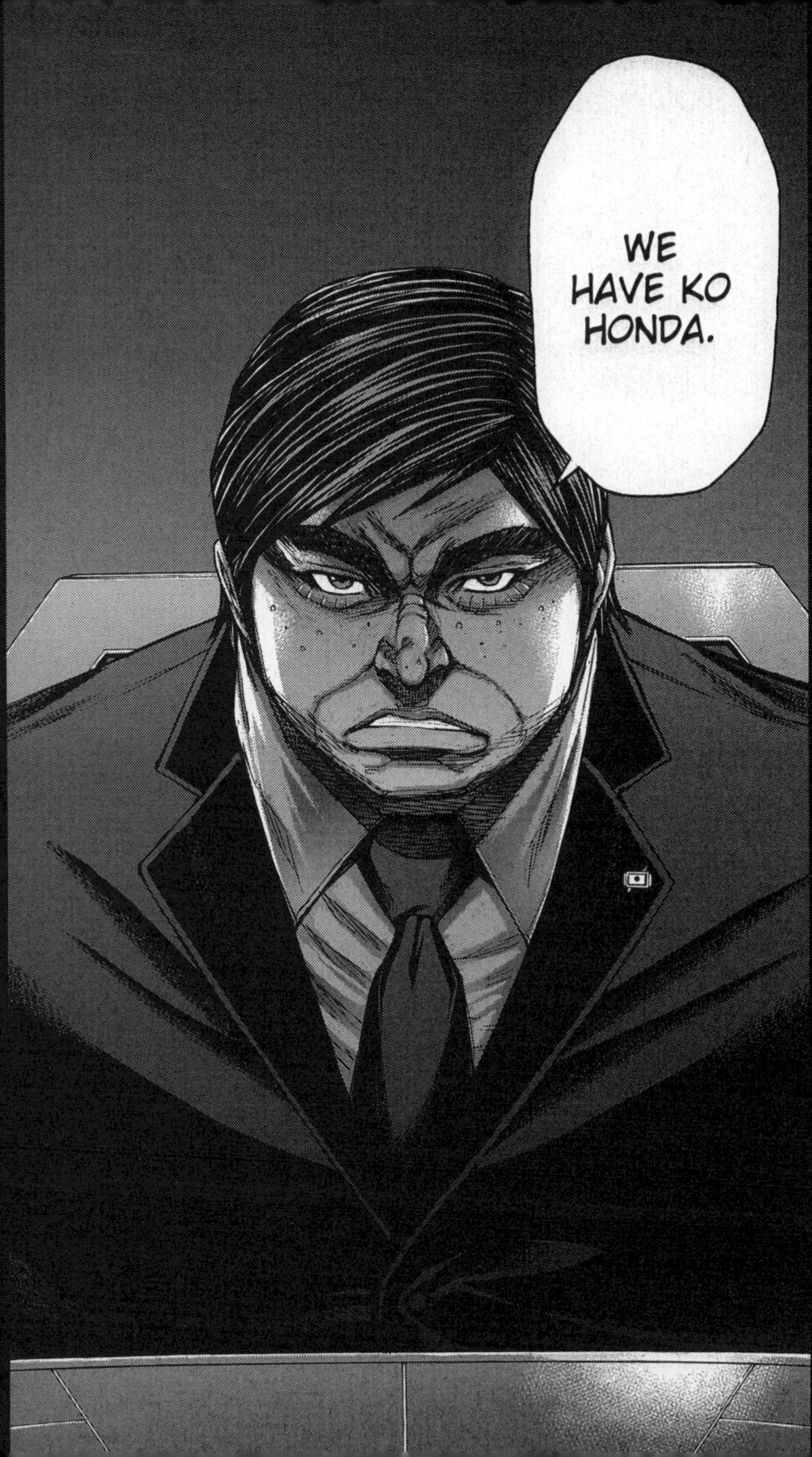
WE HAVE KO HONDA.

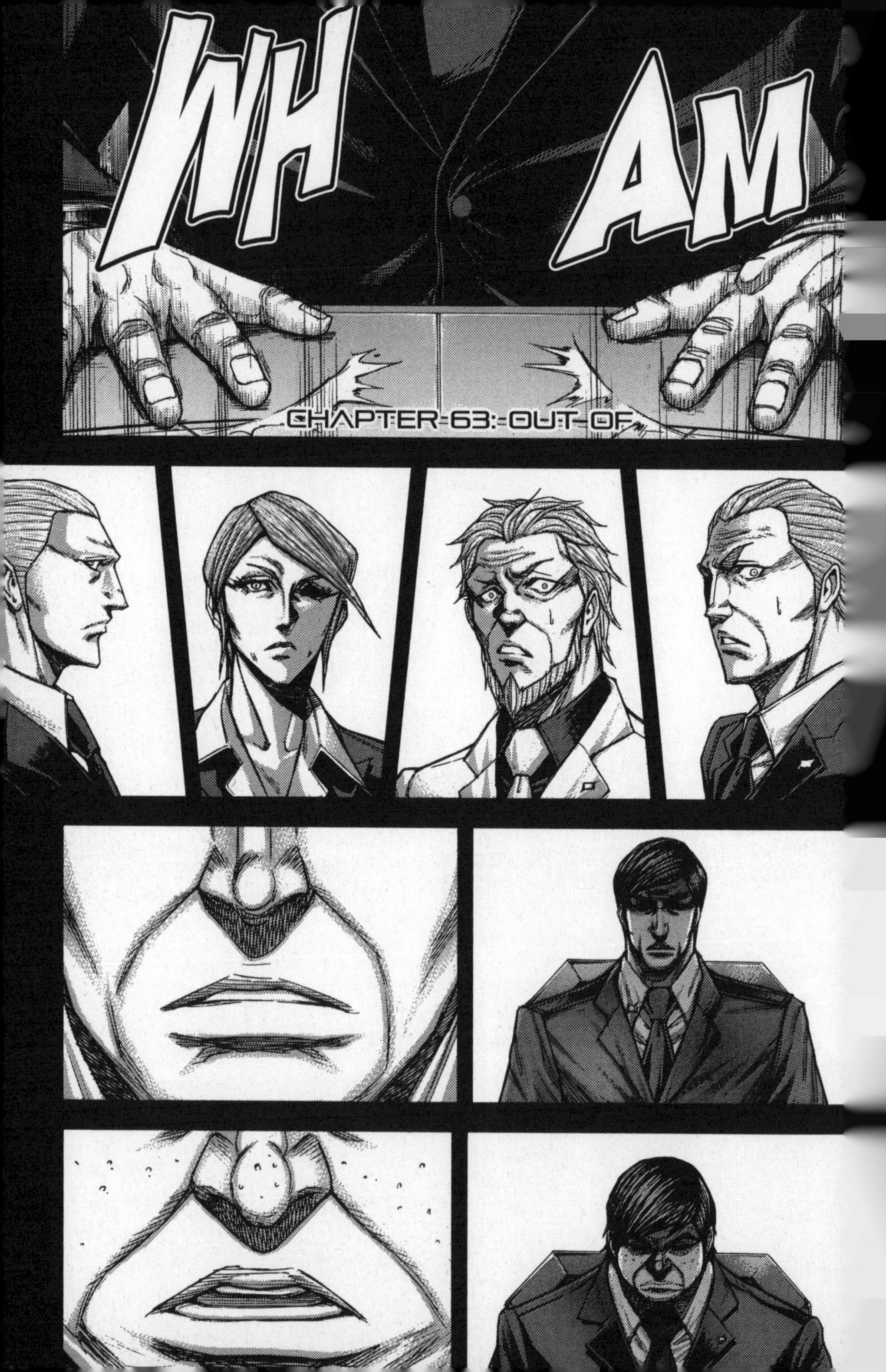
WHAM
CHAPTER 63: OUT OF

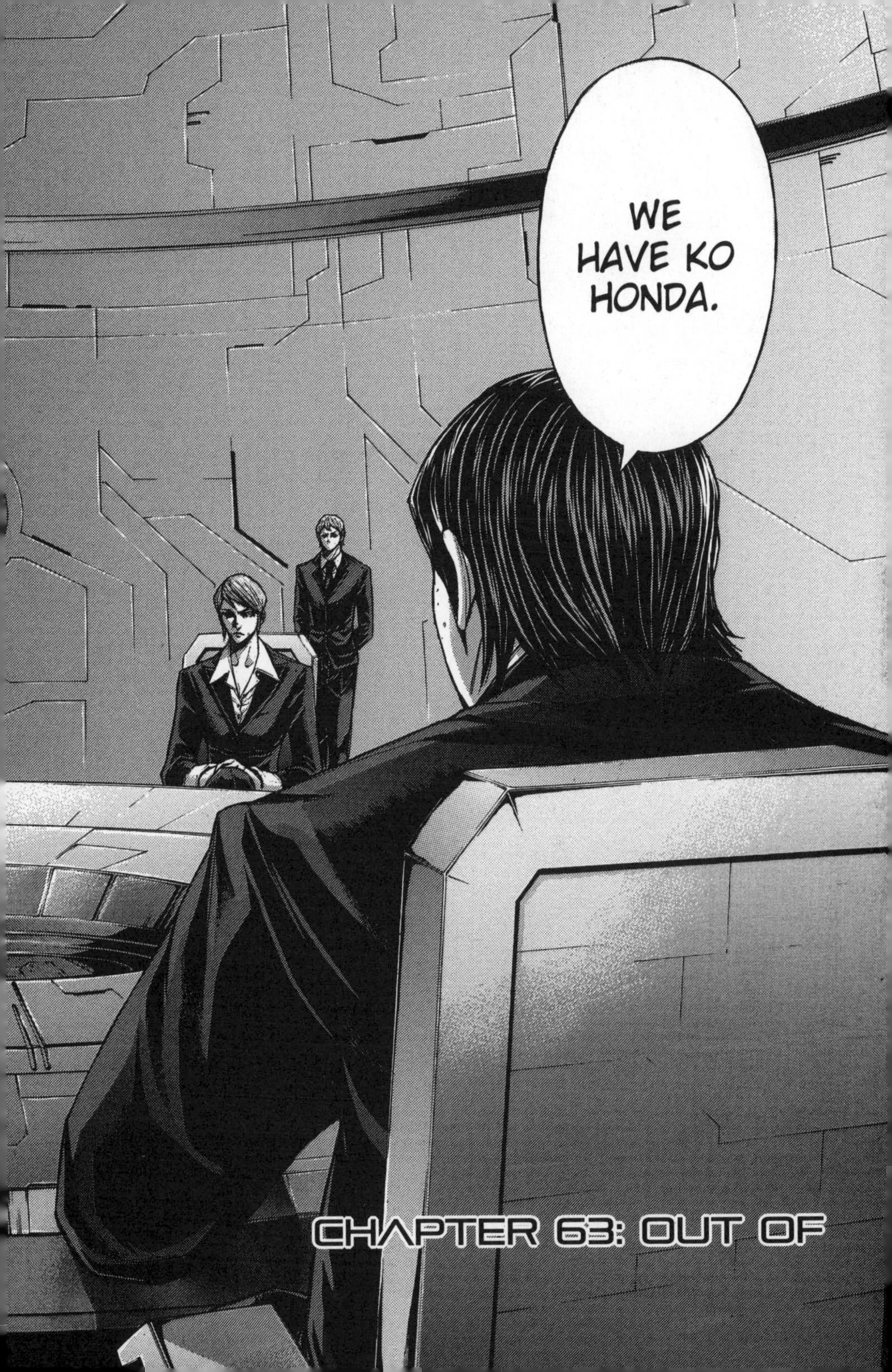
WE HAVE KO HONDA.
CHAPTER 63: OUT OF

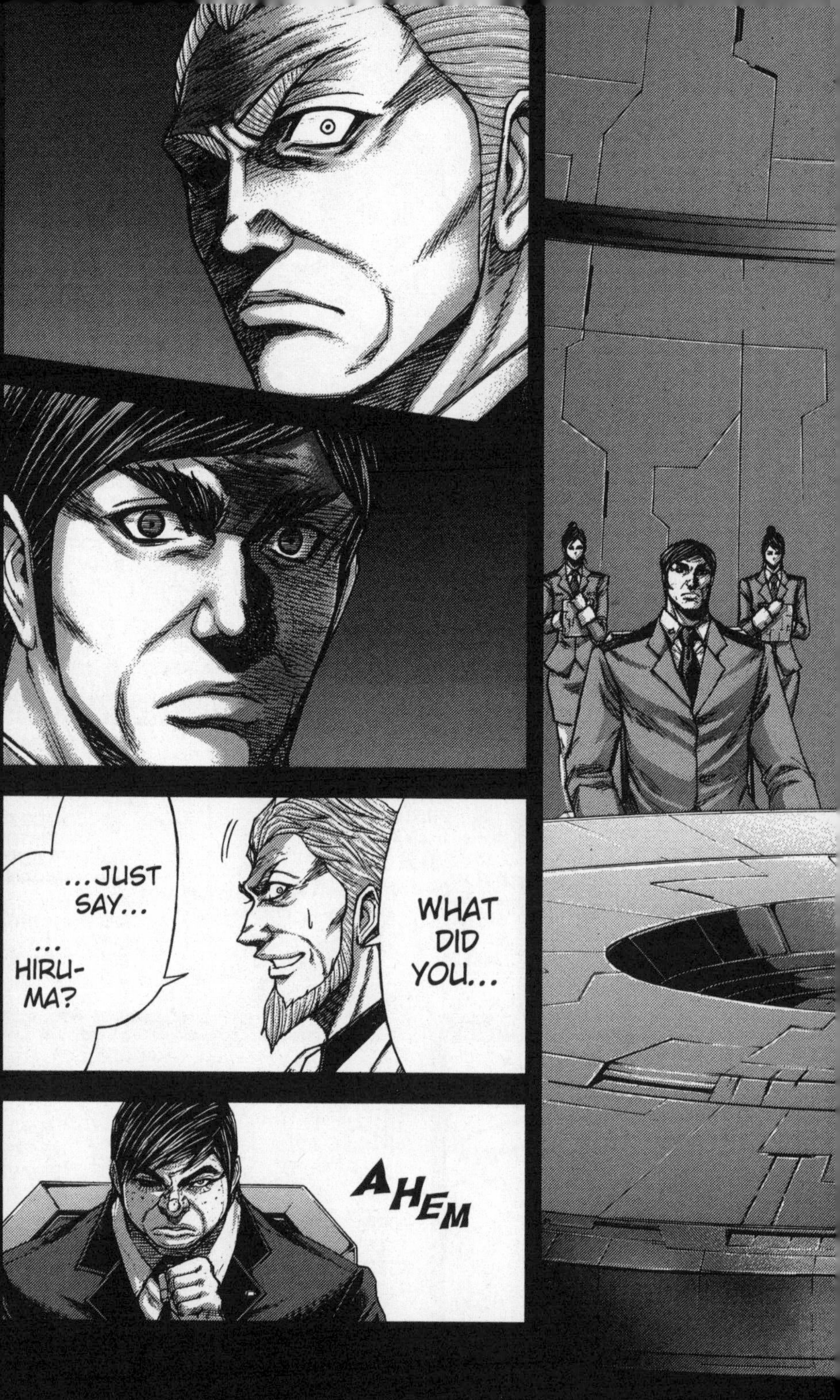

WHAT DID YOU...
...JUST SAY...
...HIRU-MA?
AHEM

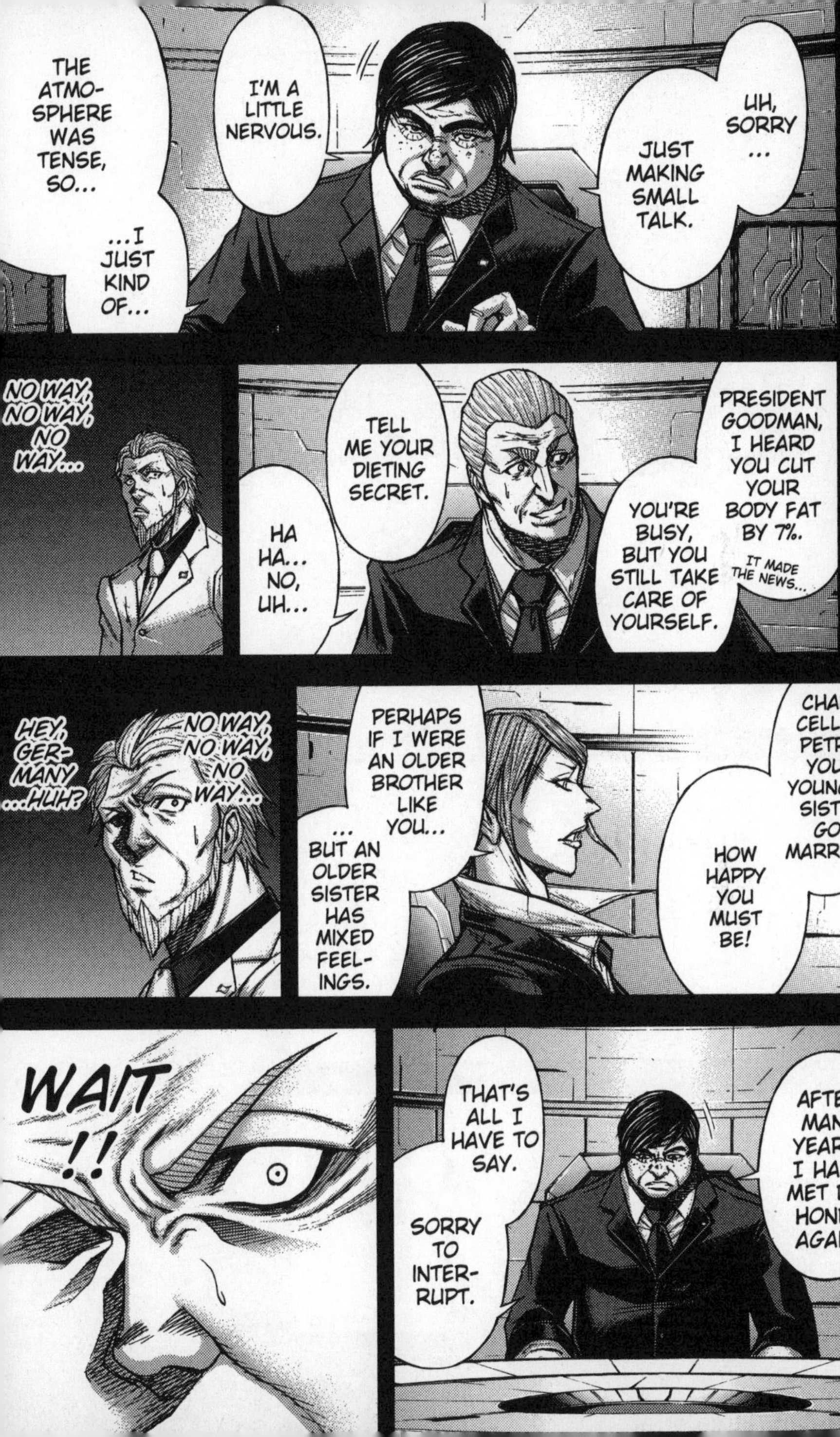
UH, SORRY...
JUST MAKING SMALL TALK.
I'M A LITTLE NERVOUS.
THE ATMOSPHERE WAS TENSE, SO...
...I JUST KIND OF...
PRESIDENT GOODMAN, I HEARD YOU CUT YOUR BODY FAT BY 7%.
IT MADE THE NEWS...
YOU'RE BUSY, BUT YOU STILL TAKE CARE OF YOURSELF.
TELL ME YOUR DIETING SECRET.
HA HA... NO, UH...
NO WAY, NO WAY, NO WAY...
CHANCELLOR PETRA, YOUR YOUNGER SISTER GOT MARRIED?
HOW HAPPY YOU MUST BE!
PERHAPS IF I WERE AN OLDER BROTHER LIKE YOU...
...BUT AN OLDER SISTER HAS MIXED FEELINGS.
NO WAY, NO WAY, NO WAY...
HEY, GERMANY ...HUH?
AFTER MANY YEARS, I HAVE MET DR. HONDA AGAIN.
THAT'S ALL I HAVE TO SAY.
SORRY TO INTERRUPT.
WAIT!!

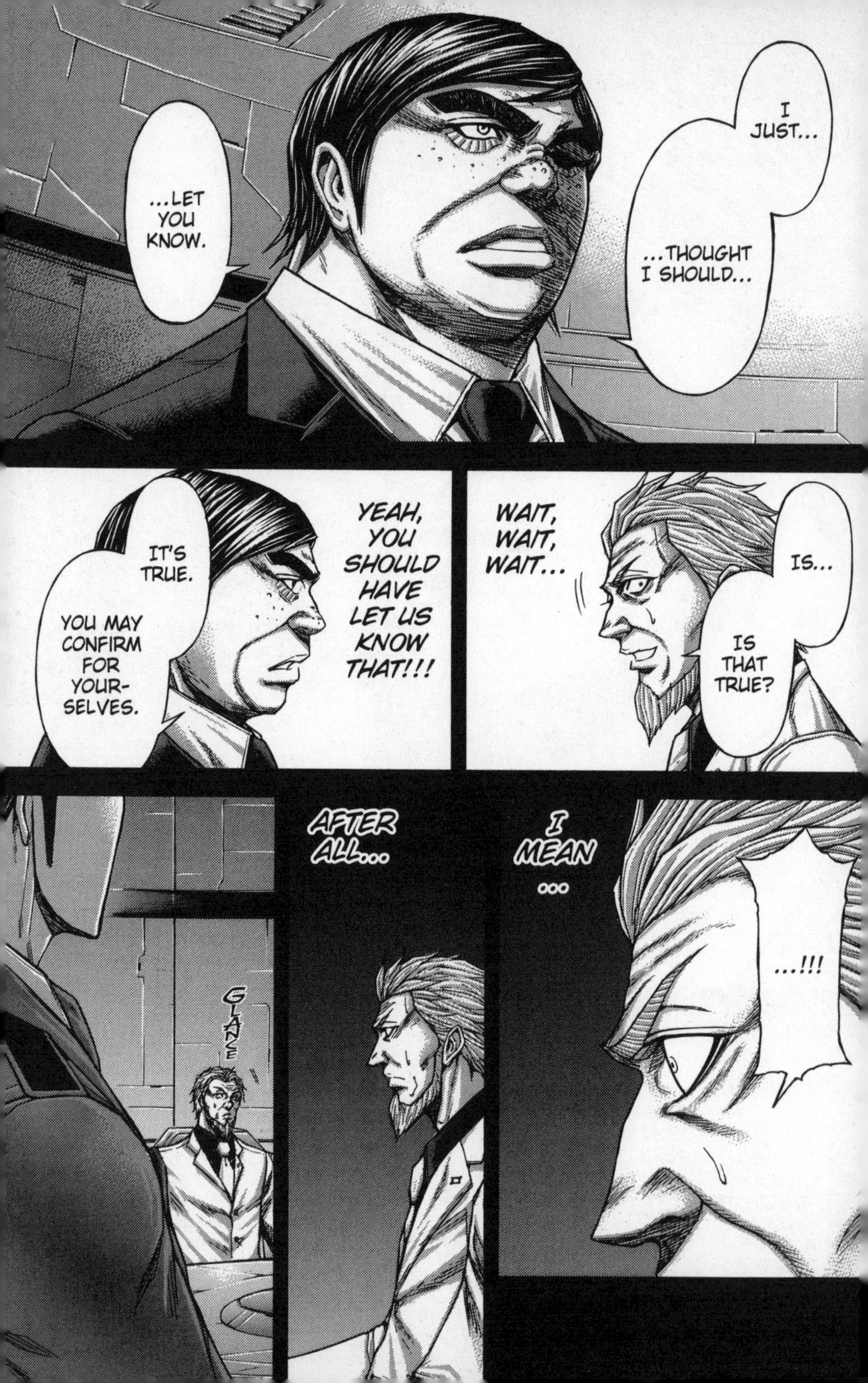
I JUST...
...THOUGHT I SHOULD...
...LET YOU KNOW.
WAIT, WAIT, WAIT...
IS...
IS THAT TRUE?
YEAH, YOU SHOULD HAVE LET US KNOW THAT!!!
IT'S TRUE.
YOU MAY CONFIRM FOR YOUR-SELVES.
I MEAN...
...!!!
AFTER ALL...
GLANCE

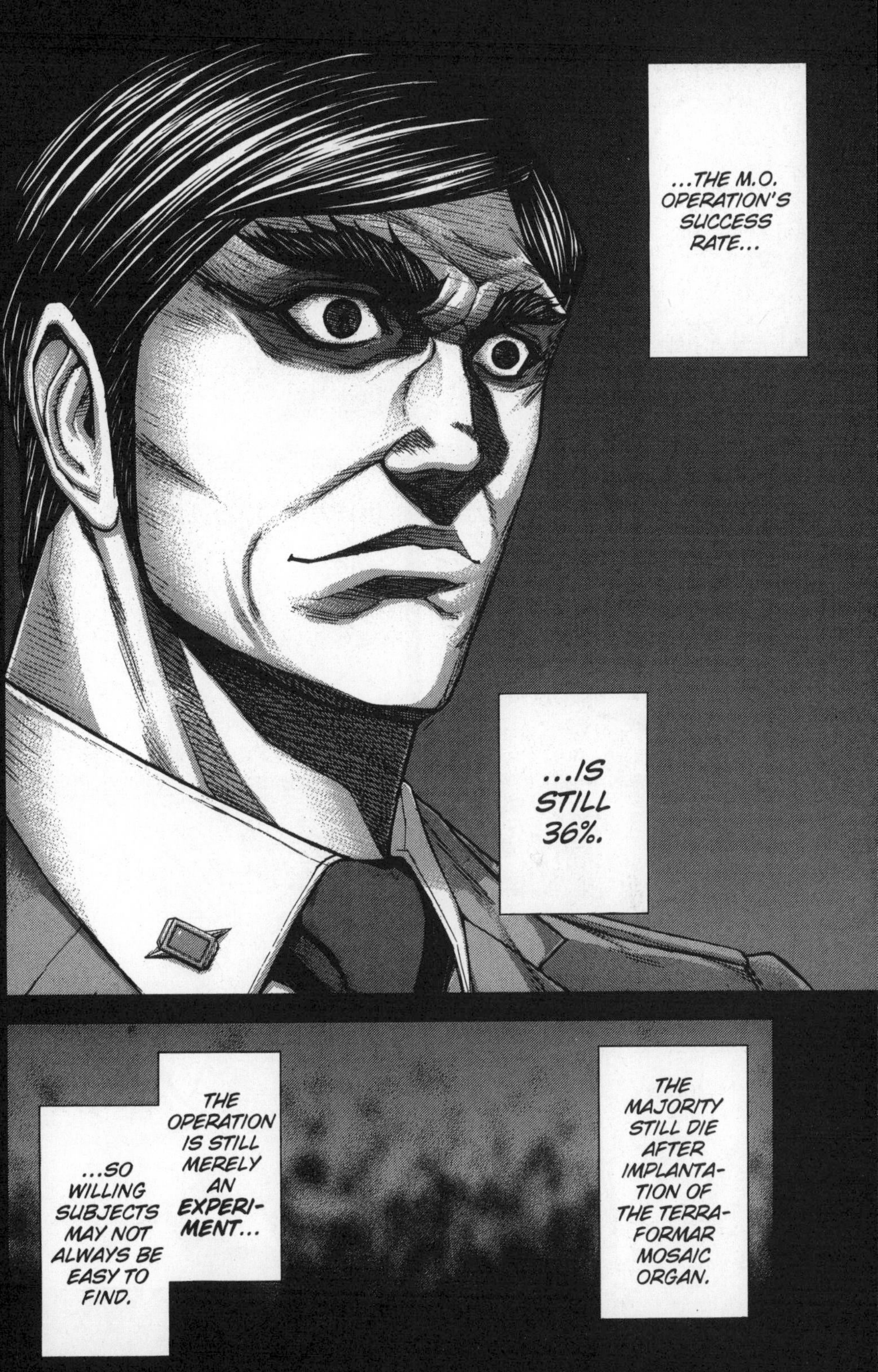
...THE M.O. OPERATION'S SUCCESS RATE...
...IS STILL 36%.
THE MAJORITY STILL DIE AFTER IMPLANTATION OF THE TERRA-FORMAR MOSAIC ORGAN.
THE OPERATION IS STILL MERELY AN EXPERIMENT...
...SO WILLING SUBJECTS MAY NOT ALWAYS BE EASY TO FIND.

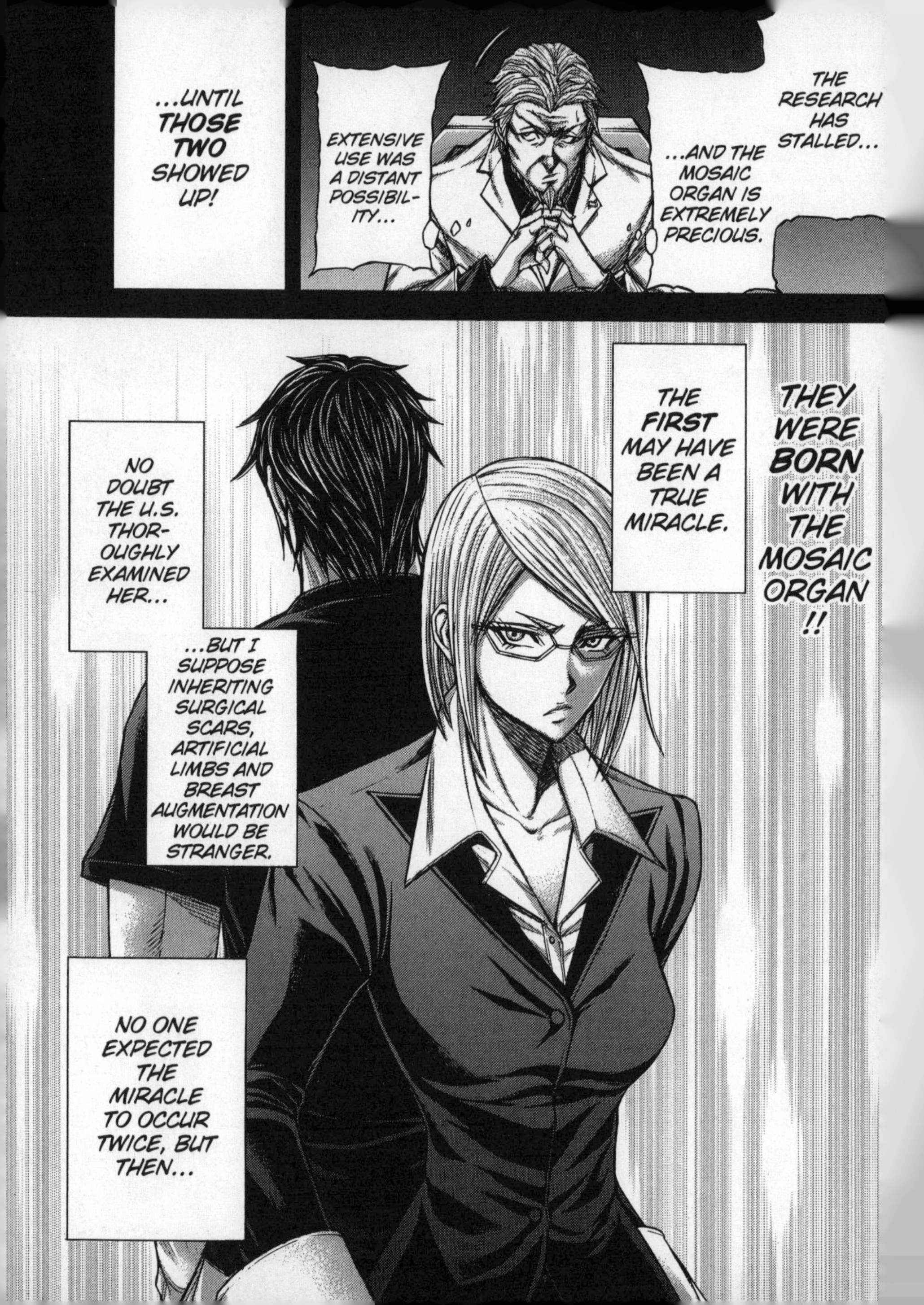
THE RESEARCH HAS STALLED...
...AND THE MOSAIC ORGAN IS EXTREMELY PRECIOUS.
EXTENSIVE USE WAS A DISTANT POSSIBIL-ITY...
...UNTIL **THOSE TWO** SHOWED UP!
THEY WERE BORN WITH THE MOSAIC ORGAN!!
THE **FIRST** MAY HAVE BEEN A TRUE MIRACLE.
NO DOUBT THE U.S. THOR-OUGHLY EXAMINED HER...
...BUT I SUPPOSE INHERITING SURGICAL SCARS, ARTIFICIAL LIMBS AND BREAST AUGMENTATION WOULD BE STRANGER.
NO ONE EXPECTED THE MIRACLE TO OCCUR TWICE, BUT THEN...

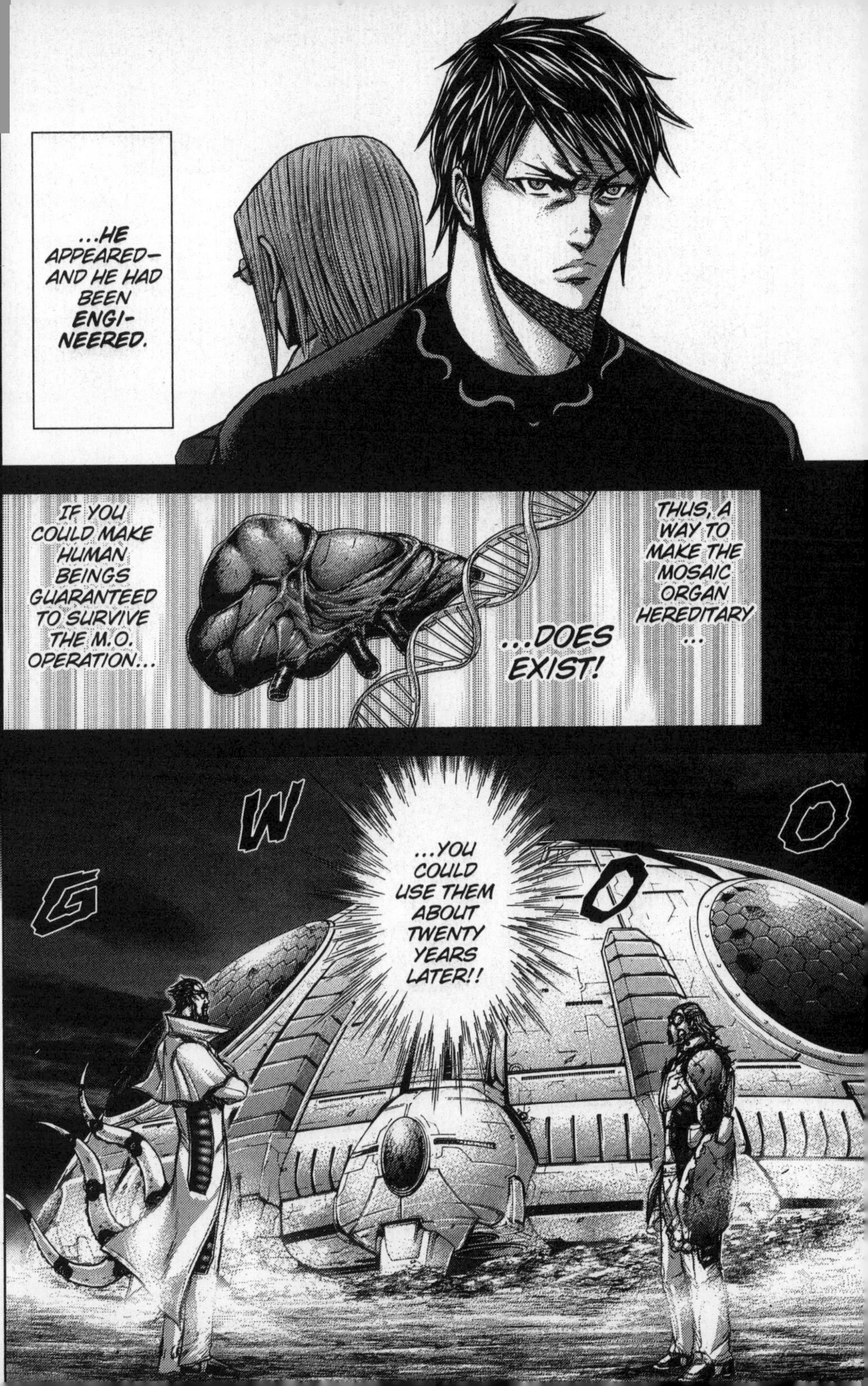

...HE APPEARED— AND HE HAD BEEN ENGI- NEERED.
THUS, A WAY TO MAKE THE MOSAIC ORGAN HEREDITARY ...
...DOES EXIST!
IF YOU COULD MAKE HUMAN BEINGS GUARANTEED TO SURVIVE THE M.O. OPERATION...
...YOU COULD USE THEM ABOUT TWENTY YEARS LATER!!
GWOO

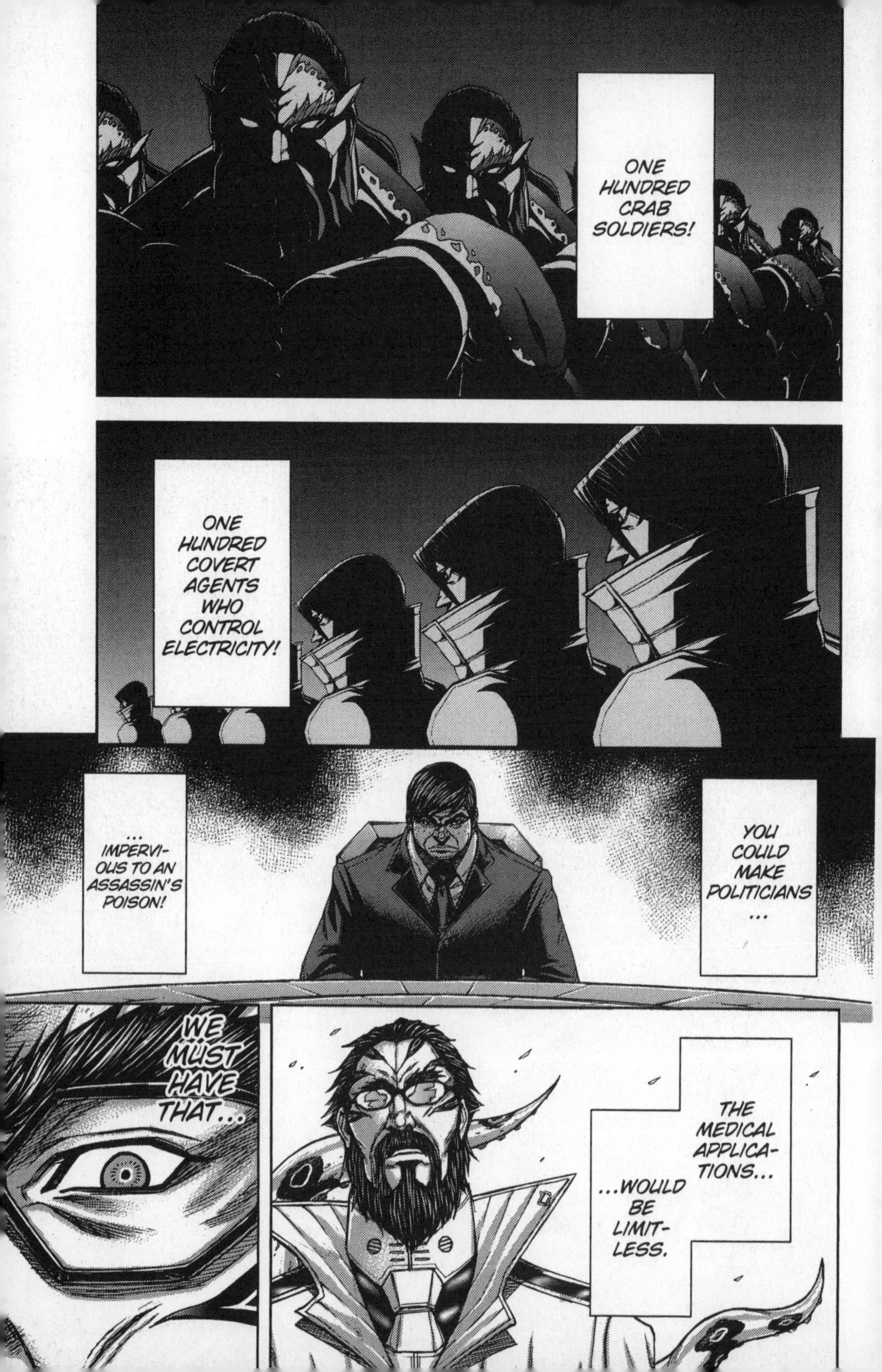
ONE HUNDRED CRAB SOLDIERS!
ONE HUNDRED COVERT AGENTS WHO CONTROL ELECTRICITY!
YOU COULD MAKE POLITICIANS...
...IMPERVIOUS TO AN ASSASSIN'S POISON!
THE MEDICAL APPLICATIONS...
...WOULD BE LIMITLESS.
WE MUST HAVE THAT...

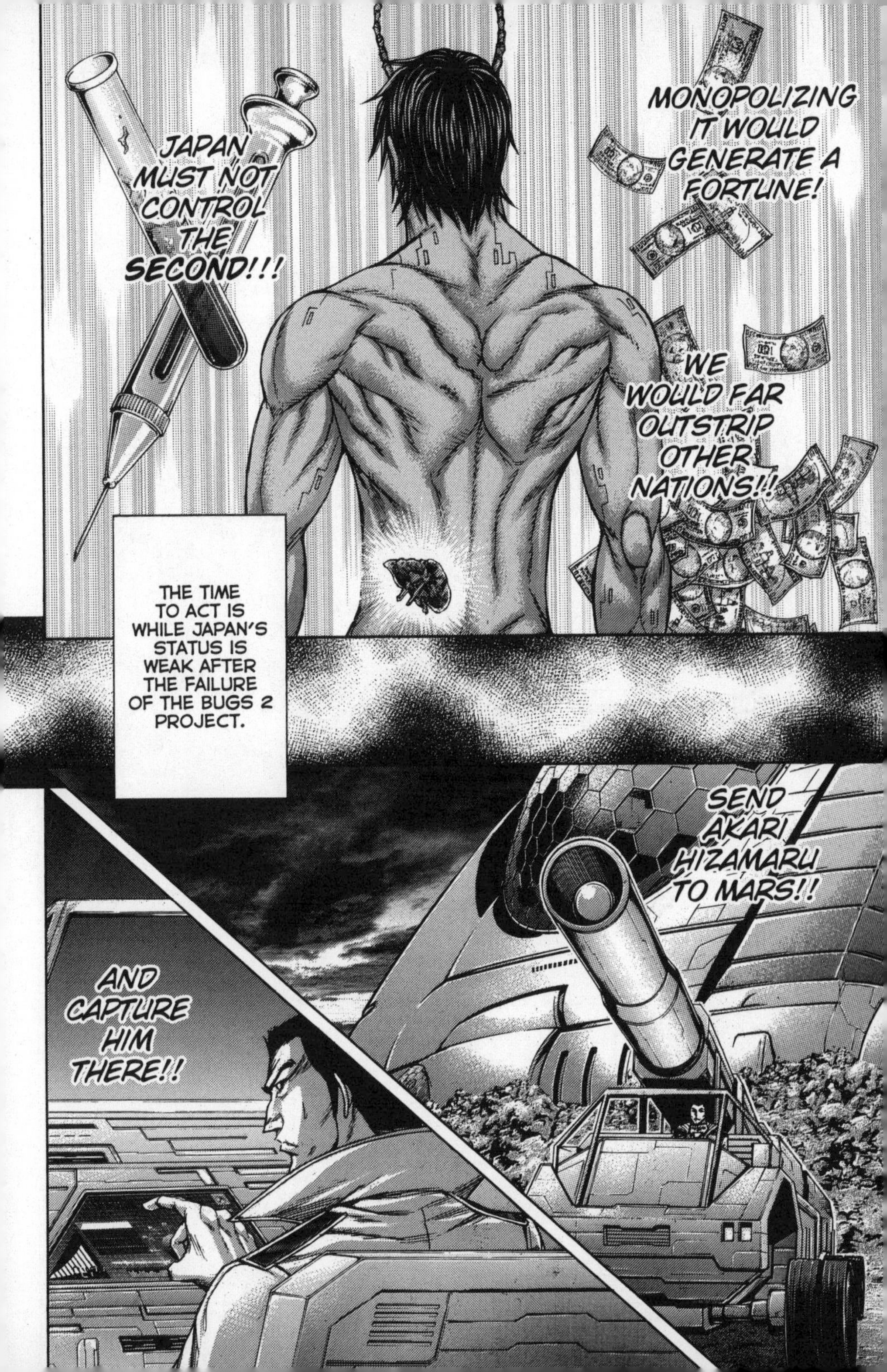
MONOPOLIZING IT WOULD GENERATE A FORTUNE!
JAPAN MUST NOT CONTROL THE SECOND!!!
WE WOULD FAR OUTSTRIP OTHER NATIONS!!
THE TIME TO ACT IS WHILE JAPAN'S STATUS IS WEAK AFTER THE FAILURE OF THE BUGS 2 PROJECT.
SEND AKARI HIZAMARU TO MARS!!
AND CAPTURE HIM THERE!!

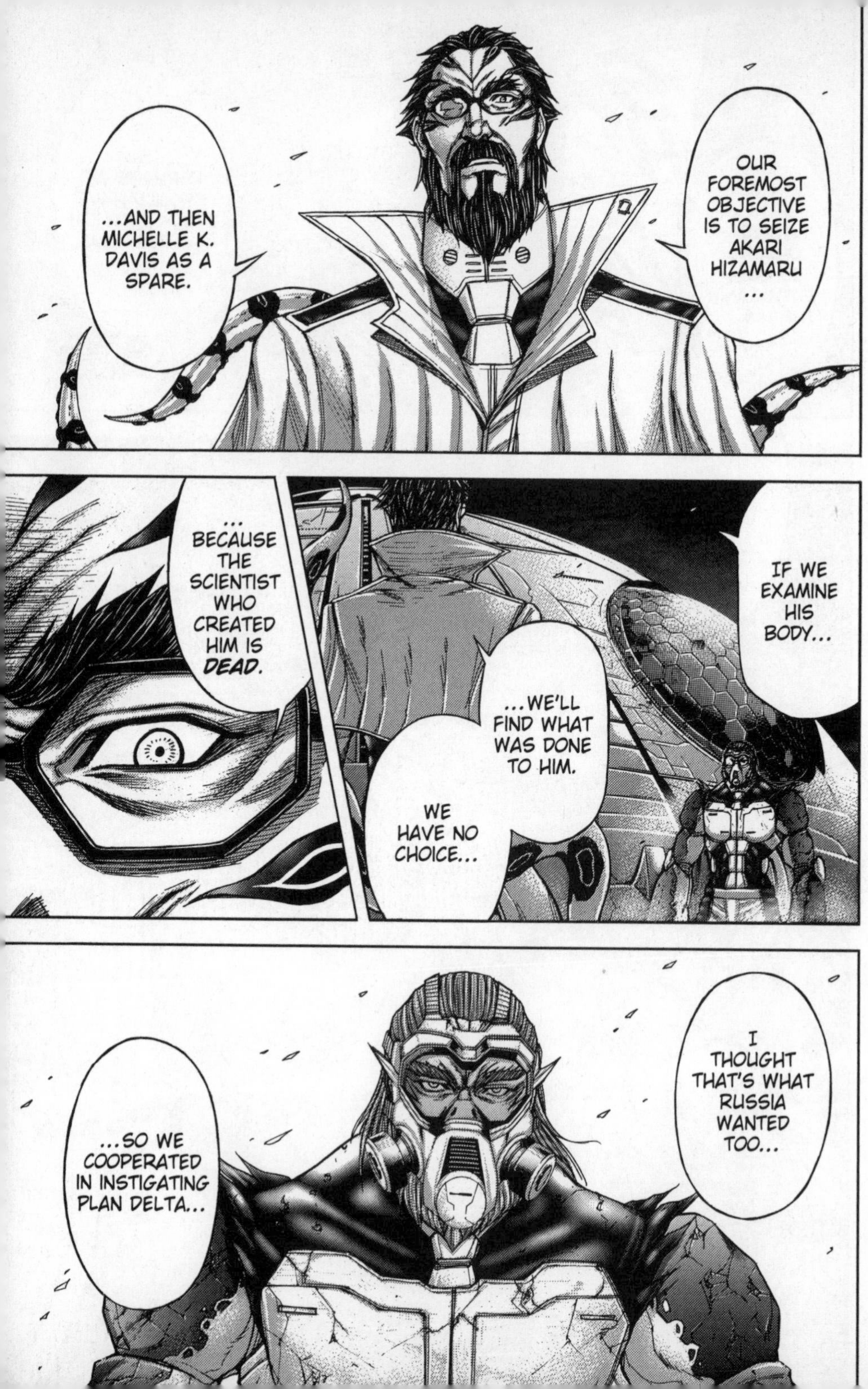
OUR FOREMOST OBJECTIVE IS TO SEIZE AKARI HIZAMARU ...
...AND THEN MICHELLE K. DAVIS AS A SPARE.
IF WE EXAMINE HIS BODY...
...WE'LL FIND WHAT WAS DONE TO HIM.
WE HAVE NO CHOICE...
... BECAUSE THE SCIENTIST WHO CREATED HIM IS *DEAD*.
I THOUGHT THAT'S WHAT RUSSIA WANTED TOO...
...SO WE COOPERATED IN INSTIGATING PLAN DELTA...

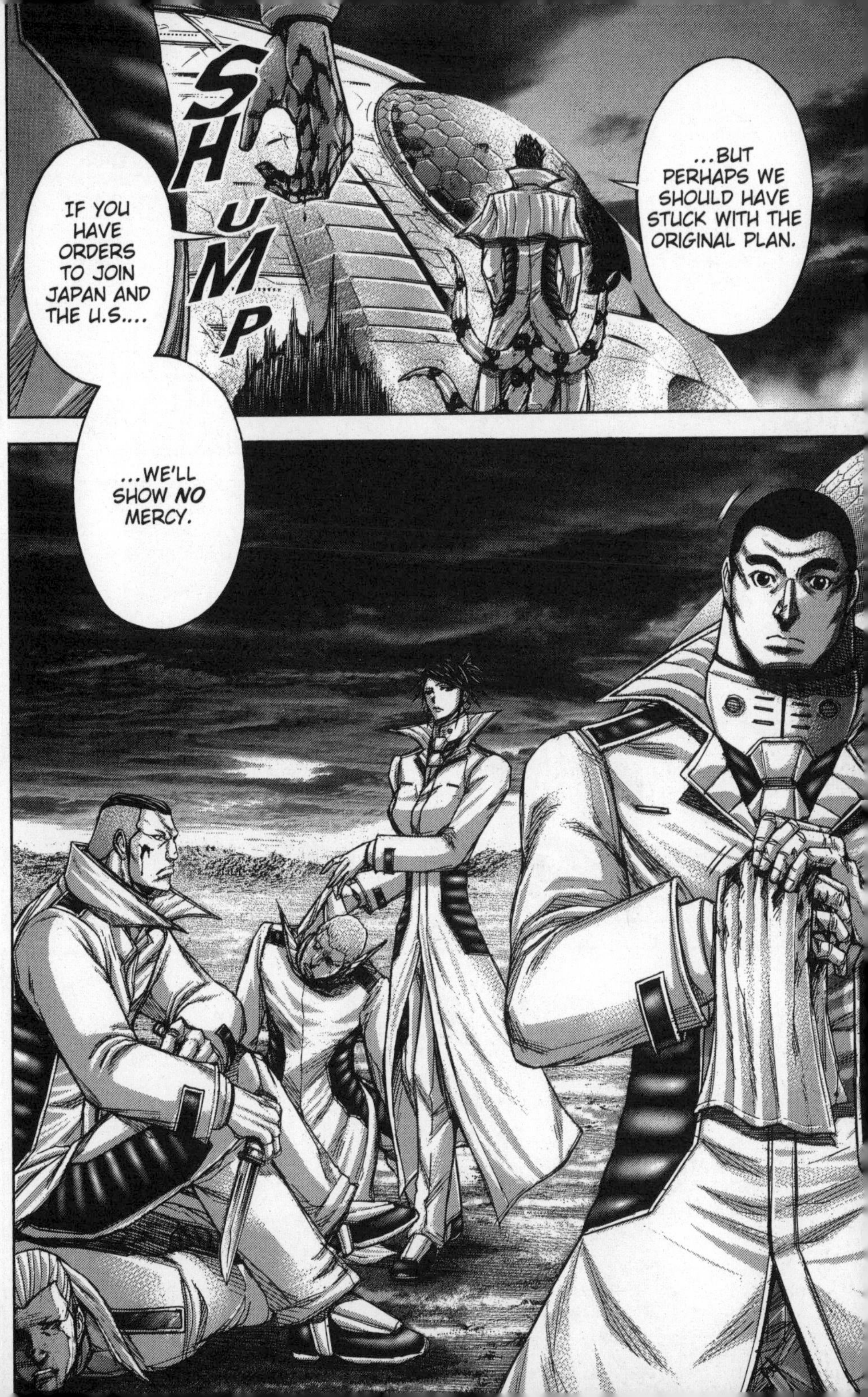
...BUT PERHAPS WE SHOULD HAVE STUCK WITH THE ORIGINAL PLAN.
SHUMP
IF YOU HAVE ORDERS TO JOIN JAPAN AND THE U.S....
...WE'LL SHOW *NO* MERCY.

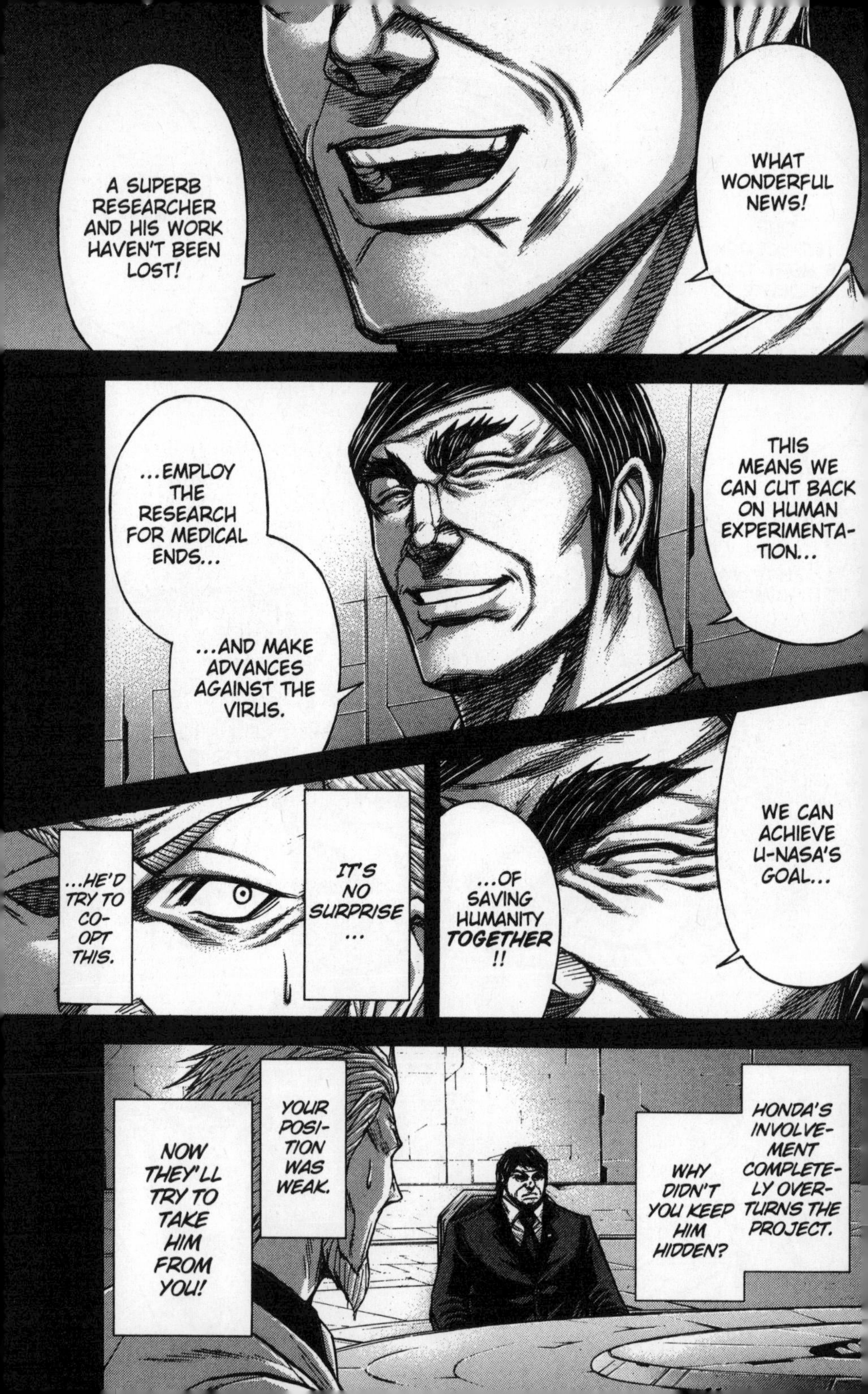
WHAT WONDERFUL NEWS!
A SUPERB RESEARCHER AND HIS WORK HAVEN'T BEEN LOST!
THIS MEANS WE CAN CUT BACK ON HUMAN EXPERIMENTATION...
...EMPLOY THE RESEARCH FOR MEDICAL ENDS...
...AND MAKE ADVANCES AGAINST THE VIRUS.
WE CAN ACHIEVE U-NASA'S GOAL...
...OF SAVING HUMANITY *TOGETHER*!!
IT'S NO SURPRISE...
...HE'D TRY TO CO-OPT THIS.
HONDA'S INVOLVEMENT COMPLETELY OVERTURNS THE PROJECT.
WHY DIDN'T YOU KEEP HIM HIDDEN?
YOUR POSITION WAS WEAK.
NOW THEY'LL TRY TO TAKE HIM FROM YOU!

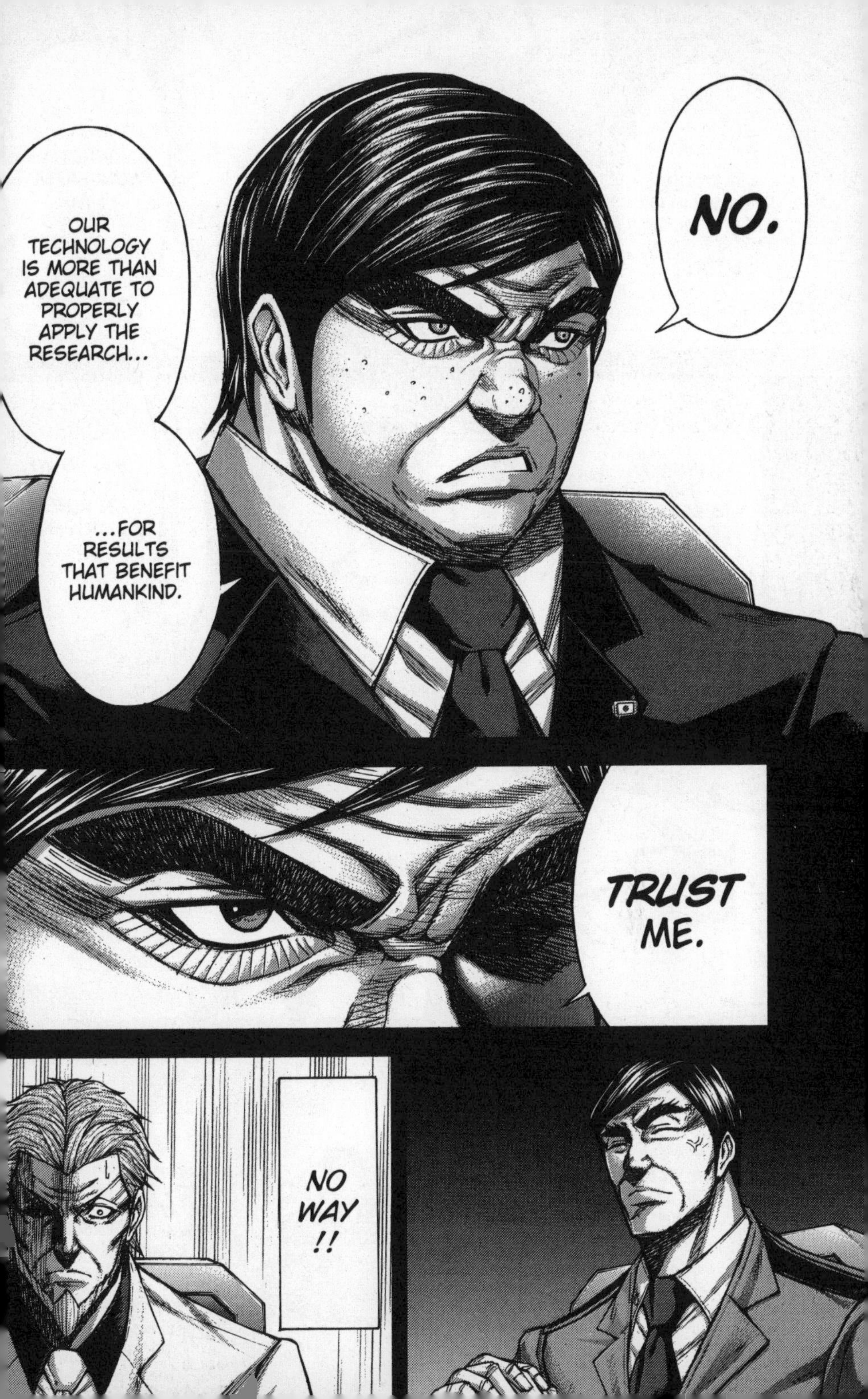
NO.
OUR TECHNOLOGY IS MORE THAN ADEQUATE TO PROPERLY APPLY THE RESEARCH...
...FOR RESULTS THAT BENEFIT HUMANKIND.
TRUST ME.
NO WAY !!

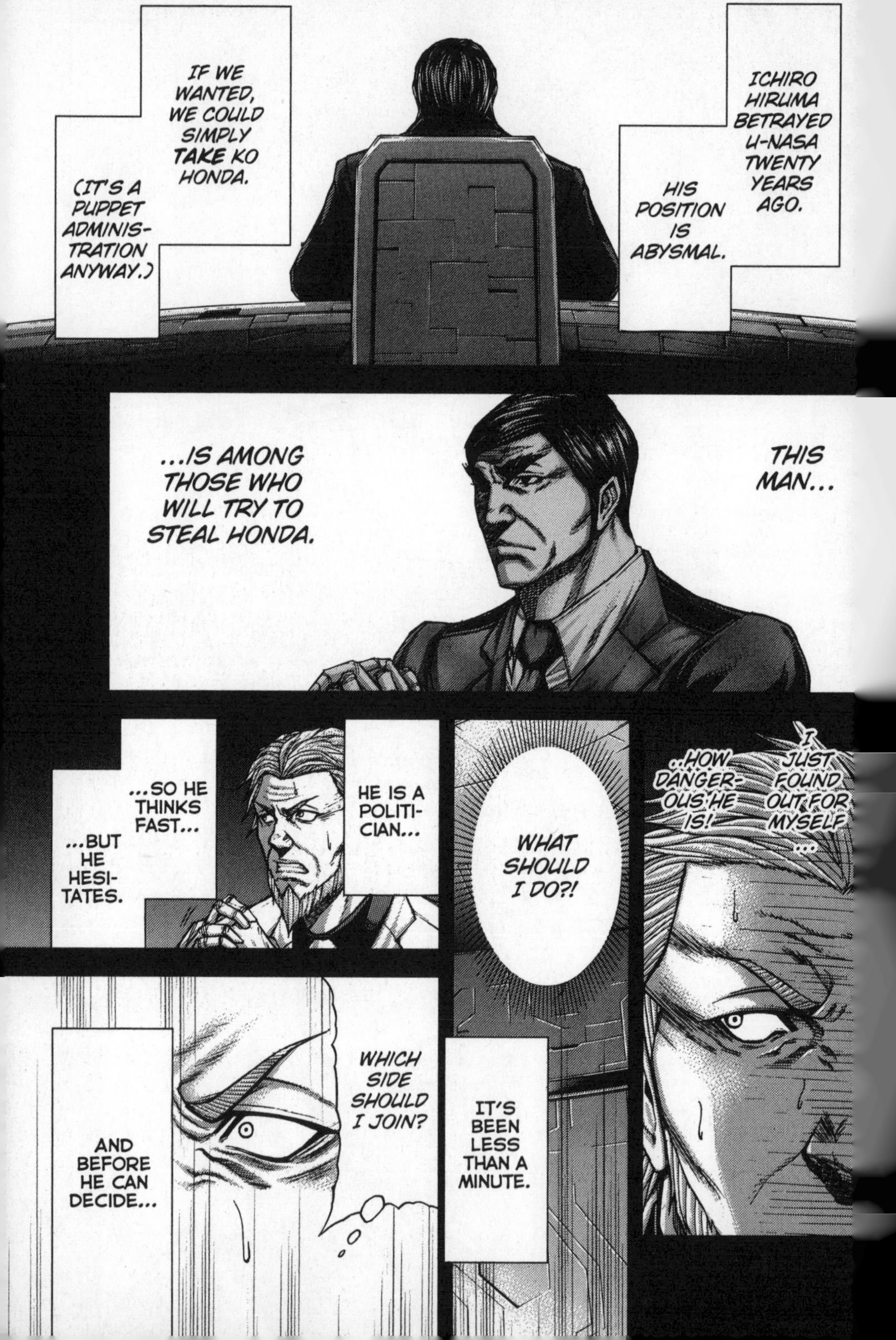

ICHIRO HIRUMA BETRAYED U-NASA TWENTY YEARS AGO.
HIS POSITION IS ABYSMAL.
IF WE WANTED, WE COULD SIMPLY TAKE KO HONDA.
(IT'S A PUPPET ADMINISTRATION ANYWAY.)
THIS MAN...
...IS AMONG THOSE WHO WILL TRY TO STEAL HONDA.
I JUST FOUND OUT FOR MYSELF...
...HOW DANGEROUS HE IS!
WHAT SHOULD I DO?!
IT'S BEEN LESS THAN A MINUTE.
HE IS A POLITICIAN...
...SO HE THINKS FAST...
...BUT HE HESITATES.
WHICH SIDE SHOULD I JOIN?
AND BEFORE HE CAN DECIDE...

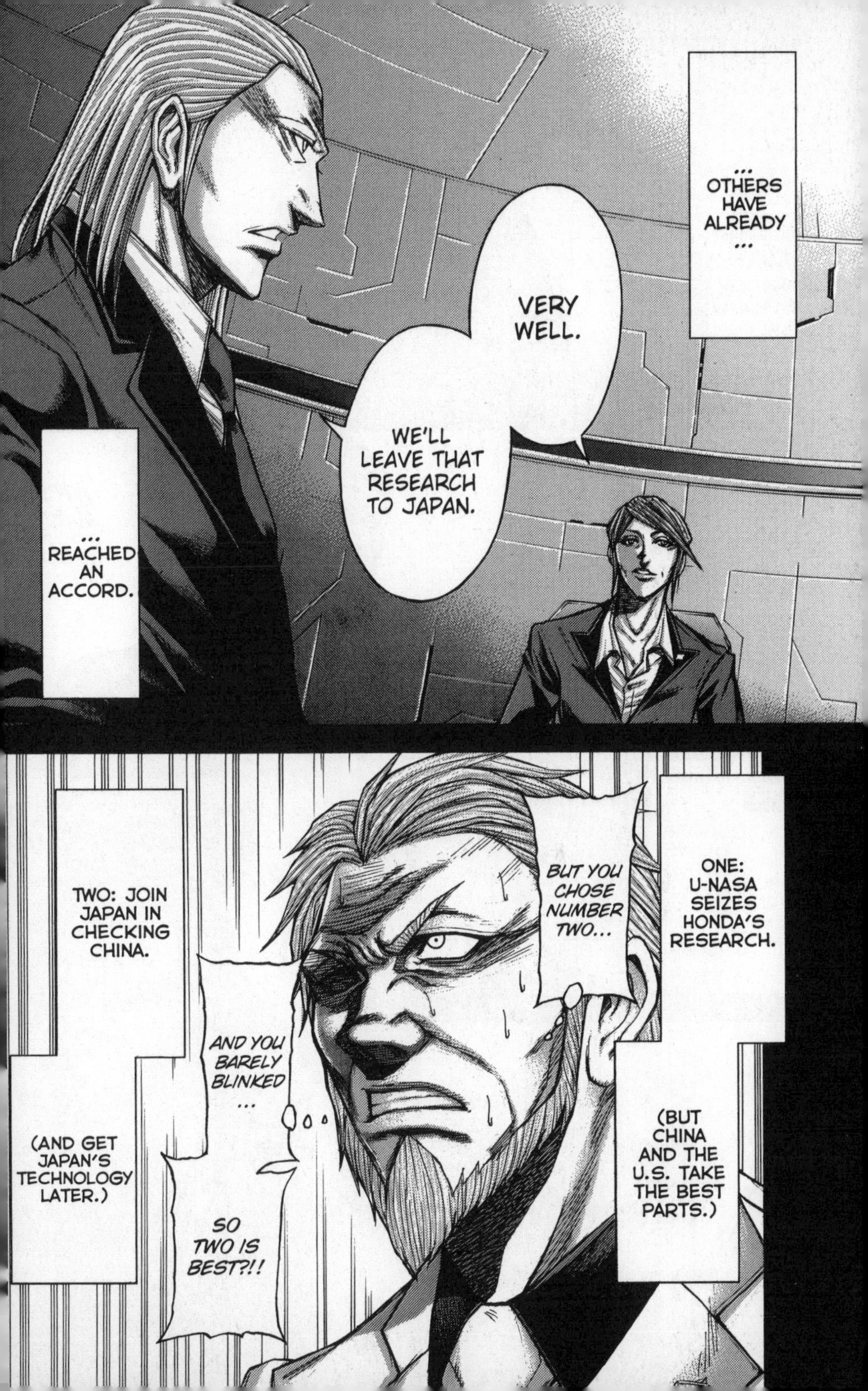

...OTHERS HAVE ALREADY...
VERY WELL.
WE'LL LEAVE THAT RESEARCH TO JAPAN.
...REACHED AN ACCORD.
ONE: U-NASA SEIZES HONDA'S RESEARCH.
(BUT CHINA AND THE U.S. TAKE THE BEST PARTS.)
TWO: JOIN JAPAN IN CHECKING CHINA.
(AND GET JAPAN'S TECHNOLOGY LATER.)
BUT YOU CHOSE NUMBER TWO...
AND YOU BARELY BLINKED...
SO TWO IS BEST?!!

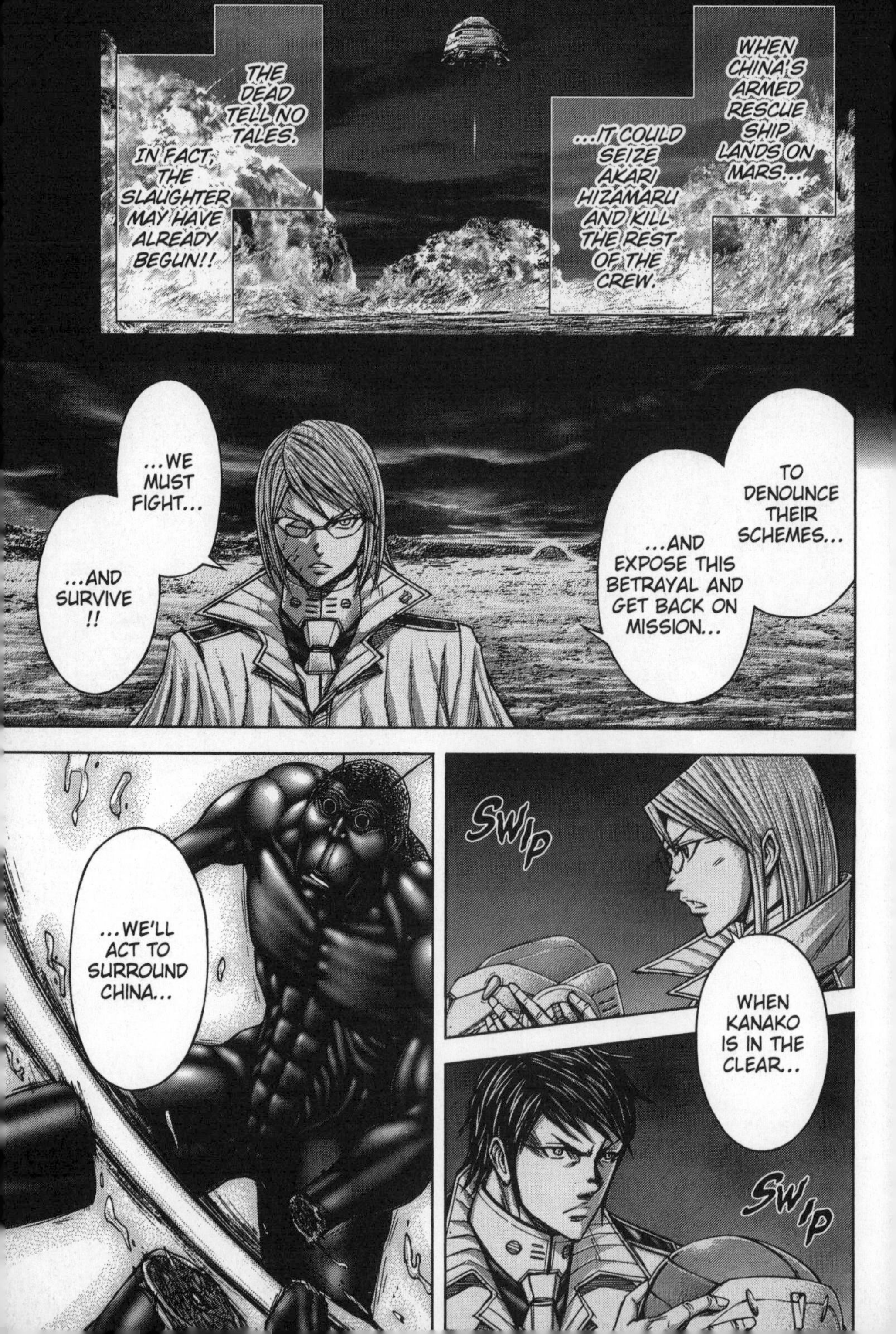
WHEN CHINA'S ARMED RESCUE SHIP LANDS ON MARS...
...IT COULD SEIZE AKARI HIZAMARU AND KILL THE REST OF THE CREW.
THE DEAD TELL NO TALES.
IN FACT, THE SLAUGHTER MAY HAVE ALREADY BEGUN!!
TO DENOUNCE THEIR SCHEMES...
...AND EXPOSE THIS BETRAYAL AND GET BACK ON MISSION...
...WE MUST FIGHT...
...AND SURVIVE!!
SWIP
WHEN KANAKO IS IN THE CLEAR...
SWIP
...WE'LL ACT TO SURROUND CHINA...

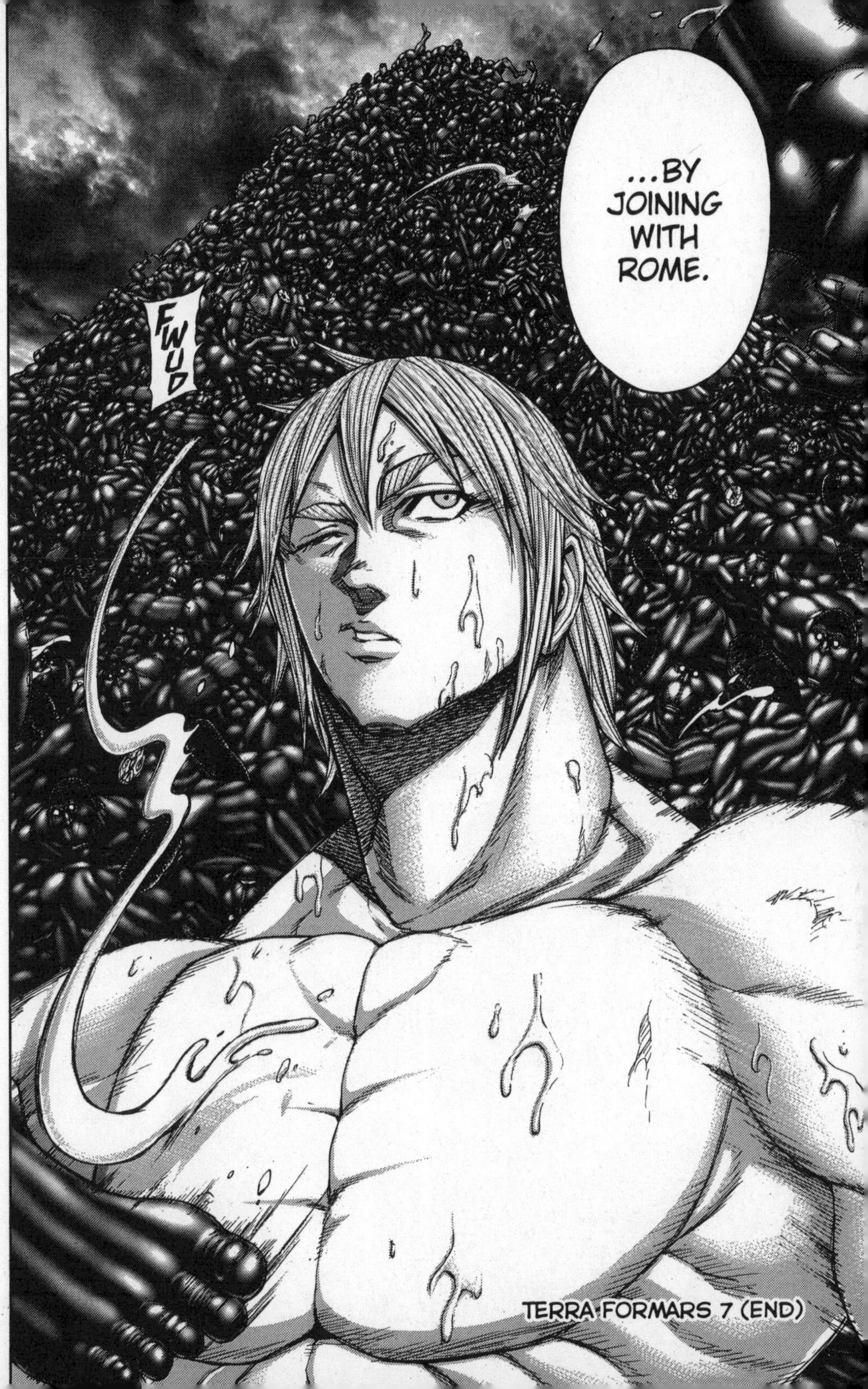
...BY JOINING WITH ROME.
FWUD

TERRA FORMARS 7 (END)

TERRA FORMARS

Character

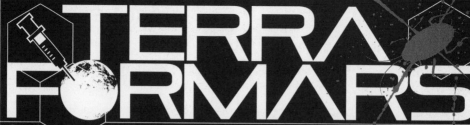

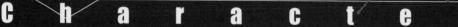

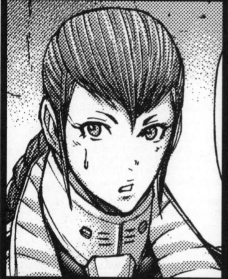

Nina Yuzic ♀

Russia 26 yrs. 168 cm 61 kg

Operation Base: Deathstalker

Favorite Foods: Mont Blanc and anything with chestnuts
Dislikes: Bookstores where the new releases are hard to find
Eye Color: Dark brown Blood type: B
DOB: November 12 (Scorpio)
Hobbies: Collecting manga

She was born the youngest of eight or nine sisters to parents too irresponsible to keep count of their own offspring. It was a fight every day to get something to eat, so that's how she polished her sambo skills. Then she joined the military in order to get three square meals a day. She joined the Mars mission after hearing that judo master and living sambo legend Asimov was participating.

Recently, she hasn't wanted to reveal her zodiac sign. Married.

Sergei Seleznyov ♂

Russia 29 yrs. 188 cm 100 kg

Operation Base: Japanese Mountain Mole

Favorite Foods: Oden sausage, sake
Dislikes: Erotic manga with impressive art that's vague about nipples
Eye Color: Dark green Blood type: AB
DOB: July 5 (Cancer)
Hobbies: Reading (and not returning) other people's books and manga

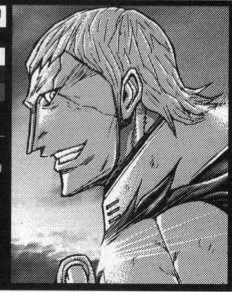

Born into a strict military family, his dislike for study was exceptional. Overcoming his parent's wishes, he joined the military as a soldier, but even then he was dismayed to find he had to study a little for promotions and such.

Because of his family's influence, he thinks of himself as irresponsible and pitiful, but others see him differently, and his grades are actually exceptional. He joined the Mars mission after hearing that Asimov—whom his parents described as "superhuman" and a "military god"—was participating. Judo: 4th-dan. Japanese Language Proficiency Exam: Level 2.

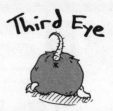

Third Eye

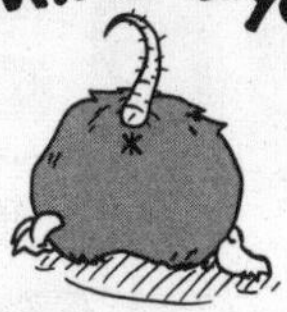

U-NASA PRELIMINARY FILE 4 – MOLE

- IT IS SAID THAT DIGGING THROUGH THE EARTH REQUIRES FROM 30 TO 3,400 TIMES THE ENERGY NEEDED TO SIMPLY RUN ACROSS THE SURFACE.

- FOR THAT REASON, MOLES EAT HALF THEIR WEIGHT IN WORMS AND INSECTS EACH DAY AND SLEEP FOR HALF OF EACH DAY.

- MOLES ARE CARNIVORES WHO DON'T EAT VEGETABLES. CLAIMS THAT THEY CHEW ON ROOT CROPS STEM FROM FIELD MICE. HOWEVER, THEY DO DESTROY THE RIDGES IN AGRICULTURAL FIELDS, SO FARMERS DON'T LIKE THEM.

- IT'S DIFFICULT TO TELL THE DIFFERENCE BETWEEN NIGHT AND DAY UNDER THE GROUND, SO MOLES GENERALLY WAKE AND SLEEP IN FOUR-HOUR CYCLES.

- THE MYTH THAT MOLES DIE IN SUNLIGHT AROSE BECAUSE LONG AGO MOLES WERE MORE COMMON, SO PEOPLE WOULD OCCASIONALLY FIND ONE DEAD ABOVE GROUND.

- MOLES RAISE THEIR YOUNG AND SLEEP UNDERGROUND, SO THEIR NESTS OF FALLEN LEAVES AND THE TUNNELS LEADING TO THEM ARE DEEP ENOUGH TO REQUIRE SPECIAL KNOWLEDGE TO LOCATE. THEY HAVE A SEPARATE ROOM NEARBY FOR BODILY WASTE, WITH MOST OTHER PASSAGES DEDICATED TO FINDING FOOD. ALTOGETHER, A BURROW MAY STRETCH 200 METERS.

- SOME SPECIES OF MOLE HAVE LARDERS WHERE THEY KEEP WORMS. IT IS SAID THEY BITE THE WORMS IN THE HEAD, THEN STORE THEM ALIVE FOR ONE TO TWO MONTHS.

- ACCORDING TO ESTIMATES, MOLES DIG ONE METER IN THREE TO THIRTY MINUTES. IF YOU CONSIDER IT TAKES A SHIELD EXCAVATOR TWO TO THREE HOURS TO TUNNEL THAT FAR, IT'S CLEAR THAT WHILE MOLES MAY BE SMALL, THEY'RE FAST. BUT BEFORE LONG, THEY TAKE A NAP.

- MOLES CAN QUICKLY DIG TUNNELS DESPITE UNDERGROUND OBSTACLES, SO MANY COMMERCIAL PRODUCTS FOR COMBATING MOLES ARE SAID TO HAVE LITTLE EFFECT.

- A MOLE'S TAIL IS HIGHLY SENSITIVE, SO IT CAN TELL WHERE IT'S GOING EVEN WHEN BACKING UP.

- BOTH MOLES AND MOLE CRICKETS LIVE UNDERGROUND. THE MOLE'S PAWS AND THE MOLE CRICKET'S FRONT LEGS EVOLVED SEPARATELY, BUT THEY STRONGLY RESEMBLE EACH OTHER IN AN EXAMPLE OF WHAT IS CALLED CONVERGENT EVOLUTION.

–WHAT DO YOU THINK ABOUT THIS?

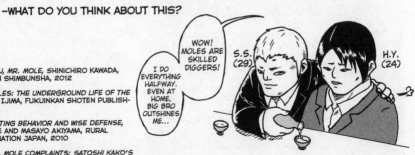

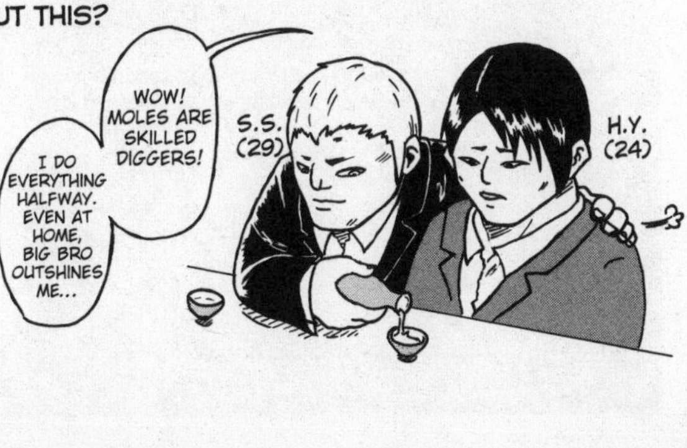
WOW! MOLES ARE SKILLED DIGGERS!
I DO EVERYTHING HALFWAY. EVEN AT HOME, BIG BRO OUTSHINES ME...
S.S. (29)
H.Y. (24)

REFERENCES:

NICE TO MEET YOU, MR. MOLE, SHINICHIRO KAWADA, SHONEN SHASHIN SHIMBUNSHA, 2012

THE LIVES OF MOLES: THE UNDERGROUND LIFE OF THE MOLE, MASAHIRO IJIMA, FUKUINKAN SHOTEN PUBLISHERS, INC., 2010

MOLES: INTERESTING BEHAVIOR AND WISE DEFENSE, MASATERU INOUE AND MASAYO AKIYAMA, RURAL CULTURE ASSOCIATION JAPAN, 2010

MOLE PROBLEMS, MOLE COMPLAINTS: SATOSHI KAKO'S ILLUSTRATED BOOK OF NATURE MYSTERIES, VOL. 6, SATOSHI KAKO, KOMINE SHOTEN, 2001

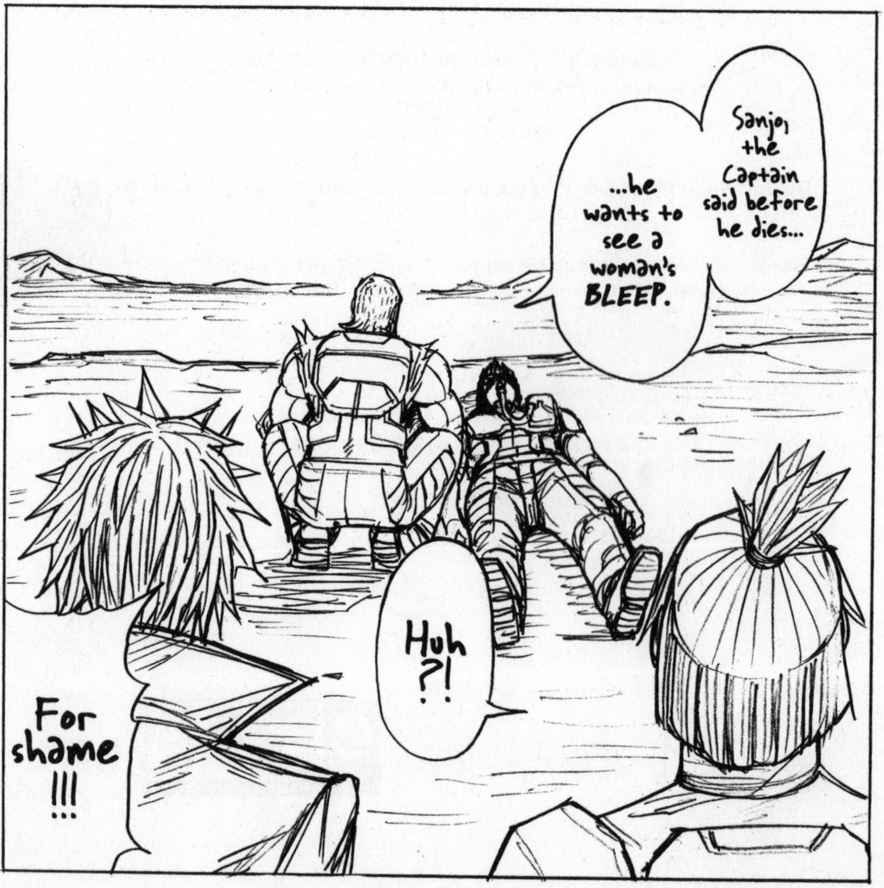
Sanjo, the Captain said before he dies...
...he wants to see a woman's BLEEP.
Huh?!
For shame!!!

TERRA FORMARS

Volume 7
VIZ Signature Edition

Story by YU SASUGA
Art by KENICHI TACHIBANA

TERRA FORMARS © 2011 by Ken-ichi Tachibana, Yu Sasuga/SHUEISHA Inc.
All rights reserved.
First published in Japan in 2011 by SHUEISHA Inc., Tokyo.
English translation rights arranged by SHUEISHA Inc.

Translation & English Adaptation/John Werry
Touch-up Art & Lettering/Annaliese Christman
Design/Izumi Evers
Editor/Mike Montesa

Printed in the U.S.A.

Published by VIZ Media, LLC
P.O. Box 77010
San Francisco, CA 94107

10 9 8 7 6 5 4 3 2 1
First printing, July 2015

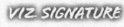

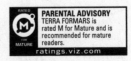

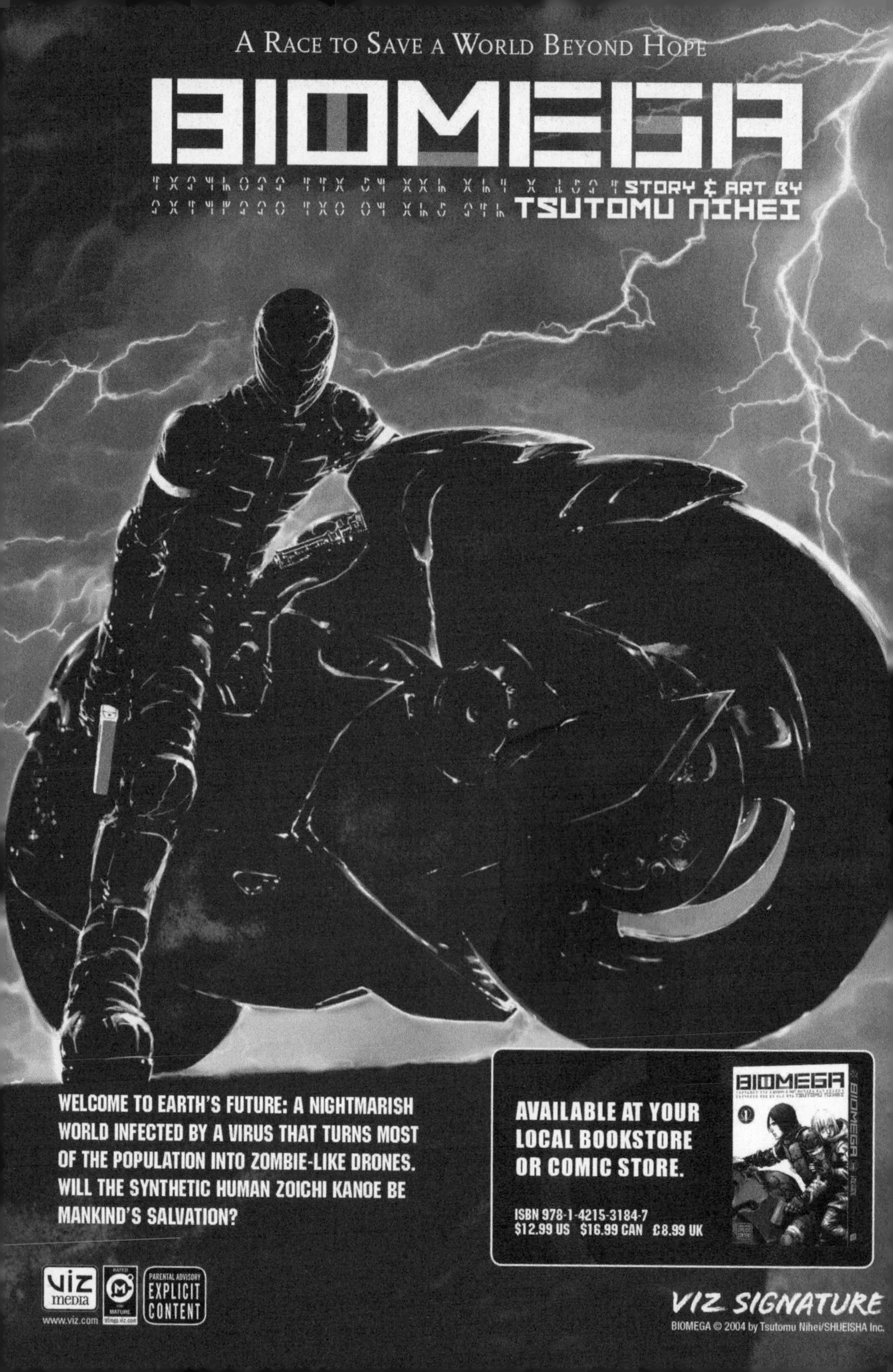
A Race to Save a World Beyond Hope
BIOMEGA
STORY & ART BY
TSUTOMU NIHEI
WELCOME TO EARTH'S FUTURE: A NIGHTMARISH WORLD INFECTED BY A VIRUS THAT TURNS MOST OF THE POPULATION INTO ZOMBIE-LIKE DRONES. WILL THE SYNTHETIC HUMAN ZOICHI KANOE BE MANKIND'S SALVATION?
AVAILABLE AT YOUR LOCAL BOOKSTORE OR COMIC STORE.
ISBN 978-1-4215-3184-7
$12.99 US $16.99 CAN £8.99 UK
viz media
www.viz.com
PARENTAL ADVISORY EXPLICIT CONTENT
VIZ SIGNATURE
BIOMEGA © 2004 by Tsutomu Nihei/SHUEISHA Inc.

Hey! You're Reading in the Wrong Direction!

This is the *end* of this graphic novel!

To properly enjoy this VIZ graphic novel, please turn it around and begin reading from *right to left.* Unlike English, Japanese is read right to left, so Japanese comics are read in reverse order from the way English comics are typically read.

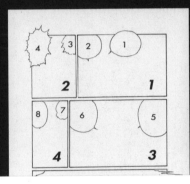

This book has been printed in th~~~ format in order to preserve the original artwork. Have fun with